P9-DXM-538

A
Movable
Feast

This book, based largely on *The Cambridge World History of Food*, provides a look at the globalization of food from the days of the hunter-gatherers to present-day genetically modified plants and animals. The establishment of agriculture and the domestication of animals in Eurasia, Africa, the Pacific, and the Americas are all treated in some detail along with the subsequent diffusion of farming cultures through the activities of monks, missionaries, migrants, imperialists, explorers, traders, and raiders.

Much attention is given to the "Columbian Exchange" of plants and animals that brought revolutionary demographic change to every corner of the planet and led ultimately to the European occupation of Australia and New Zealand as well as the rest of Oceania.

Final chapters deal with the impact of industrialization on food production, processing, and distribution, and modern-day food-related problems ranging from famine to obesity to genetically modified food to fast food.

Kenneth F. Kiple did his undergraduate work at the University of South Florida, and earned a PhD in Latin American History and a PhD certificate in Latin American Studies at the University of Florida. He has taught at Bowling Green State University since 1970 and became a Distinguished University Professor in 1994. His research interests have included biological history applied to the slave trade and slavery, the history of disease, and more recently, food and nutrition. He is the author of approximately fifty articles and chapters, and three monographs, and the editor of five volumes including *The Cambridge World History of Disease* and (with K. C. Ornelas) *The Cambridge World History of Food*, in two volumes.

Professor Kiple has been a Guggenheim Fellow and has received numerous other grants and fellowships from organizations such as the National Institutes of Health, the National Library of Medicine, the National Endowment for the Humanities, Tools Division (and two other National Endowment for the Humanities Fellowships), the Earhart Foundation, the Milbank Memorial Fund, the American Council of Learned Societies, the Rockefeller Archives, the American Philosophical Society, the Social Sciences Research Council, and the Fulbright-Hays Foundation.

A MOVABLE FEAST

Ten Millennia
of
Food Globalization

Kenneth F. Kiple

Department of History, Bowling Green State University

CAMBRIDGE UNIVERSITY PRESS
Cambridge, New York, Melbourne, Madrid, Cape Town, Singapore, São Paulo

Cambridge University Press
32 Avenue of the Americas, New York, NY 10013-2473, USA

www.cambridge.org
Information on this title: www.cambridge.org/9780521793537

First published 2007

Printed in the United States of America

A catalog record for this publication is available from the British Library.

Library of Congress Cataloging in Publication Data

Kiple, Kenneth F., 1939–
A Movable feast : ten Millennia of food globalization / Kenneth F. Kiple.
p.   cm.
Includes bibliographical references and index.
ISBN-13: 978-0-521-79353-7 (hardback)
ISBN-10: 0-521-79353-X (hardback)
1. Food – History.   2. Globalization.   I. Title.
TX353.K55   2007
641.3 – dc22   2006028231

ISBN   978-0-521-79353-7 hardback

For Coneè

Contents

Preface

*An ungainly term, globalization often suggests a troubling deter-
minism, a juggernaut that destroys rain forests, while multinational
agribusinesses plow under family farms and capitalism forces peasants
to move into cities and work for wages, thereby eroding social relations,
undermining local customs, and subverting taste in culture and food.*

Raymond Grew (1999)[1]

Friday I tasted life. It was a vast morsel.

Emily Dickinson

*Who riseth from a feast
With that keen appetite that he sits down?*

Shakespeare, The Merchant of Venice II, *vi*, 8.

"GLOBALIZATION" is a hot topic, at the center of the greatest issues of
our time, and one that has roused economic, political, and cultural historians
to grapple with the big question – is it a good thing or a bad thing? Book and
article titles like *One World, Ready or Not: The Manic Logic of Global Capitalism,*[2] *The End of History and the Last Man,*[3] or *The Silent Takeover: Global
Capitalism and the Death of Democracy*[4] take a gloomy Hobbesian view of
the process; others radiate the optimism of Voltaire's Dr. Pangloss such as
A Future Perfect: The Challenge and Hidden Promise of Globalization.[5]

Similar passion is evident wherever Western activists, the youth of Islam,
and other dissidents gather to protest that synergistic interaction of technological revolution and global capitalism that we have come to call globalization. Notable recent examples include the more than 50,000 protestors at
the World Trade Organization that turned downtown Seattle upside down

and the 2001 protestors at the Group of Seven meeting in Genoa, Italy, who slugged it out with the police. Most protesters view globalization as bristling with threats to the environment; many also feel that it is a menace to cultural integrity, even to state sovereignty, and some express the concern that globalization will promote even greater inequality among the world's peoples. Their opponents point out that a global community is preferable to the nationalism (and some of its component parts such as ethnocentrism and racism) that has occupied the world's stage (often disastrously) throughout the past half millennium and that poor countries, which have changed their policies to exploit globalization, have benefited most from it.[6]

Many of globalization's perplexities are evident in the history of foods and food ways. Some are obvious. Culture, for example, always a tough opponent of globalization, is defended whenever people defend their cuisine. On a biological level the people of developing countries require an adequate supply of the right kinds of foods for the creation and maintenance of healthy and productive populations. But in between these cultural and biological poles lies the murky political and economic question of what happens to those who resist the forces of globalization.

In the case of food, can or will a global community make enough food available to those holdouts who, for cultural or biological reasons, do not buy into the existing technologies? Today, for example, we have starving countries that refuse aid because that aid is in the form of genetically modified (GM) foods. And they refuse to sidestep future crises by planting genetically modified rice or maize or millets even though such GM crops not only deliver substantially higher yields than unmodified counterparts but are resistant to pests, weeds, and droughts, and consequently to famine.

Other big questions are "when did globalization begin" and "where and how will it end?"[7] In terms of food globalization, our answers are thankfully simple. It began with the invention of agriculture some ten thousand years ago in at least seven independent centers of plant and animal domestication. Throughout the ensuing ten millennia the agricultural fruits of all of these centers became so dispersed that today, in the West at least, diets are no longer tied to regional food production and, consequently, regional cuisines are fast disappearing. For the rest of the world such food homogenization means that for the first time in human history, political will alone can eliminate global inequalities in the kinds and quantities of food available. The next big question is whether the phenomenon of greater food availability will be canceled out by swelling numbers of food consumers.[8]

Acknowledgments

THIS BOOK is based on *The Cambridge World History of Food* published by the New York branch of Cambridge University Press in 2000 and edited by myself and Kriemhild C. Ornelas. Indeed, the contributions of every author in that two-volume work have been utilized and are cited in this one. I am very grateful to all of them; to the board members of that project who recommended contributors and read their essays for accuracy; and to Steve Beck and his squad of graduate assistants who nudged the project toward completion. I will be eternally grateful to Rachael Graham, whose efforts on an earlier project helped us to establish rules and regulations for this effort.

Readers will notice that I have employed a number of other sources in addition to those of Cambridge contributors. This was not because of incompleteness or sloppiness on their part. On the contrary, their contributions constitute the very finest scholarship in the fields of food and nutrition. The additional sources have been used to bridge gaps and with the hope that new scholarship will add fresh insights to the narrative. Freedom to do this reading and research came from funding supplied by the National Institutes of Health in the form of a National Library of Medicine Grant for the years 1998–99; the Institute for the Study of Culture and Society, where I spent the spring semester of 2001 as a Scholar in Residence; and a Bowling Green State University Faculty Research Leave during the autumn of that year.

This book has also benefited from another project – our ongoing encyclopedic effort to provide historical entries for every important food on the planet. While I was writing this book, that work has proceeded under the direction of Kriemhild Coneè Ornelas with the help of Steve Beck, who spent a summer researching and writing animal and fish entries. I am grateful to Coneè as well for the countless hours that she labored on this effort, catching errors, making corrections, and offering suggestions. She refused co-authorship, so the least I can do is dedicate the book to her. Finally the students in my Globalization of Food Seminar have been assiduous, if not relentless, in locating new data and shaping new perspectives.

Publicity to introduce *The Cambridge World History of Food* began in the fall of 2000 in New York with a reception and press conference hosted by *Gourmet* magazine. A nomination for the Kitchen Aid Best Book and a Writing and Reference Award from the James Beard Foundation followed; the books were listed as one of the "Outstanding Reference Sources for Small and Medium-Sized Libraries," and named one of the top 100 food events of the year 2000 by *Saveur* magazine. At Bowling Green State University, Teri Sharp, Director of Public Relations, was instrumental in working with Cambridge to arrange these events, along with scheduling (what seemed to be) scores of telephone and television interviews. We are grateful as well to Kathie Smith, Food Editor of the *Toledo Blade*, for a lovely spread on the culinary possibilities of the project and how the books came to be.

Vivian (Vicky) Patraka, director of the Institute for the Study of Culture and Society arranged forums for the discussion of our research, and Georgia and John Folkins, Provost of Bowling Green State University, who supported us, put their money where their mouths were when they bought one of the first sets of *The Cambridge World History of Food*. My debt to Frank Smith was made even more enormous when, despite his heavy duties as Publishing Director at Cambridge University Press, he found the time to read this manuscript and offer many splendid suggestions. And lastly I want to thank Graduate Assistants Stephen Pedlar and Teresa Pangle for their sharp eyes in scrutinizing the footnotes and scientific names in the text; Mary Madigan-Cassidy for her splendid copyediting of the manuscript, and Cathy Felgar of Cambridge and Peter W. Katsirubas of Aptara, Inc., for their joint efforts in that magical process which transforms a manuscript into a book.

Kenneth F. Kiple

INTRODUCTION
From Foraging to Farming

*"We will now discuss in a little more detail the Struggle for
Existence" said Charles Darwin in his 1859* Origin of the Species *–
a struggle which Thomas Malthus had earlier called
"The perpetual struggle for room and food."*

On Populations (1798)

PLANT LEAVES absorb the sun's energy and construct nutrients through
photosynthesis. These are passed along to animals that swallow them when
they eat the plants; to animals that eat animals that eat plants; and to other
animals, including humans, who eat both plants and animals. Because such
nutrients are basic to human survival, finding or producing food has been
the most important historical preoccupation of humans and their ancestral
species in an evolutionary journey to the top of the food chain.

The pages that follow look at the thousands of years of food finding and
food producing that have carried us to the brink of food globalization – the
latter a process of homogenization whereby the cuisines of the world have
been increasingly untied from regional food production, and one that promises to make the foods of the world available to everyone in the world. Food
globalization has grabbed headlines as cultures have circled wagons against
the imperialism of multinational companies such as McDonald's and Coca
Cola. But such standardized food production in which "McDonaldization"
has become synonymous with food globalization is a distortion of the concept that has been going on for some 10,000 years since humans first began
to control the reproduction of plants and animals;[1] since the first wild rye

was brought under cultivation in one place, wheat in another, and maize in another; since the jungle fowl of southeast Asia was transformed into the chicken of Europe and the wild boar, first domesticated in the eastern Mediterranean, became the pig during its long eastward dispersal (with many more domestications) toward Indonesia, before sailing off with the human pioneers who spread out across the Pacific.[2]

Yet food globalization means much more than simply food diffusion. Animal and plant domestication fostered sedentism, and sedentism in turn nurtured deadly diseases that became globalized. It also caused populations to swell, inviting famine to shrink them again and impelling humans further and further afield to occupy less desirable portions of the world's surface. Out of sedentism sprang organized religion, and religious wars; states, and wars between them; nationalism, trade, and wars for empire, all of which brings up another theme – the often-negative impact on human life and health wrought by technological advances.[3]

The Neolithic Revolution(s) was and remains the most momentous of all such technological advances, and in a very real sense today's food biotechnology can be regarded as just the latest chapter in those revolutions set in motion millennia ago. Collectively they have constituted an ongoing, often uncontrolled, revolution, laden with unforeseen and unknowable consequences for humankind's ecological relationship with the planet's flora and fauna, as well as for the planet itself.[4]

But this is a mega- – almost metaphysical – example and historical hindsight can spy smaller technological examples that are easier to grasp. One might be the quick dissemination of the newly discovered New World plants around the globe because the Spanish and the Portuguese had developed technologies that permitted them to stay at sea for long periods of time – long enough for their seamen to develop scurvy, a nutritional deficiency disease that killed at least a million and probably closer to two million sailors before it was understood that vitamin C deprivation was the cause.[5]

Another, more recent, example could be the late–nineteenth-century and early–twentieth-century steam mills that polished rice. The mills represented technological progress; but by efficiently stripping away the thiamine-rich outer layers of the kernels they triggered epidemic beriberi that killed thousands of Asians.[6] And finally, in a very recent (and more complex) example, the Green Revolution was supposed to end world hunger with genetically engineered plants, and in the long run it may do just that if population growth can be curtailed. However its most apparent short-run impact, ironically, has been to encourage population explosions in the "revolutionized" countries so that every one of them is an importer of the staple foods they had expected to produce in abundance.[7]

These are but a few illustrations of the unintended consequences of new technologies on the food front. Countless others can be found in recorded history and doubtless many more took place in a prehistory that we know little about. As of today, humans have spent less than one-tenth of one percent of their time on earth as sedentary agriculturalists and, consequently, much less than one-tenth of one percent of that time in the light of recorded history – which brings up a third theme.

For 99.9 percent of humankind's stay on the planet (and around 90 percent of that of *Homo sapiens*) our ancestors made a living by hunting and gathering, which means that millions of years of our food and nutritional history will forever remain obscure (recent molecular phylogeny indicates that the hominid species split from the ancestral chimpanzee line between 6 million and 8 million years ago). Nonetheless, it makes considerable sense that it was during those millions of years and not the past 10,000 that most of our nutritional requirements were shaped – shaped even before *Homo sapiens* emerged as the sole survivor of a succession of several dozen hominid models launched on, as it turned out, unsuccessful evolutionary journeys.[8]

There are numerous methods employed by bio-anthropological investigators to determine the diet (the foods consumed) and the nutritional status (how those foods were utilized) of our ancient forebears.[9] Plants and animal remains unearthed in archaeological sites across the globe, along with human remains including coprolites (dried feces), bones, teeth, and, occasionally, soft tissue, have been scrutinized using techniques of radiocarbon (14C) dating, chemical analysis, and microscopy; and all have something to say about prehistoric diets.[10] Moreover, the study of the diets and nutritional status of modern-day hunter-gatherers has helped in understanding and interpreting these findings.[11] To be sure, plenty of room still exists for bio-anthropological dispute (and there is plenty of it), but agreement has increasingly jelled that ancient hunter-gatherers did quite well for themselves in matters of diet and nutrition, and considerably better than the sedentary agriculturalists who followed them.[12]

Such a consensus may seem blatantly heretical in light of the Western teleological spin given to the history of human progress. Yet it would seem that the lives of our hunter-gatherer ancestors, living in a state of nature, were not "poor, nasty, brutish, and short" as Thomas Hobbes pithily put it in his *Leviathan*.[13] Instead they were a relatively healthy lot – at least those that managed to survive a rigorous selection process. Life only entered the nasty and brutish stage with the invention of agriculture, according to what is present in, as well as what is missing from, humankind's archeological record.

For example, rickets (caused by vitamin D deficiency) and scurvy (occasioned by vitamin C deficiency) are diseases documented in literary and archival sources from Greek and Roman times onward but there is little evidence of such ailments in prehistoric populations.[14] Or again, the incidence of anemia increased steadily from Neolithic times through the Bronze Age so that the lesions of porotic hyperostosis and cribra orbitalia (a pitting and expansion of cranial bones that are signals of iron deficiency anemia) found in the skeletal remains of Fertile Crescent farmers living from 6500 to 2000 BCE indicate that about half of them were anemic.[15] By contrast, only 2 percent of the skeletal remains of hunter-gatherers dating from 15,000–8000 BCE) show evidence of anemia, which seems testimony to an iron-rich meat diet.[16] In addition hunter-gatherers had far fewer dental caries, knobby joints, and abscesses. And finally, as a rule, hunter-gatherers were significantly taller than the village agrarians who followed them, indicating a much better intake of whole protein.[17]

In fact, among some foraging groups meat may have constituted as much as 80 percent of the diet and for most it was at least 50 percent – but this was an intake that decreased precipitously after foragers became farmers.[18] Hunter-gatherers also ate an amazing variety of wild fruits and vegetables and, in fact, still do. Modern-day hunter-gatherers like the Kung! San of the Kalahari Desert region of southern Africa utilize more than 100 plant species and more than 60 animal species in their diet, and it has been estimated that our ancient ancestors knew the natural history of several thousand plants and several hundred animals.[19]

The diet of latter-day hunter-gatherers during the last 100,000 years or so of the Paleolithic (nearly modern human skulls recently unearthed in Ethiopia were dated at around 160,000 years ago) was apparently even more varied than that of the Kung! San. It was high in meat, vitamin C, and calcium, and low in simple carbohydrates. It offered much fiber in fruits, tubers, and leafy vegetables but featured few or no cereals and no dairy products. Although meat accounted for much of the food energy, the meat was lean and a high proportion of the fat in wild meat is polyunsaturated.[20] Moreover, judging from the ancient middens of shellfish and fish bones found on all the continents save Antarctica, seafood (with its omega 3 fatty acids) constituted still another important source of good quality protein.[21]

Diet also molded humans during their evolutionary journey in ways that influence the physiology of their modern descendents. Plants, for example, synthesize thiamine, but humans and the rest of the animal kingdom lost that ability. It conferred little advantage on animals that ate plants or other animals or both. With vitamin C, however, although most animals retained the ability to synthesize it, humans did not, confirming among other things that our hunter-gatherer ancestors consumed much in the way of plant foods and raw meat (which contains vitamin C) – and consequently were among the few animals to enjoy an abundance of the vitamin.

But abundance was a relative state of affairs. The feast part of "feast or famine," and certainly the famine part – hunger and its appeasement – were the forces that propelled hunter-gatherers from their early days of mostly gathering and scavenging throughout the world in pursuit of an increasingly carnivorous diet. However, during their long and arduous trek to reach the various parts of the globe and the process of adapting to them, natural selection planted the seeds of some of humankind's modern health difficulties. Energy was stored as fat against seasonally decreased food intakes, and those who stored fat efficiently survived during bad times, whereas others did not.[22] The trouble is that our bodies are genetically programmed to store calories against lean times that nowadays (at least for affluent populations) never come. Lifestyles have become increasingly sedentary but our diets are more energy-packed, with less fiber and more refined carbohydrates.[23] As a consequence, the "thrifty mechanisms" of carbohydrate metabolism that saved our forebears now curse us with obesity, diabetes, and heart problems.

And finally, it was during the last 200,000 years that *Homo sapiens* – the wise man – appeared on earth with a brain as large as our own. Evolution had transformed him from a scavenging and gathering, ape-like australopithecine to a fully modern human being – the large brain facilitating the exploitation of a wide range of food sources and the colonization of marginal environments. However, an enhanced brain size was metabolically expensive, accounting for only 3 percent of the adult body weight but demanding around 20 percent of its energy. Calorie-dense meat, shellfish, and fish became even more nutritionally important to supply that energy and the larger brains devised the strategies, weapons, and tools necessary to acquire them.

In that symbiotic process, Hiam Ofek points out, the body managed to compensate for the enlarged brain and bring about some balance by paring down its digestive system to around 60 percent of that expected for a similar-sized primate. This paring was also the result of a large brain that relieved much stress on the gastrointestinal (GI) tract by thinking – thinking to remove dirt from foods, to peel them, to husk and crack them, and to chemically alter them by cooking. In the end, the increase in the size of the brain was balanced almost exactly by a reduction in the size of the gut. At that stage humans became omnivores with the GI tract of a carnivore – and the ability to eat large quantities of meat is a cardinal difference between humans and the other primates.[24]

LAST HUNTERS,
FIRST FARMERS

Animals feed, man eats; the man of intellect alone knows how to eat.

Anthelme Brilllat Savarin (1755–1826)

Acorns were good until bread was found.

Francis Bacon (1561–1626)

OUR ANCESTORS began the deliberate and systematic hunting of animals some 700,000 years ago in Africa. Before this their diet had been based mostly on plant foods, occasionally enlivened with meat from scavenged carcasses – other animals' leftovers. But by the time we became *Homo sapiens* – Our Kind – which happened in eastern Africa some 100,000 years ago, we were hunters, not scavengers – opportunistic hunters who apparently became so good at it that those ancestors put a considerable dent in their food supply. Around 80,000 years ago they began to radiate out of northeast Africa to western Asia, where they once again encountered plenty of protein on the hoof, and in this larger world they mustered the momentum to out-compete all others of the genus *Homo* that had preceded them.

This was the modern human species, which began colonizing Australia around 50,000 years ago, moved from the Asian steppes into Europe from around 40,000 years ago, and into the Americas 15,000 to 30,000 years ago. And it was in these wanderings that the progressively larger brains of humans gave birth to progressively better tools and weapons and increasing social organization.

There is evidence of specialized hunting strategies by 20,000 years ago that allowed our big-brained ancestors to consistently bag really big game. In the middle latitudes of Eurasia large gregarious herbivores such as horses, wooly mammoths, reindeer, and bison were victims of these strategies. Elsewhere the prey consisted of buffalo, wild pig, aurochs, and camel. Large animal carcasses had numerous advantages over plant foods. A day of foraging for plants produced the food value of just one small animal, whereas by eating animals humans took in a highly concentrated food that contained all the essential amino acids. Moreover one large animal could feed an entire band, and food sharing seems to have been the norm for hunter-gatherers.[1]

Others of Our Kind made a living from the water. Ancient rock art the world over depicts fish, although it is relatively silent about how they were caught. Probably, until late in the Paleolithic – when bows, arrows, and harpoons appeared, large animals were on their way to extinction, and flimsy dugout canoes and reed rafts were replaced by more reliable watercraft – fish procurement was largely limited to rivers. There fish could be taken with clubs, spears, nets made of twisted fiber, and lines (the fish-gorge, a kind of hook, dates from around 27,000 years ago) often after damming the water. Then, too, hunter-gatherers were surely familiar with the annual "runs" of various anadromous species such as salmon that swim from the ocean into and up ancestral rivers to spawn.[2]

The exploitation of coastal, as opposed to riverine environments, involved not so much fish, but shellfish – mussels, oysters, cockles, scallops, whelks, clams and the like – whose shells comprise the myriad middens of both Paleolithic and Neolithic origin found on seacoasts and rivers around the world. The succulent nuggets within these shells represented easily collected, high-quality protein (and also bait for fishing) – the drawback being that the food came in small increments so that large-scale gathering efforts were required. Sea slugs and sea anemones were also collected (still eaten by the French), as were lampreys – too many are famously said to have killed England's Henry II in 1189. Inland, mollusks such as snails also offered a living to gatherers – their discarded shells contributing to still other middens.

Many coastal and inland middens indicate intensive activity during the early years of the Neolithic – perhaps another indication of big game disappearing? In any event, collecting mollusks must have been a pleasant alternative to the rigors (and dangers) of the hunt or labor in the fields. So too was the collection of health-giving algae – excellent sources of vitamins, minerals, even fats.[3] Perhaps the only reason that beaches were not jammed was that the coasts could not provide enough food for everyone.

Giant sea turtles were another vital marine resource for many, although reliable watercraft were required to exploit their eggs, which were often deposited on uninhabited offshore islands.[4] The eggs, of all of the six or seven species (the number is in dispute) of these giant marine reptiles have long been good food for humans but the sea turtle most favored for its veal-like meat is the green turtle (*Chelonia mydas*) – named green not for its color but for the green gelatinous substance found underneath its lower shell, called "calipee." When scraped out, calipee is the base for the justly famous green turtle soup.[5] Even though sea turtles are easy to catch when out of the water, turtle flesh – but not turtle eggs – is avoided by many around the world. For others, however, like the coastal Miskito population of Nicaragua, whose home coasts are one of the principal feeding grounds for green turtles, they are a staple.[6]

Many of these foods, including turtle eggs, were eaten raw throughout much of humankind's time on earth and some still are, like oysters, clams, mussels, fish, and fish eggs (caviar and its pretenders). In Japan eating raw fish (called *sashimi* since the seventeenth century) has been traditional since ancient times.[7] Meats, too, are still eaten raw, such as hams (although cured or smoked) and beef (as steak tartare and carpaccio).

Insects consumed, sometimes raw and sometimes cooked, served as another important food source for hunter-gatherers and their descendents. To name but a few of the many more than one thousand species that have figured into the practice of entomophagy: North American natives ate the larvae of moths, grasshoppers, crickets, and caterpillars; in Mexico several hundred species of insects, including caterpillars, dragonflies, ants, bees, and wasps, are still eaten; and in South America giant queen ants are not only thought tasty but are depended on as an aphrodisiac as well.[8]

In the Old World the ancient Greeks and Romans enjoyed grasshoppers and large grubs, and European peasants continued to make insects important sources of protein until the nineteenth century. In Africa entomophagy is still practiced on a large scale with caterpillars ("the snack that crawls") a widespread favorite. Locusts, termites, and palm grubs are also commonly eaten. Until recently locusts were regularly popped into human mouths in South Asia and the Middle East. Beetle consumption has long been popular in Southeast Asia, where ant larvae and pupae are not only regularly

consumed but also canned and exported to specialty food outlets, as is bee brood. Silkworm pupae are shipped to the United States from Korea and regularly consumed in China. The Japanese are fond of wasp pupae and larvae, and locusts are regularly consumed throughout East Asia. In Australia the black honey ant, a special kind of bee, and witchetty and bardi grubs (the larvae of a moth and a beetle, respectively) were all local delicacies for hunter-gatherers that have recently found their way into restaurant menus – a modern reminder that these were all important Aborigine foods, along with moths collected during migrations.[9]

Vegetables and fruits comprise other groups of foods often eaten raw. Lettuce has been fried and boiled, but as a rule it is not. One does not say raw oranges to differentiate them from cooked varieties because they are seldom cooked – a good thing, too, because heat kills the vitamin C they contain. But, this having been said, although numerous food items have been, and still are, eaten raw, cooked food is generally the best tasting and the best for us. Heat destroys toxins in plants and unwanted wildlife in meat and fish such as worms and a gamut of smaller pathogens.[10] It increases the nutritional value of many foods, makes others more digestible by the denaturation of protein and the gelation of starch, even makes some inedible foods edible. Cooking softens tough foods by breaking down animal and vegetable fibers while simultaneously liberating protein and carbohydrate materials – indeed, starch requires heat to release its sugars.[11]

The domestication of fire, then, was not only the first but the most important of all the domestications that humankind has managed. Although its permanent acquisition is told in a thousand myths and legends, generally of divine gift-giving, in reality fire must have been acquired only to be lost again countless times over millennia as (often painful) trial and error led from the capture of naturally occurring fire (fire collecting) to its preservation in embers that could later be fanned into flame. Tamed fire (fire production) was probably initially employed for illumination, to frighten away dangerous carnivores, and for hunting rather than for cooking. However as cooking became routine, more reliable tools for fire kindling such as flints, fire drills, and other friction devices came about, and the art of making charcoal was developed to fuel human progress from the Stone Age to the Iron Age to the Backyard Barbecue Age.

Cooking almost certainly came about by accident, and one suspects that there were an infinitesimal number of accidents that called human attention to the process, such as the fanciful account of Charles Lamb. Appearing in an 1823 issue of *London Magazine*, the essay posited a litter of piglets trapped in a burning dwelling in China. In the aftermath of the fire the swineherd noticed the appetizing odor of roasted pig, and tasted the crisp flesh. Soon pigs were being immolated in other buildings deliberately set on fire until, finally, it dawned on the arsonists that the cooking fuel need not be an edifice.[12] With apologies to Lamb, however, cooking was underway and fire had been domesticated long before the pig entered this state.

Some credit Peking man, a hominid living around a half million years ago with the first use of fire.[13] Others have placed the event in Africa some million years earlier, but few dispute that fire has been the property of almost all humans for the last 100,000 years. It is true that earthen hearths baked by repeated fires were not numerous until around 40,000 years ago, but this does not mean that fire was not used with regularity. Rather it merely reminds us that hunter-gatherer bands regularly changed their address, and there seems little doubt that at this point humans had graduated from fire collecting to fire producing.[14]

Presumably roasting foods directly over the flame was the first method used. But they were also steamed in bags made with skins and stomachs suspended over the fire. Charred flat stones from ancient sites suggest that grilling may have taken place, and hot pebbles and stones were placed in wooden vessels for making porridges whereas holes dug in the ground served as ovens for baking roots and tubers. Pit-cooking a variety of foods came next, and the rudiments of cookery magic were established – a magic that became even more powerful with the use of pottery vessels that began in the Middle East around 8,000 years ago (earlier in Japan and China), which simplified boiling, even promoted frying.[15] Grains that had previously been toasted could now be boiled, and this, coupled with their domestication – a procedure that involved the selection and propagation of desirable traits along with the elimination of those deemed undesirable – made them more digestible. Interestingly, regularly cooking foods promoted a substantial reduction in human tooth size. We simply no longer needed large teeth for tearing at raw meat or chewing tough fibrous plants.

But fire served humans in many ways besides cooking. With it they could begin rearranging environments to suit themselves, clearing land to stimulate the growth of wild foods and opening landscapes to encourage the proliferation of food animals, that could be later driven by fire to a place chosen to harvest them. In addition, fire stimulated the growth of grasses – a kind of bait for herbivores.[16]

Fire, as a weapon in the arsenal of early humans, was useful for driving away unfriendly animals too dangerous to spear (especially in the dark), but more importantly was applied to cornering game, even driving large numbers off cliffs. Other weapons entered that arsenal over time such as the atlatl and bow and arrow. These were more powerful than the spear – so much so that they confused the instinctive flight distance of prey – the range that an animal will permit a predator to approach before fleeing. Such technologies, in turn, promoted increasingly sophisticated hunting strategies that took a quantum leap forward with the transformation of the wolf into a hunting dog around 16000 BCE. As Alfred Crosby points out, humans were now substituting cultural evolution for genetic evolution[17] – a substitution that in progressively removing humans from nature's rhythm was fraught with myriad consequences.

One of these consequences, not long in coming, was to thrust humankind onto the horns of the Malthusian dilemma. Increased food production, coupled with cooking, delivered more in the way of whole protein to the young, which ensured that more individuals survived to adulthood. Yet as humans grew more numerous, this meant more pressure on the large game animals (megafauna) they fed on. These dwindled in numbers and in the end became extinct as several genera and numerous species disappeared. Human populations were expanding to the outer limits of a food supply now diminishing in the face of the planet's champion predator, and – to spread the blame – in the face of climatic change as the Pleistocene epoch came to an end.

One way out of the dilemma was for people to become more celibate, but this was apparently not an option for Our Kind, who dug in to invent agriculture instead. They could not have realized that they were trading in a life of ease (contemporary hunter-gatherers work only about a dozen or two hours weekly to get food together and to make, maintain, and repair weapons and implements) for one of back-breaking labor from sunup to sundown with a narrow-minded concentration on a single crop.[18] And they had no way of knowing that they were exchanging good health for famine and nutritional diseases, not to mention swapping plenty of elbowroom for crowded living conditions – conditions that helped open the door to plague and pestilence.

But even had people been more prescient, would population pressure and resource depletion have left them with any other choice? Or had leaders recognized that settled agriculture would increase their control over resources and consequently enhance their own personal power? Or was it simply that people, previously confined to remote bands, began to enjoy the excitement of living in seasonal settlements and converted them into permanent villages? No matter what the precipitating factors, the people who made the transition from foraging to farming only gradually discovered the pitfalls because the transition was a leisurely one.

It had its beginnings around 17000 BCE, several millennia before the one million years of the climactic tumult of the Pleistocene shaded into the Holocene. It was then that wild emmer and einkorn grains were first harvested in the Fertile Crescent of the Middle East, as were broad beans in southwestern Asia, and a couple of kinds of broad beans may have even been domesticated in northeast Thailand. Eleven thousand years ago is the date generally assigned to the start of the Holocene, which saw the beginning of agriculture and is the age we live in today.

Such early agricultural experiments were stimulated by the changing climate at the close of the last great Ice Age. It was a gradual, but cataclysmic, process that lasted for nearly 100 centuries and ended only at the start of the Copper Age. Rising seas, caused by melting glaciers, exacerbated the population problem by inundating land bridges to those New Worlds of the planet that had been safety valves for excessive numbers. However, left behind in compensation for those not following the animals retreating with the glaciers was a stable climate favorable to the spread of wild cereal plants and, consequently, also favorable to the multiplication of herbivorous animals. That stable climate has continued to persist for the last 10,000 years during which the human diet that had leaned heavily on animal protein tilted back towards plants – and this despite the domestication of barnyard animals.

BUILDING THE
BARNYARD

*There is in every animal's eye a dim image and gleam of
humanity, a flash of strange light through which their life looks
out and up to our great mastery of command over them, and
claims the fellowship of the creature if not of the soul.*

John Ruskin

HUNTING WAS THE MAJOR preoccupation of people everywhere
around 18,000 years ago and there were plenty of caribou and bison to
be hunted – these animals still staring out at us from cave paintings at
Lascaux in southwestern France and Altamira in Spain. But over millennia,
as temperatures grew warmer, herds were nudged northward. The caribou,
probably the most important game animal in Europe, had long sustained
humans and some followed the animals. Others, however, faced up to the
problem by taking charge of the caribou, leading them between winter
and summer feeding grounds, and harvesting individuals as needed for
food.[1] Does this mean that animal domestication preceded that of plants?
Not really. These animals were probably no more domesticated than the
wild grasses being harvested at the time. Most experts are convinced that
domesticated plants came before domesticated animals, save the dog, and
that the former were vital to the domestication of the latter.

Climatic change at the tail end of the Ice Age produced forests on what
had been bare steppes and crafted a habitat of wild plants that fed smaller
creatures such as deer, hare, boar, and various birds.[2] Sheltered in the new
forests, they began to proliferate as the larger animals either relocated or

passed into extinction. At first they were merely new prey for human hunters, but later on many of them, especially those that were gregarious and herd-oriented, became our domesticated animals.[3]

Domestication, among other things, means to change genetically. These changes involve physical ones to be sure, but also behavior changes such as a loss of defensive alertness and fearfulness, along with relaxed territorial attitudes. Physical changes include alterations in size. Skeletal elements and teeth change as well; those of domesticated animals becoming morphologically distinct from those of their wild ancestors.

Despite such blatant modifications, however, dates indicating when the various barnyard animals underwent domestication remain hazy because it was generally a very lengthy transformation. It began with people who had settled into sedentary agriculture and, anxious to ensure good harvests, captured animals for sacrificing to gods they hoped would do the ensuring. As animals accumulated, some taming took place and then, ultimately, breeding.

The places where such domestication occurred are similarly obscured because of multiple domestications – and domestications in which the animals may have cooperated because of a need to adapt in a world made increasingly uncertain by growing human domination.[4]

DOG

However, the first animal to be domesticated, the dog (*Canis familiaris*) did not fit this pattern. Taming and breeding transformed the Asian wolf into a dog long before the invention of agriculture – around 16,000 years ago toward the end of the Paleolithic – and at about this time fossil remains from Iraq indicate that dogs had been put to work tracking game (the many dog varieties are mostly a nineteenth-century phenomena).[5] If the hypothesis is correct that humans and wolves – both pack hunters – had joined together to pool their respective hunting skills, then domestication seems a natural outcome of such a partnership.[6] Wolf pups that lost parents and were raised by humans were imprinted with substitute family leaders. Those animals displaying the most tameness were bred with one another, and the domestication process was underway.[7]

And there were doubtless multiple domestications. Dogs were in the British Isles around 7300 BCE; the Swiss lake dwellers had dogs by 6000 BCE; and sometime between 5,000 and 10,000 years ago dogs walked into the Americas with human masters and rode in the canoes of Pacific voyagers.[8]

However, this union of humans and dogs did not, and does not, preclude the dog from becoming dinner, and probably on occasion vice-versa. In fact, dogs, along with pigs and chickens, most likely served as portable food on many such long distance treks.[9]

SHEEP AND GOATS

Wild goats and sheep, captured while munching on crops, have long led the list of animals domesticated in the early Neolithic. In fact, such crops may have doubled as lures to draw the animals to places where they could be easily killed (garden hunting). But many were also captured, again for sacrificial purposes. Taming came next and then, with domestication, average size began to decrease. Evidence dating from 9000 BCE of goat domestication (from *Capra aegagrus*) and sheep domestication (from *Ovis orientalis*) has been found in the foothills of the Zagros Mountains of Southwest Asia (in the eastern sector of the Fertile Crescent). The domestication process was hurried along after humans learned to herd these animals. The herders led them to food, protected them from predatory animals, and looked after the newborn. In short, the animals became dependent on humans.[10]

Domesticated goats (*C. bircus*) thrive in a subhumid environment and achieved a vital place in the Middle East and North Africa, as well as in Mediterranean countries like Greece and Turkey, where summer drought conditions could make the production of enough fodder for cattle problematical.[11] The domestication of sheep (*O. aries*) included selection for "hornlessness" (a process not yet complete), wool fibers (their ancestors were hairy), and fat tails (a delicacy in the Mid-

dle East). Sheep are more uniformly spread across the Old World than goats, but the milk of both becomes cheese, yogurt, and butter (ewe's milk stars in such illustrious cheeses as the Roquefort of France, the Romano of Italy, the Feta of Greece, and the Manchego of Spain).[12]

PIG

In a recent development the pig (*Sus scrofa*) has been put forward as a challenger of sheep and goats for the distinction of being the oldest domesticated animal after the dog. In part, this is because of multiple, but undated, domestications of wild boars in a range that extends eastward from the British Isles and Morocco to Japan and New Guinea. Yet in addition, just a few years ago, bones were uncovered in the foothills of the Taurus Mountains of southeastern Turkey that sug-  gested the presence of a domesticated pig around 10,000 years ago. If true, this indicates that the pig probably beat goats and sheep into domestication. It also opens the possibility that domesticated animals may have preceded domesticated plants after all, which would precipi- tate considerable rethinking about the early Neolithic.[13]

The Chinese have laid claim to priority in pig domestication. But although they most likely carried out an independent domestication, this seems to have taken place later than pig domestication in western Asia.[14] Paradoxically, however, today western Asia is largely devoid of pigs because of the religious proscriptions of Islam and Judaism, whereas China has 40 percent of their global population.[15]

An argument against pig priority as a domesticate is that pigs can be troublesome. On the one hand, they need shade and dampened skins to prevent heat stroke, so they are choosy about locales. Moreover, they do not give milk, do not pull vehicles or plows, are difficult to herd, and instead of eating grass, utilize many of the same foods as humans. On the other hand, as village life began, that food was generally human leftovers – garbage that pigs polished off to clean up human settlements. And in addition to these janitorial duties, pigs provided sweet and succulent meat as well as skins for a variety of uses.[16] Finally, pigs are great reproducers. After a gestation period of only four months sows give birth to an average of 10 piglets that can potentially increase their weight by 5,000 percent.[17]

CATTLE

Cattle (genus *Bos*), although among the stragglers into the barnyard, have with their contributions of meat, milk, draft power, hides, and manure, long been the world's most valuable animal.[18] Like other ruminants, they convert cellulose-rich foods that humans cannot eat into proteins and fats that they can eat. Also, like other barnyard animals, they probably experi- enced multiple domestication efforts from aurochs (B. *primigenius*) – a now extinct (since the seventeenth century) beast so large and ferocious that it

must have inflicted a substantial body count on its would-be domestica-tors. Its domestication was almost assuredly a largely accidental outcome of a search for sacrificial animals because, as Eduard Hahn argued at the turn of the twentieth century, it would have been impossible to look at an aurochs and even begin to imagine the usefulness, and relative docility, of domesticated cattle.[19]

The earliest evidence indicates that domestication took place in western Asia between 8,000 and 7,000 years ago, perhaps in Anatolia, perhaps in the Fertile Crescent. But according to DNA research, the zebu cattle of India (B. *indicus*) came from a subspecies of aurochs different from that of European cattle (B. *taurus*), suggesting an independent domestication, and it is possible that yet another domestication occurred in northern Africa. Although cattle domestication took place after cereal domestication, the animals were on hand to help power the emerging agricultural civilizations of Mesopotamia, Egypt, and the Indus Valley.[20]

HORSE

The ancestry of the domesticated horse (*Equus caballus*) goes back to North America, where it became extinct as the Pleistocene came to an end. Fortunately, horses had migrated to Asia a few million years earlier to spread out across the Eurasian grasslands. Featured prominently in European cave art of the Paleolithic, horses were a popular prey of hunter-gatherers. They were domesticated in the Ukraine around 4000 BCE to be mounts and later were hitched to wheeled vehicles. Horse domestication spread from the Ukraine to the south and the west so that they were soon present in the Indus Valley and, by 2500 BCE, well-established in Western Europe and around the Mediterranean.[21] Curiously, however, Chinese archeologists tell us that the first evidence of horse domestication in their part of the world only dates from around 1300 BCE.[22]

Hippophagy – horsemeat consumption – never again achieved the popularity it had with hunter-gathers and, in fact, most people have also avoided the consumption of equine relatives such as the mule and donkey. However, although farmers not eating their horsepower is understandable, the avoidance of mare's milk is less so, the Mongols being notable exceptions. Such reluctance was probable tied to religious hostility to hippophagy because Jews, Hindus, Moslems, and even Christians at one time or another, all proscribed the practice. But in tropical regions geography could also be hostile. Such climates do not easily meet the food requirements of horses and, in addition, large sections of Africa harbor trypanosomiasis, a disease spread by the tsetse fly that is deadly to large animals.[23]

CAMEL

Like the horse, the camel originated in North America and, like the horse, became extinct there. But it too had migrated to Asia millions of years before leaving behind its relatives, the llama and alpaca. Camels are browsers, able to eat some plant species that others cannot, and come in a couple of models: the one-humped dromedary (*Camelus dromedarius*) of the deserts of Africa, India, and Arabia, and the two-humped bactrian (*C. bactrianus*) of the higher deserts of the Iranian plateau, and Central and East Asia.[24]

Camels may have been among those animals that practically domesticated themselves. According to archeological evidence, by about 10,000 years ago, at the beginning of the Holocene they had become rare in eastern, central, and southwestern Asia, even teetering on the edge of extinction because severe droughts limited their access to water. Yet, when they did congregate around water sources, their exposure to growing wolf populations increased. A solution was association with humans who could show them to water and keep wolves away. In exchange, humans got rich sources of protein in camel milk, blood, and meat, along with transportation.[25]

Reaching the transportation and real domestication stage, however, took time, and it was only about 3,000 years ago that Chinese sources confirm the domestication of the bactrian camel. Apparently the Assyrians had begun keeping the dromedary camel for its food value earlier and they had put the camel to work as a mount about 3,500 years ago – the approximate date that saddles were developed for the beasts. After this, the importance of the Camel increased enormously.[26]

WATER BUFFALO

Massive and powerful, the domesticated water buffalo (*Bubalus bubalis*) is well suited for wet rice cultivation. It also eats the fibrous vegetation of tropical regions that other animals cannot and, with a highly efficient digestive system, does a better job than cattle of converting what it does eat into protein. Water buffalo first appeared on earth around three and a half million years ago in the northwestern part of the Indian subcontinent. They subsequently migrated eastward into China and southward into South and Southeast Asia where their skeletal remains discovered at human sites indicate that hunter-gatherers consumed their meat.[27]

As with camels there are two types of water buffalo – the swamp buffalo found from the Philippines to India and the river buffalo, ranging from India to Egypt and the Balkans. The swamp buffalo is usually employed as a work animal, whereas the river buffalo is valued for its milk production – a milk much higher in butter fat than cow's milk – that lends itself to cheese-making. In Italy, for example, river buffalo are kept for making mozzarella cheese, and their milk is also made into cheeses in the Balkans and Southwest Asia.[28]

Where and when water buffalo were domesticated is a matter of controversy. Evidence from the Indus valley might place the date as early as 4,000 years ago. But it is likely that this evidence points to wild buffalo – present in the riparian environment of the Indus River and its tributaries – and that domestication there was delayed for another 1,000 years.

Water buffalo probably also lived in the swamps of the Tigris and Euphrates rivers and some scholars support the notion that the Sumerians or Akkadians domesticated them. But the most likely place is the Yangtze Valley of China, where wet rice cultivation has been underway for some

7,000 years and where an unusually large number of buffalo bones have been found, indicating a heavily exploited resource (and thus probably one that was domesticated).[29] Religious sacrifice seems to have played its usual important role in water buffalo domestication, with meat, milk, even shoulder blades (used as spades) important bonuses, along with their labor for puddling rice fields, although it was only later, with the invention of the plow, that the animal became fully identified with wet rice cultivation. The first indication that water buffalo were used in this fashion comes from northern Thailand, dating to around 3,600 years ago.[30]

YAK

The penultimate four-legged domesticate of the Old World under scrutiny is the massively built yak (its classification as B. *poëphagus* is a matter of dispute).[31] For Tibetan and Himalayan folk, yaks are beasts of burden whose powerful bodies and lungs permit them to navigate mountains in bitterly cold temperatures at high altitudes.[32] They also pull plows and thresh grain, but first and foremost these animals are a vital source of food. Yak milk, cheese, and butter are dietary mainstays for their keepers, as are products of their blood – extracted by men and prepared by women.[33] Their meat is also consumed, even though the animals are primarily kept by Buddhists whose

religion forbids killing them. But in this case piety does not get in the way of a good meal because Muslims and other non-Buddhist butchers do the killing (and are believed damned for the transgression). Consequently, practically everybody eats yak flesh – fresh, salted, smoked, and especially dried.[34]

CARIBOU

The last four-legged animal to enter domestication in the Old World was the "reindeer," the domesticated caribou. Caribou (*Rangifer tarandus*) seem to have been the most important game animal in much of the world toward the end of the Paleolithic and humans have continued to take advantage of their dense aggregation into bands of dozens and herds of thousands. Yet the domesticated reindeer is only 400 to 500 years old.[35] It entered this state in northern Scandinavia and Siberia, apparently because an increasingly numerous human population wanted to ensure a reliable source of food. But reindeer were also employed as draft animals, not to mention for pulling sleighs as in the familiar nursery poem about the reindeer-powered sleigh that goes airborne to transport the patron Saint of children.[36]

PIGEON

Appropriately, this mention of flight brings us to fowl and to pigeons whose flesh and eggs were enjoyed by hunter-gatherers for hundreds of thousands of years before they were domesticated in the Neolithic. There are some 300 different kinds of pigeons that have been eaten by humans but none more important than the easily captured rock pigeon (*Columba livia*). Its domestication took place around 5,000 to 6,000 years ago, probably at many locations but certainly in Sumer whose art prominently depicts them and where ancient recipes feature them.[37]

The most likely scenario for pigeon domestication has the birds colonizing the early cities, nesting in niches of stone and mud walls, and feeding on nearby fields of grain. Squabs from these nests were easily taken into captivity to become dovecote pigeons – domestics that foraged for food during the day and returned to the pigeon house or dovecote at night. Their eggs and meat were especially valuable during cold months when food was often scarce.[38]

Pigeons later figured into elaborate banquets of the Middle Ages, and in post-Renaissance Europe huge flocks of dovecote birds were maintained by the privileged classes – those flocks ravaging the crops of angry peasants who were forbidden to kill them. In fact, some assert that aristocratic pigeon-keeping in France contributed to that rebellion against social privilege which turned into the French Revolution.[39]

CHICKEN

The ancestors of the chicken (*Gallus gallus* or *Gallus domesticus*) were jungle fowl of Southeast Asia. Sacrifice was probably the initial reason for their domestication that took place around 6000 BCE or even earlier, but cockfighting, divination, even decoration were also motives for keeping the bird – all of these ranking ahead of egg and meat production. In fact, to this day in parts of Asia chickens are used exclusively for these purposes and their eggs and flesh go uneaten.[40] Chickens spread out in Asia so that bones of 5,000-year-old domesticated birds have been turned up in China, and at about that time they could also be found in Austronesian canoes sailing off to assist in the colonization of the Pacific.

Chickens were carried across the Asian landmass to reach Europe around 3000 BCE, and at about the same time they were also introduced to the Indus Valley and Persia. The Chinese were enthusiastic egg users and partial to brooded eggs (with a well developed fetus). They also prized those abominations in the eyes (and nostrils) of Westerners – 100 year-old eggs – really just buried for a few months in a mixture of saltpeter, tea, and other materials that makes them look old by turning the egg shell black and giving the interior a hard-boiled appearance knitted together by green veins.[41]

For thousands of years the Chinese encouraged peoples around the China Sea and the Indian Ocean to use eggs and even distributed chickens. There also seem to have been other chicken introductions into sub-Sahara Africa from Ethiopia via the Red Sea and into India across the Indian Ocean. Chicken domestication was widespread during the Iron Age and, by Roman times, breeding efforts had significantly increased the size of the bird. In the Middle Ages chicken-rearing in towns became commonplace, although eggs were classified as meat by the church and consequently frequently off the menu.[42]

DUCK

The mallard (*Anas platyrhynchos*) is the ancestor of most domesticated ducks, and southern China was the place of its first domestication, perhaps as early as 2500 BCE but probably a millennia or more later. In Europe, however, although the Romans kept several species in captivity for eggs and meat, it seems that the duck was not fully domesticated until the Middle Ages.[43] Today some 75 percent of the world's domestic ducks are located in East and Southeast Asia, at least in part because the duck carcass has a high percentage of fat (up to 35 percent), a nutrient badly needed in many Asian diets. Duck eggs are also much more appreciated in the East than in the West.[44]

GOOSE

Goose eggs were eaten in ancient Mesopotamia and Rome, but like duck eggs, have long been out of favor in the West. Geese are rendered flightless by too much weight and consequently force-feeding became an important method of domestication. But, although unable to fly, geese are not immobile. Rather they were used in places as guard animals and could be herded over long distances. Today's common geese come from two species, the greylag (*Anser anser*), and the swan goose (*Anser cygnoides*) of East Asia. Little is known of the early career of the latter, but the greylag is thought to have entered Egyptian barnyards during the Middle Kingdom sometime after 2300 BCE. When it became a fixture in European barnyards is a matter of dispute, but geese were not widespread in Europe until Roman times.[45]

Together this domesticated hoard gave meat, milk, fibers, blood, eggs, and hides to early agriculturalists of the Old World. But some were also important as farming "implements." The defoliating talents of browsing sheep and goats helped ready land for cultivation; cattle were called upon to tread seeds into the ground and fertilize them with manure; later they, along with horses, pulled the plow; water buffalo were employed in wet rice cultivation; and pigs were useful in cleaning up the garbage and feces that littered the burgeoning settlements.

PROMISCUOUS PLANTS OF THE NORTHERN FERTILE CRESCENT

When tillage begins, other arts follow. The farmers, therefore, are the founders of human civilization.

Daniel Webster (1782–1852)

HUNTER-GATHERERS, who had previously made a living based on their solid knowledge of plant life and an understanding of animal behavior, continued to follow many of their old ways even as they engaged in agricultural activities. Consequently, the Neolithic Revolution, as we have come to call the invention of agriculture, although the most momentous of humankind's achievements, was not revolutionary in that it brought abrupt change. Rather, beginning about 11,000 years ago, grain gathering began to shade into grain cultivation in the Jericho Valley and, at about that time or a little later, hunting started giving way to herding in the Zagros Mountains.[1] Millennia later surpluses were generated, giving rise to agricultural civilizations such as of Mesopotamia, Egypt, northern China, and the Indus Valley, and with them came more complex and stratified societies.[2]

It is probably not coincidental that all of these first civilizations emerged within a relatively few centuries of one another, despite the distances separating them. Each one was located on a river and dependent on annual flooding for moist, rich soils rather than on the vagaries of rainfall.[3] Agriculture was simplified because there was little need for plowing or manuring and, as a result, despite occasional famines, populations grew larger. At least they did until around 2200 BCE when droughts and reductions in river flows caused severe and successive famines, exhausted grain stores, and brought about the collapse of the Old Kingdom in Egypt, Sumerian civilization in Mesopotamia (from the Greek meaning between the rivers), and Harrapan civilization in the Indus Valley.

These early Neolithic Revolutions link the end of the Stone Age with the beginning of recorded history, when we can see early civilizations with relative clarity. Yet, the end of the Stone Age is so obscure that we cannot be certain where the first Neolithic Revolution occurred, although as a rule pride of place is given to that large and fertile arc running from the Persian Gulf to the eastern Mediterranean and south to the Nile Valley that we call the Fertile Crescent. But since agriculture in the northern part of that arc developed substantially earlier than it did in Egypt, we employ the term "northern Fertile Crescent" to exclude Egypt from this geographic generalization.

Because of the Old World's west-east axis, the northern Fertile Crescent was a region ideally located to radiate agriculture in all directions. Its crops could and did spread westward throughout the Mediterranean and into North Africa, northwestward to Europe, and eastward to the Indus valley.[4]

Such diffusion often took place over water. The Fertile Crescent is an area surrounded by bodies of it – the Persian Gulf on its southeast, the Red Sea to the southwest, the Caspian and Black seas to the north, and the Mediterranean to the west. It is also bounded by mountains on the north and east, and desert to the south, all of which acted in concert to moderate a climate that nurtured the growth of wild grains, especially the ancestral forms of wheat and barley – seminal crops that were the foundation of food production in western Asia. These plentiful wild grains made possible (and practical) widespread cereal exploitation and, consequently, encouraged sedentism, as previously nomadic peoples discovered perennial sources of food.

WHEAT

Wheat (genus *Triticum*) is a grass that today helps to sustain 35 percent of the world's population. Its origins are in Southwest Asia where its wild ancestors (einkorn and emmer) were first manipulated by humans. Sickle blades, grinding stones, even grain storage pits have been found on Natufian (pre-Neolithic foragers) sites that were lived on year round by people who harvested wild grain, although with less than optimal efficiency.[5]

The trouble with wild wheat, and other wild grasses, is that nature intended that its seed-containing spikelets fall easily off a ripe ear to be dispersed by the wind, whereupon their arrow shapes and barbs would establish them in the earth. It is a strategy that promotes reproduction but is wasteful of food. Domestication involved reversing this procedure so that the spikelets became plumper, tended to stay put even on a ripe ear during harvesting, and sported poorly developed barbs.[6] It stands to reason that this reversal was an accidental product of a selection process whereby plants with spikelets that remained attached to sturdy stalks were the most likely to have their seeds gathered and planted the following season. But the price was that wheat that had always planted itself now depended on humans for that task.

Such accidents were often the midwives of domestication and this one must have taken place at some time before 8000 BCE – the approximate date when domesticated einkorn and emmer were being cultivated around Jericho in the Jordan Valley and at about the same time, at Tell Aswad (just to the southeast of Damascus).[7] Shortly after this a fully agricultural economy based on farming and herding emerged throughout the region. Within a few generations the "self-planting" ability disappeared and the wheat had been domesticated.[8] It has been estimated that it took 5,000 acres to support a single hunter-gatherer. In the new agricultural societies 5,000 acres of wheat could sustain 5,000 people.

After this first (but very lengthy) phase of grain domestication that also included barley (see ahead), fruits such as grape, olive, date, and fig were brought under cultivation, although their full dietary potential could not have been immediately appreciated. Wild nuts – especially almond (*Prunus dulcis*), pine nuts (genus *Pinus*) and pistachios (*Pistacia vera*) – became tame and as important in the diets of the first farmers as they had been for the foragers they supplanted. According to the archeological records of the third and second millennia BCE, new foods such as apples, garlic, and

coriander were being cultivated along with foods domesticated outside the Fertile Crescent such as millets, sesame, and rice, indicating contact with the other early centers of agriculture and early steps in the direction of food globalization.[9]

Within Mesopotamia, diets varied according to the status and location of the consumers. People in civilizations that practiced irrigation – those in the south – used wheat but favored barley and beer, along with dates and date wine. In the hilly regions, however, wheat was the favored grain and grape wine the most important of the beverages. Close to the Mediterranean wheat and wine were joined by olives and olive oil. Meat was seldom available to the lower classes, and state workers received grains as the bulk of their food rations.[10]

Following establishment of an agricultural beachhead in the northern Fertile Crescent, wheat was transformed into the banner of an expanding Neolithic Revolution. It arrived in Europe around 6000 BCE, could be found in northern Egypt after 5000 BCE, and reached south Asia and China by 4000 BCE.[11] The major early civilizations that emerged – the city-states of Mesopotamia, dynastic Egypt, and the civilization of the Indus Valley – were all dependent on wheat. But there were also other cereals and a host of legumes as well.

BARLEY

Wild barley (*Hordeum spontaneum*) was present in Western Asia and its story is similar to that of wheat. It was gathered for many millennia before evidence indicates that domestication took place in the eastern Fertile Crescent around 9,000 years ago. But although domesticated barley (H. *vulgare*) came along later than wheat, after it did barley was generally its companion. They spread together into the Aegean region and then into the Balkans, central Europe, the Nile Valley, and the western Mediterranean basin. By 8,000 years ago barley agriculture, but not yet wheat, had reached the foothills of the Indus Valley and from there it moved into South and East Asia.[12]

Much of barley's appeal seems to have been its ability to ferment, which lent it to beer-brewing. This was an important, early use of the grain in ancient Mesopotamia[13] and by 2300 BCE barley had almost completely replaced wheat in the Mesopotamian Valley. The reason, however, was not so much a desire for still more beer as it was that irrigation was turning the region's lands salty, and barley is by far the more salt tolerant of the two.[14]

RYE

Rye (*Secale cereale*) is a close relative of the genus *Triticum* (the wheats) – so close, in fact, that it was recently possible to combine the two by breeding *Triticum* and *Secale* to become the hybrid *Triticale*.[15] Wild rye grew to the north of the range of wild wheat and barley in western Asia – in the Taurus Mountains of Turkey through Iran to Caucasia, where it still grows wild today. There is some evidence of rye cultivation during the Neolithic, but very little, and the first unequivocal indication that it was being deliberately cultivated only dates to the Bronze Age in north-central Anatolia.

A major problem with dating the domestication of rye is that it existed for a long time as a contaminant of wheat and barley and was consequently unintentionally cultivated. Illustrative was the "volunteer" rye now called the "wheat of Allah" by Anatolian peasants – recalling a time when the wheat crop failed but rye (much hardier that wheat), which had inadvertently been planted with the wheat, still stood. The peasants assumed that Allah had "sent" them a replacement crop.[16]

In like manner, rye probably smuggled itself into Europe where its importance increased during Roman times when, because of its winter hardiness and ability to resist drought and grow in acid soils, it became an ever more valuable crop in northern and eastern Europe. At times, however, such virtues were cancelled out by the susceptibility of rye ears to the ergot fungus, which, when ingested, causes the disease ergotism. Often its symptoms were manifested in the nervous system dysfunction of consumers, but sometimes in gangrene, and untold thousands died during the 132 European epidemics of ergotism counted between 591 and 1789.[17]

OAT

Oat (*Avena sativa*) is another grain whose wild ancestors were richly represented in the soils of western Asia. Like rye, oat found its way into domestication as a weedy admixture in cultivated cereals such as wheat or barley,

but unlike rye there is no evidence of oat domestication during the Neolithic or even the Bronze Age. Instead it seems to have taken place during the first millennium BCE in what is now Czechoslovakia.[18] Oat does well in cool and moist climates and Roman writers later observed that oatmeal had become a staple in Germany. Shortly thereafter oat was under cultivation in the British Isles, especially in Scotland, and by the first millennium AD it had reached the other side of Eurasia to become a cultivated crop in China.[19]

LEGUMES

In addition to cereals, beans, peas, and lentils were instrumental in the early development of agriculture although not always instantly appreciated as domesticates. Rather, it is suspected that, like rye and oat they too were accidentally cultivated, perhaps even domesticated while trespassing in cultivated wheat and barley fields. But if their potential as cultivars was initially overlooked, wild legumes were nonetheless handy additions to the diet. They were consumed fresh to be sure but, more importantly, could be dried and stored for porridge during winter months.

Lentils (*Lens culinaris*) are probably the oldest of the cultivated legumes (which includes peas and beans). In late Paleolithic times they were being gathered in the wild throughout much of the Old World and especially in a range from the Fertile Crescent to Greece. Domestication took place some eight or nine thousand years ago. Seeds from an apparently domesticated plant that date from around 7000 BCE have been found in northern Israel and many other Fertile Crescent sites have yielded just slightly younger seeds. Domesticated lentils were introduced to southeastern Europe when Neolithic agriculture took hold during the sixth millennium BCE, and they were also among the new crops that diffused from Mesopotamia to Egypt in one direction and the Caspian Basin and the Indian subcontinent in another.[20]

The cultivated pea (*Pisum sativum*) today ranks second after lentils in the production of seed legumes. Its ancestors grew wild in the Mediterranean Basin and the Middle East, where they were munched on by hunter-gatherers. A number of ancestral strains contributed to what we now think of as the common garden pea. According to pea remains found in early Neolithic farming villages, the legume became one of the domesticated crops of the Middle East between 7500 and 6000 BCE.[21] Pea cultivation was associated with that of wheat and barley and, like lentils, peas joined these grains in the spread of agriculture into Europe where evidence of early pea cultivation has been found in that continent's eastern and central parts.[22] The pea also traveled southward into the Neolithic settlements of the Nile and followed the lentil eastward, reaching India around 2000 BCE and China, in historic times, perhaps along the Silk Road.[23]

Another legume called pea is the cultivated chickpea (*Cicer arietinum*) whose wild ancestors were scattered over central and western Asia. Known as a *garbanzo* in Spain, *cici* in Italy, and *gram* (from the Portuguese *grão* meaning grain) in India, the chickpea reached these diverse regions from the Middle East, where it is thought to have been closely associated with early Neolithic food production. However, physical evidence of the legume only becomes plentiful in archaeological investigations of Bronze Age sites – in Israel, Jordan, and the eastern Mediterranean Basin. Chickpeas were probably domesticated around 7,000 years ago, but unlike lentils or peas did not accompany Neolithic agriculture deeply into Europe. Rather they took firm root around the Mediterranean and in Harrapan settlements of the Indian subcontinent – a subcontinent that today produces 80 percent of the world's crop.[24]

The last member of the Neolithic legume quartet is the faba or fava bean (*Vicia faba*) also known as a Windsor bean, a broad bean, and a "horse bean" (because it was also fed to animals). There is disagreement about whether the fava bean originated in the Middle East or outside the region – perhaps in South Asia. It is a disagreement not easily reconciled because the wild ancestor of the cultivated fava has not yet been discovered and may have become extinct.[25] When it was domesticated is similarly in doubt, although large numbers of fava bean remains from the third millennium BCE appear in archeological sites in the Mediterranean Basin and Central Europe. Somewhat later favas reached China – now their major producer.

Fava beans grew well in the warm Mediterranean Basin where they were a major food source for many, even though, in the sixth century BCE, the famous sage Pythagoras along with Greek physicians warned against them. With good reason! In folklore, as in real life, favas and their pollen were associated with sudden, acute illness that could result in death and, in fact, the beans did indirectly kill Pythagoras. He refused to cross a field planted in them to escape an angry mob. We now call this disease, the symptoms of which include acute hemolytic anemia, "favism." It occurs in people with a blood enzyme deficiency (Glucose-6-phosphate-dehydrogenase deficiency), developed as protection against falciparum malaria – a disease that had been endemic in Greece and the islands of the Aegean, and remains so in Africa.[26]

OTHER VEGETABLE FOODS

Spinach (*Spinacia oleracea*) was probably in use in the Fertile Crescent eons before its known history of cultivation began in Persia during the fourth century AD. About 300 years later it had reached China via Nepal and about a century after that spinach was carried to Sicily by invading Saracens from North Africa who had earlier encountered the plant in Persia, by now centrally located on the Silk Road and a clearing house for foods bound for both the East and the West. Sometime after this the vegetable surfaced in Moorish Spain. It was slower to reach other tables of Europe where it was still regarded as an oddity in the sixteenth century.

The onion (*Allium cepa*), which seems to have originated in central and western Asia but not in the Fertile Crescent, can be found as far back

as one is able to search the historical record, beginning in Sumer some 4,000 years ago, where it was widely used in cooking and where bread and onions formed part of a core diet for the peasants. Bread and onions were central as well to the diet of laborers on the Great Pyramid in Egypt, and the consumption of onion, garlic, and leek is depicted in Egyptian tomb art.[27] Many of the ancients thought that onions were symbols of eternity because of their concentric circles (perpetuated later in onion-shaped towers – a guarantee that they would last forever) and, according to some Roman writers, the onion in Egypt was regarded as a kind of deity.[28]

The leek (A. *porrum*) was probably also in use at an early date in the northern Fertile Crescent although the Egyptians are given credit for first cultivating them. Indeed Pliny confided to his readers that the best leeks came from Egypt, although the Greeks and the Romans both grew and appreciated them.[29]

There is no evidence that the Egyptians also used garlic (A. *sativum*), which was probably a native of central Asia. It was in use by the Bronze Age, but had a mixed reception in the Classical World; the Greeks favored the vegetable but not the Romans, who nonetheless made garlic a part of the diet of laborers (to give them strength) and soldiers (to give them courage).

It was only in India, however, that alliums – every one of them – were regarded as unrespectable. Elsewhere, at one time or another, all of them including shallots (A. *ascalonicum*) and chives (A. *schoenoprasum*), were regarded as medicines as well as foods. Onions were used against everything from sore throat to foot-fungus and garlic, often employed to bring down fevers and packed into wounds, also enjoyed a reputation as an aphrodisiac.[30]

Wild nuts such as almonds and pine nuts were gradually brought under cultivation, and with domestication and breeding cultivated fruits became sweeter and orchard crops more popular. In the northern Fertile Crescent, important cultivars were pomegranates (*Punica granatum*), among the first fruits to be cultivated, and palms bearing dates (*Phoenix dactylifera*). With a sugar content of over 50 percent, dates gave its consumers energy whereas the trees provided toddy from their sap.

The original home of the date palm is lost in antiquity and no wild progenitor has definitely been established. But it is known to have been cultivated for at least 6,000 years because dates were employed to feed workers constructing the temple of the moon god near Ur in southern Iraq. The Sumerians and the Babylonians made this palm their sacred tree and initiated the date palm breeding that has resulted in the more than 1,500 date varieties available today.[31] From Mesopotamia the date moved east through Iran to the Indus Valley and Pakistan, and west to Egypt, where it was growing along the Nile in the first millennia BCE. It was also grown in the Maghreb and Sahel regions, and later became a holy fruit for both Jew and Muslim. Christian legend has it that it may have been the date palm, not the apple, that was the fruit Eve offered to Adam.[32]

The fig (*Ficus carica*) was another early Middle Eastern favorite apparently native to Southwest Asia. Figs served as a cheap and staple food for many, had the virtue of tasting sweet whether fresh or dried, and in some places they were more heavily consumed than dates. The earliest place of fig cultivation is unknown, although they were apparently being grown in prehistoric Egypt.[33]

The apple (genus *Malus*), also thought to have its origin in southwest Asia, was one of the earliest tree crops to be widely cultivated, even before the transition from hunting and gathering to agriculture.[34] Apples were enjoyed by the ancients of the Middle East, but attained a more important position as an orchard crop in classical times and today there are over 7,000 varieties worldwide.[35]

And the Old World grape (*Vitus vinifera*) – thought to be a native of Asia Minor – was exploited for wine in Mesopotamia as early as 7,500 years ago (from grapes also came vinegar, an important pickling agent) although the viticulture passed on to the Mediterranean region seems to have been practiced more enthusiastically beginning around 3000 BCE.[36]

Finally, a native of the Middle East and the Mediterranean, flax (*Linum usitatissimum*) was among the first crops cultivated in Egypt, Syria, and Turkey (dating from at least 5000 BCE) for its fibers and, even more importantly, for its oil (linseed oil) used in cooking. Around 3,000 years ago flax cultivation spread to Europe where the plant was widely utilized in Greece, Rome, and northern Europe. It later entered medieval Russia, where it continued to be employed into modern times because the Orthodox Church did not proscribe its oil during days of fasting.[37] It has been largely forgotten that linseed oil was once an important food because today it used mostly for paints and varnishes.[38]

DIETARY SUPPLEMENTS

The flesh of sheep, goats, and pigs occasionally invigorated the Fertile Crescent diet, with the fat-tailed sheep a special favorite. But, as a rule, meat was consumed only on festive occasions and in dishes that stretched the meat such as kibbeh (about 6,000 years old) consisting of pounded lamb, *burghul* (cracked wheat), and onions.[39] Most animal protein, however, came from fish taken from the rivers, canals, and fishponds, along with that furnished by eggs and by cheese made from the milk of goats, sheep, and camels.[40]

Cheese making radiated out of western Iran where some claim it was invented around 4000 BCE. More likely it was a process discovered much earlier in the Neolithic, when humans began milking animals. Milk spoils quickly, but cheese is a different matter and all it took to get cheese was to leave skimmed milk out in the sun to ferment.[41]

FOOD AND NORTHERN FERTILE CRESCENT TECHNOLOGY

The dawning of the Bronze Age around 5,000 years ago marked the end of the Neolithic in Southwest Asia. At that time Sumerian civilization was in full flower. It had developed in the valleys of the Tigris and Euphrates rivers where annual floods delivered new deposits of fertile silt and where some 2,000 years earlier sophisticated irrigation agriculture techniques had been developed.[42] This momentous agricultural advance also made it possible to build fishponds (*vivaria*) and to maintain large stocks of aquatic animals such as those present in Sumerian temples around 2500 BCE.[43]

The sheer numbers of sedentary peoples provided an overwhelming military advantage over the remaining hunter-gatherers and other enemies, and before the beginning of the Bronze Age the Sumerians had put captives to work in their fields as slaves.[44] Such numbers also meant more brain power to draw upon. The sickle and the wheel were both pre–Bronze-Age inventions, and by the time of the Bronze Age domesticated animals were being harnessed to plows and wheeled vehicles. Such innovations extended agricultural areas, increased production, and facilitated the transportation of crops from field to market, while trade brought new plants, such as rice, millets, and sesame, to the region from the East.

The surpluses generated by this sort of agricultural activity, in turn, gave rise to the growth of towns housing as many as 10,000 people that began to dot the landscape; then city-states, such as Uruk, arose around 3500 BCE. Like other city-states that followed in western Asia, Uruk was administered by a priestly class made powerful by their control of food and its production. In a temple-complex priests determined the allocation of the city's lands, recorded agricultural production, oversaw its storage, and kept track of livestock. This agricultural record keeping led, in turn, to pictographic writing. Specialized scribes maintained temple archives on clay tablets that first recorded agricultural health but then branched out to codify laws and preserve religious mythology. The many segments of modern civilization were falling into place.

4

PERIPATETIC PLANTS
OF EASTERN ASIA

*We must also take into account the wheat pasta eaten in northern
China and Japan, countries usually thought of as consumers
of rice or pasta derived from rice.*

Giovanni Rebora (1998)

TROPICAL TUCK OF SOUTHEAST ASIA

Asia, sprawling over the eastern portion of the Eurasian land mass as the
largest of the world's continents was, not surprisingly, the site of many more
Neolithic upheavals than those that took place in the Fertile Crescent. Far to
its south and east – in East and Southeast Asia (Indochina) – parts of this vast
region can claim a close second in agricultural development.[1] Unfortunately,
monsoon Asia, with perhaps the best claim, lies in the tropical belt where
artifacts do not preserve well. Consequently there are considerable gaps in
the archeological record of foodstuffs and much remains speculative.[2]

Banana and Plantain

It has been proposed that in the islands of Melanesia – especially Papua New
Guinea – around 9,000 years ago, or even earlier, bananas were cultivated by
Australoid peoples whose predecessors reached these Asian outposts by crossing Indonesian land bridges that were later submerged. Geographically there
is no problem with this assertion. The wild ancestors of the domesticated

banana, *Musa acuminata* and M. *balbisiana*, (old usage designated the domesticated banana M. *sapientum* – "fruit of the wise men" – and the plantain M. *paradisiaca* – "heavenly fruit") were located in a region extending from New Guinea to Thailand.[3] But there is a big question about whether bananas were utilized as a food at that point.

Banana domestication would have been a lengthy process in which a small, seedy, inedible fruit was transformed into a large, seedless, edible one (plantains are drier and less sweet but bananas nonetheless). And it seems likely that such a transformation transpired because of another of those fortuitous accidents that so often greased the domestication process.

Because wild bananas were inedible food, the plants must have initially been cultivated to provide thatching to build shelters and fibers to make rope. Their leaves have myriad other uses including those of wrapping and serving foods.[4] In addition, banana trees (actually giant herbs) are useful for shading other crops. But out of banana-plant cultivation for these other uses a sugar-, starch-, and nutrient-packed fruit would have sooner or later emerged as an edible bonus. When this happened, we have no idea. A Burmese legend explains that humans first realized they could eat bananas only after seeing birds eating them.[5]

With this bonus the cultivation of banana plants – now capable of feeding as well as housing people – spread to South Asia (where linguistic evidence indicates that bananas have been utilized since circa 3000 BCE) and to East Asia, reaching south China toward the end of the first millennium BCE.[6] Between these dispersals another occurred as human pioneers carried the fruits into Oceania by way of western to eastern Melanesia, Polynesia, and Micronesia so that their cultivation was a familiar occupation in many Pacific islands by 1000 AD. When and how bananas reached East Africa remains a matter of conjecture, with the best guess being that they were carried across the Indian Ocean from Malaysia to Madagascar around the end of the first millennia AD. Following this, the fruit moved westward across the continent to be named "banana" on the Guinea Coast.[7]

The question of whether bananas reached the New World before Columbus has produced some lively controversy. In part the debate has centered on the claim that banana remains were found in early Peruvian tombs and, in part, on observations of early chroniclers, who assumed that banana trees were native to the American tropics because they were so widespread. Most authorities agree, however, that bananas only reached the Americas from the Canary Islands in 1516 (where they had earlier been carried from Africa by the Portuguese).[8] All of this, however, does introduce a persistent and unresolved problem dealing with pre-Columbian America's contact with Oceania that we will encounter again with the sweet potato.

Taro

Taros are among the oldest of the world's domesticated foods. There are four kinds of root crops called "taro," but only two of these – the "true taro" (*Colocasia esculenta*) and the "false taro" (*Alocasia macrorrhiza*) are widely traveled.[9] The cradle of both may have been South Asia, although they were under dry land cultivation in Southeast Asia 7,000 or more years ago, and it is thought that the time and energy lavished on ancient terraces built in Bali, Java, and the northern Philippines represents an investment in taro propagation.[10] Wetland cultivation based on irrigation techniques whereby taro was grown in prepared beds to control weeds was a later development and dry land, or upland cultivation, has always been the most widespread method of cultivating Colocasia taro.

Both taros began migrating with the Austronesians to reach the Philippines around 8,000 years ago, and Melanesia about 4,000 years ago. After this they sailed into the Pacific where they were carried by a heterogeneous people – a mixture of Austronesians and the earlier Australoids.

These were the greatest sailors of prehistory – their voyages marked by the Lapita pottery they left behind. Thanks to them taro became a highly valued foodstuff, even in the remote Hawaiian Islands where it is believed to have always been the staple.[11]

Colocasia taro also moved west to India, and reached Egypt at the beginning of the Common Era. Shortly thereafter it was introduced to Madagascar and spread throughout tropical

Africa. Around 714 AD, taro was taken to Iberia by the Moors and 800 years later was carried to the Americas. Called "dasheen" or "eddoe" in the Caribbean, it became an important food for African slaves.[12]

Yam

Several species of yams (genus *Dioscorea*) evolved separately in Asia, Africa, and the Americas. Both the greater yam (D. *alata*) and the lesser yam (D. *esculenta*) were domesticated in Southeast Asia perhaps 6,500 or more years ago to join taro as a valuable root crop. From Southeast Asia yams moved into Indonesia and reached Melanesia by 2000 BCE, Micronesia a bit later, and eastern Polynesia by 1500 BCE.[13]

Yams were present in China by the third century AD and in India about 200 years later. They traversed the Indian Ocean to Madagascar a few centuries after this (between the eleventh and the fifteenth centuries) and, by the end of the sixteenth century, D. *alata* had spanned the continent to be cultivated in West Africa. From Africa it crossed the Atlantic to the Americas in 1591 aboard a slave ship.[14]

Africa also had native yams. Two of these D. *cayenensis* and D. *rotundata*, may have been domesticated in West Africa as many as 8,000 years ago, suggesting an antiquity of agriculture south of the Sahara that some scholars have difficulty accepting. In part this is because African yam cultivation only became widespread some 2,500 years ago with the advent of iron working – a technology which provided the tools that made it possible for people to expand deeper into forests where ecological circumstances favored yams over grain crops.[15]

In most of the New World tropics, sweet potatoes, white potatoes, and manioc overshadowed the only native American yam (D. *trifida*), which was only a significant food in the northern regions of South America and in the Caribbean – areas where it is still widely cultivated today. Abroad D. *trifida* also found acceptance. It is cultivated on a limited basis in Sri Lanka and Southeast Asia. On the Indian subcontinent it is called the "India yam" and in Africa the "cush-cush" yam.[16]

Rice

Sporadic arguments among scholars erupt from time to time over the issue of whether root crop cultivation such as that of taro and yams preceded rice in Southeast Asia. Pioneers from the region spread out into the Pacific with taro and yams, but not rice, prompting the conclusion that Asian rice (*Oryza sativa*) was not an important crop in Southeast Asia when they departed. Confusion arises because their pioneering was done gradually and in stages. It began about 8,000 years ago when Austronesian peoples left Southeast Asia to fan out into the East Indies and the Philippine Islands, but it was much later – thousands of years in fact – that they settled Melanesia and then hived out into the Pacific. But – and this is the important point – they did leave the mainland before rice became important there around 5,500 years ago.[17]

An explanation for this tardy appearance of rice in Southeast Asia holds that it would have been difficult to cook it until pottery came into widespread use, whereas taro and yams could have been easily baked in earthen ovens or just tossed into the coals. A counterargument, of course, is that western Asian hunter-gatherers collected wheat or barley for food long before they had pottery. On the other hand they did not have such root crop alternatives.

Wild self-propagating stands of rice would have grown best in humid areas on poorly drained soils. Cultivation began when grains were planted nearer the home base, but much time probably elapsed before wild rice – whose original home may have been South Asia – became the domesticated O. *sativa* that now is a staple for almost half of the world's population.

The slow march toward domestication probably began at about the same time in China and India as it did in Southeast Asia – perhaps as many as 10,000 years ago – but at that early date rice was just one of many foods figuring into the diet. In Southeast Asia rice cultivation was almost exclusively of the dry variety, probably beginning in upland forest areas as well as small dooryard plots – primitive forms of cultivation that still persist in remote areas. By contrast, wet rice cultivation was not widely practiced in Southeast Asia until after the Suez Canal was opened in 1869 – an event that greatly expanded trade to the region at a time when European powers were looking for ways to feed growing colonial populations.[18]

Other Fruits and Vegetables of Southeast Asia

The eggplant (*Solanum melongena*) is an Old World relative of New World tomatoes and potatoes. Also known as *aubergines*, eggplants were first domesticated in either Southeast Asia or India. They reached Spain with the Muslims and from there moved north into Europe, south to Africa and west to the Americas. Thomas Jefferson is said to have brought them to North America.[19]

Fruits such as the sweet pomelo (*Citrus maxima*) followed the same route whereas lemons (*Citrus limon*) and limes (*Citrus aurantiifolia*), although natives of Southeast Asia, were apparently first cultivated in India (where Sanskrit names for both exist) and perhaps China as well. In fact lemons seem to have been in China about 1900 BC and reached Rome around the beginning of the Common Era aboard Roman ships taking advantage of the newly discovered route and techniques for sailing across the Indian Ocean. Lemons are depicted in frescos and mosaics found at Pompeii. But the Romans apparently regarded the lemon as an exotic fruit and there is no written record of lemon cultivation in Europe until the Arabs in the tenth century spread the fruit in the Mediterranean region.

Limes seem to have been domesticated in both India and China and were later introduced to southern Europe – perhaps by the Crusaders as well as the Arabs. Because limes were often viewed as green lemons, they are more difficult to keep track of than lemons. The latter was growing in the Azores in 1494 and both fruits began to flourish shortly after this in the New World, where the small, tart lime has alternatively been called a "Key" or "West Indian" or "Mexican" lime. (Persian limes are a recent cross between the lime and the citron.)

CHINA'S CHIEF COMESTIBLES

Rice

Although wild rice may have originated in South Asia, it was first cultivated in China, probably in the Yangtze Basin – a river practically synonymous with rice cultivation. Domesticated grains have been found there that are 7,000 years old and rice was the principal food plant for many burgeoning Chinese settlements. The cereal was originally cultivated on dry land, but with the advance of the Neolithic, irrigation techniques were gradually applied to wetland cultivation, and ultimately rice seedlings were transplanted into wet fields.[20]

As rice cultivation spread in China, it also took root in Southeast Asia around 5,500 years ago and in India some 500 years later. The grain was introduced to Korea and Japan about 3,000 years ago, and perhaps a bit later to Sri Lanka, the Malay Archipelago, the Indonesian islands, the Middle East (via the Persian Empire), and from there to Madagascar, whereupon it entered East Africa. West Africa, however, which had its own native rice (*Oryza glaberrima*), had to wait for Asian rice until a few decades after Columbus had carried it to the West Indies from whence it was transported eastward via the Atlantic slave trade.[21]

In China water buffalo began to partner with humans in wet rice cultivation, which accelerated tremendously around 1000 CE when a fast-ripening rice from Viet Nam reached the Yangtze River valley. The result was a doubling of China's population within the span of two centuries (from an estimated 60 million to 115 million).[22] Rice has continued to help spur population growth and today is a staple for billions.

Millet and Cereal Imports

Despite China's identification with rice, it was not its only important cereal, probably not even its first. Rather, in the harsh climate of the north along another of China's great rivers – the Huang Ho, or Yellow River – foxtail millet (*Setaria italica*), and proso or broomcorn millet (*Panicum miliaceum*) were under intensive cultivation by at least 5,000 to 6,000 years ago – a time when southern China was still a "foreign" (or separate) country.[23] The millets were later joined by barley and wheat – Middle Eastern contributions to food globalization along with an import from Africa – sorghum (*Sorghum bicolor*) (which reached China from Africa via India).

By at least 1000 BCE the Chinese were cultivating another grain, buckwheat (*Fagopyrum esculentum*), thought to be a native of Siberia and Manchuria. But intriguingly there is evidence that buckwheat was being grown in Japan much earlier between 3500 and 5000 BCE (it remains an important crop there used primarily for making buckwheat noodles or *soba*). Of course this raises, once again, that always pesky question about early contact between ancient cultures.[24]

Culinary Competition

These, then, were the crops that gave rise to China's first farming societies and later sustained what became China's first civilization. That civilization arose in a north that regarded the south as primitive, and because China's gradient between a cool dry north and a warm wet south did little to promote crop diffusion from one zone to another, rivalries seem to have been inevitable.[25] Wheat, ultimately, became the chief cereal in the north as did rice in the south – the crops helping to divide China into two entities, politically and economically, as well as culturally and culinarily.[26]

In the latter case, four major cuisines emerged: those of the northern region and the eastern-coastal region under the influence of the north; and those of the southern region and the central-western region influenced by the south.[27]

Vegetables and Fruits

China's stock of native vegetables and fruits was supplemented with other fruits of early globalization that originated elsewhere. By the first century BCE, cucumbers, peas, onions, coriander, sesame, grapes, and pomegranates were part of the Chinese diet, having arrived from other centers of agricultural innovation – especially the Fertile Crescent, India, and North Africa (via Central Asia). Later, under the Tang Dynasty (618–907 AD), the Persians donated spinach (now known as "Chinese spinach") to the dietary possibilities.[28]

Yet, all of these were late-comers when compared to the melon (*Cucumis melo*) – an apparent African native –and the bitter orange (*Citrus aurantium*) that reached China from Southeast Asia, via the Indus Valley. Both were growing in southern China some 4,000 to 5,000 years ago, along with apricots (*Prunus armeniaca*) and jujubes (*Ziziphus jujuba*). After their arrival in China, melons seem to have been almost rushed over to the Indus valley. Oranges, by contrast, moved more slowly. Whether the sweet orange was a native of China, or like its bitter cousin, actually originated in Southeast Asia (Viet Nam, then called Cochin China, may have been the place) has not been resolved despite its scientific name *Citrus sinensis*.

Initially, however, all oranges were bitter and used mostly for their scent – that bitterness probably the reason that they remained in China (and India) for many centuries before they became known elsewhere. The Arabs carried the bitter orange from India into the Mediterranean basin around 1000 AD, but the sweet orange from China trailed behind to enter the Mediterranean sometime in the fifteenth century, perhaps with Genoese traders or Portuguese explorers.[29]

Other native fruits reached the outside world from China. In the past the apricot was regarded as a kind of plum that had come to China from Armenia (hence the scientific name *P. armeniaca*). But there is evidence, as suggested earlier, that the fruit actually originated in China and may have been cultivated there for some 5,000 years. It arrived in Mesopotamia, by way of northern India, and later Alexander the Great introduced the fruit to Greece, leaving Roman legionnaires to spread it throughout Europe.[30]

The jujube, with a French name meaning "lozenge," is definitely a native of China that has been grown there almost as long as the apricot. From China the fruit spread out over East Asia and was cultivated in the Mediterranean circa 2,500 years ago. In fact, the lotus jujube (*Ziziphus lotus*) was the fruit of the lotus-eaters of Libya known to us from accounts by Herodotus and Pliny. In addition, cinnamon (*Cinnamomum zeylanicum*) and cassia (*Cinnamomum cassia*), natives of Sri Lanka and Burma respectively, were first mentioned as spices in China around 2500 BCE – at about the time that the Chinese acquired cassia from Burma. Roughly a thousand years later, cinnamon was passed westward as far as Egypt, where it was used in embalming, and perhaps as a foodstuff as well.[31]

Agricultural Revolution

The influence of the south gained ground against that of the north during the Song dynasty (960–1279 AD), when China's "first agricultural revolution" (after the Neolithic) took place.[32] Private land ownership and a new elite class of landed gentry did much to promote agriculture in the south, whereas the north was increasingly coming under the control of Central Asian nomadic groups. This, in turn, provoked mass migration southward into the temperate and subtropical lands along the Yangtze River and beyond with long growing seasons.[33] Agricultural abundance meant swelling urban populations and with prosperity a demand arose for such novel foods as bananas, originally from Southeast Asia, and the native litchi and apricot. Tea and sugar also came into general use during the Song dynasty.[34]

What really fueled this first agricultural revolution, however, was state encouragement, beginning in 1012, of a rice variety that had originated in central Vietnam. This was the drought-resistant, early ripening Champa rice, which Song agricultural officials imported and then handed out free of charge to farmers. Another virtue of Champa rice was that it could be cultivated in poor soils and, consequently, the amount of land planted in rice grew enormously, and an already thriving trade in rice to the cities grew exponentially. So did the population, which almost doubled in the two centuries between 1000 and 1200.[35]

Soybean

Shen Nung, a legendary Chinese emperor, known in folklore as the "Divine Ploughman" or the "Divine Husbandman" is credited with ordering (around 2700 BCE) plants classified according to food and medicinal value. Out of that list emerged five principal and sacred crops. Four of these, barley, wheat, millet, and rice, have already been noted. The addition of the soybean as the fifth may be confirmation that this piece of Chinese folklore was elaborated substantially later than 2700 BCE, because some sources do not place the domesticated soybean (*Glycine max*) in China before 1000 BCE. Others insist, however, that the wild soybean (G. *soja*) of northeastern China and Manchuria has been domesticated for at least 4,500 years, which squares with the legend while leaving the suspicion that the latter may have had something to do with the dating of the former.

Regardless, the soybean has become the most widely consumed plant in the world. Moreover, it is the only plant food that yields a whole protein (as do meat and milk) – an especially important quality in crowded countries where animal protein is in short supply. Today soy is the most important of the vegetable oils, but is also used for sprouts, vegetable milk, meal and flour, tofu, sauces, salad dressings, and margarines, and has a number of other food-processing uses. The beans are also dried and salted as a snack.[36]

Presumably soybeans were similarly employed by the ancient Chinese who even dried eggs. Tofu was the "meat without bones" of vegetarian Buddhist missionaries who made mock meat dishes from it and carried soybeans to Japan and Korea in the sixth century AD, where they gained staple status. Soybeans also found their way into the Philippines, Southeast Asia, and Indonesia at an early date, and made the journey to India, but eons would elapse before they developed into a major crop in the Western Hemisphere.[37]

Beverages

The Chinese also fostered tea cultivation[38] – now the world's foremost beverage after water. But long before tea became popular they were drinking alcohol. In fact, millennia before the advent of distillation in the West the Chinese were producing beverages with an alcohol content of between 10 and 15 percent. These were not beers, but rather the result of a "combined fermentation" process whereby an ad hoc ferment was produced to begin the fermentation of a mash of cooked cereals.[39]

Fish

And finally, well before 1000 BCE, the Chinese pioneered in aquatic farming. The common carp was a symbol of fortune in China and frequently given as a gift. Naturally one had to have a place to put such gifts, and thus, according to one story at least, fish pools became the solution.[40] Around 500 BCE, a Chinese wrote that culturing carp was one of the five best ways to earn a living and 1,000 years later, driven by an impulse to give tribute rather than receive it, the Chinese spread fish culture throughout all of Asia. For some 500 years, until the "Great Withdrawal of 1433," Chinese naval expeditions reached every inhabited place on the China Sea and Indian Ocean, telling of the grandeur of each new dynasty, distributing treasure, and passing along skills such as those of fish-farming.[41]

SOUTH ASIAN ALIMENTS

The Indus civilization, which came into being around 4,500 years ago, is the most obscure and enigmatic of the very early agricultural civilizations. It may also have been the largest, encompassing an area stretching from present-day Pakistan into India. That area contained hundreds of towns and villages and at least two major cities – arbitrarily named Harappa and Mohenjo Daro (we do not know their names in antiquity). These were close to the Indus River and its tributaries and depended on the river's annual flooding for the production of substantial agricultural surpluses. Excavation has revealed the Indus civilization to be one concerned with agriculture and trade that had links with Mesopotamia, Egypt, and Crete. Trade seems to have been conducted with the Far East as well.[42]

Much of this traffic was carried out in sailing ships called "dhows," which had been crossing the Indian Ocean for millennia to introduce new foods to places as far away as Africa and to carry away others (like sorghum and millets) back to India. And, India was not that far from Sumer – by ship along the coast of the Persian Gulf to the mouth of the Indus River or overland across Iran and Baluchistan. The active trade that developed among Mesopotamia, the Iranian Plateau, and the Indus Valley ensured that the Indus civilization, which apparently was cultivating domesticated rice by some 5,000 years ago, added wheat, barley, and millet to its list of staples; and Indian cookery was transformed into a "tale of three cereals."[43]

Rice, although eaten everywhere in India, was only a dietary mainstay in the south, where it was intensively cultivated. Wheat, by contrast, was mainly cultivated in the north, whereas millet – grown on the poorest soils – was the staple of the poor. Barley and peas, also Middle Eastern imports, were cultivated, as was sorghum. Although the dispersal of sorghum to Asia is poorly documented, the best guess is that it reached India from East Africa across the Indian Ocean in the second century BCE – probably in one of those dhows.[44]

Sesame (*Sesamum indicum*) was first cultivated in the Indus Valley. It was among history's first oilseeds at a time when oil was in great demand for illumination and as a cosmetic, as well as for cooking and food preservation. Not surprisingly then, sesame quickly radiated out of South Asia to Sumer, Egypt, and Anatolia.[45]

The mango (*Mangifera indica*), domesticated between 4,000 and 6,000 years ago in Southeast Asia, entered the Indus valley to become *the* favorite fruit. Some 24,000 couplets of the Hindu epic *Ramayana* (c. 300 BCE) refer to the numerous fruits of the region such as jackfruit (*Artocarpus beterophyllus*) and Jambolan plum (*Eugenia jambolana*) but none are mentioned so frequently as the mango which, among its many uses, was the foundation of chutney.[46] Other fruits were imported, such as oranges from China, limes and lemons from Southeast Asia, date palms from Mesopotamia, and the pomegranate probably from Persia where it is thought to be a native.

A member of the squash family and another native of India, the cucumber (*Cucumis sativus*), was most likely first domesticated in the north.[47] A mainstay of Indian cuisine, the cucumber, a member of the gourd family, had become a common vegetable in Egypt by Pharonic times, and reportedly was a part of the diet of Hebrew slaves. Cucumbers are sometimes difficult to sort out in the literature from their other melon relatives but it seems clear that they

were an important vegetable in classical times. Both the ancient Greeks and the Romans knew cucumbers – the Romans eating them in a salad of sorts, with salt, pepper, vinegar and other seasonings.[48]

An important relative of the cucumber is the cultivated melon. It may have originated in tropical Africa, but India, Southwest Asia, and Egypt are also mentioned as cradles of the melon, opening up the distinct possibility that melons may have originated, or at least become domesticated, in a belt running all the way from India to Africa.[49]

The melon is especially hard to keep track of because of its membership in the widespread *Cucurbitaceae* family. Plant expert Charles B. Heiser Jr. explains that the Latin word *cucurbitare* means to commit adultery, and melons have always been promiscuous interbreeders.[50] The bitter melon (*Momordica charantia*), however, does seem to be a native of India, grown for millennia in that part of the world where it is heavily employed in curries.

Humped cattle, pigs, water buffaloes, camels, and likely the elephant were all domesticated in the region, and milk figured heavily in a diet that was based on this liquid, bread, vegetables, and fruits, with *ghi* or *ghee*, a clarified butter, the cooking medium. The Indo-European or Aryan invasions that destroyed the Indus cities around 1500 BCE hastened the collapse of an already fading civilization and, shortly after this, the pig disappeared while cattle became sacred and therefore taboo animals. For those not committed to vegetarianism, choices narrowed to the flesh of goats or chickens. On the other hand, the Aryans, previously herders, brought with them a heavy reliance on dairy products, and the conquered peoples had no problem expanding their milk-based diets even more.[51]

LATER EAST ASIAN AGRICULTURE

The development of agriculture in Korea and Japan lagged considerably behind that of China. For the most part the Japanese remained hunter-gatherers until the very end of the Neolithic period (known as the *Jōrmon* era), gathering acorns and chestnuts, hunting game, and exploiting the marine resources within and off the shores of their islands.[52]

Rice reached Korea from China sometime between 2000 and 1122 BCE and ancient sources portray a settled village life during the Old Chosen period – the first recognized period of Korean history dating from sometime around 2300 to roughly 560 BCE.[53] Rice – the Yangtze delta grain – along with tools and techniques for cultivating it (including those of wet rice cultivation)[54] began arriving in Japan around 400 BCE with waves of migrants who passed through the Korean peninsula and others who came directly from China by sea.[55]

Rice was soon the staple grain in both countries, although peasants living in mountainous areas, where rice cultivation was difficult, grew other cereals – especially native millets that might have been eaten alone or mixed with rice to stretch it. Other grains that came from China included barley and wheat (now some distance away from their Middle Eastern cradle), along (apparently) with buckwheat, which (as previously reported) the Japanese still use to make buckwheat noodles (*soba*).

As in China, milk and dairy products failed to become popular in either Korea or Japan. This factor, along with Buddhism, whose monks from China brought with them tea, soybeans, and a taboo against killing animals, militated against an intake of good-quality protein. All three of these items had a profound effect on cuisines and cultures, with the effect most dramatic in Japan. There the ancient *Shintō* religion saw eye to eye with the Buddhist prohibition on killing animals, and meat consumption practically disappeared, whereas the eating of fish (generally raw according to the proverb: "Eat it raw first of all, then grill it, and boil it as the last resort") was made even more appealing with soy sauce – especially when it was flavored with a little grated wasabi (*Wasabia japonica*).[56]

The Koreans, by contrast, raised cattle, pigs, and chickens on a small scale despite Buddhism and thus some meat was a part of the diet, along with pickled fish and shellfish which served as side dishes to accompany rice.[57] Another side dish was a form of sushi that originated as a method of preserving fish by fermenting them in boiled rice. Sushi is a Japanese word but the same preservation practice was also employed in southwestern Korea, China, and Southeast Asia, where it appears to have originated – probably diffusing throughout East Asia from the Mekong River.[58]

Soups, bean curds, meat, fish, and vegetables were also served as side dishes for rice, and in Korea the most popular of these was (and is) *kim-chee* – a fermented vegetable preparation made with radishes, among other ingredients, to provide a little heat – until the arrival of the American chilli peppers to "kick it up a notch."[59]

FECUND FRINGES OF THE NORTHERN FERTILE CRESCENT

*Bread is a very simple manufactured article whose rise in the oven
is closely related to the rise of the sun in the sky.*

Piero Camporesi (1989)

AFRICAN VIANDS

Egypt and North Africa

For thousands of years after the beginnings of Mesopotamian agriculture, an abundance of game animals, lake and river fish, and wild cereals in North Africa did little to discourage a foraging way of life.[1] Hunter-gatherer groups adopted livestock herding, yet continued to gather wild plants – especially the root parts of sedges, rushes, and cattails in riparian environments.[2] But around 5000 BCE the Sahara began expanding, an expansion that accelerated sharply around 2000 BCE.[3] Desertification ushered people into fertile oases, and especially into the Nile Valley, where periodic migrations from the northwest brought knowledge of the Middle Eastern plant complex. It was in that valley that first barley and later wheat began to flourish, although until farming took firm hold, Nile fish (particularly catfish) and root foods continued to sustain many.[4] By around 4000 BCE, however, small states and kingdoms had arisen, supported by "taxes" levied on peasant farmers on food that went directly into the storehouses of the rulers. The small principalities gradually evolved into the two large states of Upper and Lower Egypt that were fused around 3100 BCE under the first of the pharaohs. Exploitation quickened of a peasantry that now had nowhere to go. Desertification had trapped them in the Nile Valley, where the Pharaoh owned all of the land. They worked it under the supervision of civil servants and turned over their crops to a government that redistributed them. It was a rationing process that allotted food to the peasants but could also withhold it. When the Nile flooded (late July into October), this labor force became mobile and was applied to public works projects and pyramid building.

We know something of the foods consumed by ancient Egyptians from depictions in tomb and temple art, as well as hieroglyphic writing. Nile fish, birds, cereals, breads, fruits such as the melon and watermelon, and vegetables (some names, listed in texts remain to be translated), legumes (especially brown fava beans), and onions, garlic, leeks, and radishes (used for medicinal as well as culinary purposes) were available to even the poorest, who mostly subsisted on bread, beer, and wild plants such as *melokhia* leaves (*Corchorus olitorius*).

These leaves, from a plant growing on the Nile floodplains, resemble spinach and have been turned into a soup by peasants (the *fellahs*) for thousands of years. Also ancient is *ful medames*, boiled brown beans seasoned with olive oil. Lentils were a base of soup; barley and emmer were processed to make beer; and grapes (grown in the Pharaoh's orchards) were turned into wine. In view of this it is not surprising that the Egyptians are credited with composing some of the world's oldest drinking songs.[5]

Flax and sesame from the Indus Valley were grown for oil, and it was probably from Egypt that sesame reached Arabia to later slip into literature as that famous door opening command – "open sesame!" – perhaps, some have speculated, because of the lubricating ability of its high quality oil.[6]

Clearly the Egyptian diet was mostly vegetarian, and this was so for all classes of society, although individuals in the upper strata availed themselves of greater quantities and varieties. What kinds of animal protein were consumed and by whom is more difficult to determine. The Egyptians failed to domesticate numerous African species such as the gazelle, antelope, ibex, and hyena.[7] They had some luck with monkeys – almost 4,000 years ago the Pharaohs of the Twelfth Dynasty had tamed and trained, if not domesticated, monkeys to harvest figs and grapes.[8] But they had the most success with those barnyard animals already domesticated elsewhere, like cattle, pigs, sheep, goats, and chickens.

A problem here is the extent to which religion interfered with meat consumption. Cattle, the most highly valued of Egyptian livestock, served as draft and sacrificial animals and were also sources of food. Most beef apparently went to the elite including the priests, who did the butchering, although at times Egyptian priests refrained from eating beef; and from time to time there were sweeping beef prohibitions.[9] Meat and milk for the lower classes came from sheep and goats, judging from the great numbers of their bones turned up in settlement sites.[10]

Pig bones were also plentiful in those sites and prior to 3200 BCE pork was regularly eaten in the north (Lower Egypt) but avoided in the south (Upper Egypt). Yet, when the south conquered the north, pork avoidance became broad-based. Consumption slowed, then ceased almost completely and, at best, was spasmodic for religious and political[11] reasons during the Dynastic (3100–332 BCE) and Post-Dynastic periods.[12] When Osiris worship dominated, pigs were portrayed as unclean – even a source of leprosy – and their herders were similarly regarded.[13] Naturally enough, some have seized upon Egyptian pork avoidance to explain Mosaic pork prohibitions some 2,000 years later.

Because of such vicissitudes in domestic animal consumption, Nile fish and wild fowl appear to have been the most important sources of animal protein for rich and poor alike, although even a few species of fish were prohibited for religious reasons, and a dim view was taken of fishing as a profession.[14] Both fish and fowl were abundant and cheap although *batarekh* (salted dried roe of the gray mullet) was an ancient dish that those on the lower rungs of the social ladder never tasted.[15] Great flocks of migrating birds regularly stopped over in the Nile Valley and many of their members were killed and eaten or captured and fattened for later consumption.

During the Early Dynastic period (c. 3100–2686 BCE) the diets of rich and poor were probably similar. However, by the time of the New Kingdom (c. 1567–1085 BCE), society had become rigidly stratified and, with imperial expansion that ranged from Nubia and Ethiopia to Syria, Lebanon, and Palestine, and the benefits of long-distance trade, a huge difference materialized between the two diets in both quantitative and qualitative terms. New foods such as pine nuts, almonds, pomegranates, grapes, and olives acquired from the Middle East were probably the exclusive property of the elite, as honey and beef had always been. And that elite doubtless was looking down on foods it had classified as "low status" because they sustained the commoners.[16]

Bread and beer, however, were not among them and the fertile soils of the Nile floodplain produced great quantities of emmer wheat and barley, surpluses that were the basis of state wealth and food for the legions employed in the construction of pyramids, tombs, and a vast array of other public works projects. Arabs in North Africa outside of Egypt found another use for wheat and barley in the form of couscous. Initially couscous consisted of a coarsely ground grain turned into a kind of bran pasta called *kuskussù*. But as the dish evolved, dough was employed and shaped into sizes ranging from pellets to tiny balls. These were prepared in tiered clay devices within which vegetables, and perhaps mutton were cooked on the lower level and the couscous steamed on top. From North Africa, couscous spilled out into the Mediterranean, where the pasta was regularly added to soups – a practice that gave rise to soups like Italy's minestrone.[17]

South of the Sahara

Agriculture also diffused from the Middle East and Egypt to Africa south of the Sahara where, some 9,000 years ago, everybody was a hunter-gatherer.[18] It arrived initially with nomadic herders of Eurasian animals who were drifting southward to escape the increasing aridity. These domesticated animals arrived in waves from southwest and central Asia. First there were sheep and goats, and then came cattle (although as mentioned earlier it is possible that indigenous wild cattle were domesticated in North Africa).

Africa sorely needed these new animals. Although it hosted more native cereals than any other continent, this abundance was not extended to domesticated animals. In fact, Africa only contributed two animals to the growing pool – the ass (*Equus asinus*) and the guinea fowl or hen (*Numida meleagris*).[19] And of the two (astoundingly, in view of the many large animals the continent is known for), the guinea fowl was the only one domesticated south of the Sahara.[20]

The herders followed the Nile upstream to create settlements near the junction of the White and Blue Nile. These settlements were founded some 7,000 years ago, according to archeological remains from Kadero and Esh Shaheinab (where wheat and barley may have been grown at a later date). From these bases people spread out to the southeast, reaching Ethiopia between 5,000 and 6,000 years ago.

Sometime after 1000 BCE, chickens seem to have traveled the Nile southward from Egypt (the current flows north but the winds blow to the south) and early in the Common Era, Indian Ocean seafarers probably reintroduced them to East Africa. Interestingly, although it has generally been assumed that camels, domesticated in the Arabian Peninsula, entered Africa in caravans crossing the Sinai, they may instead have been transported even earlier across the Red Sea to Ethiopia during Roman times, which would help to explain their apparent greater antiquity among Ethiopia's desert nomads.[21]

Camels were crucial to the Cushites – those livestock specialists in the Ethiopian highlands who later advanced across the desert to the Red Sea.[22] Other peoples, the southern Cushites, migrated with their livestock southward into lands that today are Kenya and Tanzania, where they introduced finger millet-based agriculture.[23] Finger millet (*Eleusine coracana*) – so-called because the seed heads look like hands with the grain contained in the "digits" – was probably native to the highlands of Ethiopia and to neighboring Uganda.[24] From there, finger millet agriculture also spread north and west into the Sudan while, at about the same time, Central Sudanic peoples, who had been growing sorghum and herding goats, sheep, and cattle on their savannas, journeyed in the other direction to enter Uganda and introduced grain sorghum (*Sorghum bicolor*) cultivation.

There are numerous variants of this important tropical African grass (bicolor, durra, guinea etc.) whose wild progenitor is the widely distributed race verticilliflorum – so widely distributed, in fact, that sorghum could have been domesticated almost anywhere across the African savanna on the fringes of the Sahara. Indeed, it was in this broad band that intensive tropical agriculture probably began with grain sorghum and pearl millet among the first African cereals to be domesticated.[25] A belt running from Sudan to Nigeria seems a good bet for sorghum's domestication since verticilliflorum is especially abundant there – that domestication thought to have occurred about 3,000 to 4,000 years ago. Sorghum crossed the Indian Ocean from East Africa to Asia around 200 BCE and later reached China, probably during the Mongol conquest.[26] Much later the slave trade carried it to the Americas.

Teff or tef (*Eragrostis tef*), which is another of Africa's domesticated grasses, also originated in and around the Ethiopian highlands, and Ethiopia is the only country where it remains a significant crop today, although it is grown in surrounding countries like Yemen, Kenya, and has been carried to India and even to North America to satisfy an Ethiopian restaurant demand.[27] The tiny teff grains are ground into a darkish flour, which is used to make a spongy, soft bread called *injera*.

In western Africa, agriculture was practiced on the edges of the tropical forest zone some 3,000 to 4,000 years ago although West Africa's oldest cereal, fonio (*Digitaria exilis* sometimes called "hungry rice" and D. *iburua* called *acha* in Nigeria) is a millet said to have been cultivated on dry savannas for a much longer time.[28] But as the pace of West African agriculture grew more lively, goats, sheep, and a dwarf cattle variety increased in importance while sorghum was planted in one place, and pearl millet (*Pennisetum glaucum*) in another.[29]

Pearl millet – another descendent of a wild West African grass – was domesticated 4,000 years ago on the southern fringes of an expanding Sahara desert, from whence it spread into East Africa and thence to India around 3,000 years ago. It is remarkably adapted to heat and aridity, easy to grow, and more disease resistant than most other grains. Pearl millet is also versatile – the grains are cracked and eaten as a porridge or couscous; if left whole, they are eaten like rice and when ground are worked into flour for unfermented bread (*roti*).[30]

Also under cultivation, at least for the past 3,500 years (if a single source can be relied upon), was African rice sometimes called "river rice." It was probably domesticated in the flood basin of central Niger and has been grown ever since mostly in the southwestern region of West Africa.[31] It is utilized in the same manner as Asian rice, and is also made into beer.

Well-traveled African plants include the cowpea (*Vigna unguiculata*), which may have been gathered in South Asia during prehistoric times, but was definitely under cultivation in West Africa (central Ghana) close to 4,000 years ago, from whence it much later entered Europe and later still journeyed to the New World via Europeans and the slave trade.[32]

Early cultivators of cowpeas and yams made extensive use of the fruits of the oil palm (*Elaeis guineensis*), a West African native whose oil nourished indigenous peoples for millennia before recorded history. The peoples in this case apparently also included North Africans because archeological evidence indicates that palm oil was available in ancient Egypt some 5,000 years ago – meaning that it was traded overland. Oil palms produce fruit in large bunches weighing twenty pounds or more, with each containing a thousand or more fruits about the size of a small plum.[33] The oil is made by pressing the fresh fruit and that oil later became an important item in provisioning slave ships destined for the Americas. It was this trade to Brazil that reunited the African oil palm with a long lost native-American cousin (*Elaeis oleifera*). Both are now important in producing American palm oil.[34]

Another domesticate from the tropical forest is okra (*Hibiscus esculentus*) often called "gumbo" and "lady fingers." Actually a fruit rather than a vegetable, okra's migration out of Africa to the forests of tropical Asia went largely unrecorded. However, we know that the Egyptians used okra in the twelfth century AD and that it entered Moorish Spain at around the same time. Like the oil palm, okra found its way via the slave trade to the Americas (probably in the latter half of the seventeenth century), and today is used in most of the hot-weather cultures of the world. From Asia to the Western Hemisphere, okra is grilled, fried, batter-fried, mixed into curries, and is a chief ingredient of stews.[35]

Kola (*Cola acuminata* and *C. nitida*) or cola nuts contain theobromine and caffeine. Consequently they are important as stimulants. Kola trees are indigenous to the forest zone of West Africa, and their nuts (about the size of a chestnut) joined gold and salt as important items of long-distance African trade. Much later kola trees left Africa with European colonizers – the British introducing them to the East Indies, and both the British and the French taking the nuts in the opposite direction to their West Indies possessions. In the recent past, kola has been used to flavor beverages and is one of the "secret" ingredients in Coca Cola, now minus the coca.[36]

There are two final forest products of West Africa. One is ackee (*Blighia sapida*), a fruit used in West African cooking whose late eighteenth-century introduction to Jamaica is erroneously attributed to Captain William Bligh (it arrived on a slave ship).[37] The second is melegueta (or malagueta) pepper (*Aframomum melegueta*) – famous as the "grains of paradise." Melegueta peppers are related to cardamom and pack a hot and spicy flavor. The Portuguese encountered the spice in the fifteenth century along a stretch of West African coast that they called Malagueta, and began importing the grains to Europe whereupon the (now Liberian) coast came to be known as the "Grain Coast." Melegueta pepper was overshadowed by American chilli peppers after their arrival and has dwindled in importance in Africa, but remains a major component of the Afro-Brazilian cookery of Bahia, which began with African slaves.[38]

Watermelons (*Citrullus lanatus*) and possibly melon are African natives, with their many names in many languages indicating that they have truly traveled the world. They had a head start in such globe-trotting because of the antiquity of their domestication. As already noted, melon was being grown in China, Egypt, India, Iran, and Greece during the Bronze Age. Watermelons were originally domesticated in the savanna zones of central and southern Africa where they were, and remain, a life-giving source of water. In desert oases such as those in the Kalahari Desert, for example, they still grow wild around water holes, and their presence alerts one to the existence of water below them, even if it is not visible. Watermelon seeds, a good source of oil as well as protein, were highly prized, along with the flesh and the rind.

Watermelons reached northern Africa and southwest Asia over 6,000 years ago and were cultivated in ancient Egypt about 1,000 years after that; the fruit is depicted in the art of the first Pharonic tombs and its seeds are found in funerary offerings.[39] Yet, the fruit was comparatively slow to reach India (800 AD) and China (1100 AD). Watermelons were introduced to southern Europe by the Moorish conquerors of Spain, but were slow to spread northward where summers were not hot enough for a good yield. Watermelon seeds came to the Americas from Africa with the slave trade, and probably from Spain as well.[40]

It was the yam-cultivating Bantu with origins in present-day Nigeria who established agricultural production in the equatorial forest. They depended greatly on fish and, around 4,000 years ago, began to enter the forest along river valleys where they planted the white yam and, possibly, the potato yam, (*Dioscorea bulbifera*) in fertile soils. Other yams from Asia reached the Bantu somewhat later as they spread throughout equatorial Africa, especially the greater or water yam (D. *alata*) from Southeast Asia, and the Chinese yam or lesser yam from China.[41]

There is uncertainty about the time that some of the Asian foods turned up in Africa because of the Malayo-Polynesians (Austronesians) from Borneo, who (incredibly) migrated some 4,000 miles across the Indian Ocean to settle Madagascar, just 250 miles off the African coast. Because this mind-boggling feat (or feats since there were apparently a series of voyages) has been dated to sometime around 500 AD, there is the very real possibility that the newcomers introduced Asian plants, particularly bananas, to East Africa sometime during the first millennium of the Common Era.[42] Alternatively, these foods may have arrived much earlier via Egypt and the Nile or with traders along the East African coast.

Either way, the Asian yams, along with bananas and plantains, were an integral part of agriculture's extension throughout the rainforest. Moreover, bananas, which grew well in forest regions not favorable to yams or millets, joined them in engineering something of a population explosion. In Africa south of the Sahara, humans increased from around 12 million in 500 BCE to some 20 million by the year 1000, to 35.5 million by 1500.[43]

EUROPEAN EDIBLES

By 5000 BCE, relatively few areas of the globe were totally dependent on agriculture and in those parts of Europe away from the Mediterranean, farming, where it was practiced at all, was a part-time means of supplementing hunted and gathered fare. The Swiss lake dwellers, for example, were fisher folk who lived in houses built on stilts and harvested wild cereal grains that they crushed to make breads, and wild apples that they dried for winter. Yet, sometime in the late Neolithic or Early Bronze Age, although still hunting and gathering, they were also cultivating lentils, fox-tail millet, and peas.[44]

Signs of the penetration of Neolithic agriculture into Europe have also been found in central Germany where what seem to have been domesticated peas were being grown between 4400 and 4200 BCE. Yet, by 3000 BCE or so, cereals were under wide-scale cultivation and herds of sheep and goats had become common sights on the landscape.[45]

What happened to speed things up? Until that time, the various Neolithic Revolutions we have examined were gradual in their transformation of foragers into farmers. But those that took place in northern Europe and the British Isles were in fact revolutions that brought abrupt change – a significant departure from the leisurely transition that had characterized earlier centers of agriculture. What happened was agricultural diffusion – a diffusion which abruptly brought much of the farming expertise developed earlier in the Middle East to a heretofore remote foraging people.[46] In the British Isles, for example, domesticated animals – sheep, goats, pigs, and cattle – all arrived at the same time (around 3500 BCE) with Neolithic immigrants from the coasts of the Continent, so that herding was instantly underway.

Pigs, sheep, goats, and cattle had also diffused in Northern Europe where the horse was well established by 2500 BCE. Crops developed in the Fertile Crescent reached northern Europe through the Balkans via the Danube to blanket river valleys. These included wheat, or rather its ancestors, einkorn and emmer, barley, peas, lentils, and flax, the most important source of oil in northern Europe during its Neolithic Revolution.

Following these waves of crops and animals, the pace of agriculture slowed down some. Spelt (*Triticum spelta*) did not reach Europe until later, and it was not until the eighth century BCE that invading Celtic-speaking tribes added geese, ducks, and chickens to the barnyard.[47] But after this, the pace picked up again with the arrival of the Romans who brought new crops to tend, such as rye and oats, along with viticulture and grove fruits. In fact, the oldest groves and vineyards in Northern Europe date from the Roman period thanks to the stability induced by the Pax Romana (Roman Peace). Before the Romans, one invader after another had made life violent and chaotic and settlements were consequently short-lived, lasting only a few decades at best – such conditions making the establishment of groves and vines a forlorn hope.[48]

CONSEQUENCES OF THE NEOLITHIC

One of humanity's most important inventions is agriculture. This decisive step freed people from the quest for food and released energy for other pursuits. No civilization has existed without an agricultural base, whether in the past or today. Truly, agriculture was the first great leap forward by human beings.

Richard S. MacNeish, *The Origins of Agriculture and Settled Life*

SOCIAL AND CULTURAL CONSEQUENCES

As we have seen, save in northern Europe, the Neolithic Revolution did not bring abrupt change. But it did bring profound change to every aspect of human existence in no small part because of the more rigorous demands of an agricultural way of life. The original impulse for animal taming and domestication was not so much a desire for the meat, milk, eggs, and hides that came later as it was a perceived need for sacrificial animals. This, of course, suggests that the uncertainties inherent in planting and harvesting crops had led to religious rituals aimed at removing some of those uncertainties. The production of agricultural surpluses meant that not everyone was needed for agricultural labor and most likely those first freed from it were individuals with explanations for the forces of nature and the gods. Formalized religion, then, grew out of the Neolithic just as surely as the crops it gave rise to.

Other cultural changes followed. As agriculture removed the constraints on the food supply that confronted hunter-gatherers, up to a quarter of the labor force was released for other activities and, at the same time, Middle Eastern priests (and later on their Egyptian counterparts) transformed themselves into agricultural administrators and invented writing to keep records.[1] Vastly increased social organization was another product of the Neolithic and, in those early civilizations that arose in Mesopotamia, Egypt, eastern Asia (dominated by northern China), and the Indus Valley, people with power evolved into rulers – although often ruling in concert with the priestly and noble classes, commanding administrators, and warriors as well as the common people. Food control was power and, in each of the early agriculture-based civilizations, governments claimed a hefty portion of its production.[2]

To be sure, those governments stored food as a hedge against famine. But this made rulers even more powerful, able to withhold food or determine who received it and who did not. Administrative centers grew from towns into cities built by those released from agriculture, containing many more who did not work on the land but made their living from those who did. The next leap was to stigmatize those who did the farming – and such social stratification soon began to dictate what could be eaten and drunk and by whom. Skeletal evidence indicates the tremendous nutritional disparities that existed between elite minorities and the common people from the beginning of agriculture onward, with the elite minorities often supplementing their already plentiful meals at royal banquets that lasted for days and featured gargantuan quantities of food – a symbol of the ruler's status. A good example was the ten day party thrown by Assurnasirpal II (883–859 BC) to inaugurate his new palace. It was not lost on the guests (numbering some 70,000) that their host commanded tributes of food and drink from the remotest corners of the Assyrian empire, nor that he was firmly allied with the greatest of the aristocratic families.[3]

Women seem to have been the biggest losers in this dawn-of-civilization stratification process – so much so that by the time the mists obscuring the Neolithic began to dissipate, almost all power was in the hands of males who controlled both religion and government. Although earlier foraging societies were not completely egalitarian and the woman's work of gathering was not as prestigious as the hunting done by males, women became far less equal as their status as gatherers changed to that of planters, tenders, and harvesters of crops, as well as caretakers of the home and caregivers to the children.[4]

Men, previously hunters, were now often herdsmen, providing more in the way of leisure time to engage in the sorts of pursuits, civic and otherwise, that further enhanced their power over women.[5] Such power increased as communities prospered to the point where they had to be defended against tribesmen on their borders, giving rise to a permanent warrior class, along with a permanent bureaucracy; and those defeated in battle were no longer killed but put to work as slaves – often to build bigger and better defenses.[6]

More important than slave labor, however, was the animal power increasingly substituted for that of humans. Sometime after 3000 BCE, horses (domesticated on the grasslands of the Ukraine about 1,000 years earlier) reached Eastern Europe, the Trans-Caucasus, Anatolia, and the Mediterranean to pull plows – a task to which oxen were also assigned.

It was also around 3000 BCE, at the beginning of the Bronze Age, that human society emerged into the light of recorded history – having accomplished the domestication of most of the vegetables, fruits, and animals that continue to nourish us today. These included such Middle Eastern staple crops as wheat, rye, barley, millet, chickpeas, broad beans, and lentils. In addition, in East and Southeast Asia there were taro, rice, yams, and bananas; in Africa, south of the Sahara, there were other yams and another kind of rice; and in the Americas, maize, manioc, squash, sweet and white potatoes, tomatoes, chilli peppers and most of the world's beans were under cultivation. And with domestication came "mutualism," meaning that in many cases plant and animal domesticates could no longer compete for habitat with wild relatives. In short, they became just as dependent on humans as humans were on them.

Food globalization accelerated after 3000 BCE as the cereals and sheep domesticated in and around the Fertile Crescent spread north throughout Europe (where the westward-moving Celts introduced dairy cattle) and south to the Mediterranean shores of North Africa. Millet, important in China, spread to India, Africa, and into southern Europe, and Asian yams may have reached East Africa to begin a millennium-long journey across the continent. Rice (perhaps from Southeast Asia) had long before entered cultivation in southern China and at the time was being introduced to Indonesia, and southern India. And finally the chicken – that jungle fowl domesticated in Southeast Asia – began to reach the Middle East, although until Roman times its most important use was probably for sacrifice and for cockfighting. One suspects, however, that chicken eggs were welcomed by peoples whose chief egg-producers had heretofore been pigeons.

ECOLOGICAL CONSEQUENCES

Hunter-gatherers harvested plant and animal foods alike without attempting to control the life cycles of those foods. But clearing the land for the cultivation of grasses and tubers and the herding of animals brought a whole train of ecological consequences to the planet. Plant and animal species were drastically reduced as complex ecosystems were simplified. Bare earth encouraged the grown of perennial weedy plants in fields that were planted with annuals. Grazing animals also created bald spots in the earth, and many of the weeds that rushed in to cover the soil became favorites of the grazers who moved weed seeds about in their bowels and on their coats. Weeds do help to prevent soil erosion, but much topsoil blows away before weeds grow large and tough enough to be effective, and pollutants – especially carbon – began their accumulation in the atmosphere. Problems of water pollution started as manure and later chemical fertilizers drained off into rivers and streams to join other animal and human wastes.[7]

HEALTH AND DEMOGRAPHIC CONSEQUENCES

With the switch from foraging to farming, human populations grew larger and denser. Hunter-gatherers, often on the move, had carried everything they owned, which limited the number of children they could have. So did the gathering duties of even semi-settled women.[8] In fact, all primates have tended to produce relatively few infants – but infants who received considerable parental attention, including nursing on demand. These frequent snacks of mother's milk, rich in protein and sugars, ensured the survival of a high percentage into adulthood.[9]

Contrast this scenario with that of the first farmers. With a dependable food supply they stayed put and could have lots of children – to provide hands for the fields and security in old age.[10] Yet the food supply for these Neolithic baby-boomers was low in fats and short on whole protein, shortages that were hard on mothers as well as their children.[11] Because women were needed in the fields, they had little time for nursing, which meant that infants often had to get along on a starchy pap instead.[12]

Unquestionably, the first farmers had lots of children. It has been estimated that, on the eve of the earliest of the Neolithic Revolutions, "Our Kind" numbered between 3 and 5 million. But after many more such revolutions and 7,000 years of farming those numbers had increased to 100 million – hardly a spectacular increase in view of the enormous time span involved, but impressive nonetheless in light of the horrendous infant mortality occasioned by the decline in pediatric care. Losses of fifty percent or more of those born, as well as high child-mortality levels, often meant that it took a considerable number of births for a couple to reproduce just themselves.

Malnutrition gets much of the blame. The varied hunter-gatherer diet based on 100 to 200 plant species was replaced by one that tended to center on a single crop that grew best in an area – wheat in one place, rye in another, and barley in yet another – in much of Eurasia (along with rice in East, South, and Southeast Asia and maize in the Americas). The breads and gruels made from such grains became dietary mainstays, supplemented as the season and customs might allow – with meat appearing in meals only on special occasions – a significant departure from millennia of heavy meat consumption.[13]

These cereals are sometimes called "super foods," which they are in the sense that they have fed billions – but they are far from "super" in their delivery of the chief nutrients and especially good quality protein.[14] Nonetheless, they constituted the bulk of the diet for everyone including, unfortunately, the very young who require protein to survive, let alone thrive. The pap given to infants in place of breast milk along with the meatless gruels fed to children would invariably have led to protein-energy malnutrition and, thus, much infant and child mortality.[15] One estimate places average life expectancy in 3000 BCE at less than 18 years, which implies a barely viable population.

Another reason for the deteriorating health of sedentary agriculturalists was that, unlike their hunter-gatherer forebears, they had numerous pathogens to contend with. Foragers necessarily operated in small bands so as not to clean out the flora and fauna of an area too quickly. Nor did they linger long enough in one place for their wastes to pile up to attract rodents and insects and to foul their water supply. In short, small groups of highly mobile people were probably little troubled by infectious diseases – and certainly not by the contagious illnesses produced by microparasites, such as measles or influenza, that require large numbers of people to host them.[16]

Moreover, hunter-gatherers had no domesticated animals (save for the dog at the tail end of the Paleolithic) to give them diseases along with their eggs, milk, meat, fiber, and hides. That pathogens of domesticated animals found human hosts congenial is underscored by numbers; humans now share some fifty diseases with cattle, forty-six with sheep and goats, forty-two with pigs, and twenty-six with poultry.[17] Sedentism, then, destroyed the prophylactic circumstances that had protected hunter-gatherers from serious illness, and people now lived cheek-to-jowl with their animals and with each other. It is easy enough to imagine them passing incubating pathogens back and forth amidst prospering disease vectors. With increasingly dense human populations, it was only a matter of time until some of those pathogens managed to jump the species barrier.

These were the triggers of the infectious ailments that sprang forth in early cities such as Jericho, Uruk, and Babylon, even though they had been conceived long before in the settlements of the first farmers. Empires arose, spawned by invading Indo-Europeans (such as that of the Hittites in the second millennium BCE), whose soldiers spread diseases about so that by the first centuries of the Common Era, modern forms of many contagious illnesses such as smallpox, measles, and influenza had emerged.

With blossoming disease acting synergistically with bad diets, it is no wonder that people developed conditions such as anemia. They also shrank. Hunter-gatherers 25,000 years ago had thicker bones and were 2 to 6 inches taller than Bronze Age farmers of 4,000 to 5,000 years ago, and evidence from a variety of sources indicates that the majority of Our Kind continued to grow shorter until the twentieth century when some, at least, began to achieve the stature of our early ancestors.[18] Exceptions sometimes prove the rule, such as the equestrian nomads of the American Great Plains. Their lifestyle, which permitted a rich and varied diet, had made them the tallest people in the world by the middle of the nineteenth century, reminding us again of one of our themes – the devastation that technological progress can dump on human health.[19]

FOOD PROCESSING AND PRESERVATION

Food preservation and preparation technologies became essential components of the Neolithic. Cereals had been consumed as gruels since the caryopses of wild grasses were harvested during the late Paleolithic. But by around 6000 BCE, people such as the previously mentioned Swiss Lake dwellers, had learned to bake flatbreads after crushing the grains although they were still gathering, not growing, those grains. Barley and millet, as well as einkorn and emmer, were all used for flatbreads, yet only the ancestral wheats contained gluten-forming proteins. And it is the Egyptians – beer brewers by at least 4500 BCE – who are credited with making the next culinary lunge forward by uniting these wheat ancestors with yeast around 4000 BCE so as to produce yeast-risen wheat bread.[20]

Such credit, however, may rightfully belong to earlier folk, because wherever they were located, people who grew grains created yeasty environments by brewing beer – environments in which a union of yeast (a single-celled fungi) and gluten would have regularly occurred. The ideogram for beer, for example, appeared in the earliest documents of cuneiform writing in Mesopotamia at about the end of the fourth millennium BCE,[21] and, because beer making began with early grain farming, some have speculated that a desire for a steady source of the beverage may have been the reason for domesticating wild grasses in the first place. This is a speculation not at all contradicted by the staggering (no pun intended) 40 percent of the grain production of ancient Sumer that went into brewing at least nineteen kinds of beer.[22]

Winemaking also stretches back into hazy times. The earliest archeological evidence indicates that wine was made at a Neolithic site in the northern Zagros Mountains some 7,400 years ago. Research has yet to pin the area down as the cradle of winemaking, but assuming that it was in those mountains, then it would appear that wine subsequently diffused in two different directions. One of these would have been into Assyria, then to the other Mesopotamian states, and from there to Egypt where people were making wine around 5,000 years ago (a bag press, used to press grapes is shown on the walls of Egyptian tombs dating from this time). By 3,000 years ago wine drinking had become widespread throughout Southwest Asia.[23]

The second route would have taken winemaking across Anatolia to the Aegean Sea, along whose shores and throughout whose islands wine became a part of the Greek culture. From there wine entered Greek colonies in the Mediterranean such as Sicily, southern Italy, and Massilia (Marseilles) to move inland along the Rhone River Valley.[24]

A taste for alcohol was doubtless also a reason for honeybee domestication. These natives of the Mediterranean region and the Middle East were making honey for millions of years before human hunter-gatherers were around to steal it from them. It was sweet, naturally good, and with the honey came wax – useful for dressing wounds, preserving foods (honey itself was also used as a preservative), and after the acquisition of fire, for illumination. Meade, which can be as simple as fermented honey and water, was almost assuredly humankind's first alcoholic beverage.[25] From Paleolithic times to the present, bees have been routinely, if rudely, smoked out of their hives, although the Egyptians long ago invented beekeeping by constructing artificial hives.[26] In the Old World, presumably because of the risk involved, males generally hunted honey and kept bees. But in tropical America where the bees did not sting, honey gathering was women's work.[27]

Cheesemaking, by simply leaving skimmed milk out in the sun to dry, would have been practiced early in the Neolithic after people began milking the animals they had domesticated, and in fact, evidence in rock art of cheesemaking dates from around 7000 BCE. Soured milk was another early dairy product, and butter was also probably discovered early as the "churning effect" on milk was noticed when it was transported in skins.[28]

Ewes and goats were probably the first to be milked, but were scarcely the only milk producers available. Cows were milked after their domestication; some northern communities utilized reindeer milk; mare's milk was consumed in central Asia; water buffaloes were milked in South Asia; yak milk was a dietary mainstay in the Himalayas; and camel's milk was highly valued in Africa, Arabia, and central Asia. The Chinese, however, excluded themselves from a dairying tradition. There is some evidence that milk products were a part of the northern aristocratic diet prior to Mongolian Rule. But because the Mongol invaders were milk users, the Chinese decided it was a barbarian practice and have not utilized milk products since. At least this is the Chinese explanation for such teetotalism. Another theory with a ring of truth is that because planting went on year round in much of China, with heavy applications of human labor, there were relatively few draft animals to provide milk. But in South Asia, for example, where the planting season was shortened by a monsoon climate, an abundance of draft animals was absolutely essential.[29]

By 3000 BCE, the preservation of surplus milk as cheese from goats, sheep, and camels, as well as that of cows, was widespread in Mesopotamia and Egypt. At this time on the eastern shores of the Mediterranean olive trees were becoming gnarled with domestication and less bushy – their fruits laden with oil.[30] The pillars of southern European civilization – bread, wine, cheese, and oil – were in place.

The origins of food preservation by drying, smoking, and salting (bacteria do not survive in dry environments) are obscure but dehydration – lowering the moisture content of food to prevent their rotting – is the objective of all three. Probably our ancestors, who learned to sun-dry fruits and wild beans such as lentils and chickpeas, also experimented with smoke and its preserving chemicals.[31] The preservative qualities of salt were well known in antiquity, but had been understood long before that – an understanding that stretched back to the hunter-gatherers.[32] Hunters of wild herbivores knew that their prey (unlike carnivores) needed regular intakes of salt and consequently waited in ambush for them at salt licks, brine springs, and marshes where they doubtless also encountered dead, but well-preserved, animals.[33] Pickling with salt and vinegar, which has been traced back to Mesopotamia, made possible the preservation of practically any food but especially vegetables which became available year round.

All these techniques of food preservation were being applied by 3000 BCE in the Near Eastern centers of agriculture to pork, fish, olives, and a score of other products and, with the production of preserved plant and animal foods, another chapter in food globalization began – that occasioned by trade in foodstuffs – with Sumer and Egypt among the first to systemize it over long distances.

CHAPTER

7

ENTERPRISE AND
EMPIRES

No nation was ever ruined by trade.

Benjamin Franklin

Vicissitudes of fortune, which spares neither man, nor the proudest of
his achievements, which buries empires and cities in a common grave.

Edward Gibbon (1776–1781)[1]

PRE-ROMAN TIMES

War, trade, imperialism, and colonialism are all powerful vectors of new tastes
that propel them across cultural barriers.[2] Invasions such as that of the Indo-
Europeans or Aryans – a warrior class using horse-drawn chariots – brought
about, after 1800 BCE, new power structures in North Africa, western Asia,
and India, with the Aryan impact also felt in Greece, Italy, and Central
Europe. One group of Aryans became the Hittites who occupied eastern Asia
Minor, while another united with Semitic raiders of the Arabian desert to
become those Hyksos who conquered Egypt's Middle Kingdom from a base
in Palestine. The Indo-Europeans, called "shepherd kings" by the Egyptians,
introduced livestock in a way it had never been introduced before.

In the midst of this cultural confusion was Phoenicia (now modern Syria
and Lebanon), the land of Canaan and a site of early olive-tree cultivation.
It was also home to the Phoenicians, who had grown sophisticated under
multiple conquerors and had become wide-ranging Mediterranean traders

and colonizers. They were also the developers of Mesopotamian writing into an alphabet. They had earlier cut their business teeth trading grain, honey, oil, and wine with Damascus, Judah (in southern Palestine), and Israel, and by 1000 BCE had expanded operations by establishing trading colonies as far away as Carthage in North Africa and Cadiz in the Iberian peninsula. They scattered Middle Eastern products such as wine, olive oil, wheat, and chickpeas across the Mediterranean, and then grew rich on the trade in oils, grains, and legumes that followed. The wines and oils of Iberia were soon famous and chickpeas (*garbanzos*) have been the poor Iberian's "meat" ever since.[3]

Phoenicia was absorbed by a resurgent and expanding Egypt for a few centuries as the latter built a Middle Eastern empire, which brought the wealth of conquered provinces pouring into Thebes and stimulated an already thriving herb, and wine, and spice trade with Palestine and Arabia. Date wine from Mesopotamia was also traded.[4] Beer had been that region's most common drink. But in southern Mesopotamia, irrigation had leached soils to such an extent that grain had grown scarce, whereas date palms grew nicely along the irrigation canals. Beer was out and date wine was in.

Meanwhile in the several centuries following 2000 BCE, the kingdoms of Persia, Assyria, and Babylon emerged, and although quarrelsome (Assyria was conquered by Babylonia which in turn was conquered by Persia's Cyrus the Great), they jointly formed a pinnacle of ancient civilization. All three were legendarily wealthy and given to gastronomic excellence. Persian cuisine, for example, influenced by India and points east, was envied for the delicacy of its rice and the sauces served with it – those sauces comprised of fresh and dried fruits along with fruit juices, spices, herbs, and nuts. Lamb was the favorite meat served with rice. Flat Persian bread and wine rounded out the meal.

The upper classes in Egypt at this time were eating a wide variety of fish from the Nile, birds from its marshes, beef, and pork (only totally discredited by late-arriving Indo-European nomads accustomed to mutton and beef), accompanied by raised bread, wine, beer, cheese, and a variety of grains, fruits, and vegetables. The peasants did not fare badly either. They, too, had beer; their bread was mostly flatbread with pockets (like pita bread); and onions seem to have been a staple. There was generally animal flesh available on the numerous festival days, waterfowl was free for the taking during winter migrations, and fish were cheap, depicted as objects of barter in market scenes.[5] The high cost of watering many of the fruits and vegetables consumed by the wealthy, however, put them out of reach for the poor, who continued to supplement their diets with wild plants.

In Greece, where figs and acorns were honored as the first human foods, agriculture arrived from Egypt (via Crete) to expand the menu.[6] And at about the time that the Hebrews left Egypt in the thirteenth century BCE to receive their dietary instructions at Mount Sinai, Greek farmers were enjoying a bounty of wheat and barley production. They kept pigs, pressed olives from their trees, and maintained fig trees and grapevines. Fruits – such as pears and apples, along with figs – became so important that a law proclaimed in Athens in 620 BCE mandated "death for fruit thieves, fruit tree molesters, murderers, and temple desecrators."[7]

Yet at this juncture the Greeks were sufficiently prosperous that population pressure coupled with Greek trade and imperialism began to impoverish the agriculturalists. The forests – cut down to build ships – were replaced with olive trees, and olive oil became the major and, at times, the only Greek export save for the Greeks themselves who, driven by the need for new food sources, were colonizing widely in the Mediterranean. To Spain and to southern Italy they carried the ancient art of salting fish, and established anchovies as a dietary staple.[8] Greek wine followed, and the Italian countryside featured little else but vines and olive trees. Basic foodstuffs were imported.

Meals may have seemed barren but they were a model of what we today regard as a Mediterranean diet.[9] Barley paste, made with sprouted grain mixed with flax seeds (linseed), was a staple as was unleavened barley bread and barley porridge. These were likely enlivened with coriander seeds, salt, and goats milk and cheese, along with the ubiquitous olives and figs and, perhaps, an occasional serving of fish or other seafood. Greece lies fragmented at the base of the Balkan Peninsula and much of it is close to the sea, yet fresh seafood was a luxury – the closest most Greeks came to it was the salted or pickled fish (especially anchovies) for which Greece was famous.[10] Oysters were probably also in the luxury category although their shells were put to political use. The Greeks who loved to vote sometimes did so to exile an individual. They used a flat oyster shell – an *ostrakon* – hence the word ostracism.[11]

Vegetarianism played a prominent role in Greek philosophy, and meat – eaten mostly at sacrifices – was rare in daily life (even for non-vegetarians) for everyone save the rich. The latter pioneered in making a point of eating exotic meats such as the ass, the fox, the camel, even puppies.[12] By contrast, lentil soup was the pedestrian staple of the poor.

The deteriorating situation in Attica – the hinterlands of Athens – was further exacerbated by the Peloponnesian Wars (beginning in 431 BCE), which drove rural populations to find refuge in the city, and Athens swelled to between three hundred thousand and a half million people. Farms increasingly fell into the hands of absentee owners and were worked by the very poor and by slaves.

Atheneaus, a second century AD Egyptian, related that Athens was more culinarily sophisticated following the Peloponnesian Wars. Lavish feasts were common among the wealthy – often featuring roast lamb or kid or both – and, in the third century BCE, the *mezze* (an hors d'oeuvre) table made its appearance with a wide range of little dishes that included artichokes, chickpeas, snails, olives, mushrooms, cheeses, truffles, even iris bulbs. Wines were fermented in vats smeared with resin (a preservative) and were sufficiently sweet that they were customarily diluted with water.[13]

There was a time during every one of the Neolithic Revolutions when the diets of the rich and poor alike were similar. In the Middle East, for example, early on both ate a barley gruel and a wheat or barley flatbread, along with olives, figs, a little salted fish, cheese, and meat on special occasions. But with urban life came vastly increased social and economic stratification. The rich drank wine, and ate meat, fish, and fowl, which the poor only tasted on rare occasions.

Nonetheless, meat was made more important by the appearance of the first towns and then the cities. Urban dwellers depended on the countryside for food, but grain was both bulky and heavy to move about, whereas cattle, sheep, and even pigs and geese, could reach the cities under their own power. This, in turn, stimulated a spice trade to preserve meats, camouflage spoilage, promote digestion, and impress the neighbors.[14]

Spices were a part of the early traffic in ancient items of trade such as precious metals, dyes, and silks moving along the silk and spice roads of the Middle and Near East. When they arrived by caravan, spices first reached Mesopotamia. If they came via the Red Sea, their port was Nabataea in northwestern Arabia.[15] Either way, most spice cargoes were next transported to Egypt – always an important destination of the spice trade that during Greek and Roman times was in the hands of Greeks and Romans residing in Egypt.[16] Later, Indian spices reached the Levant and later still the spice roads were extended to Levantine harbors. There the cargoes were put aboard ships bound for Athens, Massilia, Rome, and other parts of the ancient world.[17]

Much of this trade took place in an empire created by the conquests of Alexander the Great (d. 323 BCE). It included the old agricultural centers of Mesopotamia (by this time a part of Persia), along with Greece and Egypt, and had trade routes linking the Mediterranean with East Africa, India, and Asia. Rice had entered Persia about this time and a couple of centuries later was grown in Egypt and Syria.

THE ROMAN EMPIRE

Founded in Alexandrian times Rome expanded, very slowly at first, from a small Etruscan village on the Tiber River into the Mediterranean superpower it became. But by 266 BCE the Romans had conquered all of Italy, and the three Punic Wars from 264 to146 BCE had netted them all of the Carthaginian territories – North Africa, Sicily, Corsica, and Iberia. By 27 BCE, the traditional date for the beginning of the Roman Empire, its frontiers were – south to north – the Sahara Desert and the North Sea, and – west to east – Iberia and the Middle East.

Farming was the basis of the Roman economy, and slaves did much of the work. Olives, one of the most important of the Roman crops, was a classical fruit crop of the Old World, "the king of trees" according to the Bible, and an ancient one as we have seen (under cultivation even prior to the Bronze Age). The Phoenicians had spread olive cultivation throughout the Mediterranean, and the Egyptians had been quick to use the oil for any number of purposes – medicinal, cosmetic, and culinary. Greece was growing olives by 900 BCE and the Romans built on this experience by cultivating them within a "plantation system" borrowed from the Phoenicians. Much olive oil was also produced in Roman Iberia – an oil prized throughout the empire, and despite Italian production at home, imported olive oil was vital to the Roman economy – a staple utilized by rich and poor alike.[18]

Another vital crop was wheat, in no small part because although Roman imperialism brought order to subject peoples, it created dislocations that led to famines – Mediterranean Europe suffered some twenty-five of them during Roman times.[19] Wheat was similarly important at home, where extremes of wealth and poverty in the agricultural sector had developed. In the Italian countryside small farms gave way to large plantations, and now landless peasants flocked to Rome and other towns and cities, whereas the very wealthy headed for their villas in resort areas such as those sprinkled around the bay of Naples – communities made complete by their Greek-style temples and great terraced baths.

After Rome's sack of Carthage in146 BCE, North African wheat fields began to feed Rome. A government policy of selling wheat (and barley) to the poor at cut-rate prices (the *annona*) gave way to one of providing it free of charge, and then, for a time, distributing the wheat already baked. Egypt, Tunisia, eastern Algeria, and Sicily were also turned into giant breadbaskets for Rome, which at its height was importing 14 million bushels of wheat annually, those bushels ferried upriver on barges to Rome from Ostia, the port at the mouth of the Tiber. Often the grain was warehoused, but often too it went directly to a relieved peasantry who panicked when the grain arrived late. Fully one-third of Rome's population was receiving welfare wheat and later, free oil and wine, and even pork fat.[20]

Before whole loaves were available, people made a gruel (*puls*) with the wheat or sent it to professional bakers who were generally Greeks (by about 30 BCE there were 329 bakeries in Rome run by Greeks).[21] The wheat was supplemented with cheeses, lettuce, fava beans, lentils, cabbage, leeks, and turnips. To the north, wheat production was encouraged in England to feed Roman soldiers on the Rhine.

A third important crop for the Romans was the grape (*Vitis vinifera*), another Old World classical fruit crop. Most of the grape harvest went into winemaking, although a significant amount was eaten fresh and dried to become raisins – a major food in winter storerooms.[22] Practically every culture from the Caspian Sea to the Mediterranean claims the invention of wine and probably many of the claims are true. Wild grapes were an important seasonal food for hunter-gatherers and the accidental, as well as the deliberate, fermenting of grape juice cannot have been especially rare.

But viticulture – the cultivation of grapevines – happened only after people had settled into sedentary agriculture, sometime around the sixth millennium BCE. As mentioned earlier, the Caucasus may have been the first place where vines were brought under cultivation, with viticulture spreading westward to Asia Minor, Mesopotamia, and then on to Egypt. Save for an appreciative elite, however, wine was not a very well-liked

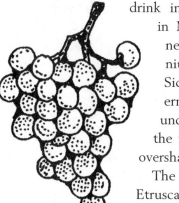

drink in Egypt until Greek wines (made first in Macedonia and Crete) gained Mediterranean-wide popularity during the first millennium BCE. From Greece, viticulture spread to Sicily, the Provencal coast, Iberia, and southern Italy (where the greco grape remains under cultivation as a kind of souvenir) and by the first century or so BCE, Italian wines were overshadowing those of Greece.

The Romans acquired their taste for wine from Etruscan settlers in central Italy, settlers they probably absorbed. They were serious wine drinkers and also serious wine exporters, with the wine contained in amphora whose interiors were coated with pitch, and the vessels sealed with clay. Viticulture also accompanied imperial expansion. The Romans followed the Greeks in introducing vines to the Mosel, Saar, and Rhine regions, as well as to many parts of Europe, and even to England.[23] Today all the important wine regions of the Continent can trace their histories back to the Romans.

There was a duality in Roman attitudes toward food, although a duality with a modern ring to it. They believed that the fresher the ingredients the more healthy they were and that processing foods reduced their healthiness – for example, a freshly picked grape was thought better for the body than grape juice. Moreover quickly-cooked foods were viewed as significantly more salubrious that slow-cooked ones, making simple dishes the ideal. But then there was a contradiction – the *cena*, consisting of elaborately cooked meals with multiple ingredients thought to be dangerous and even life-threatening to the innards, but consumed anyway.[24] Most did not have the opportunity to face up to the perils of the *cena* (and dishes such as stuffed wombs and udders, and capon's testicles), but many of the well-off bravely accepted the challenge and some conspicuously consuming Romans pointedly disregarded Cicero's advice that people should "eat to live – not live to eat," and became notorious overeaters.[25]

Among them were the gourmets called Apicius (a nickname given to gourmets), one of whom, Marcus Gavius Apicius, has been credited with penning the world's first cookbook during the time of Tiberius (13–37 AD). This particular Apicius seems to have given new meaning to the "live to eat" part of Cicero's aphorism. According to Seneca, a contemporary, although

Apicius was wealthy, he concluded that he was not wealthy enough to eat in the style to which he was accustomed. So he killed himself, choosing not to merely "eat to live."[26]

The Mediterranean was incredibly rich in seafood, with oysters, fish (especially sardines, anchovies, red mullet, and turbot), along with eels at the top of the luxury food list. Tuna was frequently on the menu and seafood was also farmed. Oysters were imported from beds along the French and Spanish coasts but were also cultivated locally. Indeed, huge breeding farms produced oysters and mussels on an industrial scale for urban markets, and practically everyone who was someone owned a fishpond or tank (*vivaria*). Rome's fish markets were also well stocked, and the brackish lagoons along the Italian coast brimmed with fish for the poor such as mullet, sea bass, bream, and eels.[27]

Romans regarded excessive meat eating as barbaric, in no small part because it was the most important staple of barbarians tribes to the north. On the other hand serving meat signified power and prestige. The Romans were not partial to beef, which was scarce anyway (although cheese was not) because cattle were used in the fields, but there were plenty of other meats available for the occasional "barbarism." The list begins with pork (wild boar was a favorite), lamb, and goat flesh, and continues through the various fowl and large fish to end with wild hares, tamed rabbits, dormice, and snails (also farm-raised). Processed meats, like sausages (first mentioned in *The Odyssey*) and cured pork (the Romans made prosciutto from smoked and salted whole pig thighs), were important foods; a delicacy was goose liver, now generally associated with the French. The Romans fattened geese with figs, then killed them by force-feeding with a honeyed wine that flavored the livers as well as the flesh.[28]

Vegetables, often served as appetizers, included (but were not limited to) broccoli, asparagus, beets, cabbages, carrots, onions, leeks, and cucumbers along with those perennial favorites, mushrooms and truffles. The latter two were believed by the Romans to originate in the spring when lightning struck the earth,[29] a more appetizing explanation for the origin of fungi than ones that prevailed later in the Christian world; because mushrooms sprang up literally overnight, they were seen as the work of the devil or of witches, a view that persisted into the nineteenth century.[30]

Like the Greeks before them, the Romans nibbled sesame seeds and pressed them for oil, ignorant of the fact that they had originated long before in the Indus Valley.[31] Fruits were both highly prized and abundant.

Pliney the Elder (23–79 AD) in his *Historia Naturalis* discussed over 100 different types including apples, figs, pears, pomegranates, quinces, citrons, medlars, and cherries.[32]

With the onset of imperial peace, wealthy Romans began to invest abroad and Mediterranean plants were carried into Gaul (along with Roman dishes such as cassoulet and bouillabaisse, now credited to the French). The Rhine Valley and the Balkan Peninsula were planted in vines and in North Africa olive groves sprang up and wheat spread out. New farming techniques also permitted lands to be cultivated in northern Gaul and Britain, where a demand for timber promoted the transformation of native forests into agricultural estates.

As the creation of large estates in Italy slowly undermined the country's agricultural base, Rome became ever more dependent on wheat from Egypt, Sicily, and North Africa, lentils from Egypt, olive oil from Spain, wine from Gaul, and all of these items and more from the Balkan peninsula – one of the richest of Rome's provinces. Germanic Europe also made a contribution in the form of Westphalian hams that were much esteemed in ancient Rome.

In addition, the Roman Empire was in commercial contact with other empires – that of Parthia and the Chinese Han Empire, after the Silk Road was opened in the first century BCE. Nor was the flow of foodstuffs invariably east to west. The idea and techniques of making thinly-rolled dough that could be turned into flatbreads, and especially dumplings and noodles, moved westward at the same time that the Chinese acquired grapevines and the knowledge of winemaking.[33] Indeed, the network of exchange routes that comprised the Silk Road represented a momentous leap forward in food globalization made possible by camels who moved swiftly across a continent of inhospitable terrain. Traveling some 4,000 miles from coastal China's Yellow Sea through Central Asia, to the shores of the Mediterranean and then back again, each camel bearing commercial burdens that probably averaged 600 to 700 pounds.[34]

Back in the third century BCE, Rome had become a naval power after building a fleet to take Sicily away from the Carthaginians, which was followed by another momentous event, the Roman discovery of the monsoon routes across the Indian Ocean. This opened yet another conduit of contact – unprecedented contact between empires – and another channel for a river of spices needed to satisfy a gargantuan Roman demand. Another source was the Middle East, with its spice streets in every bazaar crammed with condiments – a midpoint in their flow from Asia to Europe.[35] These included ginger (*Zingiber officinale*), nutmeg (*Myristica fragrans*), cloves (*Syzygium aromaticum*), cinnamon and, especially, peppercorns (*Piper nigrum*) from India.

Pliny, in the first century, complained that pepper was enormously expensive, and about three hundred years later it must still have been dear. Alaric, King of the Visigoths who captured Rome in 410, demanded 3,000 pounds of pepper as a part of its ransom.[36] But spices were not the only commodity to regularly arrive from abroad. Citrus fruits reached Rome from East and Southeast Asia, as did melons (including watermelons from Africa) and cucumbers from the Indus Valley.[37]

Despite a certain homogenization, food cultures within the Roman Empire changed as one moved north. Diets based largely on bread, wine, and oil gave way to ones featuring meat, beer, milk, and butter. Nonetheless, because of some uniformity in the use of spices, and especially seasonings such as onions, garlic (a favorite of the Greeks), and leeks, along with celery (*Apium graveolens* var. *dulce*), parsley (*Petroselinum crispum*), and dill (*Anethum graveolens*) that reached all parts of the Empire where Rome's soldiers were stationed, Roman cookery can lay claim to being the first international cuisine[38]

Also advancing northward with the Roman frontier were energy-packed legumes like broad beans and lentils as well as numerous cruciferous vegetables – those members of the mustard family, like cabbage (*Brassica oleracea*), that originated around the coastal areas of the Mediterranean and had long before been eaten by hunter-gatherers for their stems. Settled agriculturalists, by contrast, had initially cultivated cabbage for its oily seed. But by the time of the Romans, breeding had rounded its head and made it larger so that the green leaves were now the objects of culinary interest – leaves that could be eaten raw or cooked as the consumer chose.[39]

Some 400 varieties of cabbage, like kale and collards (*B. oleracea* var. *acephala*), were developed by the Romans, who planted them in northern and Eastern Europe. Not that cabbage was completely unknown in those parts. The Celts had consumed wild cabbage into the Iron Age and had developed their own cultivated variety that was similar to the wild cabbage.[40] However, with the addition of the Roman varieties, cruciferous vegetables became a fundamental part of

the northern and eastern European diet, especially important because they could be pickled (sauerkraut) and stored against long winters.[41]

Useful as well were other close relatives of the cabbage like the turnip (*Brassica rapa*) – a plant of all seasons – with greens for the warm months and roots for the cold ones. The beet (*Beta vulgaris*) was also probably a part of this plant migration (one beet variety is called "Roman") but beets were native to the Atlantic Coast as well as to the Mediterranean, and were gathered or tended mostly for their tops until the early Christian Era.[42]

Cultivated for their seeds to make oil, as well as for vegetable parts, were radish (*Raphanus sativus*) and mustard (genus *Brassica*) – both well established crops by Roman times. These, too, were relocated to the north and east where radishes became a special treat for central and eastern Europeans, and mustard seeds were pulverized and added to grape juice to prevent spoilage. In England grape juice was called "must" and mustard seeds "must seed." How could mustard have been called anything else?[43]

Well-traveled fruits that reached Rome traveled even more, so that in far-away Britain, Romans were growing peaches (*Prunus persica*), apricots (both natives of China despite the scientific name of the peach), and figs (from southwest Asia) in sheltered gardens alongside vines planted for wine. Exotic vegetables that the Greeks and Romans had pioneered in cultivating also arrived, such as asparagus (*Asparagus officinalis*), globe artichokes (*Cynara scolymus*), shallots, and endive or escarole (*Cichorium endivia*).

The Roman introduction of bread-making to northern Europe brought renewed interest in grains such as oat, rye, and especially barley, while in that portion located southwest of the Rhine River (a major artery for grain transportation) the stability of Roman rule stimulated the planting of fruit-tree groves and grape vines. Surrounding peoples were compelled to deliver crops to the towns and settlements where the Romans lived, but even those living outside of Rome's empire exported crops to Roman towns. Chickens, ducks, geese, pigs, and cattle were also delivered to the conquerors, who enjoyed these fruits of the land supplemented with foods produced by technologies they had brought with them – fish from their *piscinae* (fishponds), pigeons from their dovecotes, and thrush from their aviaries.[44]

Roman dishes were well-laced with the fishy/salty flavor of *liquamen* (also garum – similar to a Thai fish sauce), which was used as a condiment to deliver most of the salt at the table. Silphium or silphion was also employed although we do not know for certain what kind of a plant it actually was because it was apparently so overused that it became extinct. The best guess has it a kind of wild carrot-like root that gave off a resin with a garlicky taste. It came from North Africa and apparently was related to asafetida (genus *Ferula*), which the Romans substituted for silphium after it died out – probably from overcropping.

Silphium was used earlier by the Greeks, who also passed along a taste for anchovies and fish sauces to the Romans who turned their manufacture into an industry. Archeologists have unearthed sites of Roman garum factories along the Italian coasts and also those of France, Spain and the northern Black Sea.[45]

Supplemental seasoning was provided by the products of a thriving spice trade that brought a range of aromatic herbs and spices, especially pepper, from as far away as China and India.[46] Such a trade bypassed the poor, however, who made do with bread, porridge, herbs, and roots, although presumably their diet was energized with fish from the rivers and streams, and with wild hares, nuts, and berries.

But at least these poor, and even those inside Rome, were spared the lead poisoning that debilitated its aristocracy during the last four centuries of Roman rule, and that may have been a significant factor in the decline and fall of the Empire. Lead had been employed in Ur for water pipes as early as 3000 BCE and was used for this purpose by the Romans. Yet lead was everywhere in Rome – not just in plumbing, but in coins, eating and drinking utensils, and in foods themselves. Lead salts, derived by boiling grape juice in lead vessels, were consumed as a sweetener (the Romans lacked sugar) and added to wine.[47] Fortunately for the poor they were denied almost all of these lead "luxuries," and lead poisoning constituted little threat.[48]

Some late animal domestications took place during Roman times. One of these was the Fat Dormouse (*Glis glis*) a small squirrel-like rodent of southern Europe (and Asia Minor) so cherished by wealthy Romans that *gliraria* were constructed to ensure a ready supply. The dormice were fed on acorns, chestnuts, and walnuts to fatten them, then stuffed and roasted in much the same fashion that guinea pigs were cooked in the Andes half a world away.

The other late domesticate was the rabbit (genus *Oryctolagus*), which, like the dormouse, was numerous in southern Europe. Rabbits, unlike hares (genus *Lepus*), have no difficulty

being enclosed, although both were raised for the table in Roman *leporaria* – walled rabbit gardens. This earned Romans the credit for pioneering in rabbit husbandry, even though true domestication was only accomplished in the Iberian Peninsula around the beginning in the sixteenth century. Subsequent breeding has produced more than 100 breeds of domestic rabbits.[49]

Germanic peoples accelerated the process of transforming themselves from conquered peoples to conquerors with their so-called Great Migration of 406, when hoards of Vandals, Sueves, and Alans crossed the Rhine into the Roman Empire. By 410 the Goths had sacked Rome, and in 476 the Western Empire expired although the Eastern Empire, created in 395, lived on. Constantinople, its capital, became a cosmopolitan "melting pot" of peoples, as well as Roman, Middle Eastern, and Greek cuisines.

FAITH AND FOODSTUFFS

Religious contention is the devil's harvest.

Jean de La Fountaine (1621–1695)

ISLAM

The expansion of Islam began shortly after the Prophet Muhammad died in 632. By 750 the Muslims had conquered an area running from the Indus Valley westward through the Middle East to the Iberian Peninsula, and elites were speaking Arabic from Spain to Central Asia.[1]

The Arabs, like the Romans before them, learned to use the wind systems of the monsoon (the winds reverse themselves seasonally) to sail from the Persian Gulf eastward into the Indian Ocean in November, and then return to port during the summer months. Regular eighth-century trading voyages to China saw wool and iron exchanged for silks and spices. About two centuries later, when trade with China was disrupted by the fall of the Tang Empire (907), the Arabs skipped the middleman and headed directly to the East Indies, capturing the spice trade and spreading Islam as they went.[2]

Christian Europe, an implacable enemy of Islam, nonetheless admired Islamic cuisine and benefited from Islam's commercial activity.[3] That activity ensured that spices reached the Continent on a circuitous path from the East Indies, as well as new foodstuffs such as sugarcane (genus *Saccharum*), mangos (*Mangifera indica*), dates, and bananas. Moreover, toward the end of the twelfth century, the wooly merino sheep was introduced to Spain – an animal originally developed by the Romans and later exported to Africa.

The Arabs also pointed their ships south along Africa's east coast to Zanzibar and Madagascar, where they had been trading and colonizing for

a millennium or more, and bartering wine and iron implements for slaves, ivory, and edibles such as palm oil and cinnamon.

Such wide-ranging activities ushered in a widespread Muslim dissemination of existing foods within a huge region extending from Afghanistan to Spain. Under the Abbasids (750–1258), rice from India reinforced earlier introductions to Syria, Iraq, and Iran and eventually reached Spain. Saffron (*Crocus sativus*), sugar, and spices also moved freely throughout the empire, as did goats.[4] Their flesh, the favored meat in the Middle East, achieved a similar status in Islamic Africa, including that considerable portion south of the Sahara, where disease spread by tsetse flies discouraged the raising of larger animals.[5]

Mohammed had stressed that food was a divine gift to be enjoyed, and this perspective percolated throughout Islam along with new foodstuffs. However, despite the many cultural similarities wrought by this dynamic religion, a number of distinctive types of cookery emerged (or remained) – among them those of Iran, the Fertile Crescent, and Turkey, along with that of the Arabs or Bedouins, and the styles that evolved among Muslims of the Indian subcontinent.[6] The style most difficult to recognize today is that of the Bedouins. Theirs was a simple fare of meat (lamb or mutton), yogurt, and dates, a menu that practically disappeared in the whirlwind of cuisines and cultures absorbed by the expanding Arabs.

Of these, perhaps the most influential (and ecumenical) was the Iranian. Cultural influences of the Macedonians, Parthians (northwestern Iran), Greeks, and Romans were all influential in the Persian Empire and, with the imperialism of Alexander, Persia had been linked to the cooking traditions and ingredients of India. Persia's seventh-century Muslim conquerors embraced the local cuisine and, with the establishment of the Baghdad-based Abbasid Caliphate in 750, a characteristic *haute cuisine* was established that spread throughout the empire and beyond.[7] Not surprisingly it even reached renegade al-Andalus (Moorish Spain) where the Muslims introduced rice eggplant, spinach, saffron, and quince (*Cydonia oblonga*) from Persia. Later, Italian traders and returning Crusaders proved instrumental in carrying aspects of Persian cuisine to Europe.

Baghdad served as a vast warehouse of spices, fresh fruits, vegetables, grains, and preserved fish and meats for a few centuries until the Mongols (the Arabs called them Tartars) destroyed the city in 1258 along with the region's vaunted irrigation systems. They also massacred the Caliph and many inhabitants, bringing the Abbasid dynasty to an end.[8] But like the Muslims before them, the Mongols adopted the local cuisine and a couple of centuries later took it to India where Moghul (Persian for Mongol) cooking joined the many other culinary influences.

Despite Baghdad's destruction, plenty continued to prevail to the east on the Persian Gulf. When the young Venetian, Marco Polo, traveled through Persia to reach Hormuz shortly after the rape of the city, he was impressed with the great variety of available foodstuffs, reporting that even the people of the countryside ate wheat bread and meat. A favorite was the fried tail of fat-tailed sheep.[9]

The massive diffusion of food and cuisines continued as Muslim traders, soldiers, missionaries, and administrators moved even further eastward precipitating a flow of crops from the tropical and subtropical regions of the east and south to the more temperate regions of the west. The arrival of sugar cane in the Mediterranean basin has already been mentioned, as has rice from Asia, mangoes, and spinach from Southwest Asia and bananas from Southeast Asia, but to this list we might add a few more such as aubergines or eggplants from South- and East Asia; domesticated coconuts (*Cocos nucifera*), lemons, limes, and the bitter orange (also called the Sevilla orange) from Southeast Asia; and watermelons from sub-Saharan Africa.

These and other western Asian and Mediterranean foods, like almonds and saffron, were esteemed throughout the Islamic empire, the latter prized for its ability to color foods as well as its flavor. They were planted wherever there were territories to administer. Rice was grown in Moorish Spain for centuries before any other Europeans cultivated it. Only in 1468 did the Spaniards take rice outside of the Peninsula to the Lombardy plains of Italy where the Arborio variety, grown in the Po Valley, gave birth to risotto. The Moors also planted almond trees in Spain, and cultivation of the autumn crocus, if it had not occurred earlier under the Romans, commenced to produce what the Arabs called *za' faran*.

The Koran (633 AD) was initially enthusiastic about wine, then wavered, and finally prohibited it altogether. Five other food categories (blood, carrion, pork, those containing intoxicating drugs, and foods previously dedicated to idols) also made the prohibited list. Not all the faithful paid immediate attention to the wine prohibition,[10] but most were gradually weaned away from it by coffee (for more on these beverages see Chapter 15).

Initially popular in Yemen and Saudi Arabia, coffee was taken throughout the Arabian Peninsula by the mystical Shadhili Sufi to stay awake during all-night chanting sessions, and they were probably also the bearers of coffee to Egypt and Damascus. With public consumption came coffee houses and by 1500, no deal was made, no ceremony celebrated without coffee.[11]

The Muslims were also instrumental in carrying coffee far beyond the original borders of Islam to India and Indonesia, and those making pilgrimages to Mecca from these far away places took coffee beans home with them. In part, at least, this was the result of a legend that ascribed coffee's origin to Mohammed. The Archangel Gabriel was said to have given coffee to the world through the Prophet to replace the wine which Islam forbade.[12]

CHRISTIANITY

Islam was imperial and expanding while Christian Europe was fragmented, its pieces parochial and only tenuously bound together by the authority of the Roman Catholic Church. In its early years that Church taught that Adam and Eve had lived together in harmony with all living creatures. Paradise, in other words was a vegetarian place. But the Church backed off this position to hold that as the Flood was abating God let Noah know that it was all right to kill living creatures for sustenance, even for pleasure (" . . . the dread of you shall be upon every beast of the earth . . ." Genesis 10:2) With some modification and the addition of taboos, this dictum became an anchor of the Judaic dietary tradition.[13]

By contrast, the Catholic Church, and later the Church of England, were remarkably unconcerned with food taboos.[14] But they were obsessed with food (the Last Supper, loaves and fishes, bread as the body and wine the blood of Christ)[15] and relentless in imposing rules for fasting – so as to praise God by punishing the body.[16] To fast was to abstain from meat (and usually other animal products such as eggs, butter, cheese, and milk) and to limit meals to one daily. This was done routinely during the "Quadragesima" or Lent (the forty days between Ash Wednesday and Easter) and the thirty days of Advent preceding Christmas – winter months when meat was normally not on the table anyway.[17]

But in addition, Wednesdays and Fridays were designated as fast days and sometimes a third day of the week was added. In Russia, the Orthodox calendar tacked on the Saints Peter and Paul Fast which could last up to six weeks.[18] In other words, most diets were circumscribed for at least 150 days out of the year and, depending on time and place, as many as half the year – occasionally even more than half.[19] Penalties for noncompliance could be severe. That for eating meat on Fridays in England was hanging – a law that endured until King Henry VIII, wanting a divorce, broke with the Vatican.[20]

Feast days were bright spots in the gloom of this self-denial, often days that had been celebrated in earlier pagan agricultural rites and tidied up by the early church and transformed into holy days. Lamb became traditional as Easter fare, coming as it did when newborn sheep were abundant and people were starved for meat.[21] But the most spectacular of such feasts was that held a bit earlier on Martedi Grasso (Mardi Gras), the day before Ash Wednesday, when it was customary to eat all foods forbidden during Lent for a last taste, and better than letting them spoil. It was a day of gluttonous meat consumption or "Carnivale" that generally was accompanied by drunkenness, violence, and even sexual misbehavior because sexual intercourse was also taboo for the duration.[22]

Little wonder that the Church associated meat with carnal lust and dichotomized the body (feasting) and soul (fasting). Even the consumption of fish was initially proscribed only to later be judged pious; and fasting made fish a major food resource for all Europeans during the Middle Ages, and not just those living along coasts.[23] The production of preserved fish – salted, dried, smoked, and pickled herring and cod became an enormous seagoing industry.[24]

Fresh fish were also harvested from lakes, rivers, streams, and ponds. Salmon and trout were generally destined for the tables of the wealthy, but after the twelfth century, carp, which had somehow found their way west from Asia, perhaps with returning Crusaders, were available for the less well-to-do. Tuna, eel, mackerel, perch, and pike could also be procured from fishmongers.

The Baltic Sea was especially rich in fish during the thirteenth and fourteenth centuries, and it was there that Hanseatic fisheries developed a method of getting herring catches salted within 24 hours. Ships from the towns of the Hanseatic League (begun in 1241) carried salted and dried fish southward to Lisbon, Porto, Seville, and Cadiz, and returned laden with more salt from Portugal, along with olives and wines. During the second half of the sixteenth century, the politics of nation-building joined with the Church in proclaiming fast days. The idea was to relieve the demand for meat, which was becoming scarce for growing populations, while stimulating shipbuilding and training mariners.[25]

If the church fathers did European diets no good, the same cannot be said of the religious orders. Very early in the Middle Ages the monastic regimen was an ascetic exercise in monotony. By the ninth century, however, many monasteries were making up for lost time by transforming themselves into "gastronomic enclaves," where the monks took in pilgrims and turned out pastries and cheeses (Grana Padano, for example, was made by monks near Milan a thousand years ago) that remain renowned, not to mention ales, beers, liqueurs, and especially, wine, which had fallen on hard times.[26]

The raiding and pillaging of the Middle Ages had once again unsettled the countryside and made it nearly impossible to maintain vineyards, while the decline of cities and trade meant a shrinking market for wine. Yet, because wine was necessary for the Christian liturgy, bishoprics and especially monasteries managed to forge ahead with grape cultivation even in the midst of chaos. Many of today's famous vineyards along the Rhine and Mosel Rivers, and in the Saar Valley, were laid out by monks nearly a millennium ago, those monks building on the earlier efforts of the Romans.[27]

Monasteries were also the most important makers of ale during the earlier Middle Ages. The bulk of monastery-grown cereals – spelt, wheat, oat, rye, and barley – went into brewing, and monastery-produced ale, approaching industrial proportions, contributed to the fortunes of the various orders and, of course, to their reputations. Monks may also have pioneered in the use of hops to make beer – the Benedictine order is credited with this innovation sometime during the eighth century.[28]

Nor was this the extent of monastic tippling. The monks turned out liqueurs as well. Early in the history of distillation, sweeteners and flavorings were employed to mask the taste of raw alcohol and the monks became masters – albeit secretive ones – of a process that was initially aimed at producing medicine. D.O.M. (Dio Optimo Maximo) Bénédictine for example, probably the oldest liqueur in the Western World, was created in the Bénédictine Abbey of Fécamp, France, at the beginning of the sixteenth century, and Chartreuse came into being about a century later at the convent of the Grande Chartreuse in Grenoble, France.

In contrast to this monkish merriment were the food-related behaviors of medieval holy women who fasted to achieve that holiness, and made miracles by multiplying food, giving food to the poor, or exuding milk from their bodies. Some achieved sainthood, but doubtless many died from symptoms remarkably similar to those of modern anorexics.[29] Monks also "multiplied" foods in a way that might have seemed miraculous, by exchanging seeds with brothers elsewhere and experimenting with them in different climes. In so doing, they did their part in helping to homogenize the European diet.

According to evidence adduced from surviving records and physical ruins, medieval monasteries routinely maintained "stew-ponds" for fish production as did the nobility on their estates, with moats around castles sometimes serving the same purpose. Yet, feudal Europe denied land ownership (and thus stew-ponds) to peasants, and because all rivers and streams belonged to kings or their nobles, the poor were generally debarred from an easy source of good protein. Not surprisingly, when ancient laws regarding water rights and land ownership were finally changed, one of the first results, especially in Eastern Europe, was the creation of family stew-ponds.[30]

Since Roman times, cooking mediums had been one means of distinguishing European cuisines – the use of olive oil in the south contrasted with butter in the north. Pliny the Elder, for instance, in his Natural History remarked that butter was "the most elegant of foods among strange nations [of the north], one that distinguishes the wealthy from the common people." Yet during the Middle Ages such distinctions became less clear-cut, in part, because of contradictory ecclesiastical dictums about the use of fats. For instance, butter was permitted during Lent in some regions, although not in others. And there were other reasons. In parts of the south (Pliny could not have anticipated this), butter came to be regarded as prestigious and its use one of the ways elites distinguished themselves from the rest of society. Moreover, although butter was fairly uniformly proscribed in the north during fasting days, olive oil in the south was not, and this, in turn, has been blamed for retarding northern cookery, whereas southern cooks could be more inventive.[31] Elsewhere, walnut oil was popular wherever it was plentiful.[32] And in Spain, during the Reconquest, lard predominated in Christian cookery. Indeed, it became a literal "article of faith" because Jews and Muslims would not use it.[33]

BUDDHISM

Like their European counterparts, Asian monks made large contributions to the world's cuisine, although unlike those counterparts they managed to elaborate a religious basis for vegetarianism.[34] Hinduism did not prescribe a strictly vegetarian diet but with its principle of food as a moral substance – eating certain foods and avoiding others preserves purity and avoids pollution – it had established a tradition of vegetarianism long before Buddha denounced the killing of all humans and animals.[35]

Buddhism, at once an outgrowth of Hinduism and a revolt against it, began in India around 500 BCE. Like Islam and Christianity, it was a missionary religion that entered China at about the beginning of the Common Era where, in its early stages it often and inconveniently became intertwined with native Taoism. Masters from India were sent out to bring about religious order by untangling the two and they continued to be sent for the next 800 years, resulting in an exchange of religious ideas, cultural attitudes, and foods between India and China.

Buddhist monks in China embraced tea (as Arabian mystics did coffee) in no small part because it helped them to stay awake during long hours of meditation. In the fifth century they reached Japan on a missionary trek via Korea, and by the end of the sixth century, tea usage had spread to these outposts of East Asia. These same monks also introduced soybeans to Japan and Korea. This crop had become second in importance only to grains in Northern China. As the sole vegetable that provides consumers with a whole protein, the soybean delivers up to eighteen times more protein per acre than could be provided by animals nourished on that same acre, making it an ideal food in China and the rest of East Asia where pasturage is lacking, and an ideal food for Buddhists with their vegetarian diets.[36]

9

EMPIRES IN THE
RUBBLE OF ROME

To every thing there is a season, and a time to every purpose under
the heaven; a time to be born, and a time to die; a time to plant,
and a time to pluck up what has been planted; a time to kill,
and a time to heal; a time to break down, and a time to build up.

Ecclesiastes, III. 1–4

THE EURASIAN STEPPE is a plain that lies north of the deserts and mountains of Central Asia, curving from Manchuria to the Black Sea. It was home to successive waves of nomadic predators, among them the Huns. They migrated across Asia to reach Eastern Europe in the late fourth century and settled down just beyond the borders of the Roman Empire. Under Attila they so terrorized the Visigoths (western Goths) that they were driven to seek refuge within Roman frontiers. Not especially grateful, the Visigoths sacked Rome in 410 and then occupied the western portion of its Empire, the Iberian Peninsula.

Meanwhile, Attila continued to conduct bloody campaigns in the Balkans until he was finally defeated by an army of Romans and Goth allies. Undiscouraged, he attacked Italy (but spared Rome at the behest of Pope Leo I). However Attila's death in 453 (the story has it that he drank too much honey wine – supposed to enhance fertility – following his wedding to Ildico) signaled the disintegration of the Hun empire, which in turn opened the door to another group of invaders, the Ostrogoths (eastern Goths), who added Italy to their kingdom in 489.

Other nomadic groups also had a hand in redrawing the political map of the west. The Vandals were established in North Africa, the Sueves in the Galician part of Iberia, and the Burgundians in southeast France. Yet the most important of the many Germanic kingdoms was that established by the Franks over territory that would later become modern Germany and France.[1] Needless to say, this incessant plundering and pillaging was hard on agriculture although, after Attila's death, another advance into the Rhineland and on to Britain had the opposite effect. These were German-speaking farmers eager to exploit fertile lands that had only been thinly occupied by the Romans.[2]

Justinian, in Constantinople, labored to put the Roman empire back together again and reestablished some authority in North Africa, Italy, and southern Spain. But with his death another wave of steppe barbarians began to roll. These were the Avars from southern Russia, who reached the Hungarian plain to emulate the Huns by raiding in all directions. They, in turn, were eventually throttled by Charlemagne, the leader of the Franks, whose so-called Carolingian dynasty included both Germanic and Roman Europe (except for England and Scandinavia). In 800, the Pope recognized Charlemagne's power by crowning him "Emperor of the Romans."

Meanwhile the religion of Mohammed was stretching eastward. The Abbasid dynasty had overthrown the Umayyads in 750 in a bitter civil war, and moved the capital from Syria to Baghdad. Once again that city became the center of the Islamic world.[3] Ships from all parts of that world rode at anchor off the island between the Tigris and the Euphrates – an island called the "market place of the world."[4] But despite such apparent prosperity, the Dynasty found itself unable to control the vastness of Islam and increasingly became a shell, with the real power resting in the hands of newly converted Turkish-speakers.

Originally from Central Asia, these were also steppe nomads who had pressed on eastern Iran for centuries. By around 900, however, many of them were no longer nomadic but had blended into Muslim towns and were cultivating the countryside. And Turkish mercenaries were dominating the political life of Islam, which they extended into all but the southern part of India, all the while making serious inroads on the Byzantine state.[5]

Yet just as the Turkish advance was gaining momentum, another people of the steppes launched their own advance from Mongolia. These were the Mongols, nomadic herdsmen that had previously made a living by trading horses, livestock, and hides with Chinese agriculturalists to the south when not warring among themselves. But somehow they were united by the genius of Genghis Khan (ruled 1206–1227), who channeled their energies into imperialism.[6] His troops were the finest cavalrymen of the age. They moved with blinding speed because they had no logistical worries. While on the move, they needed little besides the honey-cakes and tea in their saddlebags and the blood and milk of their mares (the latter, when fermented, was *kumyss*, [or kumiss] the notorious Mongol libation). Importantly, mare and ewe's milk was high enough in vitamin C to compensate for the absence of fruits and vegetables in their nomadic diet.[7]

Their swiftness enabled the Mongols to execute an incredible series of conquests, raiding southward into China, westward to shatter the Muslim states of Iraq and Iran, and into eastern Europe via Russia, carrying out the only successful wintertime invasion of that country by using the frozen rivers as highways. Further conquests, along with political consolidation, were achievements of the sons and grandson of Genghis Kahn. They presided over an empire that stretched from Russia eastward to Korea and the Manchurian and China coasts – an empire of pacified peoples because the government was able to enforce its claim to a monopoly on violence.[8] Among the benefits of the Pax Mongolica that settled over Eurasia was the ability to travel safely across the Silk Road and, by 1250, it was said that a virgin with a pot of gold on her head could cross the Mongol empire unmolested.[9]

In China, the Yuan Dynasty (1271–1368) was launched by the Mongol "barbarians" who disdained local Persian and Chinese delicacies, much preferring their own lamb and kid dishes and, especially, mutton from their grotesque-looking fat-tailed sheep (with tails so heavy that carts were often required to help the animals support them). Traditional Chinese despised the invaders on culinary grounds alone, yet the Mongols were the conquerors after all. They not only introduced their simple, coarse fare at the imperial table (four or five sheep were slaughtered daily for the Khan's table and great vats for boiling them whole were installed in the imperial kitchen) but saw it accepted by all social classes. Shops featuring roasted lamb began to flourish in the cities.[10]

Among those taking advantage of the Pax Mongolica was the Venetian Marco Polo who claimed to have entered the service of the Kublai Khan in 1279 – the same year that the Sung dynasty ended in the south, bringing all of China under Mongol control. Later on, after Marco Polo was back in Europe and imprisoned in a Genoese jail, he described his Asian adventures to a fellow prisoner who wrote them down.[11] Marco Polo told in wonder of the "Tarters" as he called the Mongols, their cities, and especially their foods. The staple for those in the central and southern parts of China, he reported, was rice, which represented around 70 percent of all the grains consumed in China. The rice, mostly boiled for direct consumption, was also turned into rice flour and wine. The other 30 percent of grains consisted of the wheat and millet of the north that were made into noodles, bread, and gruel.

Persons of all classes ate fresh fruits and vegetables, even in the north where they were grown in protected truck gardens. Pork dominated among the meats, although mutton, kid, and lamb were making inroads on that dominance, and much fish was consumed. Sugarcane had become an important cash crop during the Sung period, and the Kublai Khan brought in Egyptian technicians to improve the quality of sugar refining.[12] Also impressive was the water pump driven irrigation system that was revolutionizing Chinese agriculture.

In 1280, Marco Polo visited Hangchow (or Hangzhou) on the East China Sea and gaped at ships laden with spices arriving from the East Indies. He was also in awe of the markets, where fish and shellfish of every description were piled high and fowl were "too many to be told." There were oranges, Mandarin oranges, and apricots, along with grapes and other fruits that had separate stalls and sellers, as did vegetables (including green leafy vegetables) and pork. Other stalls featured a variety of meats such as beef, horse, donkey, and rabbit. Candied fruits and dried bananas were also for sale.

Restaurants specialized in various dishes and methods of preparation and, in addition, there were noodle shops, teahouses, taverns, and wine halls, along with street vendors selling deep fried and barbecued foods.[13] It was this dazzling view of Yuan China that Marco Polo carried with him on his return to Venice in 1296. By contrast, Europe seemed drab and listless, although his description of spices and the spice trade would later help to galvanize it.

As time passed, the Mongols did what conquering nomadic tribes have historically done – they blended with the conquered. In China they adopted Tibetan Lamaism before they were driven out, but everywhere else they accepted Islam and assimilated into Turkish communities. As a consequence, many of their descendents found themselves on the march once again but this time under the rule of the Ottoman sultans.[14]

The Ottoman Turks were another tribe from the steppes whose roots stretched back to China. In 1354 they crossed the Dardanelles Straits and established a foothold by taking the Gallipoli Peninsula. Already converted to Islam, their state in northwestern Asia Minor attracted warriors from throughout the Moslem world to join in its raids against Christian Byzantium. By the early 1300s, the Ottomans were extending their rule over Turkish as well as Byzantine territories and, in 1389 in the battle of Kossovo, they defeated a Christian army assembled to protect the Balkan states. This opened that region to Turkish settlers and then, in 1453, Constantinople fell to the Ottomans ending the Byzantine Empire that had endured since Roman times while establishing the city – today Istanbul – as the Ottoman capital. Located on the tectonic edges of the continents of Europe and Asia, Istanbul was now the most important hub of the spice trade and the heir of Byzantine cuisine. People throughout the rapidly expanding empire flocked to the city bringing their tastes and cooking traditions.

By 1460, the conquest of Greece was complete (which dealt the Greek wine industry such a blow that it is only just now reviving), and after this the Ottoman Turks turned south to take Syria, Mesopotamia, Egypt, the Hejaz (and thus Medina and Mecca), and Yemen.[15] After Suleiman the Magnificent (1520–66) had added Algiers, and most of Hungary, to the empire, it stretched from Buda to the Nile and from the Black Sea to Tunis and Algeria, encompassing both sides of the Red Sea and the eastern shore of the Persian Gulf.[16] This gave the Ottomans control of the trade of both waterways, and that included the spice trade. In the Indian Ocean, however, they faced a determined competitor for spices in Portugal.

The Arabs had earlier absorbed the cuisine of the Persians and passed it on to the Turks, who also borrowed from the culinary traditions of Anatolia, East and Central Asia, and the Mediterranean. The Ottoman sultans were serious about food – so serious that they made a pot and spoon the insignia of their famed Janissary force and drew on the camp kitchen for military titles, such as "first cook" and "first maker of soup." The sultan's kitchen was supplied with rice, lentils, pickled meats, and sugar, as well as prunes and dates from Alexandria; other tributaries sent honey, olive oil, and butter. The sultan's ordinary diet centered around the flesh of pigeons, geese, lamb, chicken, and mutton and every day at the palace some 200 sheep, 100 kids, 10 calves, 50 geese, 100 chickens, and 200 pigeons were slaughtered. Fish, however, was not consumed unless the sultan was visiting the sea. Sugar was used with a heavy hand to produce sherbets, preserves, and syrups. The sultan, his family, and favorites ate white bread; middle quality loaves were for officers, coarse bread went to the servants, and sea biscuits to sailors.[17]

The Istanbul palace kitchen – at one time staffed by close to 1,400 individuals – was divided into four main areas: one for the sultan; another for his mother, the princes, and privileged harem-members; a third for the rest of the harem; and a fourth for the palace household. The sultan ate three or four times a day, selecting morsels from the many dishes prepared for him. After this, the substantial remainder was divided among high officers. The rest of the palace personnel dined from other kitchens.

It was here that a blending of Arabic and Persian culinary traditions ongoing since the eleventh century if not before produced the sugared sweet pastry from thin pastry sheets that we call baklava and phyllo (meaning leaf in Greek).[18] Such an intermingling of Mediterranean and Central Asian cuisines took place just decades before New World foods began to penetrate the Ottoman Empire. These were made popular by Sephardic Jewish merchants who had been invited to settle in Istanbul after their expulsion from Spain, and later Portugal. Tomatoes in particular, along with bell peppers and summer squash, joined aubergines and chickpeas as everyday ingredients in the cuisine of first the Ottomans and then much of the Middle East, that region where agriculture had first begun.

MEDIEVAL PROGRESS
AND POVERTY

*Mother Nature always comes to the rescue of a society stricken with
the problem of overpopulation, and her ministrations are never gentle.*

Alfred W. Crosby (1986)[1]

ARCHEOLOGICAL EVIDENCE now in the British Museum from West
Stow in Suffolk, England, has shed some light on the dietary changes that
came about with the fall of Rome. Sheep, goats, and pigs were retained
for food, and pigs also for their scavenging ability, and cattle as draft animals. But guinea fowl and peacocks, favorites of the Romans, escaped to
die out in the wild.[2] Many rabbits also escaped but were recaptured and
maintained in rock enclosures in both Britain and on the Continent.[3] Olive
oil vanished as a cooking medium, replaced by butter made mostly from
ewe's milk. Wine, too, disappeared with the Romans and ale became the
standard beverage.

The Catholic Church, established in England by the sixth century, imposed
fasting days and, by the time of the Norman conquest (1066), fishermen
from the British Isles had forged an important herring industry.[4] Freshwater
fish, eels and other aquatic animals from ponds, streams, and lakes comprised
a significant part of the British diet although, because the Church viewed fish
as a penitential substitute for meat, the appeal of the former suffered, and
physicians, as a rule, regarded fish as a poor nutritional substitute for meat.

In Roman times, cattle had been employed almost exclusively as beasts
of burden, yet in the early Middle Ages raising cattle for beef (although not

for milk) became increasingly common throughout Europe. Save for a few regions, such as the Alpine valleys, cheese continued to be made from the milk of sheep and goats. This pair, along with pigs, were far and away the most popular barnyard animals according to early medieval documents. They were remarkably small animals – perhaps a half or even a quarter the size of their modern counterparts.[5]

With the medieval mentality shaped by a self-conscious drive for self-sufficiency, another divergence from the days of the Romans was a move away from an intensive concentration on wheat production to fields of easier-to-grow crops such as rye, oats, pulses, cabbages, and turnips.[6] Onions, leeks, and numerous herbs were tended for seasonings in medieval gardens. In Wales, the leek became a badge after the Welsh finally paid some attention to Saint David's (c.495–589) suggestion that they wear leeks on their hats to distinguish themselves from the enemy in battle. They did this while defeating the Saxons in 633 and, ever since, the leek has been worn (then eaten) in a celebration of this ancient victory on St. David's day.[7]

The Norman conquest of 1066 brought to England new kinds of apples and pears, as well as peaches, gooseberries, medlars, cherries, quinces, and plums, and a bit later on, returnees from the Crusades carried back pomegranates, along with a variety of spices and some notions of how to use them. Cider making – the product called "perry" when made from pears – was yet another contribution of the Normans.[8]

In post-Roman Europe, rivers continued to be major arteries with goods flowing between the Baltic and the Black Sea along a network of waterways known by some as the "Amber Road." Wine and foodstuffs advanced northward along the Rhine and Oder rivers and their tributaries to be carried by Viking merchants to England, Ireland, Norway, and Jutland, while Hanse merchants transshipped them to peoples around the Baltic Sea. But these river-borne comestibles frequently glided right past peasants struggling, and often failing, to produce enough to feed themselves, let alone urban populations.[9]

Surpluses came gradually. In the sixth century, the Slavs had given Europe a new plow – later known as the moldboard plow – that could cut much more deeply into heavy soil than the scratch plough it replaced. Over time, the new plow, pulled by oxen teams, opened new lands to cultivation and initiated a shift from subsistence to market economies. Forests, the enemy of the plow, were cleared to create fields – a process that was accelerated after the eleventh century – and large collective farms that could afford the plow, and the eight or so oxen needed to pull it, come into being. Medieval Europe built tens of thousands of water mills (according to the Doomsday Book, England alone had 5,624 of them at the time of the Norman Conquest) and then, beginning in the twelfth century, the power of the wind, harnessed earlier in China and Persia, was also put to work in Europe for milling the bounty generated by the new plow. Windmill sails became familiar sights on the horizon.[10]

And yet, in returning to one of our themes, the diets of the common people worsened under the weight of these technological developments. In a society that is relatively unstratified, and one in which practically everyone make a living from food production, most everybody will eat roughly the same foods and there will be little difference in mortality levels between the rich and the poor.[11] But, as Europe moved toward a market economy, agricultural demands on the peasantry increased, a new middle class emerged, and the kinds of foods that were, and were not, consumed began to identify and differentiate. Upper- and middle-class diets improved but that of the landless changed from one of some variety to one of monotonous and restricted fare, varied only by seasonal supplements that could be caught, grown, or gathered.[12]

European secular and ecclesiastical upper classes shared a common culture of eating and drinking well. Culinary standards were mostly French and Italian, although recipe collections and cookbooks indicate that regional cuisines had yet to develop.[13] Some peoples, however, had developed specialties – the Dutch, for example, whose cheeses, butter, and horticultural expertise were renowned.[14] In fact, Catherine of Aragon had salad ingredients delivered to the English Court by special courier from the Netherlands, and the Dutch are credited with introducing garden vegetables to many areas of Europe.[15]

Meats became expensive – conspicuous consumption for the well-to-do who were also able to escape the restrictions of local food production by recourse to a burgeoning commodity trade.[16] Said to have had 2,000 cooks in his kitchens and 300 servers, Richard II of England (1367–1400) was clearly among the conspicuous consumers.[17] The less affluent ate meat sparingly and, consequently, what they could lay hands on needed to be preserved – as sausages, smoked and salted meats, and salted herring and cod – all of which came to be despised by those who could afford better.[18] For their part, the elites consumed veal and kid with gusto in the spring, when the astronomical and alimentary calendars had once more aligned, and, during the last couple of centuries of the Middle Ages, dined with considerable splendor on a very "Europeanized" menu that emphasized the exotic – centerpieces of peacocks, swans, and herons, with spices employed with abandon to flavor and color foods.

Cereals, sometimes supplemented by pulses, became the base of the diet of a peasantry that, after the ninth and tenth centuries, was unable to legally hunt animals or gather acorns and chestnuts, as wooded areas were now the property of the rich and powerful. An exception, however, lay in a belt running through mountainous regions from Portugal to Turkey, where rural peasants actually subsisted on chestnuts (*Castanea sativa*), whose trees the Romans had scattered about. These sweet nuts – loaded with starch and a staple for some since hunter-gatherer times – constituted the bulk of the diet for many from the beginning of settled agriculture until the mid-nineteenth century. Chestnuts were ground into a flour for porridge and bread-making (in northern Italy the chestnut is still called the "bread tree"), and lucky was the peasant who had several older trees. New trees do not bear fruit for 15 years after planting and their yield is less than optimal until they have been around for a half-century.[19]

Barley, oat, and rye fields that decorated the northern European countryside were joined by buckwheat (another hardy grain that grows where most other grains do not) during the fourteenth and fifteenth centuries (although legend would have it arriving somewhat earlier with returning Crusaders). This native of Manchuria and Siberia, which had traveled westward in leisurely fashion via Turkey and Russia, provided a little dietary variety for the peasants in the form of pancakes and porridge.[20]

Wheat – the preferred grain – grew well only in Europe's southernmost regions where pasta making began to flourish during the late Middle Ages.[21] In many places cheese and butter were the poor man's meat (called "white meats") – especially after the upper classes had decided to disdain dairy products – but in late winter there was only grain, root vegetables, dried beans, and pickled cabbage for the rural poor.[22]

Of course, winter had a nutritional impact on everyone, rich and poor. Dietary splurges took place when hogs were slaughtered in September, and cattle on November 11 – St. Martin's day. The offal that could not be preserved was turned into chitterlings, black puddings, and dishes of tripe and kidneys. These were feasts not to be repeated until the following year and, after this, peasantry and townspeople alike had to make do with what they had been able to raise, preserve, and store.

That these foods constituted a far from satisfactory diet was evident in early spring, when bleeding gums had people scratching beneath the snow for the first shoots of "scurvy grass" or, perhaps, for spinach that also made an early-spring appearance in their gardens.[23] Spinach had first reached Europe with the invading Moors, but it was not until the end of the Middle Ages that it showed up in a cookbook – this one published in Nuremberg in 1485. Spinach was first planted in England in 1568 and, within a century, had become one of the few vegetables that the wealthy would eat.[24]

Depending on location, virtually everyone, during good times at least, drank wine, or ale, perry, or cider (a good use for apples for over 2,000 years, especially where grapes were not grown). Yet, the gap between the diets of the rich and the poor grew ever wider to become a chasm during the two major famines of the fourteenth century. Europe had suffered more than its share of famines in the aftermath of Roman rule, and with famine came the invariable cannibalism or at least rumors of cannibalism.[25] But there had never been a Europe-wide famine before the onset of the Little Ice Age at the end of the thirteenth century, which brought appreciably colder temperatures – so cold, in fact, that the Baltic Sea froze over in 1303 and again in 1306.[26] These deteriorating climatic conditions shortened growing seasons to feed what had been steadily increasing populations (Europe's population had doubled, perhaps even tripled since 1,000), yet the famine of 1315–1317 signaled the beginning of a demographic decline that continued through the famine of 1346–1347 to culminate in the appearance of the Black Death in 1348.[27]

Ominously, rats had become prevalent in Europe by the middle of the fourteenth century and, even in the preceding century, had wrought havoc by eating grain stores, seeds, eggs, even poultry. In fact, it was in 1284 that the story of the Pied Piper first appeared – the piper who piped the rats out of the German town of Hamelin, then led the village children away after the townspeople failed to pay him.

A few decades later the plague, which had begun earlier in China, reached Europe to descend on those rats and then on humans to prune populations weak with malnutrition by some 30 to 50 percent. If there was a silver lining in this monumental demographic disaster, it was that the plague sharply narrowed the dietary gap between rich and poor. Suddenly, rural labor was in short supply and consequently better rewarded, as peasants negotiated with landlords for rent reductions, even rent forgiveness, and in some cases, became landlords themselves.

Nothing better illustrates a backpedaling elite in the face of population losses to the plague than a 1363 act passed in England ordering that artisans and craftsmen in towns, as well as the servants of the nobility, be given meat or fish at least once a day in addition to their customary milk and cheese allotments.[28] In northern Europe, livestock grazing increased relative to grain production, and a trade developed between grassland areas supplying meat and livestock and agricultural areas producing the crops. For a brief period meat became so cheap that even the poor could afford it.[29]

Because of available fuel, however, that meat, along with other foods, was cooked differently in northern as opposed to southern Europe. Despite considerable deforestation wrought by agricultural expansion, wood remained plentiful in the north where slow cooking and heavy meals were the norm. Meats were roasted for hours on spits, and even the less affluent, who at least did not have to worry about wood, simmered porridges and soups of cabbage and other vegetables, as well as some meat, or maybe just bones, in cauldrons or pots over an open fire. Bread was reserved for those who could afford an oven.[30]

By contrast, in the barren south, wood was a precious commodity. Much of the timber that was cut became charcoal for metalworking; but charcoal was also used in stoves to grill fish and vegetables and quick bake or boil sheets of unleavened bread that, when sliced, became pasta in its many sizes and shapes such as linguini, spaghetti, and the thread-like noodles affectionately known as vermicelli (little worms).[31] Moreover, many Mediterranean dietary ingredients required no cooking at all and greens were eaten in great quantities. Shoots of arugula or rocket (*Eruca sativa*), sorrel (genus *Rumex*), lettuce (genus *Lactuca*), and garden cress (*Lepidium sativum*) were chopped and torn into salads, seasoned with salt, oil, and a little vinegar. The dichotomy between northern and southern diets was noted by Giacomo Castelvetro (1546–1615) at the beginning of the seventeenth century. This author of *The Fruit, Herbs, and Vegetables of Italy* extolled the Mediterranean diet while scolding the English for an atrocious one that featured much too much in the way of meats and sweets.

Europeans had plenty of home grown spices – the aromas of thyme (genus *Thymus*), lavender (*Lavandula officinalis*), and sage (*Salvia officinalis*) still perfume the Mediterranean air.[32] But a craving for foods laced with Eastern spices, which had largely disappeared with the collapse of Rome and international trade, was reawakened during the eleventh through the thirteenth centuries by the revival of trade across the Silk Road; by Crusaders who returned to Europe with cardamom (*Elettaria cardamomum*), cinnamon, cloves, coriander (*Coriandrum sativum*), cumin (*Cuminum cyminum*), ginger (*Zingiber officinale*), mace, and nutmeg (*Myristica fragrans*), as well as pepper; and, as we already have noted, by the account of Marco Polo's travels in the "hot countries" of Asia, where "exotic" spices were not exotic.[33]

Spices are so commonplace today that it is difficult to grasp how precious they used to be. Whether they were employed to mask unpleasant tastes has been the subject of debate. So has the link between extensive fall butchering (because of a lack of winter fodder) and preservation techniques demanding spices. Most, however, agree that spices were essential ingredients in concocting aphrodisiacal prescriptions by "pepperers" and "spicers" whose guilds evolved and merged into that of apothecaries.[34] And no one disagrees that pepper acts as a preservative, adds flavor, increases the flow of saliva and gastric juices, and even cools the body.

As usual, however, the poor did not enjoy any of these benefits because pepper possession was directly correlated with status and wealth. Illustrative was Karl, the Duke of Bourgogne, regarded as the richest man in the Europe of his day, who ordered 380 pounds of pepper for his wedding feast in 1468 – no small order when one recalls that pepper fetched more than its weight in gold and, consequently, was often used as currency, and passed along in the wills and dowries of the wealthy.[35]

Shipments of cinnamon, cloves, ginger, cardamom, sugar, and especially, pepper from the Spice Islands of the Malay Archipelago and South Asia, reached the Italian city-states via Constantinople. After this they were transported along Europe's western coast to France and the British Isles, and to the North and Baltic Seas where Hanseatic merchants traded them. Spices were also sent across the Alps – through the St. Gotthard and Brenner passes – for local consumption and for transportation on the Rhine.

In 1204 the Venetians managed to divert the Fourth Crusade to sack Constantinople, and Venice, now in control of its trade, became the most important terminus for spices in Europe. Even after the Ottoman Turks captured Constantinople in 1453, Venice and Florence continued to trade in spices at Damascus and Alexandria, but the Turks were clearly a threat to the spice trade – and certainly to its profitability. The price of pepper in Venice had increased some thirty times.[36]

Port cities such as such as Lisbon, London, Dublin, and Amsterdam got rich on the spice trade, as did inland towns like Constance, Augsburg, and Nuremberg.[37] But spices from the east, with innumerable middlemen marking up prices along the way, were becoming too expensive even for the well-off. A German document from 1393 indicates that a pound of nutmeg was worth seven fat oxen and a pound of ginger would buy a sheep. Ordinary people, priced out of the exotic spice market, had to make do with local pungent plants. Among those that proved suitable were caraway (*Carum carvi*), gentian (genus *Gentiana*), juniper (*Juniperus communis*) and horseradish (*Armoracia rusticana*).

Increasing commercial activity (like the spice trade) signaled a quickening of the rise of capitalism and a growing middle class to practice it, and both helped to shake Europe awake from its somnolent centuries. Coins were increasingly minted from specie obtained from Europe's silver mines or gold from Africa but disappeared into the void of the East to buy spices and other luxury items. Spices, then sought by a capitalist-oriented middle class, became the carrots that impelled the Portuguese down the African coast and Columbus across the Atlantic. The New Worlds they reached to link with the Old brought food globalization on a cataclysmic scale.

CHAPTER

11

SPAIN'S NEW WORLD, THE NORTHERN HEMISPHERE

*. . . Christopher Columbus began a process that in the words from
a passage in one of the books of Esdras . . . "Shook the earth,
moved the round world, made the depths shudder and
turned creation upside down."*

Eugene Lyon (1992)

IN THE AMERICAS, Spain and Portugal laid claim to a vast storehouse of strange new plant foods. In the West Indies – the gateway to Spain's Americas – a sampling of the groceries that greeted Columbus and his men included zamia (*Zamia integrifolia*), manioc (*Manihot esculenta*), and maize (*Zea mays*) – these used for breads and gruels. Then there were myriad other mysterious vegetables like sweet potatoes (*Ipomoea batatas*), yautía (*Xanthosoma sagittifolium*), beans (genus *Phaseolus*), and peanuts (*Arachis hypogaea*). New seasonings were encountered, such as allspice (*Pimenta dioica*) and chilli peppers (genus *Capsicum*), along with indigenous West Indies fruits such as guava (*Psidium guajava*), soursop (*Annona muricata*), mamey (*Mammea americana*), custard apple (*Annona reticulata*), sapodilla (*Achras zapota*), pawpaw (*Carica papaya*), and pineapple (*Ananas comosus*). And these were just a few of the American foods that Europeans had never before laid eyes on nor set tooth to.[1]

Fish and mollusks had provided much of the animal protein for those South American Tainos who had settled in the Greater Antilles and the

Bahamas, but sea turtles and their eggs, land crabs (*Cardisoma* sp.), insects, and small game such as the iguana (family Iguanidae) – which became extinct in the West Indies after the Europeans arrived – also made contributions. There were few domesticated animals in the Caribbean – only dogs, Muscovy ducks, and rodents such as hutia (*Geocapromys* sp.) and agouti (*Dasyprocta aguti*).[2] Nor did the mainlands behind Caribbean shorelines have many more to offer – llamas and alpacas in the Andean region, and the turkey and possibly rabbits domesticated in Central America, Mexico, and the American southwest.

That the pre-Columbian Americans had only managed this impoverished roster of domesticated animals has not escaped comment nor speculation, for that matter. Did Native Americans mindlessly kill off most all of the candidates for domestication as they had apparently killed off the horse, the giant sloth, elephants, and the camel?[3] Or was it that the sheer quantity of large animal prey had simply delayed efforts at domestication that would have produced results had the Europeans stayed at home a little longer? Or, like the Egyptians, did Native Americans pick on animals that could not be domesticated? They did keep moose, raccoons, and even bears as pets – in other words they tamed them – but not one of these exists as a domesticated species today.[4]

Such questions go beyond diet. If, for example, one accepts the proposition that the development of wheeled transport and other technological advances were closely connected to the domestication of cattle, horses, and other beasts of burden, then this lack of domesticated animals (and the technologies they made possible) may be yet another explanation for the relatively easy conquest of Native Americans by the Europeans.

Clearly, there is much we do not know about pre-Columbian America. The fourth glaciation called "Wisconsin" for the Americas (and "Würm" for Europe) began advancing sometime between 150,000 and 75,000 years ago. The waters covering the Bering Strait gradually disappeared into glaciers that froze over 5 percent of the world's waters and lowered seas some 130 to 160 yards beneath present levels, leaving a broad (up to 1,000 miles wide), but short (only 50 miles even today), land bridge exposed (known as Beringia) from the Old World to the New.[5] In addition, the growing glaciers (some in North America reached almost two miles in height) are said to have slammed shut an inner New World door. This was the Wisconsin glacier barrier that, some experts have claimed, could not have been traversed until the ice caps receded or melted.[6]

Conventional explanations have humans crossing the Bering Straits in what is called the "first migration" from around 38,000 BCE to 18,000 BCE. But although anatomically modern humans were present in Europe around 40,000 years ago, there is no plausible evidence of Siberia being settled much before 20,000 years ago, which makes 38,000 BCE seem much too early and 18000 BCE just about right.[7] The first pioneers to set out to the east were doubtless following caribou herds and oblivious to the fact that in changing their address they were actually changing continents. Moreover, according to the conventional explanation, their new continent would have resisted any more such pioneering until they could get around the North American ice cap, which only began to melt around 10,000 to 11,000 years ago.

Yet discoveries of tools and human remains at ancient campsites dispute this. Those found in Texas and California have been dated to some 30,000 years ago, others from sites in South America a bit later, and artifacts in Pennsylvania have been dated from 19,000 to 13,000 years ago. Such finds obviously challenge orthodoxy.

It is true that the methods used to arrive at some of these dates have not always withstood rigorous scrutiny, but they have produced the concession that pioneers from Beringia did, somehow, find ways around or across the Wisconsin barrier, and it is now generally agreed that humankind had spread southward in the Americas all the way to the tip of South America by at least 14,000 years ago.[8]

A bit later, they were joined by arrivals from the "second migration" who reached the Americas from Asia and Polynesia in seagoing canoes between 10000 BCE and 4000 BCE. And latecomers managed a "third migration," crossing Beringia between 8000 and 3000 BCE before rising seas inundated the land bridge.

The first Americans to reach the Great Plains found them so loaded with protein on the hoof that some hunter-gatherer bands actually became sedentary. They lived in permanent communities and ventured out to hunt from time to time. But "good things" came to an end, and large animals – herbivores like mammoths, mastodons, giant bison and sloth, horses and camels, and carnivores such as saber-toothed tigers and huge bears – began a slow slide into extinction. Surely this was not a completely coincidental event, occurring as it did in the wake of humans entering the New World – hunters armed with newly developed and deadly Clovis projectile points that pierced even mammoth hides.[9]

Yet, climatic changes have also been blamed – changes brought about when the retreating glaciers no longer protected large animals from Arctic winds. And, after all, it was this same climatic change that had set the Neolithic Revolution in motion on the other side of the globe.[10] In the New World, diminishing big game (the very largest of the North American megafauna were extinct by perhaps 11,000 years ago) produced an increased reliance on wild plants, medium-sized and smaller game, and, ultimately, the beginnings of agriculture.[11]

By around 7,000 years ago, projectile points in both South and North America were smaller and more delicate than the Clovis points, indicating that the prey then consisted of smaller game and birds. By 4,500 years ago, grinding stones were in use, indicating that seeds and nuts had become a significant part of the diet. Such new technologies chart the Native American's journey to the threshold of sedentary agriculture. After crossing it, they domesticated some 100 of the word's 640 most important food plants with maize, white potatoes, sweet potatoes, beans, and manioc leading the list of those that would later hive out to the larger world.[12]

A final question has to do with any help Native Americans might have gotten in their agricultural innovations. Extreme diffusionists have maintained that Native Americans were taught how to cultivate plants through contact with other agricultural centers on the other side of the Atlantic or Pacific, or both. Yet, had such contact occurred, at least some plants from Africa or Asia should have become conspicuous in the Americas; instead, they are conspicuously absent. Most destructive to the diffusionist argument, however, is the long and torturous path of agricultural development taken in the Americas over millennia. In other words, there do not seem to have been any miraculous breakthroughs or visible short-cuts that could have been introduced from the outside world.[13]

MESOAMERICA AND NORTH AMERICA

In highland Central America and Mexico, many species of mammals were becoming scarce or even extinct by 9,000 years ago, just as the megafauna that had preceded them.[14] Consequently, people who had been gathering or growing nopal (genus *Opuntia*), mesquite (genus *Prosopis*), pumpkins (genus *Cucurbita*), chilli peppers (genus *Capsicum*), avocados (*Persea americana*), breadnuts (*Brosimum alicastrum*), and maguey (genus *Agave*) found themselves ever more dependent on these foods.

Maguey, now used to make tequila, was employed in the past as a food in Mexico and the desert southwest where it was generally pit-roasted. In addition, some experts believe that breadnuts (also known as *ramón*), which Mayas call the "food of our ancestors" was another valuable food-stuff for many.[15] Root crops such as jícamas (*Pachyrhizus erosus*), sweet potatoes, manioc, and malanga (*Xanthosoma* sp.) were, depending on location, also heavily utilized.[16]

In addition, early Americans relied on a species of *Setaria* – a millet, especially prominent in the valley of Mexico – and on teosinte (*Zea mays* subspecies *parviglumis*) – tiny cobs whose kernels may initially have been dried and then popped, although people apparently also enjoyed munching on the soft, sweet ears to extract the juices.[17] It has been hypothesized that a genetic mutation of teosinte gave birth to maize (*Z. mays*), but this does not preclude the essential nature of selective breeding in the development of modern maize. The earliest evidence of maize (from the Arawak pronunciation *maiz* or *mais*) domestication – unearthed in the Tehuacan valley of southern Mexico – indicates that it happened around 7,000 years ago.[18] At the time a mature ear of wild maize was as skinny as a pencil and about an inch in length, so that its growth potential could not really have been appreciated.[19]

But grow it did both in size and geographic range. By 1492, maize was a common food throughout Mexico and Central America and to the east in the Antilles. North of Mexico it was cultivated from the desert southwest throughout the Mississippi and Ohio valleys all the way to the East Coast; and in South America it was grown by both highland tribes of the Andes and rainforest peoples of the Amazon. And as maize diffused from one locale to another, Native Americans bred and cross-bred the plants to adapt to new climates, soils, and altitudes, so that by the time of the Columbian voyages there were more than 200 types. Maize was already on a trajectory to become the world's third most important crop.[20]

Maize domestication also increased the size of the ears although a satisfactory size was probably not achieved until after 2,500, and perhaps not until around 1,500 BCE, when village life began in Mesoamerica. It was a life based on cultivated plots of maize that with larger ears could, at that juncture, easily produce more food than corresponding wild plots. By about 1200 BCE, some of these villages grouped along riverbanks near modern-day Vera Cruz had fused into the first Mesoamerican culture – that of the Olmec, complete with a religious elite. Judging from the carved stelae, along with huge freestanding jade and basalt sculptures and pyramids they left behind, the people that built them prospered on maize and other foods grown on the fertile floodplains, along with fish, shellfish, and algae from river and sea. The presence of jade and basalt indicate contact with mountainous regions, most likely within an extensive trade network that ensured maize dissemination throughout the region.

Some of that trade must have been with the lofty Valley of Mexico, where Teotihuacán later achieved hegemony. At its height (450–650 AD), that city and its environs had upwards of 200,000 people, an estimated two-thirds of them farmers, showing among other things that maize had already been bred to flourish in different climates. Although it was probably eaten green in season, most of the harvest was dried for storage and eventually processed into casseroles, tamales and, most frequently, into flatbread – tortillas. Such processing involved nixtamalization – cooking water, lime, and maize together until the maize became a soft and pliable dough.

Whether nixtamalization came about by design or just good luck is anybody's guess. It was, however, vital for the health of a people whose diet centered closely on maize. Lime breaks a chemical bond so that the grain can release its niacin. Heavy maize consumers who do not obtain that vitamin from some other source become niacin-deficient and pellagra-prone – the latter an often deadly deficiency disease. Throughout the hemisphere, Native Americans who depended on maize learned this secret and treated maize with lime, even if it was lime derived from campfire ashes. They did not, however, pass along this knowledge to their European oppressors with the result that pellagra became a serious Old World disease wherever maize was introduced. Moreover, as we shall see later on (Chapter 21), the disease also erupted as a severe health problem in the southern United States during the nineteenth century and the first decades of the following one.[21]

Maize became the principal foodstuff of the Mayas, who owed much to the influence of the Olmecs. Around 400 BCE, the Mayas began construction of what has been called the most sophisticated of the pre-Columbian civilizations in America – a civilization that embraced modern southeastern Mexico, Belize, Guatemala, and western portions of El Salvador and Honduras. Importantly, these represent three distinct ecological zones with altitudes ranging from 13,000 feet to sea level, again testimony to the range that maize was developing.[22]

Modern-day Mayas practice slash and burn agriculture to grow their maize, but these techniques of shifting cultivation could not have fed yesterday's Maya millions. Rather, archeological evidence indicates that they devised an ingenious system of fields, artificially raised from surrounding wetlands and swampy areas and drained by an extensive network of canals. After investigators discovered this system they stopped puzzling over why so many of the largest Maya centers had been located close to swamps.[23]

This kind of technology produced the maize that sustained a vibrant civilization and, not surprisingly, Mayan culture was geared to the cycle of the cornfields. During the Classic Period (300–1000 AD), multiple calendrical and astronomical systems were invented to keep track of those cycles, a sophisticated glyph writing system evolved to record production, and massive architectural edifices were erected to honor the Corn God and others that watched over the fields.[24] Yet, the technology that permitted great harvests of maize also encouraged and sustained centuries of population growth. With swelling populations came a number of attendant costs, among them environmental overexploitation, ever more exposure to diseases in increasingly crowded urban areas, and terrible malnutrition. In short, population growth contained the seeds of population collapse.

The Maya, whose daily caloric intake at about the time of World War II was around 2,500,[25] were apparently taking in far fewer calories in ancient times and seem to have suffered deteriorating health almost from their first maize harvest. Skeletal evidence indicates that infants and children, the common people, and even some of the aristocrats, were suffering from multiple symptoms of malnutrition during Late Classic times. Among these symptoms were severely diminished stature, scurvy, enamel hypoplasias (indicative of growth arrest in childhood), and iron deficiency anemia, leading recent bioanthropological investigators to rank the Mayans as among the most unhealthy people to ever dwell in the Western Hemisphere.[26]

Tikal, one of the most important Mayan sites, saw its population – which some estimates place as high as 80,000 around 700 AD – drop precipitously to a small fraction of this number within a century. The Classic Maya civilization was crumbling. Religious, economic, social, and political forces were all marshaled to prevent demographic collapse, but to no avail. Skeletal evidence shows that people living on the coast, who had access to marine resources and, thus, to high quality protein were healthy enough, but it also highlights the enormous ravages inflicted by malnutrition and infection on those in inland cities. Consequently, large centers such as Tikal, Palenque, and Copán were abandoned to rainforest reclamation as survivors relocated in the Guatemalan highlands and especially, in the northern Yucatan Peninsula.[27]

Unfortunately, this kind of collapse was not confined to the Mayas. Rather, it afflicted other Mesoamerican civilizations at about the same time and apparently for the same reasons. For example, during the formative period in the Basin of Mexico (1600 BCE – 300 AD) hamlets appeared around the lakes of that intermontane valley. Population densities were low as agriculture slowly evolved.

But by the time we reach the classic period in Mexico – based on the pre-eminence of the city of Teotihuacán with its tributary and trading empire – we find maize-based agriculture turning on the people it had nurtured. Life expectancies at birth declined from 24 years during the Early Classic period (200–400 AD) to 16 years in the Late Classic period (650–750). By 750, Teotihuacán had collapsed and the population of the Basin of Mexico had dwindled by one-third.[28] Environmental degradation was one cause, prolonged drought perhaps another, and curtailed dietary diversity was still another – the whole evident in skeletal remains that reveal the same shortened stature, anemia, hypoplasias, and horrific infant and child mortality that had bedeviled the Mayas.[29]

Survivors in Mexico became divided against one another and were grouped into a number of hostile states until the Toltecs established their capital city of Tula just to the north and brought some order to the region. Warlike forerunners of the Aztecs, the Toltecs expanded by military conquest, collected agricultural tribute from neighboring tribes, established a trading network that stretched all the way to South America, and had sufficient manpower to build their pyramids. Yet, Toltec civilization also collapsed around the middle of the twelfth century. Overpopulation was again much of the reason, although, in addition, the Toltecs had to contend with hoards of desperate Chicmec refugees fleeing a prolonged drought on the northwestern frontier – a region that was similarly overpopulated.

It was a chaotic time. Waves of wild desert folk pressed in on more civilized peoples to begin an era of marching armies, war gods, and screaming captives sacrificed to them. This era of empire-building reached full flower with the Aztecs but not before much Mexican agricultural know-how had flowed north into what would later become the United States.

CHAPTER 12

NEW WORLD,
NEW FOODS

The perpetual struggle for room and food.

Thomas Malthus (1798)

MAIZE WAS ONE of the major crops collected as tribute by the Aztecs. Amaranth was another (*Amaranthus hypochondriacus* and A. *cruentus* – a third species [A. *caudatus*] was cultivated in the Andes of South America). Amaranth was a green treasure that provided edible seeds as well as leaves – both with good quality protein. Domesticated amaranth was apparently of considerable antiquity in Mexico and a part of the diet some 5,500 years ago.[1] The versatile seeds were generally boiled and eaten as a porridge but could also be made into a beverage, a candy, or could even be popped, and the hundreds of thousands of bushels of amaranth seed that reached Aztec granaries each year indicate its widespread cultivation. In addition, the Aztecs also grew their own amaranth on roughly 75 square miles of *chinampas* or floating gardens on Lake Texcoco. From Mexico, amaranth cultivation spread northward to the pueblos of the southeastern United States. It was domesticated independently in South America.

So why did this valuable plant fall into such disuse that today it is mostly a curiosity available only in health food stores? The answer generally put forward is the objection of the Spanish to Aztec religious ceremonies that employed images made of amaranth dough in what seemed to be a heretical parody of the Holy Communion. Yet, that may not be the whole story because a second tribute-crop of the Aztecs has also become obscure. Chía

(*Salvia hispanica*) – a relative of sage – is still used today to concoct a refreshing beverage. In the past, however, the mucilaginous seeds were roasted and ground into a meal called *pinole* to become porridge, a mainstay in many diets.[2]

Beans (genus *Phaseolus*) some species of which may have been domesticated at about the same time as amaranth,[3] constituted another major crop collected by the Aztecs. As was the case with Old World beans such as favas and lentils, New World beans – far more numerous than their Old World counterparts – were gathered long before they were cultivated. Discussion of the myriad varieties of the domesticated common bean (P. *vulgaris*), however, takes us straight into a terminological tangle of names such as the turtle or black bean, kidney bean (including the white cannellini), and a whole slew of other conspecific beans ranging from what we call chilli, pinto, cranberry, red, great northern, Lamon, string (snap), and Romano (Italian green), to other white beans such as pea or navy beans. Dates of domestication of these many varieties have yet to be established, but when the Europeans first reached the hemisphere, P. *vulgaris* – in one or another of its many guises – was under cultivation from Argentina and Chile in the south to the St. Lawrence and upper Missouri valleys in the north.[4]

In truth, there were probably numerous independent domestications of the common bean[5] although the epicenters of their cultivation seem to have been two – the Andean region and Mesoamerica – with legumes appearing in much of the rest of South and North America just a few centuries before Columbus set sail. Archeological evidence of bean domestication has promoted a considerable amount of wrangling because the previously used 14-Carbon dating was contextual, and small objects like beans tend to move downward and, thus, out of place, in archeological contexts.

However, with the development of 14-Carbon dating by atomic mass spectrometry, single seeds can be more accurately dated and, not surprisingly, this advance has produced some dates that contradict contextual dating by a considerable margin. All of this amounts to a tedious way of saying that the dates we give here for bean domestication are generally early ones, and domestication may actually have occurred much later.[6]

Keeping this caveat in mind, there is evidence to indicate that P. *vulgaris* may have been domesticated in the Peruvian Andes as many as 8,000 years ago and in the Tehuacán Valley of Central Mexico some 1,000 years later.[7] The lima bean (P. *lunatus*) – the scientific name indicating the "lunar-like" (actually half-moon) shape of some varieties – had its home in the Andean region where ancient Peruvians domesticated it perhaps some 5,600 or more years ago. Interestingly, although lima beans do not show up in Mexico's archeological record, a smaller cousin, the sieva bean, does. Although never grown in Peru, it was under cultivation in Mexico and Central America around 1,200 years ago suggesting that the two varieties shared a distant common ancestor but were cultivated separately.[8] Today the larger limas are called "Fordhooks" or "butter beans;" the smaller sieva is a "baby lima."

Pole beans or scarlet runners (P. *coccineus*), representing the third American bean species, are often cultivated around poles to keep them from running. Like other beans, these legumes were gathered for eons before they were domesticated – an event that some evidence suggests may have taken place as long as 6,000 years ago. There is no question, however, that pole beans were under cultivation in Mexico by at least 1,300 years ago.[9]

The fourth American bean species is the little known tepary bean (P. *acutifolius*). Of all the beans it was the most northerly in origin. Domesticated in Mexico approximately 5,000 years ago, it reached the North American southwest some 700 years before Columbus set out on his first voyage.[10] Today teparies are eaten by some Native American groups in northwestern Mexico and in the American desert southwest. In addition to baking and boiling them, the beans are toasted or parched, then emptied of their white powder. This flour, in turn, is used to make near-instant bean dishes.[11]

Squash, although not an Aztec tribute crop, rounded out the vaunted maize, squash, and bean triad upon which most Mesoamerican diets sooner or later rested. Squash was a name supplied by Native Americans and thereafter applied by North Americans to many members of the genus *Cucurbita*, which popular parlance tends to subdivide into squashes, pumpkins, and gourds.[12] The latter, however, may not be an American native but rather have African origins – and, according to plant expert Charles Heiser, floated to the Americas (it has been shown that gourds can float in salt water for upwards of a year).[13] Such a feat, however, does not call into question the American origin of squashes and pumpkins.

There were at least five separate domestications of squash in the Americas that gave us the five squash species. But none of these were initially valued as food. Rather, in the wild, all cucurbits have gourd-like qualities, and squash cultivation was probably originally aimed at securing a steady supply of hard, watertight shells to serve as cooking, drinking, eating, and storage utensils. They were also useful as floats for fishing nets, ceremonial rattles, and even for helmets and masks.[14]

When squashes were first used as food, it was for their oil-rich seeds and the tasty yellow flowers and shoot tips of immature fruits. Their bitter and stringy flesh only became edible after a long period of domestication. After this, however, squashes were regularly boiled and roasted and fit right in to the diet.[15]

Most varieties of summer squash such as zucchini, yellow, straight necked, spaghetti, and patty pan squash are members of the C. *pepo* clan, as are some winter squashes like the acorn, and most pumpkins. Collectively C. *pepo* constitutes the most popular of all squashes today, and this popularity apparently prevailed yesterday as well, because its seeds are the most common to be found in the archeological record.[16]

Arguments have been made for two independent centers of C. *pepo* domestication. One of these was in Mexico around 9,500 to 7,500 years ago, with the plant diffusing into the southwestern United States by around 3,000 years ago. The second was in eastern North America, where C. *pepo* was under cultivation between 5,000 and 3,000 years ago and where its ancestors had long been growing wild. In Florida, for instance, we now know that C. *pepo* was present before the first Native Americans moved into the peninsula.[17]

This North American center of domestication helps to explain a heretofore puzzling question of why domesticated squashes and pumpkins (from the Old English "pompion" or "pumpion") were present in what is now the eastern United States before maize. Had C. *pepo* been domesticated solely in Mexico, then presumably it would have reached the Eastern United States at about the same time as maize.[18] But Native Americans were probably not much concerned about the origin of these cucurbits, whose seeds and flesh were some of the most valuable foods in their diets.

There are other winter squashes that belong to varieties of C. *argyrosperma* (formerly denominated C. *mixta*). These were probably domesticated in southern Mexico around 7,000 years ago, although now they range through an area extending across Mexico and into the southwestern United States. They are (and presumably were) grown mostly for their seeds, although some, like the "Green Striped Cushaw" and the "White Cushaw" have good quality flesh.

The earliest archaeological remains of C. *moschata* (butternut squash is its most familiar representative) have been found close to the intersection of the northern and southern hemispheres – in southern Mexico dating from 7,000 years ago and in coastal Peru from around 5,000 years ago.[19] Whether these represent two independent centers of domestication is unclear. *C. moschata* entered North America something over 1,000 years ago, although if it spread throughout the Caribbean before or after the Spanish arrived is also unclear.

South America is the home of *C. maxima*, with coastal Peru probably the center of its domestication some 4,500 to 2,500 years ago. As the scientific name implies, these cucurbit representatives were bred by Native Americans to secure large pumpkins and squashes such as the Hubbard. Other familiar, if smaller, examples are banana and buttercup squashes. *C. maxima* did not spread to Mesoamerica and further north to North America until after the sixteenth-century conquest of Peru.

A final New World species is the relatively unknown *C. ficifolia* – a squash adapted to high altitudes.[20] Sometimes called the "Malabar gourd" or the "fig-leafed gourd," it was apparently domesticated in northern South America but subsequently moved northward to become a food for those living in the highlands of Mexico as well. In the early nineteenth century, the keeping qualities of *C. ficifolia* recommended it for livestock feed during long sea voyages and it was used extensively for this purpose in South Asia where it acquired the "Malabar gourd" moniker.

Not a cucurbit, but a member nonetheless of the New World tribe of Cucurbitaceae, the chayote or mirliton (*Sechium edule*) – also called "vegetable pear," "christophene," "custard marrow," and "*chocho*" – was domesticated in Mexico and became established in Peru after the conquest before hiving out to much of the larger world. Its squash-like fruit is generally the part eaten, although it has a large and starchy root that many find even more tasty.[21]

Chilli peppers (genus *Capsicum*) and tomatoes (*Lycopersicon esculentum*) – both members of the Solanacae family – originated in South America, where wild varieties of each are still found. However, the tomato and at least one chilli pepper species were first domesticated in Mesoamerica. Their seeds were moved northward in stages; by winds and waves to be sure, and probably by migrants and sea traders. Mostly, however, it is suspected that they traveled in the alimentary tract of migrating birds. When dropped, the seeds were enveloped in plenty of fertilizer, and when those of the cherry tomato (believed to be the direct ancestor of today's cultivated tomatoes) landed in cultivated Mesoamerican fields of a tomato relative – the tomatillo or husk tomato (*Physalis ixocarpa*) – they would have been automatically cultivated along with the similarly-sized tomatillos – and thus automatically domesticated.[22]

Chilli peppers were already fairly widespread when the first humans set foot in the Americas. By 1492, the descendents of those first humans had domesticated the four or five (there is taxonomic confusion) species that we utilize today. Two of these, both domesticated in South America, are only now becoming known in the wider world, whereas two other undomesticated but intensely cultivated species – the bird pepper and the Tabasco pepper – are semi-wild but in the process of domestication.[23]

C. chinense, which has blossomed into the fiery Habanero, Scotch Bonnet, and Jamaican Hot, was domesticated in tropical northern Amazonia and carried to the Caribbean by South American Indians. It was there that Columbus – who was already sowing confusion by naming the islands the "Indies" and (contradictorily) the Antilles (another name for Atlantis) – encountered his first chilli pepper, and promptly sowed still more confusion. Perhaps wistfully, he called it *pimiento* because that is the Spanish name for the black pepper he was seeking but failed to find.

C. annuum, the species domesticated in Mesoamerica, is the most commercially important of the peppers, giving us sweet ones such as the bell peppers and livelier ones like the cayenne and jalapeño.[24] Chilli peppers constituted the most important condiment for Mesoamericans, and after 1492 they achieved a similar status in the larger world so that today fully one quarter of its population use them every day.[25]

The tomatillo or husk tomato that preceded the (let's call it) "real tomato" in the fields of Mesoamerica was originally berry-sized, as was the wild real tomato. Unfortunately, the husk tomato and the real tomato were not distinguished by sixteenth-century Spanish writers, although it seems that the husk tomato was the more popular of the two in Mexico.[26]

Nonetheless, although real tomatoes were small to begin with, careful cultivation by Mexican growers brought forth ever-larger ones that were made into sauces, mixed with chilli peppers, eaten with beans – and in some instances apparently with human flesh. When the Spanish were on the march from Vera Cruz to Tenochtitlan in 1519, Bernal Diaz wrote that, as they were passing through Cholula, the Aztecs "wanted to kill us and eat our meat" and that "they had their cooking pots ready, prepared with chile peppers, tomatoes and salt . . . ."[27]

When the Spanish did reach the Aztec capital Tenochtitlan (now Mexico City), they noted that tomato sellers "offered large tomatoes, small tomatoes, green tomatoes, leaf tomatoes, thin tomatoes, sweet tomatoes, large serpent tomatoes, nipple-shaped tomatoes, coyote tomatoes, sand tomatoes, and those which are yellow, very yellow, quite yellow, red, very red, quite ruddy, bright red, reddish, [and] rosy dawn colored."[28] But despite this cornucopia of tomatoes, the tomatillo continues to be more appreciated in many parts of Mexico even as it remains relatively unknown elsewhere on the planet, whereas the tomato is wildly popular and one of the most important vegetables on the world market.[29]

Like the tomato, another out-of-place American plant was cacao (*Theobroma cacao*). We tend to associate chocolate with Mesoamerica, where Columbus first encountered cacao beans or "nibs" and where Cortés amassed a great store of them after discovering that they could be used as money.[30] The prevailing scholarly view, however, is that the origins of cacao (there is more than one type) lie in the Amazon region of South America, even though the Mayans were writing about cacao (an Olmec word) in their hieroglyphics as if it were their property (the Mayan glyph for cacao is *ka-ka-wa* from which the word cacao was derived) long before the Europeans showed up. And, as Cortés discovered, cacao beans were being used as currency throughout much of Mesoamerica at the time of their arrival. Cacao consumption was monopolized by the Mesoamerican aristocracy, and the Aztec nobility was especially fond of a drink made from the beans. Yet, cacao had to be imported from the Caribbean coast because the valley of Mexico was too high and dry for the beans to grow.[31]

Seventeenth-century pirates off the Spanish Main appreciated cacao as valuable plunder and also drank it for breakfast.[32] In 1663, cacao ventured westward to the Philippines, but it had traveled in the opposite direction much earlier. It reached Europe when Columbus returned from his second visit to the Americas, again in 1528 with Cortés, the conqueror of Mexico, and probably with the pirates as well.

As we shall see later on (in Chapter 15), the Europeans enthusiastically adopted cacao, along with vanilla (*Vanilla planifolia*). Like cacao nibs, vanilla beans are another pod fruit (from the diminutive of the Spanish *vaina* or pod) – in this case the fruit of the vanilla orchid, which is one of the few orchids cherished for something besides its flowers. Vanilla is indigenous to those

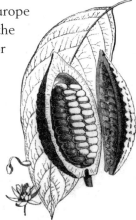

same low-lying Caribbean areas running from Mexico to northern South America that yielded up cacao. Its exploitation, however, was delayed because neither the vanilla flower nor its fruit give off that now familar enticing aroma that would have demanded further investigation.

It was about 1,000 years ago that the Totonacs, living in what is now the state of Vera Cruz, somehow learned to bring out the flavor and aroma of the beans by "sweating" them in the sun for several days, then drying them for several months. The Aztecs who conquered the Totonacs loved the flavor of vanilla. They added it to their chocolate drink and both cacao and vanilla beans became a part of the tribute extracted from conquered peoples.[33] It was a beverage of vanilla and cacao that the Aztecs served to Cortés upon his arrival in Mexico.

Alcoholic beverages in Mesoamerica were made of fermented maize products such as pozole, and *pulque* from the sap of maguey – a spiny plant but not a cactus. Pulque was employed in Aztec religious ceremonies, although, reportedly, it was disdained by most of the Aztec warrior class whose normal drink was high-status chocolate.[34]

The papaya (*Carica papaya*) was another native of South America, whose first recorded use was in the Central American lowlands. The fruit was subsequently transferred north into Mexico, south into Peru, and east into the Caribbean.[35] Related to gourds, melons, and pumpkins, papayas – with their yellow, orange, and pinkish flesh – were among those fruits the Mayas hastened to bestow on the first Spaniards to reach Yucatán.[36]

Avocados had a Central American beginning, where they have been cultivated for close to 7,000 years. The fruit was a domesticate in Mexico about 2,000 years later and, sometime after that, traveled to Peru, where it was called a *palta*. The Spaniards transliterated the Aztec name *abuacatal*, which meant testicle because of its shape, as aguacate that was transliterated again to become "avocado" in English. Avocados (also known as butter pears) join olives and coconuts as the most oily of the fruits, with their fat especially important in those crowded portions of the ancient Americas like Central America, Mexico, and the Andean region, where fats were in short supply.[37]

The Spanish and Portuguese later disseminated these fruits throughout the world's tropics and subtropics, along with the pineapple. Pineapples had their origin in Brazil and Paraguay, but were carried north by Native Americans so that by 1492, they were well distributed in coastal Mexico and throughout the West Indies. In 1493, Columbus became the first European to taste a pineapple, but not the last. Visitors to the New World were nearly unanimous in their praise for this "marvelous fruit."[38]

Some foods continued their journey northward beyond Mesoamerica. Squash had earlier blazed a migratory trail out of Mexico to join local varieties of *C. pepo*, and was diffused throughout the southeastern woodlands of North America by around 2000 BCE. Some have read this as evidence of an early "Mexican connection," or at least a Maxican influence connection, behind the construction of the Adena mounds of the Ohio Valley built around 500 BCE. These include the famous Serpent Mound and the mounds at Poverty Point in Louisiana built as early as 1200 BCE.

The assumption was that the mound builders had, like the Olmecs, been farmers sustained by the Mesoamerican triad of maize, beans, and squash, and, like the Olmecs, had plenty of labor to spare. Further investigation, however, revealed that the mound builders were not really farmers but lived by efficiently harvesting wild food. And no maize was found at any of the sites, probably because it had not yet arrived.[39]

The migration of maize northward out of Mexico apparently began as a trickle sometime around the start of the Common Era, when it first joined squashes and beans in fields irrigated by an ingenious and extensive network of canals. These were the work of the Hohokam, who inhabited a stretch of the Sonora desert where Phoenix now sits. The name "Hohokam" means "vanished ones" but, in this case, not without a trace, as they seem to have been immigrants from Mexico whom the Pima Indians claim as ancestors. They were clearly in touch with Mesoamerica, and new strains of maize bred in the interior regularly reached them on the northern frontier.

Later, after 660 AD, the Pueblo people of New Mexico embarked on what by now has become a familiar road to disaster. Agriculture was intensified in response to increasing population. Society became highly stratified, greater emphasis was placed on public architecture and trade, large regional systems appeared, warfare and violence increased, and health deteriorated.[40] Bioanthropological investigators have learned from Pueblo skeletal evidence that these early inhabitants of the American Southwest were also among the least healthy populations ever known to have lived in the Americas, even unhealthier than South Carolina slave populations of later times.[41]

From the Southwest, maize agriculture stretched eastward across North America to appear rather abruptly in the archaeological record around

1150 AD. Such abruptness was probably the result of the development (around 900 AD) of a new maize variety better adapted to North America's shorter summers.[42] And after 1200, the Mexican trinity of beans, squash, and maize became entrenched as staples among eastern North America peoples from the Algonquin in the north to the Apalachee and Guale in the south.[43]

As a rule, maize agriculture was not so destructive of human health in middle and eastern North America as it had proven to be in Mesoamerica and the desert southwest because these Native Americans continued to rely on wild foods offered by the season.[44] For example, on the Georgia coast the transition from foraging to farming (1150–1550) was based on the adoption and intensification of maize agriculture. But although this did produce something of a decline in health, it was not nearly so pronounced a decline as in the Southwest – apparently because the coastal peoples continued to take in good quality protein by exploiting marine resources for much of the year.[45]

In like fashion, although maize agriculture was adopted in the Ohio Valley at about the same time as on the Georgia Bight (and Native American skeletal remains reflect this), the people were only part-time farmers (horticulturalists rather than agriculturalists). They still relied on hunted foods – bison, other game, fish – and gathered foods such as wild amaranth, Jerusalem artichokes, sumpweed, sunflowers, maygrass, little barley, various berries (strawberry, blackberry, raspberry, blueberry, and cranberry), and nuts (especially hickory and pecan varieties). They maintained their health, in other words, by not completing the transition from hunting and gathering – and such incompletion characterized most North American Native societies.[46]

There were, of course, some exceptions. A major one that produced dramatically declining health began sometime after 900 AD when the Mexican foods, and especially maize agriculture, spurred the so-called Mississippian florescence. This brought about the population growth needed to create the most complex prehistoric society and the largest towns north of Mexico. Skeletal evidence from Cahokia, Dickson Mounds, Illinois, and elsewhere bears testimony to the nutritional lesions and physical wreckage that generally accompanied such developments.[47]

But in looking beyond this familiar sequence of events, a reasonable question might be why the florescence had to await the adoption of the new tropical foods? Could the answer be that native foods simply did not

pack the necessary caloric punch to stimulate much in the way of population growth?[48]

Chief among these native foods (from today's perspective at any rate) was the sunflower (*Helianthus annuus* var. *macrocarpus*) – North America's only contribution to the world's major crops and one of its most important oil sources. Native Americans had gathered sunflower seeds for millennia, drying and storing them for winter. But by at least 1500 BCE, substantially before the arrival of maize and other plants from Mexico, some tribes in eastern North America had taken the next step of cultivating sunflowers for their large seed-bearing heads. By 500 BCE, domesticated sunflower cultivation was fairly widespread in North America, and, later on, European observers noted that the plant had spread into Mexico. Sunflowers hit the big time in the sixteenth century when they were introduced to Europe, and particularly to Russia where, because they were recent arrivals, their oil had not made the list of proscribed foods during fasting days prescribed by the Orthodox church. Not only was the oil immediately popular, but Russia surged to the forefront of the world's sunflower producers – and continues to maintain this position.[49]

Most North American crops, however, not only failed to make it into the larger world, but faltered in the face of foreign competition. We have already mentioned a couple of varieties of *C. pepo* that were domesticated in North America sometime before 1500 BCE. Their shells were used as containers, their blossoms and dried seeds were eaten, and probably, at some point in time, their flesh as well. Yet despite such usefulness the Mexican cultivars were obviously more useful since they edged out their North American counterparts so completely after their arrival that the latter fell into disuse.[50]

Another of the North American "founder crops" is sumpweed (*Iva annua*), sometimes called "marsh elder." Although at one time a staple for Native Americans, it is one of the few plants known to have regained weed status, despite a long period of domestication, by returning to the wild. A member of the same family as the sunflower, the daisy, and ragweed, sump-weed frequents moist soils throughout North America's midsection. Generally about two or three feet in height, it has an oily seed with a nut-like flavor. Evidence indicates that it was a gathered food for Native Americans in Illinois around 3500 BCE. Some 1,500 years later it had become a cultivated food and one that remained under human control until around 1300 AD, when cultivation ceased.

Why the cessation? We are reduced to guesswork. The plant can give off an unpleasant odor, its pollen can provoke allergic reaction, and handling it can cause skin irritation; but such trifling drawbacks did not prevent three millennia of cultivation. An important clue, however, may reside in the time that cultivation stopped. Circa 1300 AD marks the advent of the Mexican foods – the arrival of maize, beans, and squash – and quite possibly the provision of more food for less work.[51]

The same explanation, namely that sumpweed lost out in the competition with foreign plants, may also account for why other local staples were also discarded. Among them were goosefoot (genus *Chenopodium*), which resembles (and is related to) spinach; the seeds of little barley (*Hordeum pusillum*); foxtail barley (*H. jubatum*); maygrass (*Phalaris caroliniana*), domesticated about 3,000 years ago; and knotweed (genus *Polygonum*), some species of which also provided greens.[52] At one time acorns (genus *Quercus*) were widely consumed by many Native American peoples, especially those of central California. There they were a dietary staple, with the nuts ground to make breads and porridges.[53]

Zizania aquatica, or wild rice, was another survivor (like the sunflower) of the Mexican trinity's imperialism. Often called "Indian rice" ("crazy oats" by the early French), it was neither a rice nor (until recently) a cultigen. This grain of a tall aquatic grass is found throughout North America but particularly in the upper Mississippi Valley and especially in the northern Great Lakes region where it grows in marshes, lakes, and along riverbanks. Today wild rice is regarded as gourmet fare, but it was a staple for those Native Americans who harvested its grains over millennia.[54]

This quick look at North American indigenous foods has only sharpened our suspicion that they were incapable of sustaining large civilizations as the Mexican crops managed to do, even if they did inflict havoc on human health. Perhaps it was just a matter of more time until selective breeding would have instilled that capability. After all, those North American plants that did undergo domestication, did so some 6,000 or more years after wheat and barley were first brought under human control in the Fertile Crescent Or maybe it was just that there was little incentive for such genetic tinkering because those who domesticated the North American plants did not rely completely on them but also continued their old hunting and gathering activities. Whatever the reason, is not surprising that their skeletal remains confirm that they enjoyed a sufficiently varied diet to ensure good nutritional health.

Some credit for this health is also due the American bison (*Bison bison*), whose availability constituted yet another reason for a lack of intensive agricultural activity. Persistently miscalled a "buffalo," there were an estimated 60 million of them roaming about when the Europeans first set foot in North America (with perhaps 70 percent scattered across what is now the continental United States and the rest in Canada).[55] Bison hides sheltered and clothed Native Americans, bison bones became utensils, bison dung fueled campfires, and, most importantly, bison meat and marrow fueled consumers with high-quality protein.

Contrast this with the Mesoamericans who seldom tasted meat and whose health slipped even more in the century of chaos that followed the collapse of Tula, when the Aztecs (probably refugees from western Mexico) entered the crowded Valley of Mexico! They settled on the swampy islands of Lake Texcoco and they created the twin cities of Tenochtitlán and Tlatelolco around 1325. Dedicated to war and imbued with a religious ideology, Aztec warriors swiftly created a predatory empire based, as we saw, on agricultural tribute extorted from an ever-expanding circle of subject peoples.

The Spanish conquistadors later showed considerable interest in the great Aztec storage bins stuffed with maize, beans, grain amaranth, chia, and cacao beans. They could not know at the time that the storehouses attested to a searing four years of drought and frost that had taken place 70 years before. The ensuing famine in the Mexican highlands not only killed thousands of Aztecs but deeply scarred the survivors and their descendents.[56]

The Spaniards marveled at the major Aztec market, writing that it was larger than its counterpart in Rome and offered vast amounts and varieties of foodstuffs, including prepared foods like tamales, tortillas, and sauces of every kind.[57] They were even more amazed by the Aztec capital of Tenochtitlán. At between 200,000 and 400,000 inhabitants (the number is debated), it was larger and cleaner than most European cities of the time, and in fact, probably the largest city that any of the conquistadors had ever seen.[58] They compared its layout to Venice, because drainage and reclamation projects had created causeways and canals – thoroughfares for canoes within the city – with bridges to the suburbs and provincial centers. On the canals and on the lake floated "*chinampas*" – artificial islands created from dredged up silt and held together by reeds, stakes, and the roots of trees growing on them. Several crops a year were raised in the rich soil of a *chinampa* – maize and amaranth among them.

Game and fish, along with turkeys and ducks were all available in the market – but went mostly to the upper classes – and dishes like the famous Aztec *mole poblano de guajolote* consisting of turkey in a chocolate sauce enlivened with chillies and nuts, were reserved for the nobility, just as hallucinogenic mushrooms were the property of the priests.[59]

However, despite the appearance of food abundance in the markets, there was actually not enough to go around. Overcrowding in the Valley of Mexico was making life short and brutish for most; yet, despite soaring infant and child mortality rates, populations continued to increase. Some have proposed that the purpose of the mass sacrificing done by the Aztecs was a means of coping with these problems. On the one hand, sacrifice was a method of population control and, on the other, it was meat production for a meat-starved people. In the words of Marvin Harris " . . . the amount of human sacrifice and cannibalism practiced in Tenochtitlán remains unique in human history."[60]

We should note, however, that human sacrifice in the Americas was hardly invented by the Aztecs. It was practiced by many other South American and Mesoamerican peoples, including the Mayas and the Toltecs – although perhaps never with such single-mindedness as the Aztecs, who demanded sacrificial victims as well as agricultural produce from subject peoples. Moreover, that the victims may have been a source of animal protein is a notion not easily dispelled when one can read of Aztec cannibal stews and receive assurances in the literature that Montezuma customarily ate human thighs cooked with chilli peppers and tomatoes.[61] Yet no one has demonstrated that human flesh was available in Aztec markets which, presumably, it would have been if sacrifice had been intended as a method of meat production.

As for a population pressure explanation, people were definitely crowded – some million and a half people are alleged to have lived within a twenty-mile radius of Tenochtitlán, which might account for why the Aztecs were not inclined to keep captives and put them to work but preferred to sacrifice them instead.[62] However, unless it can be shown that theAztecs sacrificed one another in wholesale fashion, it is not clear how the practice would have promoted Aztec population control.

What this means, then, is that we may need to take at face value the Aztec explanation, which was their belief that the gods craved human hearts and would destroy the world if that craving was not regularly satiated. Casting about for other, more practical, reasons does not seem to lead anywhere and, after all, we have also had to accept that the original impulse for animal domestication was a need for sacrificial animals – not food.

NEW FOODS IN THE
SOUTHERN NEW WORLD

A mountain climate means frost, and hail, and storms, against
which desirable domesticated plants should be able to protect them-
selves . . . [R]oot crops provide the remedy to those conditions, and
among them the potato is preeminent.

Sophia D. Coe (1994)[1]

IN SOUTH AMERICA, as in Mesoamerica, hunter-gatherers encountered
those many difficulties that eventually thrust practically everybody into
sedentary agriculture. Around 11,000 years ago people in the Andean
region were large-animal hunters, employing fluted points to bring down
the giant sloth or the horse – their preferred prey. As these animals became
extinct, fluted points disappeared and were replaced by others that indicate
a switch to smaller game – deer, camelids, birds, rodents, and the like. Gathered foods such as amaranth and chenopodium seeds (especially quinoa)
supplemented the diet, along with beans and white and sweet potatoes.

Archeological evidence in the Andean region from around 9,000 years
ago, however, indicates some sidling toward sedentism. There was increase
in the number of camelid bones that, in turn, suggests the beginning of
camelid herding, which eventually begat the domesticated llama (*Lama*
glama) and alpaca (*Lama pacos*). These wild South American members of
the camel family were serious sources of food in the Andean highlands of
Peru and Bolivia and may have been domesticated for their flesh as well
as for their labor, that flesh freeze-dried to become *charqui*, which lasts

indefinitely. Native Americans who kept llamas and alpacas did not milk them, however, which meant they passed up a good source of protein. Lactose intolerance is often the explanation offered but even the lactose intolerant can consume milk products such as cheese or yogurt in moderation.[2]

Guinea pigs (*Cavia porcellus*) were trapped and eventually became domesticates as did Muscovy ducks (*Cairina moschata*). Muscovy is a misnomer for this tropical American duck, which has no special association with Moscow, but is a duck that can mate and produce offspring with the common duck (*Anas platyrhaynchos*), even though the offspring are not able to reproduce. By the time of the conquest, the Muscovy duck could be found from Argentina to Mexico and the Caribbean, and although the turkey was a fowl competitor in Mexico, it had no such competition in South America.[3]

Unlike the common duck, wild Muscovies roost in trees, although their truly domesticated counterparts cannot fly. In the Americas the birds were kept for their flesh, their eggs, and especially for their badly needed fat. Like so many other American foods, Muscovy ducks also wound up in sixteenth-century Europe although the names they acquired like "Turkish" duck in Germany, bird from the "Barbary Coast" in France, or Muscovy for that matter, show near-total confusion about the bird's origin. It was in France, that the Muscovy and the common duck were crossed to produce the *mulard* duck, whose hypertrophied livers are, along with goose livers, the makings of pâté de foie gras.[4]

Plant foods overshadowed the few domesticated animals of the Andean region by a considerable margin. In fact, there were more than fifty South American plants domesticated by pre-Columbian peoples and four of these – white potatoes, sweet potatoes, manioc, and peanuts – today rank among the world's most valued crops.[5] In the Andes, where mountain climates at the higher altitudes can spell disaster for above-ground crops, it is not surprising that underground crops such as potatoes were highly valued.

White potatoes (*Solanum tuberosum*), the fourth most important of the world's food crops today and the major highland crop of the Andes, were probably domesticated in the neighborhood of Lake Titicaca at least 5,000 years ago (although the Chilean lowlands also claim a potato sub-species). Icy temperatures at night, alternating with the heat of the day, made it possible to freeze-dry them for storage, an ingenious process of freezing, soaking, and drying used to make *chuño*, a processed food that would keep well for several years.[6]

The Pizarro expedition reached Peru to find potato (initially they thought it a white truffle) cultivation widespread throughout the Andean region, along with what might be termed a "potato culture." The Aymara people, for example, calculated time in terms of how long it took to boil a potato.[7] Curiously, however, at the time of the conquest white potatoes, unlike sweet potatoes and maize, were not widely dispersed elsewhere in the Americas and, in fact, even after the conquest they were slow to move about despite the wide range in which they can grow, and despite their health-giving properties.

Of the world's major staples – potatoes, corn, rice, and wheat – the potato provides by far the most nutrients and the most meals per acre. It also delivers variety, although North Americans, with only eight varieties of potatoes readily available to them, might not think so. But in Peru there are countless kinds – breakfast potatoes, luncheon potatoes, supper potatoes, dessert potatoes – all with different colors, shapes, and tastes.

The sweet potato (*Ipomoea batatas*) by most reports was domesticated in Peru at about the same time as the white potato, although remains of what may have been a domesticated sweet potato have been dated to around 10,000 years ago.[8] If they were a domesticated plant at that point, sweet potatoes would rank among the very first food crops to be cultivated anywhere in the world. Such an antiquity may be hinted at by the more than 150 varieties of sweet potatoes that were under cultivation when the Spaniards first reached the Andean region. But the antiquity of its domestication is by no means the only controversy this mysterious plant has sparked. As we discuss in Chapter 13, sweet potatoes are also suspected of somehow finding their way to Australia, New Zealand, and many of the Pacific Islands long before the Europeans reached the Americas – let alone remote (for them) Oceania.[9]

Oca or occa (*Oxalis tuberosa*) a root crop second only to potatoes in the Andes, has the virtue of growing at altitudes where potatoes will not. The *Oxalis*

part of its scientific name means "acid" in Greek but, fortunately, the acidic taste of its tubers vanishes after a few days of sun-drying. Oca only became one of the globe-trotting Andean plants in the nineteenth century, when it was taken to Europe to supplement the potato. This did not prove successful but oca next moved on to New Zealand, where it did catch on. Today it is commercially cultivated as the "New Zealand yam."[10]

Arracacha (*Arracacia xanthorrhiza*), apparently domesticated before the potato, is another Andean staple. Although related to celery, parsnips, and carrots, it is the only member of this family with a New World pedigree. Sometimes called the "Peruvian carrot," it grows carrot-like roots that replace the potato in some mountainous areas because it costs less to plant and harvest. At one time or another arracacha spread throughout Latin America as far north as Costa Rica, and to Cuba and Haiti in the Caribbean.[11]

Other plants also migrated within the Americas. Sweet potatoes, as already mentioned, were in the Caribbean and were a Maya comestible when Columbus arrived. Evidence indicates that although maize is of greatest antiquity in Mesoamerica, it reached Ecuador by both land and sea routes. In fact, if maize was slow to move northward out of Mesoamerica it moved in the other direction like lightening, reaching the Andes as early as 6000 BCE, where it must have been subjected to those breeding trials and errors that, as in Mexico, gradually increased the size of the ear and made the plant more adaptable.

On the south coast of Ecuador, peoples who had previously been hunters, fishers, and gatherers began to specialize in growing the grain. By about 1,000 BCE, maize cultivation had spread into the Amazon region and to the Orinoco floodplains to stimulate the growth of populations and the concomitant development of stratified societies.[12] Later, maize was a favored foodstuff of the Incas, who used it in a variety of ways, not the least of which was to mass-produce a beer they called *chicha*.[13]

After maize, the preferred grain of the Andean region was quinoa (*Chenopodium quinoa*) – a high altitude plant of the goosefoot or pigweed family that today is planted from Columbia to Chile and Argentina. Its seeds are toasted and made into a porridge. But, although delicious and nutritious (with an average protein yield higher than that of wheat and a better array of essential amino acids), quinoa, unlike maize, has never traveled outside of its American homeland.[14] A relative of quinoa, *cañihua* (*Chenopodium pallidicaule*), raised in the mountains of southern Peru and Bolivia, is used much like quinoa and, because it is tolerant of frost and dry soils, does

better at even higher altitudes. Also known as
quañiwa and *cañahua*, botanists believe that its
domestication is not yet complete.[15]

Getting back to underground crops, although
there is evidence of the peanut being grown in
Peru some 3,000 to 4,000 years ago, the plant
is believed to have been first domesticated in
that region where modern-day Paraguay borders
with southwestern Brazil. Not a nut at all, but a tropical
legume that develops underground (hence the name "groundnut"), the peanut had done considerable diffusing by the time of the Columbian voyages,
so that it was being cultivated in Hispaniola when the explorer came ashore.
The Spanish and Portuguese subsequently introduced peanuts to all of the
world's tropics.[16]

Manioc (from *manihot* in the Tupi language of Brazil) is also known as
"cassava," (from the Arawak kasibi), and "yucca," (from the Carib Indian
word), and may have initially been domesticated in central Brazil. However, other likely possibilities are the lowland tropical forests of Ecuador,
Venezuela, and Columbia. The Caribbean islands and Central America,
too, have been put forward as candidates.

Manioc is a perennial plant grown mostly for its starchy roots that weigh
from a pound or two to over six pounds, although young shoots and leaves
are also edible. Manioc griddles dating from approximately 4,000 to 2,000
years ago have been found at sites along the Orinoco river – finds that
do not necessarily dispute those who believe that manioc domestication
took place as many as 7,000 years ago. Generally thought of as a lowland
tropical crop, manioc was sufficiently adaptable to achieve important food
status in the Andean region, where it was grown in valleys as high as 6,000
feet above sea level.

Manioc defies drought and insects and its cyanide content discourages
root-digging animals, but not human animals who somehow discovered
how to render its tubers edible. It was a complex process of removing
the poison by heating, scraping, and leaching that made this tuber a staple throughout much of South and Central America and, of course, the
Caribbean.[17] It was on the day after Christmas in 1492 that a local chief
treated Columbus to a manioc feast on Hispaniola,[18] and in his log the
explorer (who thought the tubers were a kind of turnip) provided a partial
description of manioc preparation: "They shred those turnips on certain

stones that look like cheese graters . . . then they put on the fire a very large stone on top of which they place that grated root, and they shape it in the form of a cake and use it as bread and it keeps for fifteen to twenty days, which bread several times was very handy for us."[19]

As a matter of fact, manioc was so handy that it became the bread of the American conquest.[20] It is easy to grow and prepare and, best of all, when dried, it keeps for several years, making it an ideal ration for military and naval activities."[21] Following the conquest, manioc became the most important staple in sixteenth-century Brazil, eaten by both masters and slaves settled along the coast. When the Dutch invaded the northeast of that Portuguese colony in the following century, they mastered the techniques of sugar production and discovered manioc's usefulness for feeding sugar slaves. Later, after they were driven out of Brazil, the Dutch took what was now known as the "Brazilian system" to the Caribbean, where manioc became a part of the slave diet there as well.[22]

Other root crops were *ullucu* (*Ullucus tuberosus*), and *añu* (*Tropaeolum tuberosum*), probably domesticated before the potato but today little known outside of South America. As in Mesoamerica, the tubers of jícama were eaten for their crunchy sweet taste in South America, as were *ajipa* tubers (*Pachyrhizus ahipa*). The fleshy rhizomes of *achira* (*Canna edulis*) were an ingredient in Andean Valley stewpots, and the yellow paste made from them is now marketed from Chile to Venezuela and the Caribbean and in places light-years away from achira's homeland, such as Java and Viet Nam.[23]

A final, little known underground plant – the American taro (*Xanthosoma* sagittifolium synonym = X. *violaceum*) – is thought to have been a South America native originating in its Caribbean lowlands. From there it spread throughout the northwestern portion of that continent and into the Caribbean Islands and Central America, eons before Columbus learned how to sail. It was one of the first American plants described by the Spaniards, who noted that it was cultivated for its stem and heart leaves (later called callaloo by the slaves). Named *yautía* by the Tainos (a term that Puerto Ricans continue to use), American taro became malanga or tan(n)ia for most everybody else. The Portuguese and Spaniards carried malanga to West Africa where (wrongly called a coco yam) it became a food of some consequence, often used in the preparation of the regional dish "fufu." It also hived out to tropical Asia to be united with the other taros and widely cultivated in Malaysia, Indonesia, and the South Pacific Islands.[24]

Vegetables and fruits rounded out the diet. As noted previously, South America is home to several cucurbits, among them the crookneck and winter squash as well as *achokcha* (*Cyclanthera pedata*) – used in soups and stews. Similarly, the pineapple is of South American origin as is the papaya, the melon pear or *pepino dulce* (*Solanum muricatum*), the tree tomato (*Cyphomandra betacea*), and the *naranjilla* or little orange (*Solanum quitoenses*).[25]

Steady improvements in South American plant yields encouraged population growth and, not unexpectedly, archeological sites have revealed the same kinds of skeletal evidence of poor health and lowered life expectancy that accompanied population increases in Mesoamerica.[26] Villages grew into towns, and by 2500 BCE, organized, stratified civilizations had developed to (among other things) undertake the construction of large temple mounds.

The *Chavin* culture began to dominate the eastern Andes around 1000 BCE. It flourished from a major religious center at *Chavin de Huantar* until 200 BCE and is known to history for its architecture, large stone sculptures, and, from an agricultural point of view, its canal building.[27] With the eclipse of the *Chavin* culture, regional cultures prospered for a few centuries, but by 200 of the Common Era, the southern portion of coastal Peru was under the domination of the *Nazca* culture (responsible for the mysterious "Nazca lines" etched in the desert) while, at the same time, the *Moche* culture (with its famous Temple of the Sun) achieved a similar dominance in the north. The social and religious organization needed for massive projects like the Temple of the Sun meant that agricultural surpluses were routinely produced, and in Peru, as elsewhere, populations grew into a kind of "critical mass," the kind that ushers militarism toward center stage while imperialism waits in the wings.[28]

Around the year 500, the centralized *Huari* empire was established. From its capital of the same name (located a little south and on the opposite side of the Andes from present-day Lima) expansion took place behind a well-organized military organization that was as good at occupying new territories as it was in conquering them. A couple of hundred years later, the *Chimú* empire arose on the north coast, while in the south, the populous city of *Tiahuanaco* on the southeastern edge of Lake Titicaca, (which had been a cultural and religious center from about the time the *Huari* Empire), came into being.[29]

These were the civilizations that the Incas learned much from and began to knit together in the early fifteenth century. A two-tiered agricultural system developed to fuel Inca enterprises in which much prestige was accorded maize grown in irrigated fields, and the now lowly potato was relegated to a food for the masses.[30] The *Huari* had built roads, but nothing like the thousands of miles of roads constructed by the Incas to bind the empire together. The *Chimú* may have had a complex and centralized bureaucracy, but that of the Incas controlled every aspect of human life with policies such as taxation, compulsory military service, forced labor, and administration at the local level. *Tiahuanaco* may have been a place of pilgrimage, but in the Inca capital at Cuzco dwelled the Inca, the son of the sun.

In the Andean region, as in Mesoamerica, we have already noted that agriculture and increased sedentism brought a substantial deterioration in health. We should also note that, as in Mesoamerica, the skeletons of those who relied intensively on maize consumption in South America reflect evidence of arrested growth in childhood, iron-deficiency anemia, and poor dental health.[31]

Yet, poor health was not the lot of all South Americans. By way of another exception that proves the rule, the healthiest ancient skeletal population turned up so far in a study of health and nutrition in the Western Hemisphere represents individuals living on Brazil's south coast from about 1000 BCE to 1000 AD. Like so many of their North American counterparts they enjoyed this good health because they remained hunter-gatherers – actually, fishermen and shell fishers – who produced highly visible mounds while consuming a varied and protein-rich diet.[32]

Not surprisingly, the Spaniards – for whom beggars on the streets, frequent famines, and outright starvation were omnipresent facts of life at home – took little notice of the malnourished nature of the New World people they conquered. Why should they when the nutritional conditions in Spain for the average person were sometimes little better? However, the Spaniards were much impressed with the vast storehouses of food maintained by the Aztecs and the Incas as a hedge against years of poor harvests, correctly understanding that such storehouses, brimming with grains and dried meats, were sources of enormous power. They were less impressed with some of the other things to eat such as insects and human flesh, and completely unaware that American malnutrition had joined with Eurasian diseases to pave the road for a successful conquest.

THE COLUMBIAN EXCHANGE AND THE OLD WORLDS

And the trees are as different from ours as day from night; and
also the fruits, and grasses and stones and everything.

Christopher Columbus[1]

EUROPE

The seventeenth and eighteenth centuries marked the maximum extension of that episode of glacial expansion we call the Little Ice Age, when
growing seasons were shortened by several weeks and altitudes at which
crops could grow were reduced. At the same time Europeans, having
recovered from the devastation of the Black Plague, were once more
increasing in numbers and in need of extra calories. It was at this point
that the American foods, whose earlier adoptions had been scattered and
spasmodic, began to achieve widespread acceptance.[2]

A good question is why it took Europeans so long to embrace the American crops.[3] They promised more calories and some, like maize and potatoes, had significant advantages over Old World counterparts. Illustrative
are potatoes. In that swath from the North Sea to the Ural Mountains, rye,
although temperamental in the face of cold winters and rainy summers,
was the only Old World grain that did at all well. But potatoes thrived in
such a climate – very like their native environment – and could produce

some four times more calories per acre than rye. Moreover, potato crops matured in three or four months, whereas rye and other grains required ten months. Potatoes could be planted on fields fallowed for future rye cultivation, and left in the ground to be dug up when needed. Grains, by contrast, had to be harvested when ripe, then stored in above-ground structures where they could be evaluated by tax collectors in peacetime and plundered by soldiers during wars.[4]

Maize – the other all-star American crop – could be cultivated wherever wheat was grown and had far lower labor requirements. It delivered substantially more calories per acre than other grains (double that of wheat) because of high disease resistance and a high seed-to-harvest ratio (maize gave back 25 to 100 grains for every 1 planted as opposed to wheat, which gave back only 5). And maize could prosper in areas too wet for wheat.[5]

Yet, despite such advantages, most of the American plants took considerable time to catch on as popular fare. One reason was that people were wary of the solanaceous ones. It did not take the Europeans long to realize that the potato, chilli pepper, and tomato all belong to the same family as belladonna (*Atropa belladonna*) also called "deadly nightshade," the European poison of choice at the time.[6] But the Old World aubergine (eggplant), also a member, was enjoyed by many; so this was a problem that could be overcome. A more serious short-run difficulty was that most New World food plants were tropical in origin and, consequently, could not readily adapt to the more climatically rigid European growing seasons. Even maize, which Native Americans had bred to grow in a number of climates, had to be reintroduced repeatedly, and many varieties underwent much tinkering before maize and other foods became major European crops.[7]

Much of this tinkering was done by botanists who initially probed the New World curiosities in the hope of discovering miraculous pharmacological properties and, outside of Spain, botanical gardens were the first European homes of the American plants. The botanists entered the new plants in "*Herbals*," whose woodcut engravings displayed them in detail and, as the plants became more familiar, some were slowly, often reluctantly, incorporated into diets.

Reluctantly, because of yet another problem – the conservatism of the peasants whose job it was to plant the new crops. Why should they jettison successful methods of cultivating familiar crops, passed from generation to generation for a cycle of centuries, to accommodate new and strange ones? And, for that matter, why should they eat foods to which they were unaccustomed and that demanded new preparation methods? Weaning the peasantry away from tried and true agricultural methods and tried and true foods was perhaps just a matter of time; yet, in many cases, it was a matter of a very long time.

In the decades following 1492, American foodstuffs entered Europe through Spain and Portugal (a possession of Spain from 1580 to 1640), where they were cultivated and then disseminated via two principal routes. One was into the Mediterranean to Spain's Italian holdings; the other was north via Flanders, also a Spanish possession at the time. But many food items such as peppers, maize, squash, and beans also reached southeastern Europe in haphazard fashion via Portuguese Africa, India, and the Turkish Empire.[8]

Maize was found on all the larger islands of the Caribbean by Columbus who, mistaking the plant for panic grass, called it *panizo*.[9] He carried maize to Spain in 1493, where it was already under cultivation around Seville by century's end. Three-quarters of a century elapsed before it became a dominant Andalusian crop,[10] a major Portuguese crop, had crossed the Pyrenees to decorate the countryside of southern France with green fields, and traversed the Mediterranean to Italy. Following this, the Venetians introduced it to the Near East, after which it doubled back into Europe through the Balkans.

All of this activity was accompanied by the usual semantic and geographic confusion. In 1542, a woodcut of maize appeared in a *herbal* of Leonard Fuchs who wrote that the plant had originated in western Asia, then dominated by the Turks, and consequently should be called "Turkish corn." In John Gerard's *Herbal* of 1597, it had become "Turkish wheat" and in Italy was called "Turkey grain." But in Spain the truth of maize's origin was steadfastly maintained by names like "wheat of the Indies" and Indian wheat."[11]

Such a problem of nomenclature, however, tends to obscure the fact that maize did not always take firm root. Despite an early introduction it was not an especially significant Balkan crop much before the beginning of the eighteenth century, and maize remained insignificant in Russia even throughout the following century.[12]

The crop eventually became established mostly as a food for European livestock whose meat and dairy products delivered maize to humans second-hand. But in some areas of cultivation – in northern Spain and Italy, southern France, and later the Balkans – maize was adopted by the poor as a food for humans, and, almost overnight it became their most important one. The cereal had some real advantages, not the least of which was that it could be propagated in peasant gardens, where it was tax exempt from both the tithe and seigniorial dues. Moreover, cornmeal fit easily enough into an already existing diet based on *pulmentum* or mush (the Italian polenta, for example), replacing more expensive millets or barley that could now be grown for market instead of local consumption.

The adoption of maize, however, boosted populations beyond previous limits, which created both a need for still more tillable land and a large subsistence farmer class to work those fields in return for a small plot conceded by landlords to grow that subsistence. As the diet concentrated ever more narrowly on maize, niacin-containing animal foods were rarely consumed and, without knowledge of the Native American method of treating maize with lime to release its niacin, pellagra became endemic. Those who contracted its curious dermatological symptoms were "the butterfly people" who died in great numbers, or went slowly insane.

But in the long run maize was health-giving. It helped improve diets by stimulating the inclusion of more high quality protein. Most Europeans have never been all that enthusiastic about eating the vegetable, but eat it happily enough after its transformation into beef, cheese, milk, chickens and eggs. And as an animal feed, the cereal made it possible to carry more barnyard animals through the winter which, in turn, meant more whole protein on a year-round basis. Before maize, what little hay was cut went to oxen, warhorses, and breeding stock, and the rest of the barnyard was slaughtered every fall.[13] And finally, copious barn manure collected over the winter meant much good quality fertilizer for the fields in the spring.[14]

A reputation for possessing aphrodisiacal properties did nothing to discourage the use of sweet potatoes, but white potatoes had a tardier and more difficult acceptance.[15] They may have reached Spain as early as 1539, with Hernando Pizarro, who returned from Peru carrying gold to the Spanish court only to be jailed for his trouble. He was the victim of crown anger that the conquest of the Andean region had degenerated into civil wars between the conquerors. These struggles dragged on until the middle of the sixteenth century and little more is heard of potatoes until peace finally broke out in Peru. After this, however, intercourse between the new Viceroyalty and the Isthmus quickened as the silver mines of Potosí came into production and the precious metal was transshipped to Spain via Panama.

Potatoes were adopted as basic ships stores for Spanish vessels operating off South America's Pacific coast between Peru and the Isthmus.

It is likely that the original Andean varieties needed some coaxing to adapt to the longer summer days of Europe.[16] Nonetheless the tubers could be purchased in Seville as early as 1573, according to the records of a hospital that fed them to patients. From Spain, potatoes followed the now-familiar route to Italy where a hungry peasantry eagerly adopted them – in some parts of the country they were garden vegetables prior to 1588.[17] At that point, however, the potato entered a turbulent sea of slander and semantics.

The slander came at the hands of the Swiss botanist Caspar Bauhin, who wrote in the last years of the sixteenth century that potatoes not only aroused sexual desire but also caused wind and leprosy – the latter a steep price to pay for an aphrodisiac. Moreover – and another difficulty for all of the American foods – in the eyes of religious fundamentalists, the potato was probably guilty on all of these counts. After all, nowhere was it mentioned in the Bible; hence it must be the work of the Devil. In fact, the strange subterranean process by which it reproduced seemed especially devilish. And finally, Bauhin sought to clinch his case by once more declaring that the vegetable belonged to the notorious belladonna family and was therefore poisonous, which was partially true, at least of the plant's leaves and flowers.[18]

Semantic confusion began when the Spaniards appropriated the Inca name, *papa* for the white potato and the Caribbean Indian word *batata* for the sweet potato.[19] Confusion was compounded because Columbus had taken sweet potatoes to Spain from the Caribbean decades before the white potato arrived from Peru. By the end of the sixteenth century, the sweet potato had been designated *Ipomoea batatas*, whereas the white potato was known as *batatas hispanorum* or the "Spanish potato" – this appearance of science confounded as white potatoes reached England from (as legend had it) Virginia with Francis Drake. He apparently had acquired them at Cartagena instead, but a Virginia origin of potatoes was given scientific blessing in the 1597 *Herbal* of John Gerard, who repeated the legend. It appeared that the world had yet another potato – the "Virginia potato,"[20] and all of this was not completely cleared up until 1936, when the great Russian botanist Nikolai Ivanovich Vavilov (who died in prison rather than recant his devotion to "western genetics") established (or reestablished) the potato's South American origin.[21]

Meanwhile, no one knew for certain what kind of potato was being referred to – a situation that grew murkier as the "Virginia potato" became the "English potato" only to be adopted by the Irish, and soon known as the "Irish potato." The aforementioned slander had helped to block the potato from spreading into Russia and Germany – slander coupled with a natural hostility of grain-growing peoples for root crops. But by the third decade of the seventeenth century – in the middle of the depredations and deprivations wrought by the Thirty Years War (1618–1648) – potatoes were turned to as a famine food by those lucky enough to lay hands on some and proved to be miracle workers wherever they were grown, yielding many more calories per acre of land than any grain – and calories especially welcome when grain crops failed.

The Thirty Years War had brought destruction to much of Europe's agriculture and, in its rebuilding, potatoes began to gain acceptance in the Netherlands. A century later, they were widespread there after ousting another white root, the parsnip. Potatoes were also adopted in England, and the same was true in Ireland, where in the span of a century, potatoes would encourage the population to triple and men to grow extra-long thumbnails to peel them.

In eighteenth-century France, Marie Antoinette wore potato flowers in her hair to emphasize the potato's virtues, and scientist Auguste Parmentier, who knew the value of potatoes having subsisted on them as a prisoner of the Prussians, duped the peasants around Paris into accepting them. He put a field of potatoes under armed guard until the plants were ready for transplanting, then withdrew the guards for a night, knowing that the peasants, now convinced that potatoes were valuable, would steal every last one and transplant them at home.[22] Elsewhere, however, in Germany and Russia, it required stern edicts, often enforced at gunpoint, to compel a peasantry that believed bread to be the natural food of man to plant potatoes even as a famine food.[23] And resistance, especially in Russia, continued well into the nineteenth century. This was some 200 years after the peripatetic potato, which had journeyed from South America to Europe, returned to the Americas – in this case to Boston – as the "Irish potato."[24]

Another American food that reached North America along a similarly circuitous route was the tomato, although not all Europeans, by now totally bewildered about where all the new foods were coming from, conceded the tomato a New World origin. In the past, new foods had generally reached Europe from the east or from the south across the Mediterranean.

The latter most likely meant the Arab world and consequently the tomato became a *pomi di mori* – an "apple of the Moor." This mistake was perpetuated in many languages. *Pomi di mori*, for example, was corrupted in French to *pomme d' amour* (love apple), and in Italian to *pomodoro* ("golden apple"). Despite these tantalizing names, however, the tomato initially enjoyed no aphrodisiacal reputation, and experts say it is unlikely that the first tomatoes in Italy were yellow or orange varieties.

But another more lascivious variation on the origin of the name "love apple" soon developed among those convinced that Columbus had discovered the Garden of Eden and that the tomato was one of its fruits. This made it another of the forbidden fruits, a red ball of oozing juices – clearly an aphrodisiac. The Spaniards, by contrast, called the fruit a *tomate* (from the Nahuatl *tomatl*). In Italy, the tomato ultimately had its greatest impact during the eighteenth-century "red revolution" when the strident colors of tomatoes and chilli peppers came to predominate in southern Italian cuisine.[25] It is sometimes alleged that tomatoes reached North America via Europe in the late eighteenth century. But they were being enthusiastically eaten in Carolina at the beginning of that century after drifting northward from the Caribbean.

Other American plants also made a culinary impact on Europe. Squash and pumpkins joined potatoes and maize to keep the poor alive, and one of the summer squashes – zucchini – became a near staple in Italy. American beans gained easy acceptance in Europe, probably because they were not so different from the cowpea that had come much earlier from Africa, and other Old World favorites such as fava beans and chickpeas. American beans were also the focus of considerable botanical experimentation, some of which led to still more semantical confusion. In France, for example, green pods (and dried seeds for that matter) became *haricot* beans and returned to the New World as "French Beans." But in England, "haricot" came to mean a dried bean; the fresh were called "French" or "green beans."

The reception of chilli peppers was lukewarm at best among most Europeans. The fiery fruits proved considerably more than lukewarm to palates accustomed to bland diets, and people had no desire to indulge in "benign masochism" as the consumption of chilli peppers has been characterized.[26] Consequently, although both the Spanish and the Portuguese introduced them to Iberia and had scattered them around most of Europe by the mid-sixteenth century, chilli peppers took hold only in the livelier cuisines of Italy, the Balkans, and Turkey. Predictably, Europeans got the idea that capsicums had originated in the east, especially in India, and began calling them "Calicut peppers" and "Indian peppers."[27]

The one animal from the New World to achieve ready European acceptance was the turkey (*Meleagris gallopavo*), which, like so many of the plants, also suffered nomenclature difficulties abroad. There was, incidentally, a second New World turkey – the ocellated turkey (*Meleagris "Agriocharis" ocellata*) of Central America and southern Mexico, which was exploited by the Maya, but there is little evidence that it was ever domesticated, let alone exported.[28] By contrast, (M. *gallopavo*) seems to have been domesticated in central Mexico around the beginning of the Common Era or perhaps even sooner, because the birds liked to hang around humans, stealing food and roosting in warm places, and hence deserve some credit for domesticating themselves. From Mexico, turkey domestication spread northward and the Coronado expedition (1540–42) reported seeing the birds in southwestern pueblos, even receiving them from the natives as gifts.[29]

Called *gallina de la tierra* ("land chicken") or just *gallina* as well as *pavo* by the Spanish, the soon to be misnamed turkey was an instant hit in Spain and a real delicacy, as testified to in typical backhanded fashion by Miguel de Cervantes (1547–1616). In his famous novel *Don Quixote* he had his hero declare that "I had rather munch a crust of brown bread and an onion [at home] . . . than feed upon turkey at another man's table."

As early as 1511, every ship leaving for the New World carried orders to bring back ten turkeys[30] and before 1530, the great American bird was not only established on Spanish poultry farms, but had spread out across a Europe where the wealthy, always seeking new ways to impress guests, placed turkeys on their tables alongside native birds like peacocks, herons, and cranes. Later the bird was to earn the enthusiastic endorsement of French gourmet Jean Anthelme Brillat-Savarin who declared that "the turkey is certainly one of the most delightful presents which the New World has made to the Old."[31]

This speed of dissemination contributed to the ensuing confusion about where the turkey had come from. By 1525 the bird was known in Italy as a *coc d' Inde* or *galle d'India* and by 1538 it was called a *coc d' Inde* in France (which was corrupted into *dinde*), whereas the Germans alternatively called the bird a *calecutische Hahn* (a Calcutta hen), and an *indianische Hahn*.[32]

Clearly, most of Europe looked in the wrong direction for the turkey's homeland, and this included the English. According to a chronicler writing in 1524, the fowl had just reached England a year or two earlier, probably with Turkish merchants because it was called a "turkie cock," which later prompted the waggish chant, "Turkeys, Carps, Hoppes, Piccarrell and Beer, Came to England in one year." A few years after the debut of the turkey in Britain, the Portuguese brought the guinea hen from Africa to Iberia and it, too, reached England, where it was assumed to be a relative of the turkey. Scientific disarray was assured when Linnaeus subsumed both the African and the American fowl under the genus *Meleagris*, the old Roman name for the guinea hen.[33]

The impact on Europe of this array of American foods was tremendous. Caloric intake, which had been less than 2,000 daily on average, rose, as did dietary quality with the inclusion of more high-quality protein, the whole contributing to what Thomas McKeown has termed the "modern rise of population." This was a synergistic interaction that snapped a centuries-long cycle of famine and disease snuffing out population gains, whereby improved nutrition cut sharply into infant and child mortality and strengthened the immune system of young and old alike to overcome the ravages of infectious disease.[34]

That "rise," in fact, snowballed into a population explosion as the number of Europeans swelled in the eighteenth century; England's population doubled between 1731 and 1816, and the French had some 6 million more mouths to feed in 1789 than they had in 1720.[35]

Yet – again the Malthusian dilemma – although improved diets are credited with bringing on the explosion, swelling populations soon created food scarcity once again so that population increases were increasingly paid for in the currency of human misery. Robert Fogel, for instance, has calculated that by the latter part of the eighteenth century some 20 percent of the people of England and France had so little to eat that they lacked the energy to work.[36] Hunger may have been at its worst in France where, as Le Roy Ladurie points out, fully one-third of the French adult male population subsisted on less than 1,800 calories daily during the early 1780s, and this was before the grain shortages that occurred in the second half of that decade.[37]

Population pressure continued to mount as the American crops found full acceptance, and local grass seed and clover were utilized along with maize to carry animals through the winter.[38] From an estimated 140 million in 1750,

Europe's people had increased to 266 million by 1850, and a whopping 400 million by 1900.[39] As we know, the population excess began spilling over into the New World – the migrants drawn in magnet-like fashion to the hemisphere whose foods had engineered their eviction from the Old World. Truly, the American foods were revolutionary – and not just for Europe.

AFRICA AND THE EAST

Africa

Europeans may have found chilli peppers less than impressive, but this was not the case elsewhere. In Africa, India, China, Korea, and Southeast Asia they were accepted as enthusiastically as the turkey was in Europe, even reaching the peaks of the Himalayas – an odd place for a tropical fruit, but making the point that chilli peppers can be grown practically anywhere.[40] Their worldwide dispersal was largely the work of the Portuguese, who had followed up Vasco da Gama's 1498 voyage to Calicut by building an East Indian empire.[41] The New World capsicums spread like wildfire in the East Indies and along the African coasts – so quickly, in fact, that within a generation or two everybody, including the Europeans, were convinced that chilli peppers were native to India and the Orient, save for the Africans, who claimed them as their own native plants.

The dissemination of chilli peppers and other New World foods in Africa was closely related to a slave trade linking that continent with Portugal's American colony of Brazil (discovered in 1500). From there American plants flowed eastward to Africa to feed westbound slave cargoes. Manioc and maize were the most important crops to take root, but sweet potatoes, squash, peanuts, guavas, paw paws, American taro and, of course, chilli peppers, all added to dietary variety. In addition, the Portuguese brought Old World fruits like oranges and lemons to the African coast.

The centuries-long slave trade was a direct result of the introduction of sugarcane to the Americas. The Iberians had concluded that Native Americans were not going to prove a very satisfactory source of labor even before a variety of newly-introduced Old World diseases decimated them and, almost by default, Africans were nominated to be the colonizers of the American tropics and, especially, the producers of sugar.

In Africa, people living south of the Sahara had, depending on location, previously relied on yams, or millets, or sorghum, or rice as their dietary mainstays, but now these choices were considerably expanded as American plants strayed away from fields around slave barracoons. In some places maize supplanted millets in the African diet. In others manioc replaced yams so that today manioc is tropical Africa's most important crop and that continent its biggest producer.[42] Peanuts (groundnuts) prospered in African soils, as did various squashes, American yams, papayas, and sweet potatoes.[43] American beans were accepted well enough in East Africa but did not make many inroads in West Africa where popular ones like the winged bean (*Psophocarpus tetragonolobus*), and cowpea continued to prevail.

Overall, the impact of the American foods on sub-Sahara Africa was as colossal as in Europe. They promoted greater population density and ultimately triggered a population explosion. A major difference, however, was that the excessive number of Europeans created by their ballooning populations migrated more or less voluntarily to the Americas, whereas the swelling African populations created by New World crops were drained off by the slave trade. Perhaps ironically, in both instances the destinations of the superfluous lay in the lands whose plants had made them so.

Asia

Another kind of trade carried American produce to the east by a west-ward route. It began in the wake of Magellan's discovery of the Philippine Islands and their conquest by the Spaniards, who founded Manila in 1571. Its vehicles were the Manila galleons, the ships named for that city – those tall, square-rigged vessels that lumbered across the Pacific from Acapulco to Manila on a southerly route and back to Acapulco on a northerly route so precisely that the Hawaiian Islands in the middle of the rectangle remained unknown to Europeans until James Cook ran across them in 1778.

American silver was the main cargo sent west to exchange for silks, spices, jewelry, and laquerware. But the galleons also trafficked in American products like cacao, which they carried to the Philippines for the first time in 1663, and returned – in later years at least – with tea.[44] And tucked aboard the galleons were many of the American plants, or at least their seeds, such as maize, potatoes, sweet potatoes, peanuts, cashews, chilli peppers, tomatoes, squashes, jicamas, American taro, avocados, sapodillas, pineapples, papayas, passion fruits, and guavas.[45]

These all found their way to Manila, and beyond, to spread throughout Southeast and East Asia. Illustrative is maize, that by the middle of the seventeenth century had been adopted in Southeast Asia, catching on more swiftly than the potato or manioc. In fact, it was not until the twentieth century that Thailand was heavily planted in the latter.[46]

In some cases, however, American plants had already reached the East even before the Manila galleon traffic. The Portuguese are credited with introducing maize and sweet potatoes to the Chinese provinces of Fujian and Guangdong by at least the middle of the sixteenth century, and peanuts even earlier.[47] These heralded the beginning of China's second agricultural revolution, with the Manila galleons reinforcing such introductions so that, by the turn of the seventeenth century, Chinese farmers, much more experimental than their European counterparts were routinely growing maize (called "Western" or "foreign" wheat), peanuts, and sweet and white potatoes. Yet, local Asian bean favorites such as the azuki bean (*Phaseolus angularis*), the mung bean (*P. aureus*), and the soybean stubbornly continued as favorites, forestalling widespread acceptance of American varieties, just as local beans had prevailed in West Africa.

But even without the beans, the American plants are once again credited with bringing about a mushrooming population, said by some to have reached an incredible 150 million Chinese by the beginning of the Qing (or Ch'ing, or Manchu) dynasty in the middle of the seventeenth century. We cannot know how accurate that figure is; indeed we cannot be certain that the American foods were the initial cause of a population explosion that began in China in the seventeenth century, accelerated in the eighteenth and nineteenth centuries, and produced an astronomical number of people in the twentieth century.

On the other hand, we can be certain that such population growth could not have been sustained without them. As in Europe and Africa, the new American foods vastly improved the caloric intake of the masses. Maize, for example, became a quintessential poor man's food in China because it could be propagated where the more favored crops of wheat and rice could not. As a consequence, many left the crowded Yangtze Delta and the Han River Valley to farm inland hills – to cultivate maize where it would grow and white potatoes where it would not. In addition, the Chinese were delighted to discover that peanuts preserved soil fertility. When they were rotated with rice crops, the technique facilitated utilization of the sandy soils along the lower Yangtze and the lower Yellow River, as well as those of other rivers and streams. And, finally, sweet potatoes – among the most important of the American foods in China – soared in popularity, so much so that by the 1920s, the poor in the south, where the warm climate permitted two or even three sweet potato crops annually, were eating them at every meal 365 days a year; and by century's end China was growing a huge 80 percent of the world's crop.[48]

The sweet potato spread from China to Japan toward the end of the seventeenth century, and became a food of some consequence – especially during times of famine. In Indonesia – today a large sweet-potato producer – it long served as what Alfred Crosby calls an "in-between crop," meaning that it was indispensable after the rice from the previous harvest had been used up and the current crop had yet to be harvested.[49]

Portuguese traders and missionaries also brought European foods to Japan (and probably cooking techniques like tempura) from the late fifteenth to the early seventeenth century. Cattle had been introduced to Japan shortly after the beginning of the Common Era, where in genetic isolation they developed the fat-streaked flesh that ultimately became the legendary Kobe beef, the most expensive beef in the world. But for close to two millennia, cattle were employed as draft animals. As Buddhists, the Japanese had little use for the meat-based cuisine of the foreigners, but they enjoyed Western desserts such as a sponge cake called *kasutera* – the word derived from the Portuguese *bolo do Castelo*, Castelo being the region of Portugal where the dessert originated. The Japanese also acquired chilli peppers from the Portuguese, and strived to withhold the means and knowledge of how to grow them from Korean customers who craved them.[50]

Save for peppers and sweet potatoes, however, few American foods penetrated Japan after the Tokugawa Shogunate closed the country to foreigners in 1639, creating an isolation that endured until almost the beginning of the Meiji Restoration of 1868. At about the time of their withdrawal, however, the Japanese passed along knowledge of chilli pepper propagation to Koreans (they called it "Japanese mustard"), who turned it into the most important seasoning in Korean cuisine, used lavishly in kim-chee and hot soybean paste. The sweet potato reached Korea from Japan in 1763, but white potatoes did not enter the Peninsula until around 1840 from China. Pumpkins and maize, however, had somehow materialized much earlier.[51]

Many of the same American foods that were established in China also spread into the East Indies and India as a result of the globalizing spice trade, where they were diffused from centers such as the Dutch castle city of Batavia, which maintained an inter-archipelago trade and was, for a time, a center of trade to the hinterland.[52] In fact, cashews, along with papayas, custard apples, cherimoyas, sweetsops, soursops, guavas, and pineapples all were American plants growing in Southeast Asia before the beginning of the seventeenth century.[53]

The Portuguese had led the way into the East Indies with their discovery of a sea route around Africa that eliminated Middle Eastern middlemen from Europe's trade with the east.[54] But in the developing European game of "beggar thy neighbor," the Dutch East India Company managed to hijack the spice trade from the Portuguese, only to keep a cautious eye on the English East India Company, whose officers were intent on stealing the "spicery" trade for themselves. Ultimately, they did just that, but not yet – and at the end of the seventeenth-century the Dutch were firmly in control, having captured much of the supply side of the trade by taking over Java, Malacca, Ceylon, and the Celebes, along with ports on the Malabar Coast.[55] This brought the Dutch near total domination of the world's cinnamon and pepper trade, as well as that of nutmeg and cloves. Their monopoly on cloves, however, was later weakened by the French who began to grow them on Mauritius toward the end of the eighteenth century, which, in turn, prompted the establishment of French clove plantations on Madagascar and Zanzibar.

Victory in the Fourth Anglo-Dutch War (1780–84) elevated the English to masters of the spice trade, while it sent the Dutch reeling from the war's catastrophic effects on their sea-borne commerce and led, indirectly, at least, to the demise of the Dutch East India Company. However, although the English now commanded the spice trade, they were never as dominating as their Dutch predecessors, whose draconian methods had preserved their monopoly for many decades.

At the same time that Europeans were slaughtering one another for control of the trade in tastes, New World foods were entering South Asia. Cashew nuts from Brazil enlivened rice and sweet dishes; chilli peppers from Mesoamerica vitalized curries; and peanuts from Brazil – high in fat and protein – were introduced to India, the country that subsequently became the world's largest peanut producer.[56] The Portuguese may also have carried amaranth from Brazil to the Malabar Coast of India sometime after 1500; and, by the nineteenth century, it was widely cultivated there. Yet, there is also a good argument that amaranth was domesticated independently in Asia substantially before 1492.[57]

Early in their establishment of an East Indian empire the Portuguese had captured Goa in India (1510) and made it their capital in that part of the world. Portuguese personal names, architecture, and cuisine followed, with the result that Goanese food was heavily influenced by Portuguese cuisine – including the use of pork, which is unique in India.[58]

Maize was the only American crop to have a wide distribution in India prior to the nineteenth century. It was probably introduced by the Portuguese and was listed in a western region of South Asia as one of the crops that was taxed as early as 1664 (as in China, maize was primarily a food for the Indian poor).[59] But it was in the nineteenth century and the one that followed that the American foods had their greatest impact on Indian food cultures. Potatoes, both white and sweet, found myriad uses, as did bell peppers and tomatoes, especially in seafood dishes. Manioc was introduced to southern India in the 1880s and it is still widely grown today.

American foods also traveled with migrating residents. In South Africa, for example, the Cape Malays – Indians brought in by the Dutch as laborers in the seventeenth and eighteenth centuries – and their descendents, have continued to cook their classic *bredie* – pumpkin, simmered with chilli peppers in oil. Do they know (or care) that the dish consists of ingredients entirely of American origin?[60]

THE COLUMBIAN EXCHANGE AND NEW WORLDS

Why, then, the world's mine oyster, Which I with sword will open.

Shakespeare (1564–1615)[1]

OCEANIA

In the south of Southeast Asia, Alocasia or dryland taro, perhaps originating in India or Burma, has been under cultivation for at least 7,000 years. Wetland (Colocasia) taro, yams, and (probably) dry and wet land rice came along later. Yet, as mentioned earlier, a mystery is why the Austronesian farmer-pioneers, who sailed off to settle the Philippines and the East Indies at about this time (6000 BCE), were accompanied by taro, yams, pigs, and dogs, but not rice. The most logical answer is that rice had not yet become a staple in Southeast Asia. But it is not a particularly satisfactory answer because, despite many ensuing waves of Pacific pioneers, when the Europeans first entered the world's largest body of water, rice was absent from the whole of the Pacific, save for the Mariana Islands. Did rice somehow get lost from the horticultural complex? Or were taro and yams just easier to cultivate?[2]

The pioneers originated in Southeast Asia and neighboring New Guinea, and their initial waves fanned out into the Philippines and the East Indies. These were an Austronesian-speaking people whose descendents, with their distinctive Lapita pottery, became the ancestors of the Polynesians.

Around 3,500 years ago they launched epic voyages of exploration and colonization, moving swiftly in their double-hulled canoes to establish settlements in Fiji, and then in Samoa and Tonga – the latter two islands becoming jump-off points for the eventual settlement of the rest of Polynesia, ending with Hawaii around 1,500 years ago and New Zealand some 1,000 to 2,000 years ago.[3]

These seafarers were fishermen to be sure, but also farmers, whose contribution to Pacific comestibles was as impressive as their navigation skills. They added pigs, dogs, and chickens to a region short on edible land animals, along with plant foods like taro and yams, and food producing techniques like sago palm cultivation (starch is extracted from the trunks).[4] Also introduced were domesticated coconuts, invaluable for their milk; meat, and oil;[5] bananas and plantains that became a staple for many;[6] along with breadfruit and sugarcane, all of which spread widely throughout the Pacific.[7]

Yet, incredibly, these pioneering peoples were actually latecomers when compared with their Australoid predecessors, who long before had taken advantage of lowered sea levels to walk and float across the straits to New Guinea (or Sumatra and Java) and then on to Australia where, around 50,000 years ago, they struggled ashore to enter a hunter-gatherer's heaven.[8] In addition to a plethora of wild plants, there was an abundance of large animals, including giant marsupials and flightless birds on hand for the taking.[9]

Because Australia and New Zealand had been cut off from the rest of the world for close to 100 million years, the evolutionary process was given free rein to elaborate plants and animals that were decidedly different from those found on the Eurasian land mass.[10] Australian kangaroos, for example, are browsers. But as marsupials they bear little resemblance to European cattle or North American bison, browsers also, but placental animals. In New Zealand, penguins roosted in trees and sea lions stretched out for a nap in forest clearings. And its huge ostrich-like moa birds, some around nine feet in height, were unique.[11] But they, along with many other flightless birds, are extinct now, victims like so many other species the world over, of hungry humans.

Plants that became staples for the Australian Aborigines had also taken a different evolutionary path, despite apparently familiar English names for "bush tucker" such as "sunrise lime," "bush tomato," "bush banana," "bush bean," and "Australian carrot." Desert Aborigines received an estimated

70 to 80 percent of their dietary bulk from plants such as these, and in the humid southeast, approximately 140 species of plants were eaten – foremost among them the roots and tubers of lilies, orchids, native yams, and a variety of fruits and seeds.[12]

In New Zealand, bees buzzed, making honey from the flowers of the Manuka tree that was employed by the Maori as a medicine as well as a food.[13] The Maori consumed much bird flesh starting earlier on with that of the moa and working their way through penguins, ducks, and a variety of "bush birds" – pigeons, various gulls, albatross, and the like. They also ate substantial amounts of fish and shellfish, as well as human flesh from time to time, although the latter was apparently a ritual form of cannibalism reserved for those killed or captured in war.[14]

Over the span of millions of years, watertight, buoyant seeds had floated from Southeast Asia to Australia and to other parts of the Pacific, or had caught a ride in the plumage or bowels of birds. But it was only with the arrival of humans that Oceania, and especially Australia and New Zealand, experienced a genuine reunion with the biota of the larger world.

In returning to a mystery mentioned earlier, most Pacific peoples were eating sweet potatoes when the Europeans first encountered them, and, according to their folklore, had done so for a very long time. But because the tuber was an American plant, it obviously must have been introduced at some juncture, and three different hypotheses attempt to shed some light on how and when this occurred.[15] The first, and most intriguing, of these would have the sweet potato introduced to the Eastern Pacific sometime between 400 and 800 AD and diffusing from there – which, of course, fits right into another riddle of Oceanic prehistory. How ancient was its contact with South America?

One interesting tidbit of linguistic evidence is the Polynesian word for sweet potato (*kumala* or *kumara*), which is strikingly similar to the Quechua word for the tuber (*cumara*) suggesting to some that the sweet potato reached Polynesia from Peru, with Quechua speakers somehow implicated in that transfer. But if so, why only the sweet potato? Why not other useful Americans foods like white potatoes, manioc, or maize?[16]

A second hypothesis would have the sweet potato, taken to the East by the Portuguese in the sixteenth century, somehow finding its way into the Pacific a couple of centuries before Captain James Cook arrived (during the years 1768–71 and 1772–75) to report on its presence there. A third, and more pedestrian, hypothesis has the Manila Galleon traffic introducing the sweet potato to the Pacific, where it spread so rapidly that it seemed like a long-established foodstuff to the members of the Cook expeditions.

Still another possibility is that, although sweet potatoes cannot float, their seeds could have hitched a ride in the bowels of birds such as the golden plover – a strong flyer that ranges over Polynesia, but visits western South America now and again. Clearly, when and how the sweet potato reached Oceania are still open questions. But what is not disputed is that whenever the tuber made a Pacific appearance, it readily fit into the diets of the peoples of that vast region.[17]

There were no pigs in Australia and New Zealand before the Europeans brought them. Chickens they had, along with the "dingo" of Australia, a descendent of the Asian wolf that must have accompanied a later wave of settlers from Southeast Asia because it had to be domesticated first. Cook introduced pigs to New Zealand in 1778 and the wild ones are still called "Cookers."[18] Pork was much esteemed by the Maori and added some variety to diets whose animal protein had previously been provided by birds and only two four-legged animals – the dog and the rat. In Australia pigs came ashore with the British colonizers and, with no natural enemies, proliferated to the point where in the twentieth century the Australians went to war with their wild pig population.

Less troublesome were Merino sheep, introduced in 1833, to add meat to the diet and wool to the economy. Today, pastoralism has produced the world's largest sheep population in Australia and one of the highest human-to-sheep ratios in New Zealand. Cattle flourished about as well as pigs in the absence of predation. Two bulls and six cows arrived with the First Fleet in 1788 to become the progenitors of the millions of cattle that, in the nineteenth century, were first a nuisance and then, along with mutton, the foundation of Australia's meatpacking industry.[19]

These grazing animal legions opened the door for opportunistic European weeds such as white clover, and with the introduction of the honeybee to pollinate the clover, Old World animals were once more munching on an Old World favorite. It is not surprising that both Australia and New Zealand became nations of meat eaters. It was a matter of self-defense.

As for plant foods, white potatoes carried by the colonizers were promptly utilized by the Aborigines in part, at least, because they were easier to grow than sweet potatoes. Maize was the first cereal to gain acceptance in Australia and New Zealand. Wheat only became widespread around the middle of the nineteenth century, as did European and American vegetables, Eurasian fruit trees, and grapevines. Winemaking was first tried in Australia in the late eighteenth century, the vines brought from Europe and from South Africa where winemaking was already established. The earliest vineyard in New Zealand was planted shortly before 1820.

As one might expect, long geographic isolation triggered the occasional ecological nightmare as new fauna reached both Australia and New Zealand. The brown rats from Europe that jumped ship in New Zealand all but exterminated their local counterparts and grew to enormous sizes – which, at least, provided more good quality protein for the Maori. In Australia, a few rabbits were imported in 1859 by a farmer to provide a little sport for hunters. He was apparently ignorant of the rabbit's spectacular reproductive capacity (females can deliver up to eleven litters each year) in the absence of natural enemies and got far more sport than he had bargained for.[20]

In fact, that sport soon became a grim, but fruitless, campaign of extermination as the Adam and Eve rabbits multiplied into an estimated 20 million within 30 years, and hordes of them spread across the continent to compete with livestock for grazing land.[21] The rabbits did provide food for the lower classes, however, and in the 1880s rabbit meat was being canned in Australia, and hundreds of tons were exported. More recently, Australian possums have invaded New Zealand to destroy forests and spread tuberculosis among its cattle. Fortunately, most other Pacific peoples were spared this sort of ecological excitement and, despite missionary meddling, their diets remained more or less traditional until the middle of the next century.

Aside from officers and cabin passengers, the first settlers to wobble down gangplanks in Australia were convicts sentenced to "transportation," along with their guards – hardly representatives of British Isles elites.[22] Aboard ship their "rations" had centered on salted meat and bread, and such "prison food" continued to be issued ashore to the rural work force until the first half of the twentieth century. Called "Ten, Ten, Two, and a Quarter" the weekly rations consisted of 10 pounds of flour, ten of meat, two of sugar, and a quarter pound of both tea and salt. Many who migrated voluntarily after the 1830s were spared this "crew culture," although not those who began the settlement of New Zealand from Australia in the 1840s. The New Zealand Company also relied on such tried and true (not to mention cheap) rations.

The success of pastoralism meant a surfeit of available meat, and quantity not quality determined the success of a middle-class meal. But the upper classes, with a penchant for French-style cuisine, enjoyed a variety of viands, thanks in no small part to the naturalist Joseph Banks. He had sailed with Cook on the 1769 expedition, equipped the founding expedition to Australia, and expected Botany Bay to have a Mediterranean air about it. Accordingly, Mediterranean citrus fruits, peaches, apricots, grapes, and figs were imported to change the landscape and perk up the fare of the genteel, although peaches became so plentiful they were used to fatten hogs.[23]

The preference of most, however, was plain food and plenty of it. It was a part of their British heritage and a far cry from today's globalized and sophisticated cuisines of the Antipodes. Change in this direction was gradual. Beginning in 1842, religious persecution drove German and Prussian Lutherans to South Australia where they planted fruits and vegetables and began making wine to found the Barossa wine industry. Shortly after, as early as the 1850s, Chinese immigrants, with no luck in those gold fields that had lured them to Australia, turned to gardening and became Australia's vegetable and fruit specialists.[24] Next, steamships, railroads, and refrigeration expanded the initial stock of American, European, and local foods while urbanization fostered larger markets.

Change accelerated during and after World War II. Air transport brought Australia and New Zealand squarely into the orbit of the West. Coca Cola and Spam accompanied American troops, and after the war, chain supermarkets began to spring up. Meat pies and fish and chip carts gave way to Kentucky Fried Chicken, McDonald's, and Pizza Hut restaurants. More Asians arrived with their cuisines, and immigrants from the Mediterranean brought their recipes and methods of food preparation so that Chinese food, gyros, and kebabs all joined in the fast food competition.

Everyday cuisine was also transformed as local resources such as kangaroo, quandong, and Macadamia nuts were blended with a variety of Asian and Mediterranean vegetables and herbs that could be grown locally. Stir-frying became common, and new foods arrived. Some from America, like sweet potatoes ("kumara" in New Zealand), had been on hand from the very beginning of European colonization and white potatoes that followed were joined by tomatoes, feojoas, tamarillos, pepinos, avocados, babacos, passion fruits, and guavas. Other foreign fruits, like the Chinese gooseberry (kiwifruit) and persimmon, appeared in "down under" orchards while garlic, ginger, soy sauce, and tomato sauce became staple condiments in the new Antipodal cuisine. Almost unnoticed was the virtual annihilation of the British culinary heritage.[25] And uncommented on was that, unlike the

Americas, Oceania had little to give the world in the way of foodstuffs and practically everything to receive.

THE AMERICAS

In 1492, the only land animal in the Antilles was the hutia, a large rodent. But the second voyage of Columbus changed that. The seventeen ships that dropped anchor at Hispaniola in 1493 were veritable Noah's Arks, disgorging horses, pigs, dogs, cattle, sheep, and goats – meat animals for a hemisphere where good quality protein was in short supply[26]

Pigs – eight of them – from the Canary Islands trotted ashore to flourish in a hemisphere that harbored few natural enemies. With a reproductive capacity some six times that of cattle, and a willingness to eat practically anything, pigs conducted their own conquest of the Americas with the help of Spanish explorers who scattered them about to assure a supply of meat for those that followed – dropping them off on Caribbean islands as well as the mainland.[27] To say simply that they multiplied, trivializes the ensuing feat of fertility. In the case of Cuba, for example, its conqueror Diego Velázquez wrote the Crown in 1514 that the two dozen pigs he had earlier introduced to the island had already increased by some thirty thousand.[28]

Pigs swarmed everywhere that offered water, shade, and food. In New England they rooted for clams at the water's edge; in the Carolinas they ate peaches; in the jungles of Brazil they munched on wild roots, lizards and frogs. As early as 1531, Gonzalo Pizarro introduced swine to Peru, and in 1539 the Hernando de Soto expedition drove a herd of them from Florida to Arkansas, where they became the feral razorbacks that later on lent their name to athletic teams of that state's university.[29] Pork had almost instantly become the preferred meat in much of the Americas, and there was plenty of it to eat – too much, in fact, wherever swine populations ballooned to the point that they threatened crops.

Cattle from Spain and from the Canary Islands also came ashore in 1493 and, like pigs, proved excellent colonizers, especially on open savannahs, although they multiplied so prodigiously in the Antilles that ranching developed very early in Hispaniola. A century and a half after their introduction, all West Indies islands supported great herds of wild cattle (and pigs) that were more hunted than herded, and their hides and smoked meat sold to passing ships by – among others – those European outcasts who later on promoted themselves to buccaneers.[30]

Cattle reached Mexico from Cuba in 1521 and thrived. Ponce de Leon brought them to the North American mainland in that same year, and just two decades later, when Coronado crossed the Rio Grande and the Pecos rivers to reach the vast prairies west of the Mississippi, he reported huge herds of wild cattle preyed upon by "primitive peoples."[31] By century's end, in northern Mexico, a herd of a "mere" 20,000 animals was sneered at as small.

Cattle invaded South America with the Portuguese. Those introduced to the Brazilian "Sertão" south of São Paulo and the upper São Francisco valley were the progenitors of the great herds that occupied the Argentine and Uruguayan Pampas. In both Mexico and South America, cattle ranching was done with semi-feral animals, on large fenceless tracts of land, by mounted cowboys.[32] By 1600, wherever cattle were numerous, beef was the cheapest food that could be purchased; by contrast, and perhaps ironically, it remained a luxury item in the Old World that had supplied the animals to begin with.

Although wild sheep had preceded the Spaniards in the New World by many millennia, Columbus brought the first domesticated ones. There was, however, no immediate prodigious procreation of sheep like that accomplished by pigs and cattle. Tropical lowlands were not their ideal habitat. But in the sixteenth century, sheep were taken to highland Mexico and to the high meadows of Peru, after which they were moved south to Chile and southeast to Argentina, and Uruguay.[33] All of these regions emerged as important sheep-ranching centers.

The goat, a close relative of sheep, also sailed with Columbus in 1493. This "poor man's cow" dedicated itself to climbing the cliffs and browsing the mountainous terrain of most Caribbean Islands. In Mexico, goats of the poor –an early part of the rural tradition – grazed on the countryside's sparsely vegetated slopes whose offerings the nannies converted into rich milk. The resulting butter and cheese were generally the sole source of animal protein for their owners, although on festive occasions roasted goat, in Mexico as around the Mediterranean, served as the centerpiece.[34]

Horses were essential to the Iberians in their conquest of the Americas and, like most other barnyard animals of the Europeans, needed little encouragement to multiply. In 1580, just 60 years after their introduction to the La Plata region, it was reported that horses were already the property of Native Americans, and that they had become excellent horsemen.[35] It took another century before their native counterparts in North America managed to acquire their own horses. This happened during the Pueblo Revolt of 1680 when horses were forcibly liberated from the Spaniards – after which Native American traders and raiders spread horse ownership across the Great Plains and into Canada.[36]

The Spaniards drove horses into Alta California during the 1770s. Seventy years later, at the time of the gold rush, there were so many of them in the region grazing on grass that stockmen figured should go to their cattle, that thousands of them were driven off the cliffs at Santa Barbara – a repetition of one hunting technique used by Amerindians during the late Pleistocene to help bring the horse of the New World to extinction.[37]

Whether chickens were already in the Americas when the Spanish arrived has been the subject of some speculation. South American natives had names for what may have been a chicken and, if so, the only one in the world to lay blue and green eggs. Most agree, however, that even if these South American curiosities were chickens, they probably were not natives but rather had reached the hemisphere with Pacific Island voyagers – those other pioneers who became Native Americans.[38] Chickens that the Europeans were accustomed to only arrived in the New World via Hispaniola in 1493.[39]

Bees were producing honey in tropical America before humans set foot on the earth, and the Spaniards, famous for their honey, probably brought bees with them. But North America had no honey bees until the English turned them loose in Virginia in the 1620s and in Massachusetts a couple of decades later. They thrived, multiplied, and, although the Appalachian Mountains blocked them for a time, by the end of the eighteenth century they had buzzed their way west of the Mississippi. Their honey made a fine addition to the Native American diet, although the latter called the bee an "English fly" – its very presence announcing the advance of the white man, and a harbinger of wrenching change to come.[40]

Seeds and plant cuttings also rode in the holds of those ships that put into Hispaniola in 1493. Wheat, however, although eventually the most important of the Old World cereals introduced to the New World, did not do well in the Antilles where the Spaniards reluctantly made do with zamia and manioc breads. But wheat grew well enough in Mexico, so much so that in the eighteenth century that country served as a breadbasket for the many sailors and soldiers garrisoned in Havana. Argentina and Chile became even greater wheat producers and were joined later on by California, although the transformation of the Great Plains (with its tough soils impervious to pre-industrial tools) into a vast granary that is now regarded as the "world's breadbasket," did not take place until after the Civil War.[41] Wheat was in the vanguard of this transformation, but ironically, although Native Americans accepted the new food animals readily enough and had long before adopted maize, they were always slow to adopt wheat.[42]

Columbus gets no credit for rice – the second most important cereal to reach the Americas. Pedro de Alvarado introduced it to Central America in 1524, and it quickly became a backbone of Caribbean cookery, a staple of some slave populations, and, in the nineteenth century, a familiar food for East Indian and Chinese contract laborers who replaced the slaves after abolition.[43] Rye showed up in Mexico to be welcomed by the colonists because of a hardiness that let it grow at altitudes where maize had difficulty, as well as on lowlands where high winds frequently threatened wheat crops.[44]

The chickpea that the Spanish called *garbanzo* – and a food that had been in Iberia since the days of the Phoenicians – sailed with Columbus to take up New World residence, as did grapevines offloaded for winemaking. A few years later, Hernando Cortez invigorated Mexican viticulture with his decree that 1,000 grapevines be planted for every 100 workers on an estate.[45] Bananas were carried to Hispaniola by a friar from the Canary Islands in 1516, and they, along with Asian melons, oranges, lemons, limes, and European peaches, radishes, and salad greens worked such a dietary transformation that just five years after the conquest of Mexico they had become so familiar that their prices were being set by the government in Mexico City.[46]

In 1519, when the men of Cortez were marching on Tenochtitlan, Bernal Diaz reported seeing Eurasian onions, leeks, and garlic.[47] Could this be more tantalizing evidence of contact between the pre-Columbian Americas and the larger world? Or was it the case that the alliums planted by Columbus' crews on Hispaniola in 1494 had somehow managed to spread to the mainland? Probably not, because the Aztecs had words for their plants, suggesting a longer acquaintanceship than a mere quarter of a century. More likely, Diaz mistook the Eurasian allium varieties he was familiar with for the bulbs and leaves of the chivelike, native American allium representatives *Allium shoenoprasum* var. *sibericum*.

Unhappily, we cannot be certain of this, and most likely never will be because wherever the Eurasian varieties were introduced, they spread like wildfire. Cortez grew garlic in Mexico, and it was adopted by the natives of Peru. By 1629, onions were under cultivation in Massachusetts and, by 1648, in Virginia. Even the Choctaw Indians, in what later became the states of Mississippi, Louisiana, and Alabama, grew onions as a garden esculent. Garlic was later cultivated in California – its town of Gilroy proclaiming itself the twentieth-century "garlic capital of the world," although most of the tens of thousand attendees at its annual Garlic Festival might be surprised to learn that Gillroy now imports most of its garlic from China.[48]

California was also the recipient of olive trees (that had reached in Americas in the early sixteenth century), and oranges, and grapevines that had come with Columbus. These, along with date palms, were all first planted by Franciscan friars at their San Diego mission around 1769, and accompanied the Fathers as they pushed their missions northward to number twenty more. Within a few decades, olives were being pressed and wine made at most all of them.

Spices from the East flowed into the Americas to be packed over the mountains to Mexico City and Lima, and in Mexico experiments were launched in growing them. Some were failures but ginger, introduced in 1530, was not among them. Rather, by the 1580s Spain was importing two and a quarter million pounds of Mexican-grown ginger.[49]

Coconuts may have floated to the Americas in earlier times, but with Vasco da Gama's 1499 return to Lisbon from India and East Africa, a "final phase" of coconut dissemination around the globe got underway.[50] Within a half-century of that epic voyage, coconuts were growing on the Cape Verde Islands and had reached Puerto Rico and Brazil to become a source of food and liquid for conquerors and explorers alike.[51]

Early explorers and colonists also introduced cabbage, kale, collards, radishes, and turnips to their Caribbean gardens and these, too, diffused throughout the mainland.[52] Because turnips do best in cooler climates, they became a North American summer crop in the north and a winter crop in the south, where they were highly prized for their greens. By contrast, cauliflower, other mustard varieties, and rutabaga arrived tardily, although seed catalogues indicate that they were firmly ensconced in nineteenth-century gardens.[53]

An important downside to the invasion of all these Eurasian plants and animals was their devastating impact on the native flora and fauna they elbowed aside. European weeds like clover followed Eurasian animals (as they later did in Australia), to provide good forage, but in so doing they smothered indigenous plants and crops. So did "Kentucky Bluegrass"

(a European import despite the name) and a host of others such as thistles and nettles that flourished along with cattle and pigs from North America to the Argentine pampas.[54]

And then there were the rats – stowaways that poured off every European ship to run riot throughout the hemisphere. In sixteenth-century Peru multitudes of them gnawed at plants and their roots and colonized granaries. During the early settlement of Buenos Aires rats swarmed "among the grapevines and the wheat"; and at Jamestown they very nearly cut short the history of that settlement by devouring the food stores.[55]

But by far the worst ecological downside to Europe's invasion of the Americas was the onslaught of diseases unleashed on "virgin soil" peoples. Influenza, smallpox, measles, tuberculosis, and numerous other lethal Eurasian infections were followed by a train of African illnesses headed by falciparum malaria and yellow fever. These, together with European colonial practices (ranging from the importation of garden-gobbling Eurasian animals to forced Indian labor), are held up as the proximate causes that reduced a pre-Columbian population – that may have stood at somewhere around 100 million – by some 90 percent.[56] Moreover, this demographic disaster presaged another, because as Indian labor became scarcer, the demand for African slaves increased.

It was this demand that first lured Englishmen such as John Hawkins to the Caribbean.[57] But despite his initial incursions, followed by those of Francis Drake, it was the Dutch who mounted the first serious challenge to Spain in the region. And the reason was food-related. The Dutch needed salt. At first, their ongoing war for independence from Spain was not a total war and, consequently, hostilities notwithstanding, the Dutch continued to trade with the Iberian Peninsula and maintained their access to the salt deposits of Spanish-controlled Portugal.

Such access was vital. The mineral was central to the Dutch food industry, especially to the production of salted herring, but also for butter and cheese. Therefore, when Madrid did finally make the war total by denying salt to the Dutch, it precipitated a crisis that was ultimately resolved by resort to still another source of Spanish salt – this one off the coast of present-day Venezuela.

With this move the Dutch struggle for independence spilled over into the New World, and it was not long before the Hollanders, with an eye on their bottom lines, stopped sending ships out in ballast to pick up the salt and began replacing the ballast with trading goods to be smuggled into

Spain's American colonies. Nor were they content to just carry away salt; they also stuffed colonial products like hides, cacao, and tobacco (for an incipient cigar industry) into their ships' holds.

Having gained an inch, they reached for a mile by grabbing real estate in the Caribbean sun. Between 1630 and 1640, the Dutch West India Company (chartered in 1621) seized the islands of Curaçao, Saba, St. Martin, and St. Eustatius. Of these Curaçao, taken in 1635, proved the most valuable. It was an entrepôt for smuggling and, as a bonus, had valuable salt-pans. From this location off the Spanish Main the Dutch began financing mainland cacao growers, whose produce they marketed in Europe, and for years they controlled the supply of cacao beans in Europe.

Momentously, as it turned out, the Dutch also snatched northern Brazil, where they learned the secrets of sugar cultivation, and to this knowledge they spliced their control of the African slave trade. It was a mercantilist's dream come true, with profits rolling in from sugar harvests, sugar-marketing operations in Europe, and still more profits piling up from trafficking in the labor applied to cane cultivation.

When the Dutch were finally expelled from Brazil, the dream may have turned briefly into a nightmare. But not for long. In Barbados, then elsewhere in the Caribbean, they had begun financing tobacco planters willing to grow sugar instead. The new sugar planters needed factories to make the sugar and slaves to work the fields – the slaves arriving and the sugar departing in Dutch bottoms. Soon a "sugar revolution" was underway – a revolution that transformed the Caribbean demographically, making the region an extension of Africa, and sugar its chief crop. And on the northern rim of their American empire, in "Nieuw Amsterdam," the Dutch introduced molasses from the Caribbean and other Old World foods of interest to nearby English colonists such as tea, cookies, coleslaw, and waffles.

Truly, the Columbian Exchange was revolutionary in every sense of the word. It reversed an evolutionary tendency for the world's biota to grow ever more distinctive, even as it began rearranging available foods around the globe. It lay behind swelling populations and their renewed migrations, and gave rise to undreamed of commerce and enterprise. It ushered in the modern world.

SUGAR AND NEW
BEVERAGES

SUGAR

Dazzling-white sugar, ground down from huge Dutch sugar loaves . . .
sweeter and more yielding than Venetian sugar loaves, the white gold of
confectioners and pastry-cooks. (Piero Camporesi, *Exotic Brew*, 157)

Sugar – a preservative, a fermenting agent, a sweetener of food and drink
without changing the flavor – has revolutionized the food processing
industry; and sugar cane was the most revolutionary of all plants to
reach the Americas.[1] Today sugar – actually the chemical sucrose,
extracted from the cane – is the world's best-selling food, surpassing
even wheat.

This giant grass with stems juicy with a sappy pulp is generally believed
to be a native of New Guinea, although India and China are often put
forward as alternative cradles because it was cultivated in both places in
ancient times. Much later (around 500 BCE) the Persians came across sugarcane growing in the Indus Valley and, although humans had doubtless
coaxed sweet juice out of bits of cane by chewing on them for eons, the
Indus Valley growers may have been the first to use the cane in a more
sophisticated fashion by pressing it for its juice, then concentrating that
juice by boiling it.[2]

In any event, the Persians quickly adopted cane cultivation and, by
the seventh century AD, had refined the process sufficiently to produce
a nearly white loaf. Some of these sugar loaves entered Europe through
Venice as one more spice called "white salt." Its price, however, was

astronomical – only the rich and powerful ever tasted its sweetness, save perhaps those taking one or another of the various medicinal preparations that sugar was almost immediately incorporated into.

The Arabs, who conquered the Persians in the ninth century, took over the sugar-making process and established sugarcane plantations in a number of places, including Muslim Spain. Some seven centuries later, both the Spanish and the Portuguese transferred sugar cultivation to their possessions off the African coast, where Madeira and the Canary Islands blossomed into major sugar producers. Slaves were imported from mainland Africa to work the plantations – the whole a dress rehearsal for sugar slavery in the New World.[3]

By 1518, a number of small sugar plantations had been established in Hispaniola, and in that year the Atlantic slave trade got underway, the Spanish pioneering in applying African labor to cane cultivation and sugar production in the Americas.[4] A couple of decades later, the Portuguese established a slave trade to Brazil and were even more successful in the sugar business.[5] In the following century the English, French, and Dutch grabbed tropical turf from the Iberians to launch their own sugar operations. Barbados, which the English began to colonize in 1627, led the already mentioned "sugar revolution."[6]

Initially an island of small tobacco planters whose plots were tended by white indentured servants, Barbados, by mid-century, was undergoing transformation into a land of a relatively few large sugar planters whose fields were worked by gangs of African slaves. The techniques learned in Brazil by the Dutch were passed along to the Barbadian planters, along with capital for constructing sugar-making factories and acquiring African slaves. As we pointed out, however, this was not altruism. The slaves were delivered in Dutch ships and the sugar marketed in Europe by the Dutch.

This mercantilistic model was, in turn, followed by the English, who established sugar cultivation in Jamaica (which they had captured in 1655), and who began taking control of the slave trade. Other major players in the sugar and slavery business were the Portuguese in Brazil and the French in Guadalupe, Martinique, and later on, in St. Domingue (Haiti following its independence); and, after the sugar industry in St. Domingue dissolved into the chaos of slave revolution, Cuba emerged to build its nineteenth-century sugar empire on a contraband slave trade.[7]

However, even before Cuban planters rejoiced that their turn to get rich had arrived, beet sugar (genus *Beta*) was looming on the competitive horizon. Beginning around the middle of the eighteenth century, German scientists and plant breeders had proven increasingly successful in both extracting the sucrose stored in beet roots and in breeding beets that had a greater sugar content. Then, with the dawning of a new century, a spate of beet sugar factory construction suddenly occurred. What may have been the world's first such factory went up in Prussia in 1801. Russia, hoping to stop being a customer of West Indian sugar growers, opened its first factory at about the same time (in 1801 or 1802), and Austria followed suit in 1803.

Initially the French, although they did some experimenting, mostly watched these developments from the sidelines – at least they did until 1806, when those blockades the French and the British had erected against one another cut sharply into the amount of sugar reaching the Continent from the West Indies.[8] An aroused Napoleon (known to have a sweet tooth) ordered that upwards of 100,000 acres be planted in sugar beets to free the French economy from its dependence on colonial imports. There-after, although the fortunes of beet sugar rose and fell, the new sugar made steady inroads into what had been a cane sugar monopoly. By the turn of the twentieth century, the production of beet sugar (a mostly European effort buttressed by government protection) briefly surpassed that of cane, although by century's end it accounted for only about one-third of all the world's sugar.[9]

Sugar use in beverages became more uniform after 1872 when Henry Tate, an English sugar merchant, invented the sugar cube which was instant-ly popular in both Europe and the Americas. Yet, the cuisines of these two areas also reflect differing consequences of yesterday's sugar availability. When Europeans visit the United States, they are startled at the sweet-ness of the pastries. Americans by contrast, find the lack of sugar in the cakes of Europe off-putting. The reasons for the sweetness of American versus European baked goods are that historically sugar was always rela-tively cheap in the Western Hemisphere, whereas it was always relatively dear in Europe.

A spiraling demand for sugar also had much to do with beverages, both alcoholic and nonalcoholic (but stimulating nonetheless because of caffeine). Three ingredients predominated for the nonalcoholic drinks – cacao from America, coffee from Africa, and tea from Asia. Together they fundamentally altered the drinking habits of the globe.

CACAO

Look, there's no metaphysics on earth like chocolate. (Fernando Pessoa)

Cacao, originally a native of the Amazon region, was enjoyed extensively as a drink in Mesoamerica during pre-Columbian times, among aristocracies to be sure, but probably by all classes.[10] The Maya were the first to write about the secrets of cacao bean processing – fermenting, curing, toasting, and grinding – to which an array of other ingredients were added, such as chilli peppers, vanilla, honey, and perhaps, maize. Warm water was the medium that combined them.

Because cacao contains caffeine and theobromine, it was a stimulating drink that some Spaniards initially thought to be a kind of wine.[11] Columbus was the first European to encounter cacao beans and noted they were used as coins.[12] Hérnando Cortéz and his lieutenants adopted the drink in Mexico during the 1520s and apparently introduced cacao to Spain where, enhanced with American vanilla, it became the property of that country's aristocracy.[13] But although Spain was on the receiving end of a commerce in New World cacao from the late sixteenth century, decades elapsed before sugar ensured that the beverage became popular.[14]

Hot chocolate may have started its European career as a drink of the Spanish elite, but it soon charmed elites all over Europe (it did no harm that chocolate had become known as an aphrodisiac), and by the end of the seventeenth century, chocolate houses had become commonplace from Lisbon to London to Livorno.[15]

COFFEE

Coffee, which makes the politician wise. (Alexander Pope 1688–1744)

More pervasive and permanent than chocolate in their European impact were coffee and tea. Coffee originated in the mountains of Ethiopia and probably Yemen as well, where it was first used extensively as a beverage. According to legend, around 850 AD an Ethiopian goatherd, curious about a strange friskiness among his charges, discovered that the goats were

nibbling berries from coffee trees. The first humans to use coffee probably emulated the goats by eating the berries. Mystics – especially the
Sufi monks – used the berries early on, and later on the drink, to produce
visions and to keep them awake during long nighttime rituals.[16]

Coffee was drunk in Persia during the ninth century, and the famous
physician Avicenna wrote about it around the year 1000, although at this
point it was still a rare beverage.[17] By the turn of the fifteenth century,
however, coffee beans were being roasted, ground, and brewed into a beverage, and coffee trees had been brought under cultivation. The Ottoman
Turks introduced coffee to Constantinople in 1454, and by 1500 it was a
common beverage of the Arabian peninsula.[18] Arab merchants shipped the
beans from the Yemeni port of Mocha to an Islamic world, whose enthusiastic acceptance of the beverage, after some hesitation, can be traced at
least in part to the Koranic prohibition of alcohol. Coffee provided the
same excuse for socializing and conviviality that alcoholic beverages did
elsewhere.

Coffeehouses became the location of such gatherings; the first is said to
have been established at Constantinople (Istanbul) – that wedge of land
jutting into the confluence of the Bosporus and the Golden Horn – at
the end of the fifteenth century. But coffee houses in Baghdad, Damascus,
Mecca, Medina, and Cairo quickly followed, and soon they were as much
a part of the North African landscape as the prickly pear cacti brought
from the Americas by Spain. Attempts to ban the early coffee houses were
frequent because they were suspected of housing too much conviviality in
the form of drug use, prostitution, and suspicious political activity. Yet, a
coffee craze accompanied by official disapproval of coffeehouses was not a
phenomenon confined to followers of the Prophet.

Venice, in close contact with the Arabs, the
spice trade, and the Turks who occupied Yemen
in 1536, was exposed to coffee early and apparently saw its first coffeehouse (called caffe and
elsewhere café, eponymous for the drink pur-
veyed) established around the middle of the sixteenth century. Legend, however, contradicts. It
has coffee only reaching Europeans in 1683, in
the aftermath of the Ottoman Turk's abortive
siege of Vienna, when the Austrians discovered
a veritable mountain of coffee bags left behind

by the fleeing Turks – a mountain that spurred Vienna into becoming Central Europe's coffee-processing capital.[19]

Like many legends, this one contains some truth. Coffee was a valuable commodity in the Ottoman Empire, and the Turks jealously guarded what was essentially their monopoly. But 1683 was hardly the first time coffee had gotten away from them. Decades before (in 1616), the Dutch had managed to steal a tree in Aden, and soon were spreading coffee cultivation throughout the East Indies, while simultaneously introducing the berries to Europe. England's first coffeehouse opened in Oxford in 1637. In France, Marseilles got a coffeehouse in 1671, and Paris the following year, although the Café Procope, "the first true Paris café," did not open its doors until 1686.[20]

As coffee consumption grew apace, along with the production of sugar to sweeten it, the Dutch took coffee trees to Surinam, and in the early eighteenth century saw them radiate out across the Caribbean. Martinique was the first West Indies island to grow coffee extensively, followed by French St. Domingue, and later on Spanish Cuba. On the mainland, coffee cultivation moved south from Guinea into Brazil, where slave labor was employed to tend coffee trees as well as sugar cane.[21]

Before the St. Domingue slave revolution, France was the world's biggest coffee-producer, satisfying about 60 percent of a European demand that had grown tenfold in the half-century between 1739 and 1789.[22] But after the revolution, Brazil took up the slack and bloomed into the world's largest coffee grower, producing some 50 percent of the total by the middle of the nineteenth century. And this happened despite the efforts of refugee planters from St. Domingue (about to become Haiti), who had established coffee-plantations in Jamaica, Puerto Rico, Cuba, Colombia, and Central America.

Planters with smaller scale production methods in some of the new coffee countries such as Colombia, Jamaica, Costa Rica, and Guatemala soon concluded that they could not compete with Brazilian coffee in price and switched to the production of better quality coffee grown in the soil of their mountainous regions. The champion of quality that emerged was Jamaica whose rich Blue Mountain coffee has long been widely regarded as the world's finest.[23]

After abolition in 1888, the freedmen in Brazil, as elsewhere in the hemisphere, were understandably less than enthusiastic about returning to the coffee fields as hired hands. So the planters and their agents recruited an army of southern European immigrants to replace them with the focus on a family work unit – with each family assigned around 5,000 trees.[24]

Coffee may have reached southern Europe first, but it was the northern Europeans – the Dutch, the Scandinavians, and the Germans – who ultimately became its most dedicated imbibers. In England, coffee was at first closely identified with the academic communities at Oxford and Cambridge. But soon coffeehouses abounded in London so that by 1700 there were some 2,000 of them.

As coffee percolated down the social scale, its consumption increased some ten times in the half-century from 1739 to 1789. In Vienna, coffeehouses drew the customers in with billiard tables; in France it was chess. Coffeehouses also became vehicles of social and political change. Sultans had fretted about their potential for bringing troublemakers together – closing them from time to time with blood-curdling threats – and in 1675, Charles II of England followed suit by ordering all coffeehouses closed on the grounds that they were hotbeds of sedition. As the sultans had before him, he subsequently backed down in the face of public uproar but the fears of these rulers were not groundless. In France, the 1789 assault on the Bastille was plotted in a coffeehouse (the Café Foy).[25]

Arabica – the trees of which require about four years to mature and produce a yield of berries – has been the coffee discussed to this point. But there is another species of coffee tree (Coffea *robusta* also *C. canephora*) that was found growing wild in the Congo at the turn of the twentieth century. These trees have the advantage of maturing in only one year and were quietly cultivated in many parts of Africa (as were a couple of other minor species) prior to the 1950s. Since then, however, Robusta has come out of the closet to enter the world market. By 1956, it already accounted for 22 percent of the world's coffee crop – with Angola and Kenya its top producers.

Judged by most to be less tasty than Arabica, Robusta is used in cheaper blends and is the foundation of instant coffee. War in Angola and political unrest in Uganda and Kenya have crippled African production, but Viet Nam has been the beneficiary. As of 2002, its Robusta production had helped to send world coffee prices spiraling downward at a dizzying rate.

Following World War II, globalization scattered the complicated machinery for making Italian espresso coffee over all of Europe as well as over all of the Americas – one says complicated because in the words of a couple of experts "brewing espresso . . . unlike other methods of brewing coffee . . .

is rocket science. . . ." And with espresso came a new dimension to the old European-style coffeehouses.[26]

America, on the other hand, contributed a modern version. In 1987, Howard Shultz bought a Seattle coffee bean business called "Starbucks," cleaned up its logo by covering the mermaid's breasts with her hair, and began opening coffee bars to supplement his wholesale and mail-order operations. By 1994, there were almost 500 Starbucks coffee outlets; by 2001, that number had mushroomed to close to 5,000 worldwide. Coffee globalization was well underway.

TEA

Thank God for tea! What would the world do without tea? How did it
exist? I am glad I was not born before tea. (Sydney Smith 1771–1845)

Tea (*Camellia sinensis*) was the third beverage to catapult a demand for sugar into the stratosphere. These days tea is drunk by four-fifths of the world's peoples, and daily by about half of them, making it the most consumed beverage on the planet, after water. Nonetheless, it is second to coffee in international trade because so much of the tea produced never enters that trade but rather is consumed locally.

Like coffee, the origin of tea (the word derives from Chinese dialect words such as "Tchai," "Cha" and "Tay") is shrouded in legend, although in this case one reason the legends persist is that facts are hard to come by. For this we can blame the Han Emperor reigning around 206 BCE. Clearly something of a megalomaniac, he ordered all written records destroyed; the idea was that Chinese history should begin with him.

According to the most often repeated legend, tea drinking began in China nearly 5,000 years ago when a leaf from a wild tea plant (which grows from 30 to 40 feet in height) fell into a bowl of boiling water prepared for the emperor Chen Nung.[27]

Maybe! But tea leaves were probably first not brewed but eaten as a vegetable relish, and in some places pickled tea leaves are still consumed this way.[28] Moreover, one could reasonably expect that the commercial possibilities of tea as a beverage would not have eluded the Chinese for close to 3,000 years – in fact until the Han Dynasty (206 BCE – 220 AD), when the shrub was reportedly under cultivation in central and south China. At the end of the Han era, tea got a mention in the literature as a good substitute for wine, but despite this endorsement, it was used mostly for medicinal purposes and was not widely consumed until the sixth or seventh century.

At the time this was happening (during the T'ang Dynasty 618–907), tea reached Tibet and nomadic peoples on China's northern borders, such as the Mongols and Tartars.' For the Siberian nomads tea became not just a drink but also a food – they added a paste made of meal, butter, and heavy cream to the beverage.[29]

Tea's popularity continued to grow so that by around 960 (the beginning of the Song Dynasty) it had become a tipple of an emerging middle class. With tea drinking more common, government evinced an enthusiasm for supervising tea production, controlling its trade, and especially for collecting tea taxes. The number of tea plantations in China increased dramatically during the Song period (960–1280)[30] and by the thirteenth century, tea was a staple even for the poor.[31]

Buddhism entered China at about the beginning of the Common Era to reach its zenith in the ninth century, and it too can claim credit for tea's steady gains in popularity. The beverage served as a comforting substitute for alcohol, which the strict dietary regimen of its monks excluded and, in addition, provided the "energy" for long hours of meditation. That energy, of course, derived from caffeine, which tea bristles with. A pound of tea packs more than twice the caffeine of a pound of coffee. What generally saves the tea drinker from caffeine jitters is that it takes around seven times more coffee than tea to make a cup of beverage. Or put less obliquely, a cup of tea contains about half as much caffeine as a cup of coffee.[32]

It was around 800 AD that Lu Yu, who had been raised by Buddhist monks, wrote the first definitive book on tea, the *Ch'a Ching* or *The Classic of Tea*. But the Buddhist influence on tea-drinking was not confined to China. Tea journeyed with the monks to Japan around 593 and probably reached Korea at about the same time. Civil war, however, broke out in Japan as tea was taking hold, and it fell into disuse for some two centuries, only to be reintroduced in 805 by another monk – this one Japanese – returning from China. His name was *Yeisei*, and to this day he is remembered and revered in Japan as the "Father of Tea."[33]

From Japan, tea spread southward to Java but it was only with the European maritime incursions into the East that a taste for tea moved any further westward by sea. On land it was a different story. Tea doubtless entered Afghanistan from China early on – crisscrossed, as it was, by numerous trade routes including the Silk Road – and has remained the national drink of that country. Later, after the rise of Islam, tea was adopted by the Ottoman Empire (the Turks still drink more tea than coffee) and entered Egypt – Africa's most serious consumer of the beverage.[34] Moreover, with Turkish rule, what had been a slow decline of Muslim wine usage became a rapid one – so much so that wine virtually disappeared from the region where it had first made its appearance millennia before.[35]

In the fifteenth century, China, although leading the world in maritime technology, chose to turn its back on the oceans. But just as the Chinese were executing their Great Withdrawal, the Portuguese were inching their way down the African coast in their quest for a route to the East. They found it at the turn of the sixteenth century, and in 1514, the Portuguese now leaping – from Calicut to Malacca – reached the south China coast to become the first Europeans to taste tea. They were also the first Europeans to gain the right to trade with China,[36] and the first to introduce the beverage to Europe.[37]

Other firsts followed. A Portuguese Jesuit became the first European to write about tea in 1560, and by 1580 tea was taken from China to Lisbon, making the Portuguese the first European tea drinkers. From Lisbon, tea was carried northward in Dutch ships to Holland and the Baltic countries.

Unfortunately for the Portuguese, the year 1580 also marked the beginning of Spanish sovereignty over Portugal, making its empire fair game for the Hollanders who, at the time, were waging their war for independence against Spain. Consequently, by the turn of the seventeenth century the Dutch had become Portugal's enemy in the Americas and in the Orient where they set about seizing Portugal's empire. The Dutch also picked up where the Portuguese left off in introducing tea to Europe.[38]

As early as 1610, Holland received its first tea directly from East Asia, although not from China, but from a Japan that had not yet fully shut out the Westerners. As with other novel plants, early European interest in tea focused on any curative substances it might contain and, because the Dutch were more interested in capturing the spice trade than the tea trade, both demand and supply were anemic. But by the middle of the seventeenth century, the Hollanders had become masters of the spice trade and tea was being drunk by elites in Holland and France. Tea's commercial possibilities began to dawn on the Dutch, but the new Tokugwa shoguns had now closed Japan to Europeans, so they had to sail directly to China for tea cargoes.[39]

The John Company – forerunner of, and often confused with the British East India Company – was formed a year before its Dutch counterpart, but initially its achievements in exploiting the East Indies were more modest. Although the English made some inroads in India, they lagged behind the Dutch in "energy and ability" to say nothing of "capital and material resources."[40] This changed radically, however, as the seventeenth century drew to a close, and in the one that followed it was the aggressive English East India companies that stole the tea trade from the Dutch and presided energetically over the rise of tea in the West.

Tea's debut in Britain was as a health food that coffeehouse-owner Thomas Garraway (also spelled Garrway, and Garaway) advertised in 1657 as a cure for "dropsies, scurvies," and a drink that made "the body active and lusty."[41] The British government, always alert to lucrative possibilities for increasing revenues, soon slapped a tax on tea imports that remained in place until the 1780s; and much of the time it was a tax worth evading. In 1684, tea sold for less than a shilling per pound on the Continent but carried such a whopping import duty (five shillings a pound) in Great Britain that smuggling became rampant and more than half the tea consumed by the British was said to have escaped the import duty. Nonetheless, the 20,000 pounds of legal tea that Britain imported in 1700 rose to a prodigious 20 million pounds by century's end.[42]

The tea trade also opened up other profitable avenues. Tea is bulky but not heavy, which meant that ships returning from the Orient, although laden with tea, nonetheless required some kind of ballast. As a rule, ballast produced no profits, but in this case it did. The solution was to use porcelain or "china" as ballast, which buried Europeans under hundreds of tons of Chinese porcelain before they finally learned to make it themselves in the eighteenth century.[43] Moreover, because Europeans drank tea at a much hotter temperature than the Chinese, when they did learn, they put handles on the cups.

The rise to prominence of tea in England is also the story of a long-term decline of coffee. One says long-term because it was only around 1850 that tea became less expensive than coffee (because the East India Company's tea monopoly had been broken in the 1830s), enabling British tea consumption to catch up with coffee.[44] As already seen, coffee was so enthusiastically adopted in that country after its mid–seventeenth-century introduction that, within a decade after the first coffeehouse opened for business, there were over 3,000 of them in London and nearby cities. And these many establishments were on hand to also serve tea after its arrival. The increasing demand for both coffee and tea elevated the demand for sugar, and West Indies plantations responded with an avalanche of the sweetener as British per capita consumption rose from four pounds in 1700 to twelve pounds by 1780.[45]

Some of the coffee/tea houses were called "Penny Universities," because for a penny a person could get a pot of tea, a newspaper, and intellectual conversation. A pioneering extortive device improved the quality of service – a small coin placed in a box marked "T. I. P." ("to insure promptness").[46] Other establishments catered to specialized clienteles – attorneys, military officers, literary people, merchants, ship owners – that tended to frequent establishments where like-minded customers congregated. These were the forerunners of private gentlemen's clubs, and some, like that owned by Edward Lloyd (which attracted ship owners, shippers, and marine insurers), evolved into other businesses – in this case into the world's largest insurance company – Lloyd's of London.

Another such success was Tom's Coffee House opened by Thomas Twining in 1706. It became a major tea importer and distributor. In short, coffeehouses were instrumental in ensuring that tea was introduced to all walks of life in England where, as a consequence, tea eventually became a democratic drink. By contrast, in the Latin countries – Spain, Italy, France – tea was always a privilege of the upper classes, whereas coffee was the drink of the masses.[47]

Yet another factor elevating tea consumption in England had to do with a decline in that of alcohol. Gin crossed the English Channel from the Netherlands with William and Mary to capture the fancy of the working classes – so much so that by 1735 English distillers were producing a gallon annually for every man, woman, and child. An alarmed Parliament raised taxes on gin so that by mid-century the poor could no longer afford it and were forced to switch to beer, coffee, or tea. Duties on tea were reduced in 1723, after which it began its slow rise as the drink of England's working classes – a process that was accelerated after malt was taxed, causing beer to be more expensive – whereas further duty reductions in 1773 and 1784 made tea even cheaper.[48]

If the English were gradually weaned from coffee to tea, the weaning ran in the opposite direction in England's North American colonies. Tea was being served in New Amsterdam around the middle of the seventeenth century and two decades later – with the colony no longer Dutch – a veritable "tea craze" was underway in what was now New York City. Tea gardens opened everywhere. By century's end, tea had become a staple of the American colonists and, thanks to the British tax on tea, an important item of illegal, as well as legal, trade.[49]

American smuggling to circumvent the Navigation Acts – especially of tea, molasses, and rum – was one source of friction with the Mother Country. Taxation (which created smuggler's markets) was another, especially after the French and Indian War of 1756 to 1763 (the Seven Years War in Europe), when the British (with some justification) decided that the Americans should help to pay for a war that, in eliminating the French threat to the colonies, had certainly benefited them.[50]

The Revenue Act of 1764, the Stamp Act of 1765 (which laid an excise tax on a wide range of items), and the Townshend Acts of 1767 that taxed still more items, including tea (the third most important American import after textiles and manufactured goods), precipitated such an outcry that the Stamp Act was repealed and the Townshend duties rescinded, save for the one imposed on tea – this one deliberately retained as a reminder of Parliamentary authority. Yet, this was balanced by the Tea Act of 1773, which reduced the cost of tea to the colonists by permitting the East India Company to ship it directly to North America from China. The latter, however reasonable and conciliatory, was a move that threatened the economic well-being of American tea merchants and smugglers.

They and their supporters made much of the fact that the Act retained the Townshend duty on tea, claiming that payment of the duty was a surrender to Parliament's insistence that it had a right to tax. American unhappiness came to a head in December of 1773, when colonists, dressed as Indians, threw hundreds of pounds of tea into Boston Harbor, at the same time that tea was left to rot on docks at New York, Philadelphia, and Charleston. Stern English measures to ensure enforcement were met with colonial countermeasures, and revolution followed. Practically forgotten is that one of the supporters of the "Boston Tea Party" was John Hancock, an illicit tea smuggler put out of business by the Tea Act.[51]

Severance from Great Britain, however, meant that Americans had to fetch their own tea, and in 1784 the first U.S. vessel reached China to do exactly that. Within three years the American tea cargos totaled a million pounds annually and the first three of four millionaires in the United

States, John Jacob Astor of New York, Stephen Girard of Philadelphia, and T. H. Perkins of Boston, all made their fortunes in the tea trade. The other millionaire, Elias Haskett Derby, made his fortune in the pepper trade but like the others was able to do so well, so quickly, because of the ever-faster ships being designed – designs that ultimately produced the famous Yankee Clippers – and ironically, by the mid-nineteenth century, American clipper ships were delivering tea to British ports.[52]

This came about in part because the British had abolished their Navigation Acts and gone to free trade and, in part, because the American demand for tea had fallen precipitously. Coffee consumption had increased in the wake of the Boston Tea Party and the events of the Revolution, again during Jefferson's Trade embargo between 1807 and 1815, and once more because of the British blockade during the War of 1812. These events combined to make tea less attractive to Americans at a time when Caribbean and Brazilian coffee prices were much cheaper than ever before. Coffee flowed into the fledgling United States in ever increasing quantities and by 1830 the tea weaning was complete. U.S. citizens had transformed themselves into dedicated coffee drinkers.

It was at about this time that the British had finally managed to unravel the secrets of tea cultivation – secrets that the Chinese had wisely kept quiet about for so long. With the establishment of the great English tea plantations of Assam and Ceylon in India, the Chinese monopoly was broken. Yet, demand was such that the British still needed great quantities from China, and it was a demand which promoted a perpetual headache. The Chinese insisted on payment in precious metals, which played havoc with British trade balances.

Opium turned out to be the palliative. In 1773, the East India Company had broken the Portuguese hold on the illicit drug traffic to China, and following this, the Company had increasingly looked to opium – a Company monopoly in India since 1758 – to finance its tea purchases. Because the Chinese had declared trafficking in opium illegal, the British were forced to resort to subterfuge – to employ go-between companies and merchants to get the narcotic into China from India. It was sold at auction at Calcutta for the sake of appearances, then carried to China by the intermediaries who exchanged it for silver and gold coin. These precious metals were then used to buy Chinese tea.[53]

The Chinese were not fooled, however, and in an effort to stop the traffic jailed some British sailors. This touched off the so-called "Opium Wars"

(1840–42), with England going to war for the principle of free trade – in this case the right to sell opium – and on behalf of "free traders" determined to see China "opened" to the West. China had no chance against the Royal Navy, and in the peace settlements the British wrung concessions from Peking to continue opium trafficking in China until 1908. Hong Kong became British, and Amoy, Fuchow, Ningpo, and Shanghai were other ports legally opened to the West. Additionally, China was "opened" even more during wars in 1851, 1861, 1871, and 1894.[54]

Meanwhile the British public got the notion that the fresher the tea the better it tasted, and clipper ships – the tea clippers of North America and Great Britain – entered into a lively competition to see how quickly tea could be hurried from China to England. Although starting a half a world away, the ships could frequently be spied racing neck and neck up the Thames, separated only by seconds. The record voyage was that of the American clipper, the *Oriental*, which rushed tea from China to London in 97 days.[55]

In addition to this record, there were a couple of other American contributions to the culture of tea. One of these was iced tea, invented, so the story goes, at the 1904 St. Louis Fair by a tea merchant whose samples of hot tea went begging in the St. Lois heat. But when he dumped a load of ice into the brew, his chilled tea became the talk of the fair.[56] Actually there is no credit for the invention here because iced tea had been drunk in the United States – especially in the South – for over half a century, although this event in St. Louis helped to popularize the drink. Indeed, just a few years after the fair, the author of *The Grocer's Encyclopedia* gave his readers a detailed recipe for making iced tea.[57]

The second American contribution was even more inadvertent. In 1908 Thomas Sullivan, a New York coffee and tea merchant, started delivering samples of his various teas to customers – mostly restaurants – in hand-sewn bags rather than in the customary tins. Some of those customers discovered that they could brew the tea right in the bag, and Sullivan was swamped with orders for tea bags. He wasted no time in complying and soon was using a machine specifically designed to bag tea. Today, more than half of the tea consumed in the United States is bagged.[58]

The health benefits of tea have been extolled over the centuries, and it is currently enjoying a reputation as a cancer fighter.[59] Yet, although the herb may well be salubrious, its place in Western history is one of violence. It was said (by the French at least) that even during the fiercest battles, British armies ceased fire for tea at five o'clock.[60] In 1942, Winston Churchill asserted that tea was more important to his troops than ammunition. He was echoing Rudyard Kipling, who earlier had proclaimed that "tea fights." Earlier still John Adams had written of the Boston Tea Party that "this destruction of the tea is so bold, so daring, so firm, intrepid and inflexible . . . that I cannot but consider it an epoch in history."[61]

Such belligerence contrasts starkly with the Chinese association of tea with tranquility and health.[62] "Gunpowder" was the name given to a Chinese green tea by the British because the pellets reminded them of lead ball shot. The Chinese, however, were clearly reminded of a more serene substance. They have always called it "Pearl Tea."[63]

SOFT DRINKS

A great variety of temperance beverages are made by putting a sufficient
quantity of flavoring syrup in bottles and filling with Carbonated Water.
(Artemas Ward 1911)[64]

Soft drinks were around long before there was sugar to sweeten them. In fact, water, the major ingredient in soft drinks, was also the first soft drink. Long understood to be life giving, waters from springs, streams, and rivers were associated with divinities from earliest times. The Ancients also gave attention to the various tastes of water. Rainwater was best of all; that from mountain streams was better than water from streams in hot plains or from wells; river water taste varied depended on the riverbed.[65]

But it was well known that water could also be life-threatening. Premodern Chinese thought cold water damaging to the intestines and their preference for heated, even boiled, water must have had a sterilizing effect that spared people, who lived in close proximity to one another and practiced a paddy rice cultivation that commonly employed human excreta for fertilizer. Boiling was also done to purify water in the Arab world, although classical and medieval authors knew about filtration. Where there were public waterworks (such as the aqueducts of ancient Rome), water quality was an important responsibility delegated only to experts. Clearly, the concept of water-borne disease, if imperfectly understood, was nonetheless well-engrained eons ago.

By the seventeenth century the best water was "mineral" water, derived from springs that imparted iron, sulfur, salt, or other minerals believed to be effective against myriad ailments. Less desirable was well water, and least desirable of all was "common" water from public fountains and pumps – its contamination often proving extraordinarily deadly in the spread of typhoid and other waterborne diseases such as cholera during the pandemics of the nineteenth century.

Out of that experience with cholera came a greater understanding of water safety and, between 1840 and 1940, public water supplies in the industrialized world were subjected to intense filtration and chemical treatments. In the early twentieth century, with the advent of chlorination, public confidence in the water supply was high. But by the beginning of the twenty-first century that confidence had clearly slipped a bit and Americans were leading the West in a mineral and bottled water craze that returned water to its former soft drink status.

Throughout the ages, fermentation and brewing processes turned out attractive alternatives to raw water such as "small" beers, ales, and new wines containing little alcohol that were available to everybody. The first concocted nonalcoholic soft drink may have been lemonade (which probably originated with the Arabs). Italians were sipping lemonade in the sixteenth century, and by the following century its popularity had spread to the rest of Europe.[66] In France, the beverage (often sweetened with honey) provided employment to a host of limonadiers, who dispensed the drink on the streets from tanks on their backs.

In 1772, Joseph Priestly laid the foundation for the modern soft drink industry with his publication of *Directions for impregnating water with fixed air*. The "fixed air," or carbon dioxide gas, was first used to carbonate mineral waters, a procedure that Jacob Schweppe perfected to produce artificial mineral waters in large scale fashion. Like mineral waters, these carbonated beverages were understood to have medicinal properties, as were other drinks such as lemonade or orangeade. And as the nineteenth century got underway and sugar was no longer dear, effervescent lemonade and other sweetened fruit-flavored drinks, along with spruce beer, ginger beer, and seltzer waters, could be purchased at market stalls. But now, these were drunk for their refreshing (as opposed to medicinal) qualities.

In the United States, mid-century pharmacists were producing carbonated waters, flavored with various syrups at their newly-installed soda fountains. Sarsaparilla, root beer, and the ice cream soda also debuted on their counter tops. Soda fountains caught on as well in Europe, where they became Germany's *Trinkhallen* and France's *buvettes à eaux gazeuses*.

During the second half of the nineteenth century, quinine water came into production. It was originally intended for British malaria sufferers who had picked up the disease in the tropics and, along with ginger ale, was exported to the American market where (as in Great Britain) temperance drinks were increasingly in demand and soda fountains were flourishing. In fact, by 1891, New York had more soda fountains than saloons.[67]

Kola, made from the African kola nut, was a popular soft drink in late Victorian England. So was coca wine, derived from the leaves of the coca shrub, its leaves chewed for millennia by natives of the Andean region. But it was in North America in 1886 that the two were married by Atlanta pharmacist John Styth Pemberton. The drink, "Coca-Cola," was initially sold in soda fountains and billed as an "esteemed Brain Tonic and Intellectual Beverage" although, in fact, it was originally intended to be a hangover and headache cure.[68]

Asa Chandler, who bought Coca-Cola in 1891, continued Pemberton's practice of marketing it as a syrup for soda fountains, and by 1895 he could boast that the soft drink was sold in every state in the union. Coke was bottled for the first time in 1899 – just after U.S. troops on their way to Cuba toasted one another with "Cuba Libres" (rum and Coca-Cola) served up by a bartender at the Tampa Bay Hotel.

Exactly when the marriage of cocoa leaves and kola nuts was put asunder is an unanswered question. When Coca-Cola was invented, coca (from which cocaine is derived) did not have the evil reputation that it subsequently acquired. The name merely promised a little zip in the drink. And although there was subsequent legal pressure to remove coca from the drink, it was not removed from the name. The alliteration and consonance were perfect – always a frustration for competitor Pepsi-Cola (introduced in 1898). Yet, if we do not know exactly when the coca was removed from Coca-Cola (the recipe remains a fiercely guarded secret), we do know that it did not hurt sales and "Coke" quickly became the world's biggest selling soft drink.[69]

Other soft drinks that were introduced in the last decades of the nineteenth century and are still around today include Dr. Pepper and Hires Root Beer (both in 1886) and Canada Dry Ginger-Ale (in 1891). And if temperance was good for soft drink manufacturers, so was prohibition, with Seven-Up and Nehi both starting up business during the 1920s.[70]

"Coca Colonization" is not a bad way of putting a name to the spread of soft drinks from the United States and Europe to the rest of the world.[71]

Developing countries initially imported them but then, through twen-tieth-century franchising mechanisms, acquired their own bottling and manufacturing operations. This was especially typical of Muslim countries, whose hot climates, youthful populations, and prohibitions on alcohol consumption made them excellent soft drink markets.

Soft drink manufacturers have had their eyes on the health market since the 1960s, when low calorie soft drinks first appeared, and now New Age drinks are upon us – drinks you can see through – that rely on natural fla-vorings, shun additives, and are only lightly carbonated. Available as well are isotonic or sports drinks designed to supply energy and replace fluids lost in exercise.

ALCOHOLIC BEVERAGES

John Barleycorn was a hero bold, of noble enterprise.
For if you do but taste his blood, Twill make your courage rise,
Twill make a man forget his wo;
Twill heighten all his joy. Robert Burns (1759–1796)

Before cacao, coffee, and tea, European beverages were generally of the alco-holic variety, especially wine and beer ("small" beer or ale called *kavas*, or *braga* in Russia – for the poor) because, among other things, the alcohol made water safer to drink.[72] Boiling water for the new beverages achieved the same end but, needless to say, they did not displace those of the alcoholic variety.

In the case of wine, after the advent of the new beverages, growers col-lectively began to concentrate on quality and consistency, whereas coun-tries like England and the Netherlands, with climates that did little to encourage viticulture, became good customers.[73] England, which had sev-eral small vineyards prior to the Little Ice Age but none after its advance, got much of its wine – especially claret – from France. The trouble with this arrangement was that it depended upon relations between the two countries that were often tenuous when they were not downright hos-tile. A British search for a more reliable source took them to Porto and the Douro Valley of Portugal. But this was a good deal further away than France, and to ensure that the wine reached the British Isles without going bad, some brandy was added to it. The result was Port wine.

Similarly, in Spain, after the expulsion of the Jews in 1492, English mer-chants began to dominate the wine trade around Jerez de la Frontera and came up with another fortified wine – this one Sherry (an English corruption of Jerez).[74]

By the end of the Middle Ages, beer was no longer the purview of monks and the church (although church bells still tolled at ten and two to let workers know it was time for a drink).[75] Breweries and drinking establishments proliferated in private hands and governments jumped in to regulate and tax. A classic example of regulation was the *Reinheitsgebot* or "Edict of Purity" instituted in 1516 by the Duke of Bavaria, which stipulated that the only ingredients permitted in beer were water, barley, malt, yeast, and hops (the latter coming into widespread use to extend the shelf-life of beers and for the tastes they imparted). The decree is still in effect for all German-made beers intended for consumption in Germany.

Until the fifteenth century, distilled beverages were mostly produced by alchemists and regarded as medicine. The Scotch and Irish, however, may have put the products of their stills to recreational use at an earlier time. The Scots called theirs *uisge beatha* ("water of life") and the Irish *uisce beatha* with the word "whisky" deriving from the pronunciation – "wisky-baw." Aquavit (another water of life) was the name initially given to brandy (from the Dutch *brandywijn*, meaning "burnt wine"), that became popular in the fifteenth century. But brandy, distilled from fruit or wine, was more expensive than beverages distilled from grains. Brandy for the poor was made from grape skins and seeds leftover after winemaking (called *marc* in France, *grappa*, in Italy, and *aguadiente* in Spain).[76]

Other waters of life dating from the fifteenth or sixteenth centuries are gin and vodka ("little water") – the latter now made in Russia from rye, although potatoes were used in the past and still are in some Eastern European (especially Polish) vodkas. This was a Russia whose leader had, according to legend, chosen Christianity over Islam in 988 because Islam prohibited the strong drink that was "the joy of the Rus." It is also a Russia where people still believe that it was the 1914 decree by Czar Nicholas II outlawing vodka which brought on the Communist Revolution.

Gin or *genever* (the Dutch name for juniper berries) became a grain-based favorite in the Netherlands and, according to some, the source of "Dutch Courage" in battle. With William and Mary, gin came to England and later gained the distinction of having saved the British Empire. It made bitter quinine water easier to drink – quinine that warded off malaria.[77]

Obviously, rather than drawing a sober breath with the arrival of coffee and tea, Europeans doggedly expanded their repertoire of alcoholic beverages, and these began to navigate the road of imperialism as surely as Old World plants and animals.[78]

Grape-growing was introduced to Mexico in the early sixteenth century and spread quickly southward to Peru, Chile, and Argentina and northward to California in the eighteenth century. But European wine grapes did not do well in the thirteen colonies and, although beer had been brewed since the days of the Puritans, it was rum that was the most cherished North American beverage until the Revolution. First made in Barbados in the 1630s, the cane spirit was soon produced throughout the West Indies, and distilleries making rum from molasses could be found from South Carolina to New England and to the maritime provinces of Canada.[79]

Rum made from sugarcane was one of the most important commodities in the slave trade, exchanged in Africa for people transported to the Caribbean to make even more sugar. The Revolution severed much North American contact with the Caribbean (and therefore with its source of rum), but many Scotch and Irish settlers in the south had brought with them the techniques of whisky making and stood ready to take up the slack. By the 1830s, Americans annually consumed more than five gallons of corn whisky on a per capita basis.

CHAPTER

17

KITCHEN HISPANIZATION

And I can assure your Majesty that if plants and seeds from Spain were to be had here . . . the natives of these parts show such industry in tilling land and planting trees that in a very short time there would be great abundance. . . .

Hernando Cortés (1485–1547)[1]

THE SCOPE of the known world doubled for the Europeans over the course of the sixteenth century, but it was only in the New World that the planet's cuisines as well as foods and peoples were first amalgamated on a vast scale. Had the European conquest occurred without a massive Native American die-off, its history might have been more like that of China or India, where it was only a matter of time before huge native majorities tossed out ruling foreign minorities to reclaim their lands and cultures. But in Mexico, Peru, and in most of the rest of the Americas, shrinking native populations left the door wide open to a flood of European and African and Asian peoples and cultures that came to stay.[2] The ensuing blending of New and Old World foods was a giant stride in food globalization, even though it was sometimes hobbled by Latin American tariff rates that were among the highest in the world between 1820 and 1929.[3]

During the Hapsburgs stay on Spain's throne (1516–1700), elites in the Americas, like those in Europe, ate the cosmopolitan foods of the Hapsburg Empire – "roasted kids and hams, quail pies, stuffed fowl and pigeons, *blancmange* and *escabeche* of chicken, partridge, and quail" were some of these foods that Cortéz and the new Viceroy of New Spain served at a feast in 1538.[4]

But after 1700, when the French Bourbons took over Spain's helm from the defunct Hapsburgs, French cuisine became the vogue for the elite of the Americas and remained so until well into the twentieth century. French food and the French language were identity cards for the upper classes who were sufficiently distanced from Indians and mestizos, blacks and mulattos, even poor and middle-class whites, so that in Mexico, one of its upper class members recently confessed that when she was growing up "we never ate Mexican food."[5]

For most everybody else, however, stews and soups were central to the diet, just as they were for pre-Columbian peoples who, like the Spaniards, used ceramic pots for cooking them. Called *puchero* in Argentina, *cazuela* in Chile, *chulpe* in Peru, and *ajiaco* in Columbia, such stews blended Old World ingredients – beef, salt pork, sausage, mutton, and cabbage, rice, and peas – with those of the New World – sweet and white potatoes, manioc, maize, annatto, and chilli peppers.[6]

With some exceptions, South Americans have not used chilli peppers as enthusiastically as the Mexicans. Fresh coriander has been a favorite in the Andean countries as in Mexico, but avocados were and are underutilized in South America. Garlic and onions are universally employed with a heavy hand, but salads of uncooked greens were rare before the twentieth century. Bananas and plantains were the most important fruits, especially in lowland locales, although citrus was everywhere. Flan, long the favorite dessert in the Hispanic countries, was a caramelized milk custard straight out of the Spanish heritage.[7]

THE ABC COUNTRIES

Iberians and Italians were the primary European settlers of Chile, Argentina, and southern Brazil. In the latter two areas the diet has tended to focus on grilled or roasted beef, often sun-dried – hardly the near-vegetarian Mediterranean diet they left behind. After their early introduction, cattle multiplied on the pampas so that in the 1840s, beef was so plentiful that it was even fed to poultry. Today the Plata region (Argentina and Uruguay) boasts the highest per capita beef consumption in the world, with southern Brazil not far behind. Wheat was the most important of Old World cereals to reach the region. As in Spain, Italy, and Portugal, it goes mostly into white bread, and together meat and wheat transplanted from Europe to Argentina and Uruguay have helped to feed the world.[8]

Mutton is another popular meat in Argentina, where seafood is curiously underused.[9] In Chile, however, the long, indented 2,600 miles of coastline yields seafood in abundance, which is consumed in large quantities. Central Chile also produces olive oil, another southern European staple.[10]

The Italians have contributed pasta to the cuisine as well as tomato-processing techniques to sun-dry tomatoes and turn them into sauce, puree, and paste. The Germans, for their part, have played a leading role in the charcuterie industry. In addition to tomatoes, many other American foods are routinely employed. In Brazil, toasted manioc meal (*farofa*) is invariably sprinkled over meats and black beans, which constitute the foundation of *feijoada*, the country's national dish – a blending of beans, rice, dried meats, and sausage.[11] And throughout southern South America potatoes, pumpkins, squash, green corn, and other corn dishes such as grits are commonly served.[12] Around São Paulo, the dish "*Cuscuz paulista*" may have been inspired by the couscous of North Africa, but cornmeal, not semolina, is used to make it.[13] Coffee, although a nineteenth-century arrival in Brazil, has become South America's leading hot beverage, although the native *yerba maté* tea, made from the South American holly (*Ilex paraguayensis*), remains popular, especially in Paraguay where Native American males, in particular, suck the brew from straws, preferably silver, inserted into gourd-like containers.

Iberian colonization brought viticulture to the Americas so that Europe is very evident in the vineyards that are common in southern Brazil and blanket the Andes foothills on both the Chilean and Argentinean sides.[14] Long ago, Spanish settlers and Jesuit missionaries elaborated a complex, but efficient, system of irrigation for both countries, using water sent down the mountainsides by melting snowcaps to solve the problem of uncertain rainfall in a hot and arid climate.[15] Chile produces less wine than Argentina or Brazil, for that matter, but its wines are better known, although the Malbec wines of Argentina's Mendoza region have recently become popular, led by a number of "Super Mendozans."

Without vast pampas, Chileans import most of their beef from Argentina but have many dishes based on pork and mutton as well. Apart from viticulture, Chile's agricultural efforts are aimed at the production of stone fruits and vegetable crops, many of these for export to the United States. Potatoes are native to the region; other important American foods are beans (foremost among them the cranberry bean), corn, and squash.

Interestingly, one of the ancestors of the hybrid garden strawberry is also a Chilean native.

To journey from the coffee country of southern Brazil to the sugar-growing regions of the Northeast is to leave an area settled voluntarily by European immigrants for a region reluctantly peopled by victims of the African slave trade. It is also to seemingly enter Africa because the region centered around Bahia showcases many of West Africa's contributions to New World cuisine. The American plant manioc is a staple in the Northeast, but major cooking ingredients like palm or dende oil, okra, and melegueta peppers are all African in origin.

Bahian cooks lavishly use ingredients such as the meat and milk of coconuts, onions, parsley, bananas, plantains, peppers, and peanuts. Their dishes are generally based on fish, shrimp, and chicken, with dried cod and dried shrimp both Portuguese contributions to what is otherwise a very tropical cuisine. Even the names of dishes like *vatapá* or *moqueca* evoke the exotic – fish, shrimp, or chicken stews that, when served with rice, represent a globalizing melding of foods native to the world's principle continents of Asia, Africa, the Americas, and Europe.[16]

THE ANDEAN REGION

Emphasizing European and African contributions to the American diet is not meant to minimize native input to New World cuisines. After all, Native Americans are the ones who domesticated major league crops like manioc, potatoes, peanuts, and maize, and not surprisingly, today's diet among the indigenous peoples in the Andes – in Bolivia, Chile, Peru, and Ecuador – remains a traditional one, relatively unchanged by the relative newcomers. Meals rest heavily on a wide variety of potatoes, along with quinoa, maize, and manioc, often laced with chilli peppers and ground annatto. Meat is eaten much less frequently in the highlands than elsewhere in South America, although dishes are sometimes flavored with the flesh of chickens as well as that of the guinea pig (*cuy*), a universal favorite that is generally roasted.[17]

On the coast, where the Humboldt Current rides herd on a seemingly inexhaustible supply of seafood, the diet becomes more tropical, utilizing bananas and plantains, side by side with potatoes but never excluding them. The minorities of European ancestry clustered in the large cities do most of the meat-eating and in the nineteenth century, if not before, European favorites such as beef, mutton, salt pork, and pigs' feet were all available in Lima.[18] Nonetheless, in a land where Quechua is spoken more commonly than Spanish, outside culinary influences are minimal.[19] This is not, however, the case in the Spanish Main countries of Venezuela and Columbia. Their llanos, like the pampas to the south, are fenceless ranges filled with cattle and cowboys to tend them.[20]

MESOAMERICA

In Mesoamerica (Mexico and Central America), Native American influences have also prevailed after the Europeans arrived. The diet centers on corn, eaten as *posole* (hominy), as a green vegetable in season, and, especially as tortillas. But it also features squash and beans, along with maize, the trinity of the Mesoamerican diet for millennia, and amaranth. In some places that plant is utilized for its greens as well as its grains. Produce includes avocados, tomatoes, tomatillos, chilli peppers, and cacao for a drink and to make mole. Yet, unlike the highlands of South America, even traditional Mesoamerican diets contain at least a modicum of globalizing influences.[21]

Wheat and rice, introduced by the Spaniards, have had a significant impact on what is eaten, even replacing maize in some cases. Animal protein supplied by pigs, sheep, goats, cattle, and chickens has had an equally profound dietary impact, their fat especially useful in flavoring dishes such as refried beans and quesadillas, and milk has become central to a flourishing cheese-making industry.

In the cities – especially in Mexico City – the diet has become truly international. Sushi bars, Thai and East Asian restaurants, French-Mexican cuisine (continuing the French tradition established under the Bourbons and reinforced during the reign of Maximillian), and traditional Mexican dishes (although most of these were not prepared before the conquest) such as chicken and turkey in mole, gorditas, infladas, empanadas, quesadillas, enchiladas, and refried beans. These join hamburgers, hot dogs, and pizza in competition for consumers pesos although even some of these foreign foods get "Mexicanized." Chillies and salsas are placed atop hamburgers and mole and green chilli topping come astride pizza poblanos.[22]

Moreover, outlying regions from Puerto Vallarta to Vera Cruz and San Miguel de Allende to Acapulco serve "fusion" specialties to tourists and Mexicans alike. Examples include crepes with *huitlacoche* (a corn fungus), Caesar salad (said to have been invented in Tijuana), cream of peanut soup, beef filet with black truffle sauce and polenta. But even Mexican specialties like hominy and pork soup or mole poblano require European garlic and onions, and guacamole is often served with sour cream.

THE CARIBBEAN AND THE SPANISH MAIN

Arguably, the Caribbean region, including lowland Mexico, Central America, and the Spanish Main, has made the greatest advances in food globalization outside of North America. It was here that Europeans, Native Americans, and Africans first mingled their blood and cultures on a massive scale, with yet more mixing taking place after the arrival of immigrants from South Asia and China. The native staples were zamia, manioc, sweet potatoes, malanga (tania, *yautía*), mamey, and, in places, maize, coupled with beans, chilli peppers, pineapples, guavas, pawpaws, and an assortment of animals and reptiles such as armadillos, dogs, snakes, and fish.[23]

In most cases these items remained in a Caribbean diet, enhanced after 1492 by the flesh and milk of Old World animals, chickpeas, garden produce, citrus fruits, plantains, bananas, melons, and, of course, sugar cane. In addition, wheat flour and salted and pickled fish were imported, and the Europeans also introduced rice from Asia.[24]

Africa sent yams, cowpeas, black-eyed peas, pigeon peas, okra, and Guinea corn (sorghum), ingredients that are turned into West Indian dishes such as "accara," or akkra (black-eyed pea fritters), "jug jug" (a haggis-like dish that incorporates pigeon peas and sorghum), "callaloo" (a thick soup of greens and okra), "run down" (salted fish, coconut milk, and plantains), and "coo coo" (okra and cornmeal).[25] Later eighteenth-century additions to Caribbean cuisine include mangoes (from South Asia), ackee (from West Africa), breadfruit (from the East Indies and Pacific tropics), and coffee (from Arabia).

West Indian slaves consumed manioc and eddoes in stews to which they added allotments of rice or cornmeal and a little whole protein in the form of pickled or salted cod, pickled pork and, in the Spanish islands, corned beef from Argentina. But the caloric expenditures of sugar slaves, along with the seasonality of many of the root vegetables, often meant outright malnutrition and a gamut of nutritional diseases.[26] The fall months were the worst. However, by December the provision crops had matured and the hurricane season ended so that merchant ships from Europe and the United States could safely resume the delivery of supplies to the islands. After months of semi-starvation, the sudden glut of food often produced a condition Robert Dirks has termed "relief-induced agonism" – a period of revelry for the slaves – characterized by feasting, drinking, and a bold aggressiveness that planters watched with nervous eyes.[27]

Another hazard for slaves was lead poisoning. Cheap rum made in stills with lead fittings and pipes provoked the symptoms of the dreaded "dry belly-ache" – a tortuous attack of intestinal cramps accompanied by painful constipation.[28] And a final problem was dirt-eating, which signaled serious nutritional deficiencies.[29] Not surprisingly, in view of such myriad nutritional difficulties, Caribbean slave populations failed to reproduce themselves which, in turn, perpetuated the slave trade.

Caribbean whites worked hard at maintaining the food traditions of their mother countries, not an easy matter in the tropics where wheat had to be imported, fresh meat and cream did not stay fresh for long, and beer and wine did not keep well either. Consequently, like the meat and fish destined for the slaves, foods consumed by the planters, although of better quality, were also salted and pickled, and rum mixed with fruit juices became the beverage of choice.[30]

With the end of slavery in the nineteenth century, Asians – mostly Indian and Chinese contract laborers – were imported, and also made culinary contributions to the region.[31] They brought with them *masalas* (spice, herb, and seasoning combinations) for curries and techniques for making *roti*, a flatbread that goes well with the curries. They also introduced *ghee*, a clarified butter crucial to Hindu cooking, whereas the Chinese brought with them a knack for steaming fish, and stir-frying vegetables.[32]

Yet, to qualify an earlier assertion about the extent of Caribbean food globalization, we must note that the myriad food introductions to the region along with culinary influences remain less than homogenized. In part, this is because of a plantation past that saw huge differences between the food preparation and the diets of whites on the one hand, and blacks and Asians on the other that persist to this day largely because of poverty. If a trans-Caribbean cuisine can be spied, it is with the bean and rice dishes found in both the islands and the mainland. Yet, the real food globalization in the Caribbean today is not found in local dishes but rather in imports: canned ham, Spam, spaghetti, canned and dried soups, and Nescafe, as well as in the plethora of McDonald's, Kentucky Fried Chicken, and Burger King restaurants, and pizza parlors.[33]

CHAPTER

18

PRODUCING PLENTY
IN PARADISE

*Earth here is so kind, that just tickle her with a hoe and she laughs
with a harvest.*

Douglas Jerrold (1803–1857)

THE FIRST EUROPEANS to settle in North America survived on Native American staples until Old World favorites began to thrive.[1] As Alfred Crosby has shown, practically all Old World plants, animals, and humans did well in regions with climates similar to those of Europe (he termed them "neo-Europes") by shoving aside more fragile competitors, when there were any competitors at all.[2]

However such "Ecological Imperialism"[3] managed only a faltering start in Florida, and sixteenth-century Spanish soldiers and missionaries had to fill their stomachs mostly with native maize, squash, and beans along with sweet potatoes transplanted from the West Indies.[4] Bitter oranges had been planted by early explorers and by the end of the sixteenth century sweet oranges were growing, although no commercial possibilities were foreseen until the English took Florida in 1763 and, in 1776, began shipping St. Augustine's oranges back to England.[5] Sugarcane was also placed under cultivation but, as a rule, where sugarcane will grow, wheat will not, and wheat flour was always an import to Spanish Florida.

Old World plant vigor, however, was exhibited by peach trees introduced directly from Europe that raced across the American continent well in advance of the Europeans. Native Americans became fond of the fruits, and, by the time of the American Revolution, peaches were so well established that many assumed them to be American natives.[6]

Carrots constitute another example of Old World plant vigor. They quickly escaped gardens to revert to that wild state in which we recognize them today collectively as "Queen Anne's Lace." Carrots were one more new food for Native Americans suddenly inundated with them. Even as early as the sixteenth century they were cultivating watermelons, cucumbers, and melons from Georgia to Eastern Canada, and from the Great Lakes region to the Southwest.[7] In 1539, Hernando de Soto planted oranges in Florida, and in 1542 he introduced pigs to the peninsula. The first cattle were landed around 1550 and spread out across the southeast. Virginia Indians fattened the cattle with corn and fed peanuts to the hogs, anticipating the Smithfield hams which eighty years later were being shipped to London from that colony to be sold at the city's Smithfield Market.[8]

Yet, while the eastern North American natives had earlier managed to adopt a wide variety of tropical American plants and now embraced many of the European foods, other tribes to the north and west stayed with hunting and gathering, although for many a traditional lifestyle was not all that nomadic. Around the Great Lakes, Native Americans did not stray very far from the stands of wild rice and fish-filled lakes, streams, and rivers. And along the coastline of the Northwest, a well-developed marine fishery encouraged a sedentary lifestyle without horticulture. Deer and other animals, of course, were also harvested, and many wild plants were exploited, including a variety of berries necessary to make pemmican.[9] To their north in the Sub-Arctic and Arctic regions, native Alaskan populations continued a semi-nomadic hunting and gathering way of life until the turn of the twentieth century.[10]

COLONIAL TIMES IN NORTH AMERICA

Eurasian diseases reached northeastern America in the seventeenth century to rage there with deadly intensity – long after the devastating epidemics that had swept the Caribbean, Mesoamerica, and the Andean region subsided. Conveniently for the European settlers, such epidemics helped to soften up Indian opposition.[11] When the English dissenters, for example, who "knew they were pilgrims" to quote William Bradford, came ashore on the Massachusetts coast in December of 1620, they encountered no resistance, just an abandoned Wampanoag Indian village called Pawtuxet, which they occupied and named Plymouth.[12] It was apparently smallpox that had emptied the village and, 14 years later in May 1634, the first governor of the Massachusetts Bay Colony could exuberantly note the end of any Indian threat when he wrote: "For the natives, they are neere all dead of small Poxe, so as the Lord hathe cleared our title to what we possess."[13]

Cleared titles or not, until the nineteenth century, Europeans found many aspects of their new homeland decidedly confusing. Rhode Island, on the same parallel as Rome, was considerably colder and, consequently, the early colonists of New England and eastern Canada were caught unaware by blustery winters.[14] They were also in the dark about what would and would not grow. Like the Spanish in Florida, the English colonists who had expected to plant wheat had to import it, and this included those who settled along the Chesapeake at the turn of the seventeenth century and the Pilgrims who followed them but accidentally wound up in Massachusetts. Mostly, however, the settlers depended on native foods for survival, like maize, which provided cornbread, and "Msicksquatash" (succotash or boiled corn and bean stew) for themselves and dried corn for their animals.[15]

They were British people with British tastes, no matter how disenchanted they were with British government and society (after all, the northern settlements were called "New England"). Yet there were no pigs, cattle, or chickens, no cheese, milk, butter, or wheat and so they initially subsisted on wild animals and corn, not because they liked it, but because they had no alternative.

At least this was the case until other grains arrived. Rye did well enough in New England but, it has been hypothesized, so did ergot, a fungus especially partial to rye which makes the disease it causes – ergotism – a suspect for the strange behavior of the Salem "witches." Buckwheat was brought to North America in the seventeenth century by the Dutch – its name deriving from the Dutch word *bochweit* – which means "beech wheat" – because its triangular seeds resemble beechnuts.[16]

But save for rye and buckwheat in New England, other grains were slow to adapt to new climates so people kept on eating corn, especially in Virginia and parts south until, finally, they did like it. Yet, unlike New England, where the Puritans became farmers out of necessity, it took the Virginians a longer time to achieve dietary self-sufficiency. This was because tobacco sales gave them the wherewithal to continue importing British foodstuffs. Nonetheless, they utilized corn long enough to establish it as a southern staple while making good use of other American offerings, like the abundant sturgeon found at the mouth of the James River.[17]

American beans got an easy acceptance by the new Americans who had eaten European beans, even if the new ones did not come in the same familiar sizes, shapes, and colors. In like manner, although there were no squashes and pumpkins in England, these were apparently close enough to familiar cucumbers and melons to be acceptable. Yet, the early colonists were not at all enthusiastic about living off the land. Following their respective "starving times" they choked down mussels and clams, regarded lobsters as food only for the very poor, enjoyed eels as they had in England, found oysters acceptable, fish even more so, and adopted the Native American method of pit-cooking seafood packed in seaweed with ears of corn thrown in – the clambake.[18] But none of these were fit substitutes for mutton, pork, and, especially, beef, all imported animals. Only later did the New England cod fisheries make that region a land of cod as well as corn, although, even then, the locals did not eat much cod.

In short, although America was truly a place of plenty, Europeans did not think so until they had added to their New World all of those Old World foods they were accustomed to eating. And these included beverages such as cider and beer. Tea was a new drink that radiated out of New Amsterdam, where the Dutch were sipping tea even before it caught on in England. It also caught on with the English colonists, and as the seventeenth century came to a close, Boston had the first establishment outside of New York to serve it.[19] Not that everyone knew what to do with tea. Some colonists brewed it, then threw away the liquid and ate the leaves. In Salem, tea leaves were eaten like greens, with plenty of butter and salt.[20]

To subdue the wilderness meant clearing the land by cutting down trees and, by 1700 in New England, more than a half-million acres of woodlands had been cleared. But many trees were also planted as fruits and received serious attention. There may have been American crab apples on hand that could be used for making jellies but these were good for little else, and the Massachusetts Bay colonists wasted no time in planting Old World apple trees. This happened as early as 1629, when legend has the first American apple orchard on Beacon Hill overlooking Boston Harbor. Apples were among the few fruits that, dried, could last through the long winters and these first ones began a transformation of the American landscape. They were the forerunners of the 100 new apple varieties that had been developed by 1800, not to mention the 2,500 or so now grown in the United States.[21] Apple cider, popular in England, became an American drink, and apple pie just became "American." Apple butter may have been first introduced to

North America by the Dutch, but the Quakers, Pennsylvania Dutch, and other Pennsylvania settlers made it a renowned American treat.[22]

Fruit trees came under royal scrutiny in 1640, when English monarch Charles I decreed that every Virginian holding 100 acres must plant a quarter acre in grafted apple, pear, or other fruit trees. Such legislation continued under new management so that, in parts of Ohio at the end of the eighteenth century, the planting of fifty apple trees or twenty peach trees within three years of settlement was a legal requirement for claiming land.[23] John Chapman (1772–1845), better known as Johnny Appleseed, had paved the way and made it easier for some of these settlers by his energetic apple-tree planting in remote areas.[24] The pear arrived in America at the same time as the pips of its cousin, the apple – in 1629 – through the Massachusetts Company. Two Dutch visitors to New York in 1679–80 were excited about the peach (and apple) cultivars they encountered, and at least three kinds of peaches were growing in Pennsylvania at the time.[25]

New food also entered the South. Carolina, founded in 1670, imported rice from Madagascar and Africans who knew how to grow it. Before the century was out, rice plantations could be found throughout the Low Country. Africa also contributed cowpeas – called "black-eyed peas," "field peas," or "crowder peas" and often just "peas" in plantation records – to help feed the slaves that worked those plantations. In addition, the slave trade brought domesticated sorghum to the south, where it was utilized more as a sweetener than a cereal, and the American peanut came to the region via Africa as well.[26]

In similar circular fashion the turkey returned to its home continent from Europe, reaching Virginia in 1584 and Massachusetts in 1629.[27] In New England, sugar and syrup from native maple trees were employed to sweeten foods and drinks, but New Englanders also used molasses from the Caribbean, as did everyone else. When they could get their hands on it, honey was much appreciated. It was an Old World treat, made by an Old World insect, the honeybee, turned loose in both Massachusetts and Virginia by the middle of the seventeenth century. Aggressive colonizers, they thrived, multiplied, and hived out to the frontier and beyond, where Native Americans learned to utilize the honey from the "English Fly" – an important dietary addition for a people who had previously been limited to honey locust, maypop, sweet gum, and, perhaps, maple syrup for sweeteners.[28]

Records indicate that settlers who moved to the Massachusetts frontier also did not miss many meals. Cabbages, parsnips, turnips, lettuce, squash, beans, asparagus, carrots, onions, and a host of other vegetables were growing in eighteenth-century gardens, although not yet potatoes, which belatedly arrived in New England with the Scotch-Irish. Wheat, rye, and maize were both planted and imported. White bread was preferred but "rye n' injun" (bread made from rye and Indian corn) was more common.

Much salt was purchased by townsmen, probably for brining pork, their most valued meat, although game was also much esteemed. Large quantities of pickled fish, butter, and cheese were stored in the cellars. Dried apples were a local product, but considerable amounts of raisins, currents, and figs from the Mediterranean were purchased. Spices – black pepper, cinnamon, nutmeg, and cloves from the East Indies and allspice from the West Indies, along with cane sugar and molasses, served to enliven and sweeten foods. Tea was the major "soft" beverage, but much hard cider, beer (mostly home brewed), and, especially, rum was downed as well. Clearly, the stern Puritan view of the world did not preclude alcohol, and "rum was the oil that greased every transaction."[29]

Okra, according to legend, was carried from the Caribbean to Mobile by French girls in the early eighteenth century, where this African fruit called "gumbo" was used to make just that. However, "gumbos" were stimulating palates on the Gulf coast before okra. These were made with filé – a thickener of ground American sassafras leaves contributed by the Southeastern Choctaw Indians.[30]

Asparagus and artichokes, loved by the Romans, had only regained popularity during the Renaissance. In France, white asparagus was commonly grown. In England, both white and green asparagus were known as "sparrow grass."[31] When asparagus and artichokes were brought to the New World is not certain. The pair are prominently mentioned in late eighteenth- and early nineteenth-century American cookbooks (although one patriotically insists that the American Jerusalem artichoke is better than the globe).[32]

Spain continued its contribution of comestibles to the lands north of the Rio Grande toward the end of the eighteenth century, when olives and grapevines were carried from Mexico to California by Franciscan monks. This was just about the time that both olive-growing and winemaking had a disgruntled Thomas Jefferson contemplating two rare failures in his Monticello gardens. But as an inventory of those gardens, as well as a look at

Amelia Simmons' first American cookbook (published in 1796) indicates, by century's end almost all Eurasian plants and animal foods had joined those of the New World in expanding American plenty.[33]

One late arrival was the soybean. The introduction of this crop in 1765 gave no clue that it would one day be ranked among North America's most valuable agriculture treasures. Samuel Bowen, a sailor who had served aboard a British East India Company ship, envisioned making a fortune when he left the sea and purchased land near Savannah to grow the soybeans he had acquired in China. Unfortunately, although his first crop was processed into vetch, soy sauce, and starch, soybean products simply did not "fit" with the local cuisine.

Another, this time permanent, soybean introduction occurred in the wake of the Matthew Perry mid-nineteenth century expedition that "opened" Japan, and returned to the United States with "Japan peas." At first soybeans were cultivated on a small scale as a forage crop, but they came in handy during the Civil War when disrupted shipping meant food shortages and the Union Army used them as coffee bean substitutes. Yet, it was only with the spur of a swelling population that soybeans became serious business for U.S. farmers.[34]

THE NEW NATION

During their Revolution, it was readily apparent that Americans were a people of considerable nutritional abundance. Their soldiers were substantially taller than the British and German troops they faced as well as those of France, who came to their aid. To a large degree the protein derived by meat consumption had created these towering Americans. Indeed, a French visitor to the United States in 1793 estimated that Americans ate seven to eight times more meat than bread – an unbelievable ratio for Europeans to contemplate.[35]

In addition to ushering in profound political and economic changes, the aftermath of the American Revolution saw near earth-shaking alterations in the new nation's drinking habits. For one thing, Americans traded in tea for coffee not solely, apparently, because of unhappiness with their now ex-mother country as is commonly asserted, but also because of simple economics. Tea through British sources was suddenly hard to come by, and Brazilian coffee had become cheaper than the tea carried by American flag vessels.

For another thing, this one dealing with alcohol, severing the connection with England had meant severing any connection with the British West Indies and their molasses for making rum. This was not necessarily a hardship because Americans were accustomed to smuggling molasses from French St. Domingue. But then, this largest sugar island of them all blew up in a *fin d' siècle* revolution to become an independent, but non–sugar-producing, Haiti. With rum increasingly scarce and expensive, America turned to corn whisky, or bourbon as it came to be called (after Bourbon County, Kentucky), which was destined to be more popular than rum had ever been.[36]

Americans had always made whisky. Both George Washington and Thomas Jefferson had distilleries on their estates that gave them rye whisky made from a grain the colonists had arrived knowing something about. The distillation of corn mash however, began with Scottish and Irish settlers. They brought a knowledge of whisky-making with them, and those who settled in the rugged parts of Appalachia with little flat land to cultivate and a long way from markets, put this knowledge to work to make their corn more portable to reach those markets. A horse could carry only four bushels of corn, but could be loaded with 16 gallons of whisky made from 24 bushels of corn.[37] None of this activity was against the law until 1791, when the new government sought to tax whisky distillers. The result was the Whisky Rebellion of 1794 by western Pennsylvania farmers. The government put it down without bloodshed, but henceforth, untaxed whisky was illegal "moonshine."[38]

By this time the production of commercial whisky had spread to the Kentucky territory where it had been underway for some two decades. The Whisky Rebellion encouraged other whisky makers to relocate in the territory so that by the time statehood was proclaimed in 1792, Kentucky could count more than 2,000 distilleries. Federal taxation of whisky followed statehood, prompting many of these distillers, untroubled by conscience, to take to the hills and avoid the taxes.[39]

Kentucky's mineral-free water was an important lure for whisky makers. Cleansed with limestone, it made an exceptional liquor that was barreled and shipped to New Orleans for distribution. The inevitable delays in such transit – often lengthy – taught distillers that whisky tasted better after a stay in the barrels, and this, in turn, led to the process of aging it in charred oak barrels. Charring was done to cleanse barrels that had previously been used as containers for other alcoholic beverages or foodstuffs such as butter. But, as a substantial bonus, charring gave the whisky a darker color and called up wood sap and oils from the barrel that added taste – especially when the barrel was oak (now used exclusively).

But the Haitian Revolution brought more than just a change in American alcohol consumption. It also brought Louisiana. Haiti's independence destroyed Napoleon's dream of a New World empire and, in 1803, he sold the Louisiana territory to the United States. A few decades later the nation attained continental dimensions with the 1848 treaty ending the war with Mexico. Between the end of the eighteenth and the middle of the nineteenth century, westward expansion had coaxed much new agricultural land into production and, at the mid-century mark, cheese and other foods were flowing down the Erie Canal from upstate New York and a network of canals was getting crops to market.[40] But at this point the country, stretching from the Atlantic to the Pacific, needed more in the way of rail transport to blend its many distinctive cuisines.

The nation contained a variety of these cuisines. There was that of New England, another in the Pennsylvania-Dutch country, and yet another in the South. There were the French infused food ways of Louisiana, the Hispanic influenced cuisines from Florida to Texas to California, and the Chinese cuisine of San Francisco. Practically every food eaten today was being grown, or raised, somewhere in the continental United States and its territories. But it required the upheaval of the Industrial Revolution and its many constituent parts to engineer the homogenization of these foods and America's food ways.

One of these constituent parts was the massive immigration that followed the Civil War – the immigrants drawn by the "carrots" of jobs and free land, and driven by the "stick" of population pressure in their native lands. European industrial capitalism, built on a surplus of workers requiring a surplus of food, had created too many workers and not enough food to go around. People had to go elsewhere because, astoundingly, in spite of the 30 million who emigrated to the United States, and the 20 million more who hived out to Canada, South America, Australia, and southern Africa, Europe's population more than doubled during the nineteenth century.[41]

While the number of new people to feed were reaching Ellis Island by the boatload, railroads were spanning the continent to abet the conversion of the nation's fertile lands into a vast granary. Livestock proliferated in the west, and new meat preservation techniques were developed. Gustavus F.

Swift and P. D. Armour established their packinghouses at Chicago's Union stockyards and employed refrigerated railway cars (invented in 1867) to ensure that dressed meat reached eastern butchers without spoiling.[42] This trade also reached across the Atlantic to ensure that meat became plentiful in the diet of many Europeans because it was cheap, coming not just from the United States, but also from Argentina, Australia, and New Zealand.

This was all part of a transportation revolution in which railroads and steamships became the vehicles of a movable feast, delivering meat and other perishables like fresh milk, vegetables, and fruits to the millions. Oranges reached them from Florida, where sweet oranges had been grown since at least 1579, along with bananas whose Silver Lake plantations subsequently lost out to those of the Caribbean; peaches arrived from Georgia and barrels of oysters could be found in the Midwest during the holiday season.[43]

At about the three-quarter mark of the nineteenth century, the Mason Jar and large pressure cookers began another sort of revolution, this one in home and, especially, in commercial canning, making still more different kinds of foods available year-round to people who otherwise would have never tasted them. Among these were pineapple, grapefruit, and many fish varieties, the condensed soups of Campbell's, and what would become the "57 Varieties" of Heinz.[44] In other words, the preservation of plenty went hand-in-hand with the production of plenty.

With each step west after the Civil War, more and more land became available for the production of ever more plenty. But ever increasing production drove down commodity prices from 1870 to the end of the century – these low prices high on the American farmer's list of grievances, which ranged from disproportionately high taxes and railroad shipping charges to governmental policies of high tariffs and deflation. Understandably, many started to leave the land. In 1850, close to 85 percent of Americans were engaged in farming or farm-related occupations. By 1900, this had been cut to 42 percent and by the end of the twentieth century to less than 2 percent; yet the production of plenty never faltered because industrialization was not confined to the factories. It was an increasingly mechanized agriculture that continued to briskly add to the nation's abundance.[45]

But despite (or perhaps because of) an increasingly varied diet, American suspicion of foods grew as fast as the industries that supplied them. Such distrust was evident in the reforming currents that swirled around individuals like Silvester Graham, Ellen White, spiritual head of the Seventh

Day Adventist Church, the Kellogg brothers, and C. W. Post. Food historian Reay Tannahill has viewed such currents as one of the nation's "recurring bouts of moral vegetarianism" ("how can you eat anything that looks out of eyes?" asked the graminivorous John H. Kellogg).[46] Yet, in giving us Graham Crackers, Postum (much of Post's career was spent belaboring real coffee), and Post Toasties, as well as lectures on the evils of masturbation (caused by eating meat),[47] they helped to give us brand names. The brand revolution was facilitated by a packaging revolution of the late nineteenth and early twentieth centuries. Countless commodities previously sold in bulk were now marketed in paper bags, paperboard cartons, bottles, and cans – all bearing brands – and all of which accelerated the art of peddling plenty. The claims and counterclaims of advertisers and promoters grew shrill as Americans became increasingly brand conscious.[48]

CHAPTER

19

THE FRONTIERS OF
FOREIGN FOODS

When Samuel Clemens (a.k.a. Mark Twain) visited Europe in 1878
he complained bitterly about the food, comparing it most unfavorably
with American fare. Before returning home, he composed a wish list
of comestibles he desired upon his return including Virginia bacon,
soft-shell crabs, Philadelphia terrapin soup, canvas-back duck from
Baltimore, Connecticut shad, green corn on the ear, butter beans, as-
paragus, string beans, American butter (he complained that European
butter had no salt); predictably apple pie, and curiously, frogs.

Leslie Brenner (1999)[1]

WITH APOLOGIES to Samuel Clemens there was no such thing as
"American fare" north of Mexico when he wrote, nor had there been for
close to two centuries, the remnants of pre-Columbian foodstuffs and cooking techniques notwithstanding. Since the seventeenth century, American
cuisine has been a work in progress, kneaded, shaped, and reshaped by
African, Asian, and European immigrants. The African contribution was in
place by the time of the Civil War, as was that of Northern Europe though
somewhat distorted by Native American influences.

But following the war, millions of southern and eastern Europeans,
along with a relative handful of Asians, arrived to take their turn at stir-
ring America's culinary melting pot. The new immigrants settled on both
coasts in large numbers but some, lured by the promise of free land in the
1862 Homestead Act, spread out into the interior, planting seeds of food
globalization as they went.

Railroads were even more effective in scattering migrants about. During the war, the Lincoln government had authorized the construction of two railroads One of these, the Central Pacific, extended eastward from California while the other, the Union Pacific, ran westward from Omaha. When joined with a golden spike at Promontory Point, Utah in 1869, the nation's first transcontinental railroad was completed, and by then two foreign cuisines – Chinese and Italian – had also become transcontinental.

TSAP SUI: CHINESE INFLUENCES

The Chinese had been West Coast settlers since the 1820s. With the beginning of the Gold Rush, many more arrived and some got into the San Francisco restaurant business to feed hungry miners. They later stayed in business by catering to more arriving Chinese: laborers to work in California canneries and agriculture, and those who laid track for the railroads. This clientele was mostly male – single men hoping to put together enough money to return to China, take a wife, and buy some land. Since the construction crews hired by the Central Pacific were mostly Chinese who wanted the same food they had eaten in San Francisco restaurants, Chinese cooks were employed to provide it.

And still more Chinese immigrants came to California seeking jobs so that the 7,500 counted in the 1850 census had increased to 105,000 by 1880. As a rule they were Cantonese, from southern China, whose dishes were based on rice and vegetables quickly cooked. The art of stir-frying, the use of spices such as raw or preserved ginger, ingredients like bean sprouts, and dishes such as fried rice, along with "Americanized" chow mein and chop suey (from the Cantonese *tsap sui* meaning "miscellaneous things") began to move east.[2]

However, the influence of Chinese food and the Chinese themselves ran afoul of American xenophobia when Congress yielded to public pressure and passed the Chinese Exclusion Act, which took effect in 1882 and was not repealed until 1946. With neither new arrivals nor fresh ideas to invigorate it, Chinese food in America became an increasingly poor rendition of the dishes of Canton.

SPAGHETTI AND RED WINE: ITALIAN INFLUENCES

In Omaha, it was European laborers and some Civil War veterans who began laying track in the opposite direction. The Irish were the most numerous among them but they were joined by a significant number of

Italians, who had been arriving in the United States since 1850. Like the Chinese, the Italians were from the southern part of their country, and from Sicily, which meant a diet based on pasta, olive oil, cheese, tomato sauce, and wine; and these foods were furnished by the railroad after the Italians rebelled at consuming any more potatoes, beans, bully beef, and whisky, the diet favored by Irish workers.

Some of the Italians never left Omaha, and a "little Italy," one of the nation's first, sprang up with restaurants that served meatballs and marinara sauce over spaghetti, and red wine from straw-thatched bottles of Chianti atop checkered tablecloths. Other Italians continued west from Utah to open more restaurants, transform themselves into truck gardeners, cultivating cherished old country vegetables like artichokes, zucchini, and broccoli (California now grows 90 percent of the nation's broccoli crop), and become movers and shakers in the burgeoning California wine industry.

America's new transcontinental railroad made it possible to ship California produce to the east in less than a week – lightning fast when compared to a 120-day voyage around Cape Horn – and immense wheat farms sprang up in the Livermore and San Joaquin valleys. Their production of 16 million tons in 1870, although just a fraction of the nation's total 1869 crop (of almost 300,000 million bushels), represented nearly a quarter of its 70 million bushels produced in 1866.[3] In like fashion, California wine production, which totaled around 4 million gallons in 1870, increased to over 20 million gallons by 1890.

CHILLIES AND GARBANZOS: HISPANIC INFLUENCES

The real estate acquired through war with Mexico abruptly made Americans out of many Mexicans, and both Spain and Mexico continued to exert a vast influence over the cuisine in a belt running from southern California to Texas. From Louisiana to Florida, Spain's influence continued along the Gulf Coast. Hispanic cuisine is bean based, utilizing New World legumes like pintos and black beans, along with the Old World chickpeas (garbanzos).[4] It is also tortilla based, with their preparation (before *masa harina* and tortilla presses) claiming many of a woman's waking hours even before the tortillas were metamorphosed into tacos, tostados, and enchiladas.

Chilli peppers, tomatoes, tomatillos, pumpkin seeds, pine nuts, garlic, onions, squashes, cheeses, and spicy sausages also figured into meals for many in Texas and the desert Southwest, with beef, often barbequed, central to the diets of practically everyone. But why not beef, with Texas sending an average of some half-million head of cattle a year up the Chisholm Trail to Abilene?[5] These were longhorn cattle, descendents of the same breed still raised along the Guadlaquiver River in Spain. They were first brought to America in 1493 and, as in Spain, tended by mounted cowboys.[6] The first serious cattle drive north of Mexico took place during the last years of Spain's tenure in Louisiana, when a large herd was driven from Texas to help feed Spanish troops during the American Revolution.

Beef also entered the diet in chilli con carne, a dish popular in Texas while it still was a territory of Mexico. The "Bowl of Red" has suffered from the allegation that it was a Texas invention and not truly Mexican. But this is a definitional argument. Stews containing chilli peppers, beans, and assorted bits of animal protein have been eaten in Mexico for thousands of years. So the charge must be because the Texas contribution has often been to eliminate the beans and base the dish almost solely on beef, the one ingredient the Aztecs and their predecessors did not have. Chilli con carne lies at the heart of Tex-Mex cuisine that is also disparaged in some quarters, but is a part of a fusion cuisine that represents an early triumph of globalization, in the case of chilli, Old World animal flesh and New World plants with or without the beans.

Given today's popularity of buttery guacamole, it seems strange that avocados, until recently, were not a part of the fusion. They were first used by pre-Columbian Americans, then by the Spanish conquerors of Mexico and Central America. In 1651, a Spanish priest, Bernabé Cobe, described three kinds – Mexican, West Indian, and Guatemalan, and a century later, George Washington, then a nineteen year old visitor to Barbados, tasted the West Indian variety (he didn't like it). By 1825, American avocados were growing in Africa, Polynesia, and the Sandwich Islands (Hawaii), but it was not until 1871 that the Mexican variety was commercially cultivated in California and, later still, that the Mexican and the Guatemalan varieties were combined to become the Hass avocado.[7] Toward the end of the nineteenth century avocados were popular in New York, and the West Indian variety was growing in Florida by the early twentieth century. Yet, only belatedly did avocados become an integral part of the "Hispanic" food influences.[8]

Spanish influences, of course, were not limited to Texas and the American southwest. Much of the cuisine of coastal Florida was Spanish Caribbean in orientation, and Cuban cuisine could be found from Tampa to Key West to St. Augustine on the Atlantic seaboard. Black beans and rice ("Moors and Christians" when the rice is not yellowed with saffron) are at the core of Cuban-American cooking. So are soups made from black beans or garbanzos (chick peas), chicken and rice, roast pork, fish and shrimp, bollitos (deep-fried nuggets of mashed black-eyed peas and garlic), olive oil, Cuban bread, and Cuban coffee.

CREOLE AND CAJUN: FRENCH AND AFRICAN INFLUENCES

In 1533, Catherine de Medici moved from Florence to France to become the Queen of Henri II. Her love of spinach brought forth the still-used the designation of spinach dishes as "Florentine." These dishes were prepared by the entourage of Italian cooks who accompanied Catherine, and her cooks profoundly altered French cooking techniques and ingredients, leading later on to the famous French *haute cuisine*.[9] In some ways these events influenced Louisiana cookery, but French influences also arrived from the French Caribbean and French Canada, and it is sometimes forgotten that many other cultures took part in its creation.

Among them were German culinary traditions, thanks to thousands of farmers, mostly from Alsace-Lorraine, who were lured to Louisiana early in its history with the promise of free land. Spanish cuisine was well-established during Spain's three decades or so of rule and, just before it ended at the turn of the nineteenth century, Sicilian settlers arrived to be joined by some 25,000 Irish refugees from the potato famine by the middle of that century.[10] Arguably, however, the greatest influence was that of West Africa because both slaves and free blacks seem to have been in the forefront of fashioning those cuisines that are now called Cajun and Creole.[11]

The French Revolution impelled refugees from the "Terror" and its guillotine to Louisiana at the same time that it touched off the slave insurrection in San Domingue. That revolution evicted thousands of whites, many of whom relocated in Louisiana along with their slaves and free colored retainers to continue sugarcane cultivation under old management in a new locale.[12] But in addition to sugar-making skills, the slaves and free coloreds carried with them the cuisine that had been elaborated in a now independent Haiti – a blending of French and African influences that relied heavily on local seafood (especially oysters, shrimp, and crayfish), along with sausages and rice.

The Spanish word *criollo*, employed to mean "born in America," was used in Louisiana to connote roughly the same thing and therefore "Creole" cooking, by definition, had an American birth even if the midwives were foreign. In New Orleans's Vieux Carrè, which burned in 1788 but was rebuilt under Spanish rule, Haitian cookery was infused with Asian rice, brought to Louisiana in 1718 by the British; chicory from southern Europe; American plants such as tomatoes, potatoes, red beans, squash, chayote (called a mirliton in New Orleans); chilli peppers, introduced from Mexico; okra and cowpeas from Africa; and filé powder (dried sassafras leaves) from the Choctaw Indians. As in San Domingue, however, the foundation of the cuisine was constructed of fish and crustaceans.

So was the cuisine of the Acadians whose exile from Acadia in French Canada had transplanted around 5,000 "Cajuns" (a corruption of Acadian) settlers to south central Louisiana by 1800. Cajun cookery employs roughly the same ingredients as Creole cookery and is often called "Creole," which it is, because it too was born in America. Historically, at least one distinction has been that Creole is city cooking and Cajun its rural counterpart. Either way, Cajun with its hot and spicy flavors is typical of everyday Caribbean meals. Crawfish (crayfish, crawdads, mudbugs) which arguably characterize Cajun as opposed to Creole cooking, are found all over the hemisphere, but are seldom eaten outside of Louisiana. They are eaten hot and boiled, inhabit gumbos, and when deep-fried are known as "Cajun popcorn."

Gallic cooking did some migrating from Louisiana. Eighteenth- and nineteenth-century settlers carried it up the Mississippi and its tributaries to influence the cuisine of St. Louis, Terre Haute on the Wabash, and Louisville on the Ohio. The introduction of the steamboat – the first was the *New Orleans* in 1812 – transformed the city it was named for into a major port, and thereafter river traffic, including that of luxury steamboats, ensured the reinforcement of Creole cookery in all river towns.[13]

GRITS, GREENS, AND BEANS: AFRICAN INFLUENCES AGAIN

Along coastal Florida, Hispanic hands often guided food preparation, but inland the diet was that of the Old South, shaped around the "hog and hominy" core of southern cooking that first took root in Virginia. Save for a few sections of the south, beef was rare and fresh milk even more so. The Old South enjoyed a cuisine that, like its Creole counterpart, was crafted largely by African cooks. They worked with familiar foods from Africa, like okra, yams, collard greens, cowpeas, and watermelons to feed their own families or, on some plantations, all of the slaves. These were complemented by molasses, corn bread, grits (similar to millet porridge in Africa), chitterlings, fried fish, salt pork, fat pork, and the occasional ham. The African cooks for the big house, however, also put together dishes of greens and beans and cornbread to go with the roasted pigs, turtle soups, steaks, boiled mutton, deep-fried turkeys, fried chicken, chicken and dumplings, and sherbets. As in the southwest, during warm weather much of the meat was barbequed outside to escape the heat of the kitchen.

In Africa, foods were highly seasoned with native melegueta peppers as well as American chilli peppers, and southern dishes were equally well seasoned but mostly with red peppers. The slaves also employed sesame oil, peanut sauce, walnuts, and Jerusalem artichoke pickles as condiments. In and around Charleston, rice has been used since its introduction in the seventeenth century – a classic Charleston dish is "Country Captain," a curried chicken dish that blends African cooking with the spices of India served over steamed rice. Other slave-inspired favorites of the Carolina Low Country include red rice (rice cooked with tomatoes and seasonings), rice pilaf (pronounced perloo from the English pilau), and she-crab soup, which counted among the "fancy foods" as did that grand dessert, "syllabub."

Southern cooking depends heavily on the frying pan (with lard or oil and cornmeal for breading). This is where catfish are fried, okra turned into fritters, and corn-batter deep-fried (the results were later called "hush puppies"); where cowpeas, pork, and peppers become "Hopping John," and batter is transformed into corn bread or, when cracklings are added, crackling bread.

BRATWURST AND BEER: GERMANIC INFLUENCES

In the north, by contrast, people relied more on the oven and baking than on the stove top and frying. Stovetop cooking had the advantage of keeping houses cooler in summer, whereas baking helped to warm a house in cooler weather. It was an advantage much appreciated by the Dutch in New York, who introduced cole-slaw (kool = cabbage, sla = salad), the baked cookie (koekje), and waffles. In Pennsylvania, baking, which had often been done in three-footed redware, became more of a science after the first American iron cook stove was cast in 1762 – a stove put to good use by immigrants from Germanic Europe, mostly from the Rhineland, who had begun arriving during the last years of the seventeenth century. These were the Mennonites who, along with their cooking, were erroneously labeled "Pennsylvania Dutch" instead of "Pennsylvania Deutsch."

That cookery focused on the pig – all of it – from the ears and snout for head cheese, to the feet for souse. Leftover scraps were mixed with corn-meal, shaped into a loaf, and called "scrapple," one of Pennsylvania's most famous dishes, rivaled only by "Philadelphia Pepper Pot," also a Pennsylvania Dutch creation. This cuisine is distinctive, among other things, because of its seasonings, which have always featured sage and coriander for sausages but became a trinity after the autumn crocus, whose stamens yield saffron, was introduced by the Schwenkenfelders from Silesia in 1736.[14]

For Europeans sugar was still dear, but in America it was cheap, and the term "Pennsylvania Dutch" is nearly synonymous with sweet baked goods. Cakes, cookies, and pies were inevitable at every meal. So, too, were their renowned cinnamon buns, puddings, apple butter, and applesauce, all good reasons why the Pennsylvania Dutch are said to bear much of the respon-sibility for America's sweet tooth. Pickles, also generally sweet, are another of the Pennsylvania Dutch specialties – everything from beet pickles to bread and butter pickles to watermelon rinds.

This was the cuisine carried west to Ohio, Indiana, and Illinois by the Amish Mennonites. Other Germans also moved west – on flatboats down the Ohio River to Cincinnati, southern Indiana, St. Louis, and Missouri's interior – and via the Erie Canal and the Great Lakes to Wisconsin and northern Indiana. Iowa, equidistant from both Missouri and Wisconsin, got German settlers from both directions.

At Cincinnati many Germans left the river to help transform the town into "Porkopolis" – the place where mast-fed pigs from the Appalachian Mountains arrived on Ohio River flatboats. Their flesh was packed into brine-filled barrels for long-distance marketing, and their fat became the foundation of Cincinnati's soap manufacturing empire.[15]

The German taste for pork also spawned the Wisconsin and Indiana sausage industry, which turned out Thueringer blood sausage, summer sau-sage, liver sausage, knackwurst, beerwurst, and bratwurst. Still another of their sausages was the frankfurter wurst reminding us that the Germans gave America its two most famous sandwiches – the hot dog named for

Frankfurt in Germany, and the hamburger, named for Germany's port city of Hamburg.

The Germans also raised dairy cattle, made butter and, in collaboration with their Swiss immigrant cousins, began the Wisconsin cheese industry. Until then cheese in America had been produced under an English influence which meant that most varieties were versions of cheddar. But Limburger, and brick (an American milder version of Limburger) were among the first German cheeses produced, and as the Italians entered the business, Wisconsin began duplicating most all of the famous Old World cheeses.

Dumplings, sauerkraut, schnitzel, sauerbraten, rye and pumpernickel breads were still other German specialties that were blended into cuisines originally introduced by the English – the whole accelerating a Europeanizing of American cuisine.

German beer, yet another specialty, was welcome in a country where beer (actually ale) had fallen on hard times. In the absence of barley malt, English settlers had from the beginning of their residence in North America brewed ale from persimmons, pumpkins, maize, maple sugar – just about anything they could get their hands on that would ferment. That the result was not always satisfactory can be discerned from the great quantities of English ale they imported. But whether homemade or imported the ale was made the English way – a top-fermented brew that was heavy, dark, and cloudy.[16] Hard cider, therefore, was always a serious competitor of ale, or at least it was until the techniques of brewing lager beer (also called pilsner) reached America with German immigrants.[17]

Lager was a bottom-fermented brew ("top" and "bottom" signifying where yeast collects in the vat) that turned out light, clean, and crisp – well suited to America's warm summer temperatures, and a beverage that sparkled when served in glasses the consumer could see through. This was a much different experience from heavy, opaque tankards containing heavy, opaque ale. But to produce lager and store it (lager means to store), cold temperatures were required. In fact, because bottom fermentation needed ice for the kegs to rest on while the bubbles worked and because the final product required caves and tunnels to keep it cool, the brewing season did not include the summer months. Milwaukee and St. Louis both satisfied these beer brewing requirements and became its early centers, as well as centers of German populations.

Milwaukee had three rivers – the Milwaukee, the Kinnickinnic, and the Menominee. All converged on Lake Michigan to provide water, ice, and caverns. Tunnels could also be bored into bluffs along the lake. In 1844, Jacob Best took note of what seemed to be an ideal location and founded breweries that a few years later became the property of Frederick Pabst and Frederick Miller respectively. A third brewery was founded by August Krug who died in 1856, whereupon a young bookkeeper of the firm, Joseph Schlitz, took the helm. Together, Pabst, Miller, and Schlitz made Milwaukee famous.

Meanwhile, in St. Louis, the Busch brothers, Adolphus and Ulrich, had each married daughters of brewer Eberhard Anheuser. Adolphus, who worked for Anheuser, ultimately gained control of the brewery, and in 1879 it was named the Anheuser-Busch Brewing Association, launching another goliath in the brewing business. More firms followed as Copenhagen's Carlsberg brewery developed a pure brewer's yeast that brought an end to brewing failures, and ice machines were invented so that breweries were not necessarily tied to rivers and lakes that froze.[18] Cincinnati, Detroit, and Chicago – also centers of German immigrants – began to boast of their breweries and from this Midwest beginning, lager brewing spread across the land to both coasts.

There was a concomitant spread of barley and hop cultivation. Prior to the brewing boom, hops were either imported from England, cultivated in small plots, or gathered in the wild. But supply uncertainty ultimately stimulated commercial growing. New York State was the big hop producer until the 1940s, when its cultivation spread to California, Washington, and Oregon. Now the latter two states and Idaho account for most of the U.S. hops, and North Dakota leads the nation in barley production.

None of this is to say that German foods and culture were always enthusiastically received by mainstream America – not after warring with Germany twice in the first half of the twentieth century. In fact, altering food appellations became part of the conflicts. The name "sauerkraut" was temporarily changed to "victory cabbage" during the first of these wars, and "German toast," became (permanently) "French toast."

TEA AND BOILED PUDDING: ENGLISH INFLUENCES

Despite foreign culinary intrusions, a stubborn adherence to English foods and English ways of preparing them continued to dominate – especially in New England. The colonists had brought a British sweet tooth with them and used maple sugar and syrup, along with molasses, to satisfy it. Later the sweetener became cane sugar, and falling prices for both cane and beet sugar in the nineteenth century meant that British-style puddings, always sweet, became even sweeter. Tea was sweetened and served at teatime with sweets, as were tisanes made from elderberry or any other handy local plant. Tart cranberries, an American fruit (*Vaccinium macrocarpum*) (also known as bearberries because bears are fond of them, and called bounce berries because their ripeness can be determined by bouncing them) begged for sugar and a good deal of it went into pies, puddings, and tarts. Cranberry juice, loaded with sugar by the New Englanders, has been pointed to as the beginning of the American soft-drink industry.[19]

Nor did the colonists abandon an extravagant use of salt – so excessive in fact that the average Englishman in the eighteenth century is said to have taken in so much salt that it should have killed him but did not because of a well-developed tolerance for the mineral. This was probably the case in New England as well where beef was corned, pork salted, fish dried with salt, and heavy doses of salt were tossed into the cooking pot.

One-pot boiled meals, such as corned beef and vegetables or beef a la mode, which evolved into the "Yankee pot roast," were frequently on the table followed by a boiled pudding for dessert. An elaborate dish called succotash, constructed with corned beef and fowl, along with beans, corn, and turnips also made for a hearty meal. Cornmeal was turned into johnnycake, porridge, and flap (or slap) jacks. Beans, cooked with pork and molasses, were generally served with brown bread made from rye steamed over the pot of beans. The New England climate was cold enough to grow rye which was often combined with cornmeal to become the "rye'n'injun" (now called Boston Brown Bread) generally available at mealtime.[20] Some wheat was grown and pies made from its flour were treated as seriously by New Englanders as they were by Pennsylvania Dutch.

As early as 1640 the Massachusetts Bay Colony began to market codfish and, by the end of the seventeenth century, cod fishing had elevated New England from a starving colony to a commercial powerhouse.[21] The best cod were shipped to Iberia, the worst to slaves in the West Indies, and a "codfish aristocracy" in Salem arose to build mansions adorned with wooden codfish, and place a codfish image on coins, seals, stamps and letterheads.[22] New Englanders were never great fish eaters themselves, but codfish did enter their diet as codfish cakes (or balls), often for breakfast, and in chowders.

And, finally, housewives, as their grandmothers before them, blended native corn with beans, made "hasty pudding" with sweetened cornmeal porridge, and used the plentiful pumpkin lavishly – today people think pumpkin comes only in cans or pies – in baked, boiled, roasted, and dried forms as the Native Americans had originally taught them. Indeed pumpkin went into everything from puddings to pies after first – like all vegetables – undergoing a fierce boiling.[23]

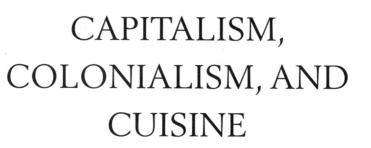

CAPITALISM, COLONIALISM, AND CUISINE

*In short, Europe's colonization of Africa had nothing to do with
differences between European and African peoples as white racists
assume. Rather, it was due to accidents of geography and bio-
geography – in particular, to the continent's different areas, axes,
and suites of wild plant and animal species. That is, the different
historical trajectories of Africa and Europe stem ultimately from
differences in real estate.*

Jared Diamond (1997)[1]

ARGUABLY, THE UNITED STATES and Europe benefited more than
most of the world's regions from the quickened tempo of food globalization that followed the Columbian Exchange because, by increasing food
supplies, it fueled their respective Industrial Revolutions.

This synergism was first seen in Great Britain, where the calories in sugar
and potatoes from the New World stoked labor.[2] In the towns and cities
where that labor was readily available, and where even more labor could
be accommodated, industries began to arise. Cities and towns, of course,
raised little food so that workers had to be fed from rural areas – the food
reaching urban centers via an increasingly complex network of railroads. As
this occurred, more and more rural individuals were attracted to city life
and factory wages, draining the countryside of manpower. Consequently,

agriculture, too, had to be industrialized, which, in turn, meant even more migration to the cities because far fewer hands were needed in the fields.

Food production also became mechanized, its transportation and distribution organized, and its processing, capitalized.[3] Railroads, steamships, and developments in canning, freezing, and chilling foods made their shipment possible over long distances. It was nothing short of a revolution in transportation and technology – a revolution in which food production, although of paramount importance for practically all of humankind's stay on the planet, came to be taken for granted in the industrialized countries practically overnight. Food processing and marketing, not production, lunged to the forefront of the food industry.

Industrialization, coupled with nationalism, also changed approaches to food and its consumption. In the Middle Ages there were no national cuisines but, then again, there was no nationalism either. As nations emerged, however, peoples and governments went to great lengths to set themselves apart, and although Europeans all had access to the same ingredients, their manner of preparing them became distinguishing features as "national" dishes emerged. The English boasted that roast beef and beer – plain food but good – was central to their being: "For your Beef-eating, Beer drinking Britons are souls, Who will shed their last drop for their country and king."[4] By contrast their French neighbors ate decadent foods dressed up with poisons so that one never knew what they were eating. The French counterattacked with the claim that beef was a common food whose fat was crippling. They also countered with another means of distinction involving a philosophy of food consumption.[5]

The *grande cuisine* of nineteenth-century French restaurants, for example, emphasized the pleasures of eating and drinking. For the diners the *grande cuisine* also symbolized the cultural superiority of France over its more puritanical neighbors, who found less joy at the table. The neighbors, however, were not impressed, and called the French "frogs" because of their partiality to frog legs; whereas the Germans became "krauts," and the English "limeys." One was, in a very nationalistic way, what one ate.[6]

Moving back to the nationalism-free Middle Ages, there were also no food fads then, save among small elites. Peasants engaged in subsistence agriculture were a conservative lot with neither the means nor the inclination to experiment with fashion, and the fashion for all classes was Roman, at least in principal, with grain on the menu but not much meat. New foods for the wealthy were spread about gradually; the use of butter radiated out from Germany, saffron from Spain, and dried fruits from southern Europe. But this relatively static situation changed with industrialization. Far fewer people were tied to the land, and food-marketing techniques were brought to bear on workers with wages. Demand was created for countless new products – especially those made from sugar and products that came in cans and bottles – beginning the food crazes we still live with.[7]

Yet, if industrialization meant a better life for the fortunate, it managed to add to the ranks of the poor. During the second half of the eighteenth century, English population growth outdistanced grain production creating, among other things, a homeless class that down to the middle of the nineteenth century comprised between 10 and 20 percent of the population. Prices for wheat and other staples skyrocketed, reducing the quantities of bread, cheese, and even turnips that could be afforded and putting meat out of reach for those not among the ranks of the fortunate. For those that were, such as the eighteenth century canon of St. Paul's Cathedral in London, it was an entirely different world. At age 77, he calculated that over the course of his lifetime he had consumed 44 wagonloads of meat and drink that could have saved 100 people from starving to death.[8]

Life got no better for the poor during the nineteenth century when industrialization quadrupled the population of London, among other cities, and bread, potatoes, and tea constituted the bulk of the diet, with perhaps the addition of a little milk and sugar once a week and a piece of bacon once a year. And average height fell precipitously during most of the century – especially for the poor – only taking a pronounced upward turn following the beginning of the twentieth century. Thus, at the close of the Napoleonic Wars, the average male worker in Britain was some five inches shorter than his upper class counterpart, close to half the children born in towns died before they were five years old, and those who did not were likely to be badly undernourished, stunted, and deformed by rickets.[9] In light of this it does not seem surprising that during recruitment for the Boer War (1899–1902) fully 37 percent of the volunteers were pronounced unfit for military duty.[10] This scandal touched off a debate, in Parliament which revealed that in 1883 the minimum height for recruits had been lowered from 5 feet 6 inches to 5 feet 3 inches and then again, in 1902, to just five feet.[11]

As the middle of the nineteenth century drew near, Irish peasants, despite, or perhaps because of, having dined almost exclusively on potatoes for a century and a half, were considerably sturdier than their English counterparts. Average potato yields were six tons per acre, as opposed to less than one ton for grains, and the "conacre" system gave peasants small plots of land to grow them on in return for agricultural labor to British (and Irish) landlords.[12] Dreary though their meals may have been, the Irish prospered demographically, their population almost doubling between 1800 and 1845 (increasing from 4.5 million to 8 million people), thanks to this New World crop. Not only were the Irish healthy, their potatoes permitted them to marry early because of food security, and younger mothers could more easily nurse their newborn through an always precarious infancy into childhood.[13]

Perhaps the landlords took Irish robustness as a signal that they could be squeezed even more. Conacres shrank as land planted in grains increased, impelling many peasants to seasonally migrate to Scotland for the harvest, their absence reducing potato consumption in Ireland while simultaneously generating money to purchase food.[14]

It was not that an Irish vulnerability to famine was unappreciated. The potato crop had failed in 1816, causing much hunger, and again in 1821, this time leaving perhaps 50,000 dead. The crop failed again in 1831, 1835, and 1836, but not yet from the fungal disease *Phytophthora infestans* that brought on the great famine that began in 1845.[15] It started in the Low Countries – the fungus apparently arriving with New World potato varieties imported, ironically, to heighten potato disease resistance – then spread to England and Ireland. Called "late blight," the disease caused apparently healthy-looking potatoes to suddenly rot, turning into a black mush, and in 1845 Ireland lost 40 percent of its crop. But the worst was yet to come. Infected potatoes had been left in the fields and the spores of P. *infestans* saw to it that scarcely 10 percent of the 1846 potato crop could be salvaged.[16]

At first the British government turned a blind eye to the Irish plight, and exports to England of grain, meat, vegetables, and dairy products continued from that ravaged land, the conservatives in Parliament arguing that the famine was an act of God, and Irish relief – giving them food – would not only go against God's will but would also paralyze trade. Yet, when America sent relief ships, international embarrassment gave free-traders their chance to get the Corn Laws repealed, which had restricted grain imports from other countries to keep prices high, a repeal that did nothing to help out the Irish. Rather it eliminated Ireland's favored status as an exporter to the British market, prompting landlords to switch from growing wheat to raising cattle, an enterprise in which peasant labor was no longer needed.[17] Eviction from their lands, hunger, and illnesses through 1848 caused the death or migration of between one and a half and two million people – a loss from which Ireland, with today's population less than half of that of 1841, has clearly never recovered.[18]

England's repeal of the Corn Laws in 1846 signaled the triumph of the industrialists and free trade over landed and agricultural interests, which meant that much of the food to feed industrial workers now had to be imported. Australia and New Zealand sent meat and butter, and the economies of countries like Ireland and Denmark were geared to an English demand for bacon and dairy products.[19] Fortunately, the nineteenth century witnessed ever greater speed in ocean crossings and, consequently, lower transportation costs that fostered trade expansion and market integration, and brought on a spurt in food globalization. Much of the latter was connected to colonial economies and not just to that of Ireland.[20]

Tea, coffee, and sugar were products that reached European countries directly from those colonies, and brightened the life of even the poor. After all, a cup of hot and sweetened tea could make a cold meal seem like a hot one,[21] and sweetened foods, like preserves that required no refrigeration because sugar is a preservative, became the nineteenth-century convenience foods for the harried families of factory workers.[22] Meats (lamb, mutton, beef), dairy products, and, later, tropical fruits flowed into the British market from Australia and New Zealand after 1870, and especially after 1882, with the beginning of refrigerated shipping, while wheat reached England from its ex-colony, North America.[23]

Iberian imperialism may have opened both Old and New Worlds to an avalanche of new foods, but other imperial powers were not far behind in moving foods around the globe. Illustrative is a rice dish on the streets of Cairo called *kushuri* made with lentils, onions, and spices – a favorite that the locals believe to be their own. Yet, it originated in India as *kitchri* and was brought to British-dominated Egypt by British forces from British India.[24] In England, a similar dish called *kedgeree* had accompanied returnees from India with appetites for curries, mulligatawny (a soup made with meat, dal, chapattis), and chutney. This, in turn, not only created a British demand for turmeric, curry powders, and gooseberry chutney to substitute for the mango chutneys of India, but made Indian restaurants ubiquitous.[25]

Similarly a taste for the myriad spicy dishes of a *rijistafel* (rice table) and other Indonesian specialties such as *nasi* from the Dutch East Indian colonies became epidemic in the Netherlands, and Indonesian restaurants to serve them proliferated (rijistafel is the closest thing to a Dutch national dish). Exotic stews served in Lisbon – *muambas, mufetes,* and *cachupas* – were inspired by the African colonies of Angola and Mozambique and the ex-colony of Brazil.[26] The ingredients like dende or palm oil and manioc are equally exotic but now readily available in that temperate city. The Portuguese also contributed to and developed a fondness for the dishes of Goa, which combined tropical foods, spices of the East Indies, and Eurasian meats and brought home recipes for dishes such as *galinha à Xanti* (chicken marinated in herbs and spices) and *bojé* (fritters made from onions, spices, and chickpeas).

In France, couscous and its companion the *merguez* sausage flavored with *harissa* (a hot chilli pepper paste) became part of the cuisine – a colonial contribution from the Magreb (Algeria, Morroco, and Tunesia). Another colonial contribution – this one from Viet Nam – helps account for the fashionable finger-foods of Paris – tidbits wrapped in lettuce leaves and spring rolls. North African and Vietnamese restaurants continue to be wildly popular in France.[27]

By the nineteenth century, chocolate as an adult drink had pretty well lost out to coffee and tea. But Dutch, English, and Swiss pioneer confectioners abruptly changed the cacao focus from a drink to a solid, and the mass production of chocolates began, culminating in the establishment of Milton Hershey's American empire in 1903, which saw a town grow into the world's largest chocolate factory. The dairy farms around Hershey, Pennsylvania supplied 60,000 gallons of milk daily, but the other components were of foreign origin. The sugar, until Fidel Castro at any rate, came from vast Hershey-owned sugarcane estates in Cuba, and the cacao originated from a variety of locales.

Latin America had been the major nineteenth-century cacao supplier, but the Portuguese spoiled this by introducing the plant to São Tomé and Principe (islands off Africa's West Coast). By 1905, this pair of islands had become the world's leading exporter of cacao beans. Yet, as demand spiraled upward cacao cultivation moved to nearby British colonies like the Gold Coast (now Ghana), the dominant producer by the 1920s. Soon, however, Nigerian and Ivory Coast production was rivaling that of the Gold Coast and other African countries also became exporters. Africa's domination of cacao also faded, however, and by the 1990s production had shifted to Indonesia on one side of the globe and to Brazil on the other.[28]

Coffee's fortunes followed a similar, if less erratic, course. In the nine-teenth century, upwards of 95 percent of the world's coffee was produced in Latin America. But during the twentieth century, colonial regimes in Africa brought coffee and its production back to its home continent in places as diverse as Ethiopia, Kenya, Angola, and Uganda. Today, in the aftermath of colonialism, Ethiopia and Uganda continue among Africa's chief producers and have been joined by the Ivory Coast.[29]

The temperance movement in England ushered in an era of record tea consumption. Millions became "tee-totalers" and tea rolled into the British Islands from British India and as well as from China – reduced in the second-half of the nineteenth century to near colonial status.[30] Other beverages, or least their ingredients, also moved about in the nineteenth-century colonial world.

Kava (genus *Piper*) has been cultivated in the South Pacific for close to 3,000 years for the narcotic properties of its roots. These are turned first into a pulp and then a soporific drink long employed in rituals but also put to a secular, recreational use. In the nineteenth century kava became a cash crop to meet a pharmaceutical demand in Germany and France, and this market remains. In addition, there was an attempt to make a kava-based soft drink in Germany.[31]

Khat (*Catha edulis*) is another plant with narcotic properties – although the origins of this one lie on the other side of the globe from kava – probably in the Ethiopian highlands. It is used by many in the Horn of Africa and southwestern Arabia. A beverage is sometimes made from khat leaves (and "bush tea" still is) but more often in the past than today; now the leaves are mostly chewed. Khat shares a geographic cradle with coffee and, like coffee, helps to promote wakefulness – important for Muslims who pray for long hours – especially during Ramadan.

But the drug was equally popular with Yemenite Jews who started migrating to Ottoman-ruled Palestine in the nineteenth century. By the time Israel was established in 1948, about one-third of Yemen's Jews had migrated and most of the rest subsequently followed. Not surpris-ingly then, khat production and consumption is legal in Israel even though it is a scheduled drug on the United Nation's 1971 Convention's List of Psychotropic Substances and, consequently, at least theoretically, illegal in nearly 140 countries. Most of these countries, however, par-ticularly those with large numbers of North African immigrants, are not rigorous in enforcing the ban. Khat parties – social events in countries like Yemen – provide an excuse for enjoying the drug with friends in a relaxed atmosphere.[32]

Kola (genus *Cola*) is the best known and most widely traveled of these relatively obscure beverage ingredients that became nineteenth century curiosities in the larger world. A native of West African forests, the kola nut (about the size of a walnut), like khat, is a stimulant and a masticatory. It delivers both theobromine and caffeine to stimulate the nervous system for which it has been prized for millennia. Kola nuts – along with gold and salt – were the most valuable long-distance trade commodities in the Volta basin of West Africa, and the nuts had spread all the way to East Africa by the time the Portuguese showed up to spearhead European colonialism.

Kola nuts impart a pleasant taste to food and water, which contributed to their medicinal reputation – a reputation that that was known in the seventeenth-century Caribbean where a Jamaican planter began growing them to perk up despondent slaves. Later, the French transplanted kola from Africa to their islands of Martinique and Guadeloupe, and the British introduced seedlings to the East Indies. During the last half of the nineteenth century, kola nuts enjoyed a brisk demand in Great Britain, France, and the United States for use in pharmaceuticals and as a flavoring for cola-based soft drinks.

Another use of kola nuts stemmed from the belief that they imparted courage to their consumers. As a result they were traditionally distributed on African battlefields. This might be written off as superstition yet, it is interesting to note that in 1890, the German War Office ordered thirty tons of the nuts after conducting experiments on their courage-inducing effects.[33]

Tropical crops, especially bananas, also flowed out of the British, French, and U.S. Caribbean, and in the case of the United States, fruit companies were engaged simultaneously in teaching people to eat lots of bananas and people of the Caribbean basin to grow them. They succeeded in both enterprises. By the 1920s, bananas were commonplace in the dinner pails of laborers and the lunch boxes of school children, while the United Fruit Company, which had begun operations in Costa Rica in 1874, had become an empire directing the affairs of numerous Caribbean basin nations.[34]

The machinery of the nineteenth-century Industrial Revolution was also greased by colonial enterprise. Harnessing the energy in water and fossil fuels, then using it to power the motors that drove vehicles and factories, required lubrication – and more of it than was available in Europe. People cooked with oils, to be sure – even used them for cosmetic purposes – but olive oil, animal fats, walnut oil, even linseed oil and fish oil were regarded as precious commodities. In the eighteenth century, just a little fat or butter for bread could be a "cherished luxury" and in the nineteenth century all of these fats and oils combined could not meet the many lubrication demands of steam-powered engines, let alone cooking and soap-making needs.[35] The Europeans were once again forced to look to their colonies – this time for the tropical oils that they could produce in abundance.[36]

Coconut oil was one of these. It flowed into Europe from India, but sailing schooners and, a bit later, tramp steamers also fetched copra (dried or smoked coconut meat) from the Pacific to be pressed in European refineries for still more oil.[37] From the 1840s on, coconuts were grown as a plantation crop in the colonies. This coconut commercialization was spurred along by the discovery that coconuts could be utilized in dynamite production.[38]

The early nineteenth century also witnessed a brisk traffic in palm oil from Africa. Around mid-century, however, West African seedlings were transplanted to Southeast Asia. This had no immediate effect on palm oil production, but in the early twentieth century the oil palm industry in Sumatra and Malaya caught fire. This was about the same time that oil palms were introduced to Guatemala, Panama, and Honduras by the United Fruit company although, again, there was a lag and commercial planting did not begin until 1940.[39]

The palm oil kernels shipped to Europe were originally pressed for candle-making and, of course, as a lubricant for machinery. But after the invention of beef-fat margarine in 1869, it was only a matter of time before European beef fats would become insufficient for the spread's manufacture and, in 1907, palm oil was put to work by margarine makers. Oils were hydrogenated for the first time in that same decade so that palm oil also became a foundation for shortenings.[40] A dividend of no small consequence was that coconut and palm kernel processing also yielded a high-quality feed-cake for livestock.[41]

Coconut and palm oils dominated the oil market for much of the twentieth century, but other oils arrived from colonies as well. By the mid-nineteenth century, Senegal was producing peanut oil for the French market, and, after the Suez Canal was opened in 1869, peanut oil reached Europe from India. Its pleasant nutty flavor earned it a place in European kitchens, an acceptance facilitated by the inability of Europe to satisfy its demand for olive oil.[42] Most peanut oil, however, was transformed into margarine and shortening, and its cake too fed livestock. Moreover at the turn of the twentieth century, George Washington Carver at the Tuskegee Institute in the United States was showing the world some 300 uses for peanuts and their by-products, including that of fashioning peanut butter.[43]

Unlike peanut oil, which comes from an American plant, sesame oil was derived from a plant native to India, where it was (and is) extensively employed for cooking in the south. Not that sesame was a total stranger in the New World. Its cultivation had spread from India to Africa, and from there sesame seeds crossed the Atlantic with the slave trade to North America, where the British encouraged sesame cultivation in what was still their American colonies. They cherished the mercantilistic hope that sesame might replace the olive oil they were reluctantly importing from European rivals.[44]

All of these oils joined to bring about a food processing revolution in the midst of the Industrial Revolution. Until the nineteenth century, people obtained their dietary fats from local sources and, as late as 1899, animal fats still accounted for 70 percent of the fats utilized in Europe. But by 1928 that percentage had fallen to just 6 percent[45] and it continued to fall even though the dominance of tropical oils diminished as the Europeans lost their colonies and as the colonies, having lost their monopolies on oil shipments to their ex-mother countries, were forced to compete on the basis of price. The European Common Market tried to help by eliminating all duties on oils, but this only served to open the floodgates to American soybeans.[46]

Soybeans were fairly late arrivals in America and only recently the focus of much agricultural attention. During the latter part of the nineteenth century, high oil prices had encouraged the extraction of oil from cottonseeds in the southern United States, which became Wesson Oil after chemist David Wesson, at the turn of the twentieth century, found a way to deodorize it. Following this, cottonseed oil became dominant in the world's vegetable oil market until the 1940s.[47]

By contrast, soybeans, although grown in the United States since the eighteenth century, were little more than agricultural curiosities as the twentieth century began. This began to change in 1915, when the nation's cotton fields became infested with boll weevils, and a shortage of cotton seeds in tandem with elevated oil prices caused by World War I prompted a new look at the virtues of soybean oil. Throughout the Great Depression

and the next World War, soybean oil was increasingly applied to the manufacture of margarine, shortening, salad dressing, and, of course, cooking oil. By the beginning of the 1950s, the United States, which had been the world's biggest importer of fats, was becoming its biggest exporter thanks to soybeans, accounting for a whopping three-quarters of the world's soybean crop.[48] Soya was well on its way to achieving the status of being the most widely consumed plant in the world.[49]

The process of industrialization helped mechanize fishing fleets while simultaneously polluting Europe's inland estuaries and rivers – both these events coming at a time of increasing demand for iced seafood as railroad networks opened large urban markets. On the one hand, the situation produced a booming marine fishing industry; and on the other, it stimulated the application of science to the new field of fisheries.

Administrators in the colonies of India and Africa established fisheries departments during the last decades of the nineteenth century. The original intent was to stock familiar sports fish, but in India, where a large portion of the population did not eat meat, an effort was made to introduce (or reintroduce) Chinese carp and African tilapia for public consumption. In Africa, in addition to sports fish, mosquito-eating fish were cultured to help control malaria.[50]

In the first few decades of the twentieth century it was becoming clear that the days of the colonial empires were numbered. In India, Mahatma Gandhi led his famous "march to the sea" in 1930 to collect salt in defiance of a government monopoly. Such "civil disobedience" was just one of many strategies to break the imperial yoke. But despite this kind of local resistance, the real imperial train wreck came only in the aftermath of World War II with the vanishing empires scattering colonial tastes and culinary influences all over the globe. Millions emigrated from Africa and Asia to ex-mother countries to nurture these traditions while, conversely, European colonizing influences and ingredients greatly expanded the range of foods employed in the ex-colonies. Can one imagine the cuisines of the West Indies without salt cod, salt pork, salt beef, and rice, the dishes of India without potatoes and chilli peppers, or the West African diet without peanuts, sweet potatoes, and maize?

Because racism drove nineteenth-century imperialism and colonialism which, in turn, drove scientists of the time to discover physical reasons that would help to account for the alleged inferiority of subject peoples, it seems appropriate to close this chapter with a brief discussion of one of these "discoveries" that was food-related.

This was – at the risk of prurience – the (alleged) early age of menstruation in the inferior groups which, it was believed, signaled an earlier sexual maturity that put them closer to the animals.[51] Yet, the age of menarche is closely linked with nutritional status, and thus to the extent that this was true, we are confronted with the apparent paradox of middle- and upper-class white girls being less well-nourished than their poorer and darker-skinned counterparts. The most logical explanation is that the beginning of menstruation among upper class girls of the Victorian Age was significantly underreported, whereas it was exaggerated for those members of the disdained classes.

Yet, this may be too parsimonious an explanation and too dismissive of the role of nutrition. This is because "precocious puberty" was viewed with alarm among the middle and upper classes whose physicians advised that their daughters not eat much meat. Meat was still linked with carnal lust as it had been for a cycle of centuries. But denying good quality protein to maturing young ladies, for whatever reason, could easily have delayed their age of menarche, or at least, caused the amenorrhea now seen among today's anorectics. It could also have produced the greenish skin color of chlorisis – a disease that singled out upper-class young women. That disease proved ephemeral and is now gone but many suspect that it was anemia.[52]

CHAPTER

21

HOMEMADE FOOD HOMOGENEITY

Tell me what you eat, and I will tell you what you are.

Brillat Savarin – Physiologie du Goût

A man accustomed to American food and American domestic cookery would not starve to death suddenly in Europe; but I think that he would waste away and eventually die.

Mark Twain – A Tramp Abroad

AMERICA'S HEAD START in food globalization was a function of industrialized agriculture – and the concomitant growth of a large industrial agribusiness – both serious components of the Industrial Revolution.[1] The production of labor-saving machinery for the farm was given something of a fillip early on by the Gold Rush. After 1848, hired help deserted farms to head west, and thousands of farmers replaced their workers with the new McCormick reaper.

Following this, industrialized agriculture began the inexorably painful process of replacing family farming. By the beginning of the twentieth century, the introduction of many more such labor-saving machines (with the tractor just a decade away) had already halved the number of individuals depending on the land for a living. Despite a shrinking farm labor force, however, millions of additional acres were brought under cultivation, and American farmers were industriously adding to the nation's abundance at a time when the threat of famine hung over Europe – such food shortages just one more factor helping to evict those who became immigrants to the United States.

Between 1839 and 1909, American wheat production increased eight times as the center of the nation's agricultural production moved some 800 miles westward from Wheeling, West Virginia, to the Iowa/Nebraska borderlands.[2] Such food production was crucial in feeding not only the new immigrants from abroad but the other new migrants as well – ex-farmers chased off their lands to become urban laborers.[3]

But even those who remained on the land to produce national abundance did not prosper; rather, they were increasingly beset by a range of difficulties from low farm prices, disproportionately high taxes, and railroad shipping costs to governmental policies of high tariffs and deflation. Such grievances led to a the formation of the Populist Party, but the country's only agrarian revolt faded in the face of a lost election, a collapse of the Populist-Democrat coalition, the distraction posed by war with Spain and, perhaps most importantly, a new *fin de siècle* prosperity for agriculture as well as for much of the nation. Other agrarian revolts in much of the world effectively preserved small holdings, (which reinforced ethnic cuisines). America's revolt, which was barely a whimper, did not.

The twentieth century dawned with 60 percent of the world's shipping done in steamships and, with more efficient transportation, other countries began relying on the United States for cheap grain. Yet, if the Europeans were impressed with American food productivity, they were less impressed with what Americans did with (and to) their foods. Some Americans were also unhappy with American cuisine, beginning a long tradition of poking fun at U.S. foods and foodways. In large part this was the result of a British culinary heritage that Americans were thought to have difficulty shedding.[4] And there is no question that, like the cuisine of the British, that of America suffered qualitative, although not quantitative, difficulties. In 1923, vitamin discoverer Elmer McCollum estimated that 90 percent of the diet of most Americans consisted of white bread, butter, meat, potatoes, coffee, and sugar.[5] At about the same time a food commentator complained that "American cookery lags the very last of our arts" and called for Americans to jettison their "Puritan stomachs" as well as their "Puritan minds."[6]

The ensuing dietary educational campaign took place in an atmosphere of increasing vitamin awareness that significantly raised public consciousness about the importance of a varied diet that included more in the way of fruits and vegetables.[7] Yet, half a century later, food historians Waverly Root and

Richard de Rochemont once again chided Americans for rejecting " . . . any foods incorrigibly foreign to the eating habits imported from the British Isles" and criticized America for not being a "culinary melting pot."[8]

At first blush these charges seem silly. Throughout the century, diets had improved and many Americans had searched restlessly for novelty in cuisine. The middle and upper classes had long served fruit for breakfast and had experimented with salads and sandwiches at lunch or dinnertime, depending on when the family took its lighter meal: the Caesar salad was invented in the 1920s, the Cobb salad in 1937, and the club sandwich was known as early as 1899. Nor were foreign food eschewed, including mayonnaise, carried to France by a naval officer battling Britain near the the port of Mahon in Minorca (hence it was known at first as Mahonaise) in the eighteenth century, and made popular in America by Richard Hellman in the early twentieth century. Casseroles for the heavier meal were inspired by immigrant Italians, Greeks, and Hungarians – this despite a brief attempt by the New England Kitchen and other programs to teach immigrants to cook "Yankee-style" as a part of their assimilation.[9] What happened instead was that dishes like spaghetti with meat sauce or meat balls became American favorites, as did macaroni with meat or cheese and chop suey.[10]

Moreover, following World War II, Americans had adopted foreign food influences with a vengeance, as reflected in a spate of cookbooks, the appearance of magazines like *Gourmet*, and the countless contributions of Mexicans, Germans, Scandinavians, Italians, Greeks, Slavs, Chinese, and Japanese to what was becoming an American fusion cuisine. By contrast, the countries with which America's foodways were unfavorably contrasted, such as Germany, Italy, and, especially France, had cuisines that varied by region, to be sure, but were hardly experimental. Rather, they were conservative regional cuisines that eschewed "foreign" foods.[11]

Food critics, of course, seldom see eye to eye, and while Root and de Rochemont were lambasting Americans for their hopelessly "British" tastes in the decade of the 1970s, food critic John Hess and food historian Karen Hess leveled the contradictory charge that Americans were caught up in a "gourmet plague" – a quest for the fancy, the foreign, the elegant – that had consigned "good food in America" to "little more than a memory and a hope."[12] The Hesses then were blaming foreign influences and food homogenization for a decline in America's culinary standard of living, but despite an obvious polarity, the two sets of authors may have been driving at the same points.

If we substitute "food globalization" for phrases like "culinary melting pot" or "food homogenization" it becomes clear that one set of critics deplored that it had not been achieved, whereas the other was upset that it had. But their angst ran deeper. Both were troubled by the "Americanization," of foreign foods as foreign dishes were modified to fit American tastes. And at an even deeper level, both had a problem with the technology that has facilitated such food Americanization.

It is probably wise at this point to deal briefly with the concept of "melting pots." When Root and de Rochemont used the term "culinary melting pot," the reference was to America as a melting pot of peoples and cultures – a cherished American myth, but a myth nonetheless. Immigrants were not asked to make cultural contributions to their adopted land; rather, during an age of intense nationalism, they were expected to transmute themselves culturally into Americans by jettisoning their language in favor of English and obeying Anglo-Saxon, not Roman, law. Their children, in particular, were forced by a homogenizing public school system to surrender, not contribute, their cultural distinctiveness.

Similarly, as syndicated columnist, TV host, and noted cookbook writer James Beard astutely observed, foreign dishes, like immigrants, were (and are) transmuted to an American model. In his words " . . . very few foreign dishes survive in their pure form when they become nationally popular; they take on the stamp of the American kitchen so quickly that in many cases they cease to be exotic and are accepted as casually as a plate of ham and eggs."[13]

It was this "stamp" of the American kitchen that both sets of critics objected to – a stamp that includes significant technological input, which was also deplored. The just mentioned ham now comes from pigs bred to be lean; the eggs from huge automated egg factories; and when undergirded by an English muffin and topped with hollandaise sauce, the ham and eggs are transformed into "Eggs Benedict." This is a dish widely viewed as sophisticated and assumed to be foreign (although it probably originated in Manhattan's old Delmonico's restaurant), but one that has become "casually accepted."

No Parisian would recognize the Creole cuisine of New Orleans as "French" food any more that someone from Japan would feel at home in an American Japanese steak house; nor would an Italian be immediately comfortable with an American pizza. Much of the "Americanization"

process has been a function of American abundance, the addition of great amounts of animal protein to foreign dishes, particularly since the beginning of what *Look Magazine* in 1954 called the "Protein Era." Americans embraced Russian foods like kebabs and Beef Stroganov (named after the Russian Count Pavel Stroganov), which most Russians seldom tasted. They did the same with the English Beef Wellington (the name honoring Arthur Wellesley, the Duke of Wellington); and great amounts of meat were added to Chinese dishes that were low in protein when they first crossed the nation with Chinese railroad workers. American pizzas have been loaded with so much meat and cheese that visiting Europeans routinely complain about them.

But none of this means that America was not, and is not, in the forefront of food globalization or that Americans are still chained to English tastes, if they ever were outside of New England. With food globalization, it is the foreign influence compelling the adoption of new foods and the ways of preparing them that matters, and not the dish that Americanization ultimately molds. Moreover, the critics notwithstanding, Americans are hardly afraid of foreign foods. To be a bit facetious, witness the hot dog and the hamburger, which despite their German ancestry are, along with French fries, still in the fast lane of the fast food revolution. And certainly names such as "Swiss steak," "French," "Italian," and "Russian" dressings, "negimaki," "cioppino," "tetrazzini," "vichyssoise," even "Cornish game hen" – all indicating a foreign origin for what are actually American inventions – are not suggestive of an aversion to things foreign. Rather, despite their American origin, such dishes came into being exactly because they were perceived to be foreign.

The process of adopting foreign dishes for American adaptations is a complicated one that has much to do with exposure. And that exposure generally begins in the restaurants.

RESTAURANTS

We may live without friends; we may live without books; but civilized man cannot live without cooks. (Owen Meridith)

The homogenization of foreign food influences was well underway in New York City "restaurants" (French for "restore" – in this case, the diners' strength) before the nineteenth century had run its course where

Service à la Russe, (meals served in courses of individual dishes), popular in Victorian England had finally caught on. But the predominant influence was French, and Lorenzo Delmonico was the most influential of the French restauranteurs. At the time of his death in 1881, it was said that Delmonico's restaurant – founded in 1825 – had, in several subsequent locations, hosted every president from Jackson to Garfield, as well as a stream of foreign dignitaries. The restaurant helped to popularize green undercooked vegetables and salads, and despite its French food orientation, is credited as the first in the United States to feature the "hamburger steak."[14]

Delmonico's was an establishment where the rich brought their educated tastes. Many of them had seen something of the world and its various cuisines, and such individuals are often in the gourmand vanguard. Dorés, which began business in 1862, was Delmonico's only serious rival until Sherry's opened its doors in 1891. Most other restaurants in the city at the time served more pedestrian fare. Sweet's, for example, located close to the Fulton Fish Market, featured chowders, fresh fish, and shellfish whereas Cavanaugh's specialized in oysters, lobster, crabmeat, and turtle steak, as well as roast beef and filet mignon. Diners also went to Keen's English Chop House (founded in 1885 and still in existence) for thick mutton chops; to Lüchow's or Luger's in Brooklyn for German wiener schnitzel and hasenpfeffer, and, after 1902, to Angelo's in Little Italy for osso buco, risotto, and a score of other Italian dishes.

New York had hundreds more restaurants to choose from, including neighborhood ethnic eateries, among them numerous Chinese restaurants. But so did many other American cities and towns. By the 1880s, virtually every major one in America had Chinese restaurants. Caucasian palettes found chop suey, chow mein, egg rolls, and egg foo yong acceptable, and no wonder. Most of these dishes, although influenced by Chinese cookery were, in fact, American in origin.

Another cuisine that became a part of the New York dining scene early on catered to Jews, many of whom were among the new arrivals from Eastern Europe. Delicatessens were established to accommodate those who kept Jewish dietary laws, which prohibited cooking on the Sabbath. The highly spiced delicatessen meats along with chicken soup, borscht, gefilte fish, smoked fish, beef briskets, breakfast beef, unleavened bread, dark rye bread, and complex kosher dishes also appealed to gentiles. By the turn of the twentieth century, kosher foods had become an industry, turned out by firms such as Manischewitz in Cincinnati and Hebrew National Foods of

New York City. And by the end of World War I, Ratner's restaurant in New York had become famous for its Jewish cuisine.[15]

In New York during the early decades of the twentieth century, a plethora of restaurants serving ethnic foods to the rich and famous started business, and in 1911 the renowned French chef Auguste Escoffier arrived to take charge of the kitchen for the opening of the new Ritz Carlton hotel. Seven years later Louis Diat, the French chef who stayed on to run that kitchen, invented vichyssoise, which became another American dish with a foreign name.[16] Mama Leone's was established in 1915, and Sardi's Restaurant followed in 1922, both specializing in Italian-American foods. L'Aiglon opened in 1919 to serve both French and Italian dishes, and Lindy's, aiming at the sweet tooth with crullers and cheesecake, began business in 1922.

On the opposite coast, foreign food influences were ushered into San Francisco by the gold rush. In 1849, the nation's first recorded Chinese restaurant, Macao and Woosung, opened its doors, followed in 1850 by the Poulet d'Or – first a saloon but soon an elegant French restaurant. Jack's began business in 1864 with jackrabbits on the menu, along with English mutton chops and royal kidneys. San Francisco's Far East Café was established to continue the city's offering of Cantonese-American dishes in the twentieth century at about the same time that California's Nut Tree Restaurant began serving Chinese and Mexican dishes. By the 1950s, thanks to James Mitchner's *Tales of the South Pacific*, the musical *South Pacific*, and the *Kon-Tiki* expedition, the South Seas were big news in California, and establishments like Hollywood's Don the Beachcomber and San Francisco's Trader Vic's led the way in a leap from Cantonese-American to fusion cuisine.

Early restaurants in New Orleans dished up that city's version of French cuisine. Antoine's opened its doors in 1840 with specialties such as Oysters en Brochette and Chicken Rochambeau (and after 1899, Oysters Rockefeller, so named because they were so rich). Commander's Palace opened in 1880, Galatoire's in 1905, and Arnaud's in 1919, and all three remain vigorous competitors. An exception to the New Orleans Creole focus was Kolb's, an elaborate German restaurant established in 1909.

The Volstead Act of 1919 prescribed Prohibition which began the following year with a funeral for John Barleycorn, presided over by none other than the Reverend Billy Sunday.[17] The law against alcohol was hard on the upscale restaurant business, and Delmonico's, its most famous fatality, closed in 1923 after 96 years. Perhaps this folding was premature because opposition to Prohibition was mounting and just a couple of years later *Collier's* became the first major magazine to demand an end to it. After this that end seemed only a matter of time.

This emboldened some entrepreneurs to open ethnic restaurants in cities other than New York before the 13 years, 10 months, 19 days, 17 hours, and 32 minutes of Prohibition had run their course. The doors of one of these, Haussner's in Baltimore, swung open in 1926 to serve German and Hungarian specialties like sauerbraten, goulash, and spätzle, and the following year Lender's Bagel Bakery was founded in New Haven, Connecticut. In Los Angeles, Les Frères Taix dished up French cuisine in 1928, and following the end of the "great experiment," Don the Beachcomber served Hawaiian specialties on Hollywood Boulevard in the middle of the Great Depression. In nearby Beverly Hills, Dave Chasen's began as a chilli parlor in 1936, and in Chicago the Pump Room, with its European and South Asian cuisine, opened in 1938

PREPARED FOODS, FROZEN FOODS, FAST FOODS, AND SUPERMARKETS

For the hoi polloi, however, exposure to new cuisines came not from expensive restaurants but from Mason jars and tin cans. Hammers and chisels were the tools for can opening prior to 1865, after which thinner steel made the job a little easier. It got much easier and cleaner after can-top rims inspired the invention of the can opener (patented in 1870) that substituted a cutting wheel for the hand tools.[18] Life became more pleasant for the housewife, canned foods increased in popularity, and technological improvements transformed the canning industry.

At first the canning concentration was on American foods. Baked beans had been a virtual monopoly of New England – but no longer after B&M Baked Beans were first canned in 1875. Corned beef was canned in 1885 by Libby, McNeill, and Libby, and after 1890, the meat was more accessible thanks to "a key opening device for rectangular cans."[19] Residence near maple trees was no longer a requirement for enjoying maple syrup after 1887, when cans of Log Cabin Syrup were available (a blend of maple and cane syrups).

But "foreign" foods also began to find their way into cans. In 1887, Franco-American began canning frankly "Americanized" spaghetti, and in 1911 chilli con carne and tamales were canned for the first time in San

Antonio. Pineapple, an exotic fruit for North Americans despite its New World beginnings, was tasted for the first time by many in 1902 as James D. Dole's Hawaiian Pineapple Company began operation; pineapple juice from Dole followed in 1933.

Libby, McNeill, and Libby began marketing canned sauerkraut in 1904, and in 1907 bottled A-1 Sauce was introduced from England. Contadina tomato sauce was available in cans at the end of World War I, at the same time that Old El Paso brand Mexican foods started operation to develop a line of refried beans and sauces. In the late 1920s, Progresso Foods in New Orleans was importing Sicilian olive oil and soon expanded to produce tomato sauce, marinated artichoke hearts, and pignoli.[20]

In 1932, a Mexican recipe for tortilla fritas was turned into Frito Corn Chips in San Antonio, Texas, and Goya Foods (established in 1936) actively promoted Hispanic foods and ultimately distributed some 750 items. The year 1937 saw more "Italian" offerings with the appearance of the Kraft Macaroni and Cheese Dinner and Ragú spaghetti sauce. La Choy first canned bean sprouts in 1920, although chop suey and chow mein had to await the establishment of the Chun King Corporation in 1947 to find a home in a can.

One reason for the increasing availability of "foreign" canned foods was the increasing shelf space in the food markets. In 1916, the year that Piggly Wiggly of Memphis became the nation's first full service supermarket, U.S. grocery stores carried about 600 items; the supermarkets of the late 1930s and early 1940s offered several thousand. Paradoxically, supermarkets were mostly launched during the depression years of the 1930s. The venerable Great Atlantic and Pacific Tea Company (A&P) founded in 1869 had no supermarket outlets until competition from Kroger, Safeway, Publix, Piggly Wiggly, and Big Bear forced Charles Merrill (controlling stockholder of A&P and later, founder of Merrill Lynch) to begin in 1937 to open them in wholesale fashion. Not coincidentally, this was the same year that the shopping cart was invented.

Behind the supermarket excitement of the 1930s lay a good number of food globalizing technological advances. The opening of the Panama Canal in 1914, just as World War I got underway in Europe, meant that fresh agricultural produce and wines from California were now only 20 days away from Eastern U.S. markets. Another canal, this one the Houston Ship Canal, was also opened to traffic in 1914 – its 50 miles of waterway making that city a deep-water port and a major shipper of U.S. grain.[21] And 1914 was the year that frozen foods had their commercial beginning as Clarence "Bob" Birdseye pioneered in freezing fish.

After further experimentation with frozen foods, in 1924 Birdseye became one of the founders of the General Seafoods Company, which sold frozen fish fillets. Then, in 1929, General Seafoods merged with Postum Company to become General Foods, which marketed other frozen foods besides fish under the Birdseye label.

At first, these were mostly vegetables and fruits (including juices) that looked and tasted better than those from a can, and they were convenient. Like their canned predecessors, they eliminated problems of seasonal availability. During the early years of frozen foods, many took their purchases home, thawed them, and ate them the same day. But by mid-century, some 90 percent of urban homes and 80 percent of farm households had mechanical refrigeration so that families were able to refrigerate foods and maintain those that were frozen.

Swanson's, building on experience gained in shipping foods to the troops during the war, began experimenting in 1945 with frozen poultry, and a decade later was producing frozen individual whole meals. These were especially welcomed by women entering the workforce and by mothers with baby boom offspring. As televisions were added to living rooms, so were TV trays, introduced in 1953.[22] The first Swanson "TV dinner" debuted the following year. It was turkey with cornbread dressing, sweet potatoes and buttered peas – an all-American dinner – but choices soon came to include "foreign" foods such as beef goulash and chicken cacciatore, along with a plethora of pizzas. A couple of decades later the microwave oven came along to deal with frozen foods and, like the latter, revolutionized food processing. By 1988, U.S. food processors had introduced 962 microwavable products and some 90 percent of American homes had a microwave oven.[23]

To satisfy a growing American taste for the exotic was also a mission of the fast food industry. True, its beginnings were in marketing the (by now) "American" hamburger, later joined in the 1950s by "all American" fried chicken as the fast food industry took off. But Lum's, with its frankfurters steamed in beer and sauerkraut, was also born in the 1950s, and pizza parlors spearheaded by Pizza Hut, Little Caesar's, and Domino's spread across the country. In the 1960s, Taco Bell marketed its Tex-Mex cuisine; the Golden Wok and Teriyaki Express did the same with Asian food; and Au Bon Pain was created as a chain of French-style bakery-cafes. El Pollo Loco joined the "foreign" fast food list in the 1970s.[24]

How much credit belongs to World War II for the ready acceptance of such foreign influences expanding U.S. culinary horizons has been a "bone" of contention that will not be gnawed on here. Suffice it to say that the war exposed millions of Americans to foods in foreign lands, and the successive waves of service men and women who followed the World War II generation also gained culinary experience in Europe and Asia, returning home with tastes of exotic foods fresh in their mouths. So did millions of American tourists, especially during the foreign travel boom of the 1960s and 1970s.[25] In addition, many foreigners – the spouses of returning service personnel – carried their cuisines with them, and following the Immigration Act of 1965 (which took effect in 1968) millions of immigrants from a range of locations from China to the Caribbean, and from the Middle East to Mexico, brought still more foodways to America.[26]

No longer did Fannie Merritt Farmer's 1896 *Boston Cooking-School Cook Book* rule the kitchen, although it had sold over 3 million copies in the United States alone; nor did *The Joy of Cooking* (first released in 1931), an enormously popular bestseller that went through edition after edition to achieve the distinction of being the best-selling cookbook ever. As Americans found foreign foods increasingly interesting, they began paying some attention to food critics, television cooks with 100 megawatt personalities, and cooking magazines and cookbook writers who were introducing variations on French, Chinese, and Italian foods to sophisticated cooks and beginners alike. Their next step was to move beyond these to unveil a window on foods the world over, and window-shopping these foods has now become a breeze with the Internet.

Dominating this early food consciousness-raising were culinary giants James Beard (who operated cooking schools and authored twenty-two cookbooks) and Julia Child (pioneer hostess of Boston's public television cooking show *The French Chef* in the early 1960s). In 1969 and 1970 alone, best-selling cookbooks focused on the foods of France, the British Isles, the Caribbean Islands, Germany, Spain and Portugal, China, Russia, and Japan.[27] Such efforts nurtured a growing cosmopolitism, making Americans ever more receptive to foreign food influences and initiating a surging globalization of the American diet that shows no permanent sign of abating despite the chilling events of September 11. To be sure they temporarily dampened the nation's enthusiasm for things foreign. We got the message that the world was a hostile and dangerous place and for a couple of years tended to stay close to home. Travel slowed, and over 100,000 restaurant workers lost their jobs, but by 2004 American curiosity for the novel and exotic had returned.

Meanwhile, home cooks turned for exotica to supermarket shelves lined with everything from myriad pasta sauces to Chinese vegetables to Old El Paso products, while their freezer sections house a United Nations of ethnic foods from Eastern European pirogies to Italian polenta and, of course, the ubiquitous pizza.

And today those dining outside the home can find foreign foods for almost any budget. Indeed, it is hard to avoid foreign foods even if one so desired. For although there are plenty of French, Italian, Greek, German, Polynesian, Chinese, and Japanese restaurants, there are relatively few that call themselves "American" restaurants, although chains such as Cracker Barrel and Bob Evans clearly are.

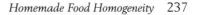

NOTIONS OF NUTRIENTS
AND NUTRIMENTS

*It is no surprise for historians of science that in any scientific field
ideas which in one generation seemed to be firmly based truths
should be overturned in the next.*

Kenneth J. Carpenter (1994)[1]

ALLAYING PUBLIC HEALTH concerns about food quality was a necessary step in America's march toward food globalization. How could one be
adventuresome about new and strange foods when even familiar ones were
suspect? Moreover, perceptions had to change. For example, throughout
most of baking history, white bread has been preferred by the elites; the
whiteness signifying purity and refinement. By contrast, brown and black
breads suggested coarseness, so that in racially-mixed Spanish America,
skin color was closely associated with the color of the bread consumed.[2]

Sylvester Graham had railed against white bread in the nineteenth
century but not for the right reasons. He thought white bread was *too*
nutritious to be digested properly.[3] Regardless, Graham's railing did little
to slow white bread production or to improve its yield of nutrients. Quite
the contrary. The steel roller mills that came into use in the 1870s made
it possible to turn out bread flour lacking both bran and wheat-germ as
well as important vitamins and minerals. Interestingly, it was only after
white bread became universally available that the upper classes, at least,
discovered the virtues of coarse bread that was high in fiber, and the coun-
terculture of the 1960s found practically anything brown (brown bread,

brown rice, brown skin) preferable to white (white bread, white skin, White House).[4] Four decades later, Tufts University researchers discovered that white bread and other refined grains are much more likely than whole grains to create an unsightly abdominal region which, of course, increases the risk of heart disease.

Graham would also probably have railed against the waterlogged iceberg lettuce, introduced in 1894 by W. Atlee Burpee & Co. Like white bread, it has little nutritional value and not much flavor. Its sole virtue is that, with reasonable care, it stays crisp. Also, like white bread, it fell from fashion among the nutrition-conscious upper classes, yet both have had recent reputation comebacks. Cheap white bread is a partner of pulled pork, and wedges of iceberg lettuce with blue cheese dressing have become standard fare in the new chophouses springing up across the country where only the lettuce is an American development – even chophouses are imports.

Food prejudices and taboos are generally constants. The Seventh Day Adventists, for example, always maintain the dietary prohibitions of the Jews found in Leviticus and Deuteronomy, and the Mormons always reject alcohol.[5] In the past we saw Romans frown on everyday meat-eating, believing it to be "barbarian," and the upper classes of the Middle Ages avoided plebian vegetables. Thus, foods such as white bread and iceberg lettuce that fall in and out of fashion do so because of fads on the one hand and health concerns on the other, with advertisers straining to exploit both.

This, in turn, has presented the public with another of what we might call the "perils" of plenty. Advertising, promotions, and packaging are the weapons of choice in a competitive struggle that aims at creating an irresistible illusion of quality, no matter what the truth.[6] But any measurable quality, in a nutritional sense, that might have reassured a jittery public remained an elusive concept until vitamins were discovered.[7]

The English had been nervous about foods since the 1850s and particularly about meat contaminated with tuberculosis.[8] And, by the end of the nineteenth century, quality as measured by purity was another, and serious, matter for a U.S. public now thoroughly alarmed by exposés of food adulteration and dangerous additives at the hands of "muckraking" journalists – and, especially, by Upton Sinclair's *The Jungle* published in 1905.[9] His description of conditions in the meatpacking industry – such as sausages made from spoiled meat, then chemically treated to disguise this fact, and handled by tubercular workers – turned many to vegetarianism, and meat sales in the country plummeted by half.[10]

The book, however, did muster support for Harvey Wiley, who, as head of the Chemical Division of the U.S. Department of Agriculture (the USDA), had been campaigning relentlessly for a federal pure food law, while at the same time generating publicity by using his "Poison Squad" of volunteers to test the safety of food preservatives.[11] It was the uproar caused by *The Jungle* that prompted President Theodore Roosevelt to order an investigation, and Wiley finally got his bills passed:[12] the Pure Food and Drug Act of 1906 and the Federal Meat Inspection Act of 1907, which he subsequently erratically and idiosyncratically enforced.[13]

These Acts, although amended from time to time by Congress to make them more effective, were routinely circumvented by the food industry and even used by big producers to force smaller ones out of business. Still, the Acts constituted an important acknowledgment by the federal government that it had both the authority and the responsibility to ensure a safe food supply for the nation.[14]

In 1907, an article appeared in the USDA yearbook entitled "Food and Diet in the United States," in which its author asserted, "in no [other] country is there a greater variety of readily accessible foods of good quality."[15] But despite such reassurances, the nation's safe food jitters were far from over. Rather, the appearance of the article coincided with the beginning of the nation's next food scandal: pellagra, a nutritional deficiency disease (see Chapter 23), had broken out among people in the south who had little access to either food variety or quality.[16] Not that poverty was immediately identified as the culprit, but corn became a chief suspect, and in 1909 the plant was put on trial for murder by the state of South Carolina.[17]

By 1913, it was clear that there were at least 100,000 cases of the illness in the south (in that year it killed 1,192 people in Mississippi alone), and the disease continued to stalk that region until the middle 1930s. In 1934, pellagra was credited with the deaths of 3,602 Americans and it was estimated that there were 20 cases for every death.[18]

The persistence of pellagra did nothing to sooth a public worried about the dangers lurking in its food supply, nor did publications like Leon A. Congdon's *Fight for Food* (1916).[19] Congdon, Division Chief of Food and Drugs for the Kansas State Board of Health, systematically criticized the food industry for adulterating and mislabeling foods, and for employing unsafe additives. He was especially hard on the milk industry, which he correctly portrayed as responsible for outbreaks of typhoid and scarlet fever as well as diphtheria and tuberculosis.[20] In fact, of the cattle supplying

Pittsburgh with milk in 1907, between 10 and 15 percent were found to be tubercular,[21] and in the following year it was estimated that from 20 to 25 percent of all dairy cattle in the nation were affected with the disease.[22]

Pasteurization, it was pointed out, was an easy remedy but hardly one consistently utilized, as a significant percentage of samples of milk, butter, and cream for sale in U.S. cities were found to be infected with tuberculosis bacilli.[23] Another turn-of-the-century problem was lead water pipes, which had come into use with the beginning of canalized water toward the close of the nineteenth century. Fortunately, this danger was quickly realized, and many municipalities abandoned their use when it became apparent that the presence of lead sharply increased infant mortality rates, elevating them from 25 to 50 percent.[24]

Congdon was similarly concerned about the safety of new food substitutes like oleomargarine and saccharin, and echoes of such concerns have continued to reverberate right down to the late twentieth-century distress caused by the use of other laboratory-produced products such as Stellar, Simplesse, and Olestra.[25] In addition to one alarm after another set off by new food-processing technologies from an industry few relish trusting with their lives, the public has gotten a century's worth of contradictory, but nonetheless "scientific," advice about what constitutes good nutrition – beginning with the remarkably high recommendations for protein and fat intake that were in vogue at the start of the twentieth century.[26]

Such advice has always commanded a wide audience, because in speaking to questions about the salubrity of various foods taken into the body, it speaks to concerns that are both eternal and global – as reflected in the Hippocratic medicine of the ancient Greeks, the Chinese yin and yang, and the Ayurvedic texts of India. But despite the antiquity of the anxiety, little more than theorizing about nutriments could be done until the advent of modern chemistry and the birth of nutritional science.

Vitamin A deficiency and the blindness (especially night blindness) it causes was probably the first nutrient deficiency to be identified. The problem was known to the ancients – both Hippocrates and Galen wrote about night blindness – and they had a cure for the condition. It was liver, high in vitamin A, although the vitamin and its assignments were not understood for another 2,500 years. In fact, the discovery of most of the chief nutrients was a strictly twentieth-century phenomenon, even though the importance of some minerals, such as iron, to human health was at least vaguely understood in the eighteenth century.[27]

In 1789, Antoine-Laurent Lavoisier published the first modern chemical textbook that used the term "calorie" and showed that all animals, humans included, were machines that burned food for energy, thereby demolishing the millennia-old theory of the "four humors." A half-century later, Justus von Liebig, a 39 year old German chemist, argued that this combustion produced animal heat and he founded the science of biochemistry while introducing the concept of proteins. These, he argued, were the only true nutrients, even as science was going about disproving him.[28]

At the beginning of the nineteenth century, it was known that blood contained iron and, by its end, numerous other minerals were understood to be vital to life itself.[29] But important as such mineral research was in advancing nutritional knowledge, it was only with the discovery of vitamins that the field of scientific nutrition experienced a truly spectacular birth. This occurred as disease descriptions in earlier texts were matched with modern counterparts suspected of being caused by nutrient deficits. Vitamins came to light in the ensuing search for their causes and cures.

THIAMINE AND BERIBERI

Illustrative is beriberi, caused by a dietary deficiency of thiamine (a B-complex vitamin). Historically those that consume a diet centered too closely on rice, and one that excludes thiamine-rich foods, particularly animal foods, have been especially susceptible to the malady. In Asia during the latter part of the nineteenth century, the disease achieved a new virulence when new steam-driven mills were applied to processing rice. In stripping away the husks and hulls of the grains (polishing them) they also stripped away their thiamine. The cardiac symptoms of "wet" beriberi, as well as the paralytic symptoms of "dry" beriberi, became widespread, as did those of the invariably fatal "infantile" beriberi that mothers passed on to their babies in thiamine-deficient milk.[30]

Recognition that beriberi was a deficiency disease began with the work of Christiian Eijkman, a Dutch military surgeon in Java, who showed during the 1890s that a diet of polished rice caused beriberi-like symptoms in chickens, but symptoms that vanished when the diet was switched to crude (unpolished) rice.[31] In the first decade of the twentieth century, the Malayan government instituted programs to warn of the dangers of consuming polished rice and to encourage the production of unmilled rice. Both programs dramatically lowered beriberi incidence.

After learning of these developments, the United States launched similar programs in the Philippines during the 1920s that were overseen by W. E. B. Vedder and colleagues. It was Vedder who encouraged R. R. Williams, a scientist at the Bureau of Science in Manila, to begin studies that led in 1933 to the isolation of the substance protective against beriberi, a substance that Williams named "thiamine."[32]

Thiamine was a "vitamin," the word coined in 1912 by Polish chemist Casimir Funk, who proposed that an absence of a dietary substance he called *vitamine* was responsible for scurvy, pellagra, and rickets as well as beriberi. He was simultaneously right and wrong, but with Funk's notion of a "vita" (life) "amine" (any chemical compound containing nitrogen) the vitamin age leaped into the twentieth century. Research during that century, however, carried us well beyond vitamins to an understanding that all nutrient deficiencies, if sufficiently severe, can either produce disease or lower disease resistance.[33]

VITAMIN C AND SCURVY

Scurvy, caused by vitamin C deficiency, is probably the nutritional deficiency disease that has caused the most human suffering.[34] It was infamous as a scourge of seamen, who regularly turned yellow, developed purple spots all over their bodies, had gums grow over teeth, teeth fall out, and old wounds open up. Such symptoms were prominent among the crews of the expedition led by Vasco da Gama that rounded the Cape of Good Hope in 1498, crossed the Indian Ocean to Calicut, and returned to Lisbon the following year.[35] In that not so tender-hearted age, it was declared a successful (and enormously profitable) venture even though scurvy and other ailments had claimed 100 of the 160 Portuguese seamen who had begun the voyage.

Progress in shipbuilding and navigation technology had reached a point where humans could remain at sea for indefinite periods of time, and consequently, away from the vitamin C contained in those fresh fruits and vegetables found ashore (many sailors also developed night blindness since the same circumstances produced vitamin A deficiency).[36] It was, therefore, "progress" with a price. Scurvy would ultimately kill substantially more than a million sailors – claiming more of them than all other diseases, shipwrecks, naval warfare, and nasty storms combined.[37]

Nor did the disease limit itself to sailors. Soldiers – such as the Crusaders in 1250 – engaged in prolonged warfare and under siege (along with civilians) developed it. So did inmates of prisons and asylums, who had little choice about what they ate. Scurvy dogged explorers searching out the North and South Poles, and others who ventured into remote places like the goldfields of California or into deserts (the onion was recommended in ancient Egypt as a cure for a disease resembling scurvy.)[38] And mild symptoms were displayed by practically everyone in northern climes during the winter months. Early spring found them scratching under the snow for the first shoots of "scurvy grass" (any number of plants with antiscorbutic properties) to heal their bleeding gums.

In fact, winter was yet another reason scurvy was particularly hard on sailors. Although the body stores upwards of a thirty-day supply of vitamin C to fall back on, this supply was already pretty well exhausted for those who generally began their voyages in the spring.[39] In the eighteenth century, experiments in the British navy by James Lind (1854) – some would also credit the observations of James Cook during his voyages of the 1770s – and later, advocacy by Gilbert Blane and Thomas Trotter, finally convinced the Admiralty that citrus juice could both cure and prevent scurvy.

One says "finally" because it was only at century's end (1795), some forty years after Lind's observations were published, that lime or lemon juice became a regular part of the rations of a Royal Navy sailor (hence the term "limey," not generally an endearing one). Moreover, although citrus juice was demonstrably successful as a scurvy preventive, unaccountably, another half century elapsed before citrus rations were extended to the Merchant Marine.[40] Nor did other navies follow suit, let alone armies. Scurvy was rife during the Napoleonic Wars, the American Civil War, and the siege of Paris during the Franco-Prussian War.

In short, the British example did not galvanize many medical decision-makers to follow suit. Most remained skeptical of any theory linking nutritional deficiency with disease causation, theories that were almost totally derailed by the advent of germ theory, which sent investigators scurrying off on wild goose chases for a scurvy-causing pathogen. Yet, the skeptics made some good points, among them that Eskimos who consumed no fresh fruits or vegetables did not suffer from scurvy.[41]

Fortunately, Casimir Funk's proposal that diseases like scurvy were caused by some crucial (but missing) dietary substance was never totally forgotten, especially by vitamin researchers of the 1920s. And in 1932 the missing substance was isolated and identified by the Hungarian scientist Albert Szent-Györgyi and American researcher Glen King. It was called "vitamin C," and with this discovery many scurvy riddles were resolved. In the case of the Eskimos it turned out that they derived the vitamin after all, by eating their meat raw (cooking destroys vitamin C) and, in addition, they ate the stomach contents of caribou and other herbivorous animals. Finally, the Eskimos had long before learned to doctor any scurvy-like condition with an extract of evergreen needles.[42]

NIACIN AND PELLAGRA

Since 1937, science has known that pellagra is associated with a deficiency of niacin – another of the B-complex group of vitamins. It was a disorder known to present with unlovely, and generally protean, symptoms, like severe dermatitis (hence the Italian *pelle* agra or rough skin), diarrhea, and dementia, with death the ultimate symptom of this "disease of the four D's."[43] Historically, pellagra has dogged the heels of heavy maize consumers but it was only in the middle 1950s that we learned why. Maize contains plenty of niacin, but contains it too well, in a chemically-bound form that makes it unavailable to consumers without special treatment.[44]

Yet, other questions remain. We now know that a little fresh meat or milk in the diet permits human bodies to manufacture tryptophan (an amino acid and niacin's precursor) and be pellagra-free no matter how much maize is eaten.[45] However, science continues to puzzle over the importance of other amino acids and proteins in pellagra's etiology. And for the longest time investigators had wondered how maize-dependent Native Americans managed to elude the disease for millennia.[46]

It turned out – as mentioned earlier – that they perfected the "special treatment." Called nixtamalization, it is a complex process of soaking maize grains, then cooking them with lime (or campfire ashes). When this is done, the pericarp of the grain – a transparent skin – can be removed, and this releases the niacin, improves the quality of maize protein, and also contributes to an intake of calcium.[47]

Unfortunately, Native Americans neglected to pass along this little secret to their European conquerors who carried maize back to Europe where it became a subsistence food for the peasants of northern Spain, Italy, southern France, and the Balkans. The life of a peasant was always precarious, and when their economic situation deteriorated, many could afford to eat little else but cornmeal mush. By the first decades of the eighteenth century, pellagra had become common among them.[48]

The disease also accompanied maize into Africa, then erupted in its home hemisphere, in the southern United States among slaves in the nineteenth century, and prisoners, sharecroppers, and mill workers in the twentieth century, all people with circumscribed diets they could do little to change.[49] The U.S. Public Health Service launched a quest for both cause and cure, and progress was made after Joseph Goldberger's 1914 investigation that involved experimenting with the diets of eleven prisoner volunteers at Mississippi's Rankin prison farm.

Six of the volunteers were fed grits, cornbread, and fatback, while the other five had milk, butter, eggs, and lean meat added to this regimen. It was an elegant experiment in which none of the latter five developed pellagra but all six of the first group did. The experiment tied the disease to the kind of poverty that permitted little or no relief from the monotony of a "3M" diet of meat (mostly fat which contains no niacin), meal, and molasses. And in further experiments with dogs, Goldberger came close to discovering the pellagra-preventive by showing that yeast (loaded with niacin) prevented "black-tongue" (canine-pellagra).[50]

But the concept, let alone the importance, of vitamins, just then being discovered, lay in the future, and few of Goldberger's colleagues were willing to concede that a circumscribed diet might actually cause disease. Fortunately, the American Red Cross did make the concession, and during the Great Depression distributed yeast to southern sharecroppers and encouraged them to grow vegetables.[51] Finally, in 1937 at the University of Wisconsin, nicotinic acid was discovered. Later renamed "niacin," this vitamin was pellagra's long-sought preventive and cure.[52]

VITAMIN D, RICKETS, AND OTHER BONE MALADIES

Rickets, the last of Funk's deficiency disease suspects, is actually young peoples' osteomalacia. Symptoms appear when growing bones are not sufficiently calcified. They become deformed, with the characteristic bowing of the long bones of the legs and deformity of the rib cage, especially noticeable. The ancient Chinese wrote of such pronounced skeletal abnormalities, as did the Romans and Europeans during the Middle Ages.[53]

Their cause stems from a lack of vitamin D, which is crucial to the utilization of calcium.[54] But the only significant food sources of vitamin D (actually not really a vitamin but rather a pro-hormone) are egg yolks, animal livers, fatty fish, and fish oils. Consequently, most, if not all, of the vitamin

D required by the human body has to be produced by that body, which introduces another variable. Ultraviolet rays from the sun are required for vitamin D production – rays that, in reflecting off of the skin, stimulate the production of a cholesterol-like substance, which is the natural form of vitamin D, called alternatively cholecalciferol, calciol, or vitamin D_3.[55]

Humankind originated in, and adapted to, a region of the world where abundant sunlight ensured vitamin D production, which made rickets an unlikely event. Skeletal evidence indicates that trouble began when our restless, ancient ancestors wandered into northern climes with frigid and overcast winters that not only shut out sunshine but also made considerable clothing necessary, shutting out even more sunshine.[56] Physical adaptation to this newly adopted region would have included a lightening of the skin (another variable), because pigment has an important effect on vitamin D synthesis – the darker the skin, the less synthesis, and vice versa. In fact, because black skin absorbs rather than reflects ultraviolet rays, it receives only about a third of the stimulus to produce natural vitamin D that white skin receives.[57]

Another adaptive mechanism involved acquiring an ability to utilize the calcium in milk and milk products by developing what most of the world's peoples do not have – the lactase enzyme that makes milk digestible by breaking down lactose (milk sugars). Lactose-tolerant individuals (who maintain high levels of the lactase enzyme into adulthood) are assured a regular source of calcium.[58] But even Charles Darwin might have been startled at the speed with which natural selection must have hastened this process of evolutionary adaptation.

This is because women with dark skins and limited sources of calcium in northern latitudes would have been much more likely than their milk-drinking, fair-skinned sisters to have their pelves deformed by rickets or osteomalacia which, in turn, would have sharply limited successful births. Conversely, women with light skins who could drink milk were much less likely to have birthing problems. Not only did they enjoy a satisfactory calcium source, but the lactose in milk could also substitute for vitamin D.[59]

The tradition of June weddings in northern climes has been linked with rickets, because a couple's first baby was likely to be born the following spring and bask in plenty of spring and summer sunshine during its rapid growth phase. By contrast, fall babies were much less healthy because they lacked vitamin D during this phase.[60]

Still another variable in the etiology of rickets came with industrialization. In the cities, smokestacks spewed smoke and smog blotted out sunshine to provoke widespread rickets, especially in gloomy inner city tenements. Some called it the "English disease" as England led the march to industrialize – and the crippled Tiny Tim in Charles Dickens' *Christmas Carol* was probably all too recognizable to readers as a rachitic child.[61]

Yet, the disease was not a monopoly of England or of Europe. In the United States, young black people had been troubled by rickets as slaves, and because of migration to the cities their tendency to develop the illness accelerated after emancipation and well into the twentieth century. Indeed, rickets was so prevalent in turn-of-the-century Washington and New York that physicians believed all black children suffered from the ailment as a kind of rite of passage. An article published in 1920 suggested New York's immigrant children had a similar problem with the disease.[62]

Fortunately, by this time science was closing in on the causes of rickets. In 1917, Alfred Hess and L. J. Unger showed that the disease could be cured by what seemed to be two unrelated treatments – exposure to sunlight or ingestion of cod-liver oil. Three years later a number of researchers, especially those led by Elmer V. McCollum, resolved the apparent contradiction by isolating vitamin D in cod-liver oil and explaining that it could also be made in the skin.[63] In 1931, the chemical structure of the vitamin was identified, and two years later the Borden Company introduced vitamin D-fortified milk to help children ward off rickets.[64]

Thereafter bread and margarine were also fortified and, following the Great Depression, the illness went into spectacular decline in the United States.[65] By contrast, in the Canadian province of Quebec there was fierce resistance to vitamin D-fortification of dairy products until the early 1970s, when health authorities, under considerable pressure, reluctantly gave up the fight. The incidence of rickets at one Quebec hospital dove from 130 per thousand young patients in 1968 to zero by 1976.[66]

Yet, the battle is not over. In the United States during the 1990s, babies – mostly black – were again being hospitalized for rickets, and physicians are now recommending vitamin D supplements for all breast-fed babies. In Great Britain the government only permits the fortification of margarine (which many do not use) with vitamin D, and considerable evidence has accumulated to indicate that rickets (and osteomalacia) is now common among Asian groups in both England and Scotland. Other examples of women suffering from osteomalacia include Muslims and Hindus with a strict tradition of keeping the female skin out of public view and, thus, out of the sun.[67]

In addition, osteoporosis (bone fragility) is laying siege to middle-aged and older women because estrogen loss and aging intensifies the loss of calcium in bones. Research indicates that a lifetime intake of sufficient calcium could cut the world's burden of osteoporosis by around 50 percent (the other 50 percent is caused by non-nutritional factors).[68] The diets of our hunter-gatherer ancestors were extremely rich in calcium because of their consumption of leafy plants. Difficulties with calcium began with the cultivation of cereal grains that are low in the mineral so that hunter-gatherers took in four to six times more calcium than do today's American women.[69]

Osteoporosis is a much greater curse in developed countries because of some significant variables in calcium retention. Phosphorus intake is one of these (calcium cannot be retained in bone without phosphorous), with magnesium another (it promotes the intestinal absorption of calcium). Negative dietary factors include zinc (which inhibits the intestinal absorption of calcium) and protein consumption (high intakes increase the urinary loss of calcium).[70]

But although some phosphorous is needed for calcium retention, a low (or even adequate) calcium intake, coupled with a high phosphate intake, can also produce serious consequences for bone mass. And, incredibly, in view of an osteoporosis epidemic in the United States, food processors are adding some 40 to 50 different phosphate salts to the foods they sell. The result? For the first time in the history of humankind there is a serious excess of phosphorous in the food supply.[71]

A final variable in the etiology of osteoporosis is that in the United States its incidence is much higher among Caucasian women – especially those of northern European ancestry – than it is among those of Asian or African ancestry.[72] There is no satisfactory explanation for this as yet but it does raise questions about the nutritional adaptation of various peoples to various environments and foreshadows some of the queries we make later on about exactly who the "Recommended Dietary Allowances" of nutrients are intended for.

IODINE AND GOITER

A last deficiency disease brought to heel in the early twentieth century was goiter, caused by a deficiency of the ultra trace mineral iodine. Iodine deficiency has usually (but not always) been associated with elevated regions where soils have been leeched of iodine by glaciation, floods, melting snow, and high rainfall. By contrast, peoples living close to the sea have historically seemed immune to goiter. Their diets were rich in iodine because of seafood and algae, the latter known since early times to be a cure for goiter.[73]

Goiters (enlarged thyroid glands) and cretinism (the physically and mentally retarded condition suffered by individuals born of iodine-deficient mothers) are easily spied in the ancient literature of China, India, and Greece.[74] During the Middle Ages, the Alps Mountains were a notorious stronghold of the disease, and it was apparently also present in the interior of Britain. However, there is no way of knowing how widespread it was in England and most places on the Continent because in the medical terminology of the times the term "scrofula" was used to designate both goiter and bovine tuberculosis, another disease that presented with similar symptoms.[75]

Napoleon Bonaparte ordered a systematic investigation of the disease because so many men who came from regions where it prevailed were unfit for military service. And, as the nineteenth century progressed, those searching for a goiter cure came tantalizingly close to pinning iodine deficiency down as the cause, then shied away. If this sounds much like the story of scurvy and its citrus cure, it is, because the discovery of a bacterial cause of diseases sidetracked the search for nutritional causes, in this case sending investigators racing off to find a goiter-causing pathogen.[76]

But the iodine-deficiency hypothesis was finally substantiated on the iodine-leached soils of Ohio and Michigan close to the Great Lakes. David Marine, at Cleveland's Lakeside Hospital, showed that iodine prevented goiter in brook trout, and began giving it to his patients. Between 1916 and 1920, Marine and a colleague carried out a large-scale trial in the Akron area proving conclusively that iodine cured goiter. This, in turn, led to the first preventive use of iodized salt in Michigan, that cut goiter prevalence dramatically, and iodized salt has been in widespread use in America ever since.[77]

Unfortunately, such preventive measures were not always instituted elsewhere. In Spain, for example, the efficacy of iodine was ignored until after the death of dictator Francisco Franco, and many continued to suffer from goiter.[78] In Africa, where the soils south of the Sahara frequently lack iodine, incidences approaching 100 percent have been observed, although part of the problem may lie in goitrogenous agents such as heavily consumed manioc.[79] And globally, the International Council for Control of

Iodine Deficiency Disorders (founded in 1986) has been coordinating and facilitating international and interagency cooperation in an all-out war on goiter that has yet to be won. As of the late 1980s, some 200 million of the world's peoples suffered from goiter and more than 3 million were cretins.[80]

OTHER VITAMINS, MINERALS, AND CONDITIONS

There are also eating disorders that can be symptomatic of nutritional deficiencies but seem to have psychological causes as well. Apparently new ones (relatively speaking) like anorexia and bulimia are discussed later on. But another, pica (a craving for and consumption of non-foods) has been observed and described since ancient times – since Socrates and Aristotle wrote about earth-eating (a form of pica called geophagy or geophagia).[81]

Children and pregnant women are the most visible non-food eaters in pica literature. In sixteenth-century England both groups had representatives who nibbled on coal, although worldwide, soils, especially clays, have generally been the substance of choice. It has been hypothesized that in the past dirt-eating was a response to anemia, especially that caused by hookworm infection that drains the body of iron – a "germ of laziness" reducing its white victims in the southern United States to sorry clay-eating derelicts. Recently, however, pica usage has been attributed to a wider spectrum of mineral deficiencies such as those of calcium, manganese, as well as iron – deficiencies that pregnant women are especially likely to suffer from. But it is also conceded that the practice can have a cultural basis, and one that purportedly diffused from Africa via the slave trade, at least in part because of a belief that certain earths have healing properties.

Nonetheless, given the consistency with which pica has been tied to iron and other mineral deficiencies, nutrition apparently does have a role in this disorder, making pica a nutritional disease; and it seems likely that other such shadowy deficiency diseases still await discovery, or perhaps better recognition. The fat-soluble vitamin E, for example, was discovered in 1923, but forty years elapsed before it was shown to be as essential to human health as the other vitamins. For one thing, it stops body fat from becoming rancid. But vitamin E is also associated with muscle health. Moreover, it can attenuate the damage caused by free radicals during a heart attack, may be protective against heart attacks, and, perhaps, some forms of cancer.[82]

Vitamin K is another fat-soluble vitamin known to be essential – vitally so because it works to prevent bleeding. Its deficiency is rare in adults but its administration to mothers before birth and to their infants shortly after delivery has been recommended since 1961 to forestall hemorrhagic disease. It is also employed to correct overdoses of anticoagulants such as coumarin compounds used by patients prone to thrombosis or clot formation.[83]

Finally, the ancient Greeks employed magnesium as a purgative, but it was not until the early 1930s that the mineral was given essential nutrient status – appropriately enough since life on the planet would be impossible without it. Photosynthesis, the process that enriches the air with oxygen, depends on magnesium.[84] Low intakes of the mineral can produce the twitching and convulsions of tetany (especially in the very young), and a lack of magnesium has also been implicated in coronary artery disease.

Where the water is soft (meaning a low mineral content) and the arable soils are magnesium-deficient, cereals (a major source of the mineral) will have a low magnesium content, and the population will suffer an elevated rate of cardiovascular mortality.[85] In Western countries this sort of syndrome is mimicked when foods heavy in starch and sugar predominate in the diet along with soft drinks and distilled alcohol. All of these are very low in magnesium, with the problem compounded by an agriculture that relies on magnesium-depleting pesticides and herbicides, and accelerated growing techniques that inhibit magnesium fixation.[86]

CHAPTER

23

THE PERILS OF PLENTY

These same forces – improvements in transportation, preservation,
and distribution – liberating Americans from seasonality also con-
tinued to free them from the dictates of regional geography.

Harvey Levenstein (1993)[1]

IT IS WORTH REPEATING that many of the breakthroughs in nutritional science paradoxically occurred during the depression years of food riots, soup kitchens, and breadlines, where the hungry in the cities shoved aside dogs and cats to get at the contents of garbage cans, and rural folks ate wild roots and plants. These were years when morbidity and mortality rates caused by pellagra, scurvy, and rickets were rising alarmingly, and bowleggedness continued to be a common sight.[2]

Needless to say, it was not a time for experimenting with foreign foods, nor were the food-rationed war years that followed. Despite rationing, however, Americans ate better than ever during the war although this did not prevent the "experts" from touching off a brief episode of vitamin hysteria, beginning in 1943 when the Food and Nutrition Board erroneously told Americans – now back to work with plenty of money to spend – that their diets were *dangerously* deficient in many of the chief nutrients. Such foolishness only underscores the fact that the functions and chemistry of vitamins and minerals were still poorly understood. So did proposals for widespread vitamin supplementation, with bread, cereals, milk, and oleomargarine all fortified during the war. It was a vita-mania pot that Adel Davis would continue to stir in ensuing decades with her recommendations for an excessive, even dangerous, vitamin intake.[3] By 1994, vitamin supplements constituted a four billion dollar industry.[4]

Backyard barbeques came into vogue in the 1950s. By 1995, 77 percent of American households had at least one grill generally presided over by males who, at first limited themselves to charring hunks of meat, slabs of ribs, chicken parts, or, less ambitiously, hot dogs and burgers.[5] It was men who bought the barbequing cookbooks that began appearing in the fifties, and some became sophisticated cooks who promoted themselves to the indoor kitchen. Frequently more culinarily adventuresome than their wives, many led their families into foreign cooking.

By the 1960s dark clouds had once again built up on the health horizon, even as Americans were congratulating themselves on being the best-fed people in the world. In 1953, University of Minnesota physiologist Ancel Keys had ominously correlated high rates of coronary heart disease with high intakes of animal fats,[6] and in the United States coronary artery disease (CAD) rates had spiraled upward with CAD death rates rising from 180 to over 200 per 100,000 by the early 1960s.[7]

There were also cancer concerns. Worries about cancer-causing additives in foods prompted a 1958 amendment to the Food, Drug, and Cosmetic Act of 1938, which forbade the use of additives that had not been used long enough to be "generally recognized as safe" (GRAS). At the behest of Congressman James J. Delaney, an amendment was inserted that became a controversial clause (the Delaney Clause), which stated that if any amount of an additive was shown to produce cancer in humans or in test animals then no amount of the additive could be used. Needless to say, food processors were not amused by the joke that everything seems to give mice cancer, and they correctly pointed out that humankind would not be here if low levels of carcinogens could not be tolerated. Paracelsus, a Renaissance physician, wrote a long time ago that all substances were poisons and it was the dose that mattered; an important truth, but no Congressman wants to be known as voting for cancer.[8]

If the apparent upsurge of these chronic diseases did not give Americans enough to fret about, they also found themselves battling obesity in a way they never had before. "Plenty" was multiplying. By the late 1960s, the average output of meat per breeding animal was double that of the 1920s; the average Wisconsin dairy cow was yielding ten quarts of milk a day instead of the six it had provided in 1940; and the average farm acre was producing seventy bushels of corn, up from twenty-five in 1916.[9]

Paradoxically, however, while many wrestled with the problem of too much to eat, others were not getting enough. The Field Foundation report entitled *Hunger U.S.A.* and the television documentary *Hunger in America*, both released in 1968, touched off President Nixon's "war on hunger" as well as a debate over the methodology used by hunger studies.[10] Yet, despite the "war" there seems little doubt that food insufficiency remains a chronic problem for some 35 million Americans. During the first four years of the new century hunger was either present in or a threat to about 12.6 million American families (a bit over 11 percent of U.S. households). Obviously, this has nothing to do with food shortages. But it has everything to do with poverty caused by joblessness, the cost of housing and other basic needs, and a welfare system that does not put up a safety net.[11] Some defenders of the system, however, take a perverse delight in pointing out that obesity is more pervasive among the poor than among the affluent, brushing aside that the poor feed disproportionately on cheap and fatty fast foods.[12]

In the 1940s, obesity was defined as "overfatness," implying that one could be overweight but not "over-fat." But in the following decades such niceties were tossed overboard – people had become sufficiently concerned about their waistlines that sales of low-calorie and diet products skyrocketed and books on weight control became best sellers. In 1962, 40 percent of American families were using low-calorie or diet products on a regular basis; by 1972 the percentage had jumped to 70.[13]

There was good reason for concern. Over the past two centuries the fat intake of those on a western diet had risen five times, while their sugar intake had leaped fifteen times. Americans who were taking in less than 2,000 calories daily at the end of the eighteenth century were swallowing over 3,000 toward the end of the twentieth century – and by 1995 more than half of them had achieved the "ideal" weight of an earlier America, when slimness was regarded as a sign of ill-health and products, like Groves Tasteless Chill Tonic, promised to add "much admired heft to the figure" by making children and adults "as fat as pigs."[14]

By the beginning of the twenty-first century, there was such plenty that a mean of almost 4,000 calories was available on a daily basis for every man, woman, and child in the nation (up from 3,700 in 1990), representing over a third more than the caloric RDA for men and over twice that for women.[15] Moreover, the calories in question have increasingly come from highly processed calorie-dense foods, which means that they reach the stomach in such a compact form that we generally get more of them than we need before ever feeling comfortably full.[16] For the sake of comparison, unprocessed plant foods such as cereals, pulses, potatoes, vegetables, and fruits comprise around 61 percent of the calories consumed in Crete, and 74 percent of those in Greece. But in the United States only 37 percent of energy is derived from these unprocessed foods.[17]

These are some of the reasons behind the so-called "obesity epidemic" that has ambushed the nation, and yet another, some say, is that food is too cheap for our own good. In 1965, Americans spent an average of 18.5 percent of their income for food – down from 24.4 percent in 1955. This represented the lowest percentage ever, as well as the lowest in the world – a situation that has not changed.[18]

Paradoxically then, life-giving food has become life-threatening and not just for Americans. The World Health Organizations' (WHO) fears that the obesity epidemic would be globalized during the first part of the twenty-first century were realized in the very first year of that century when it was reported that the number of overweight people in the world had reached a bit over a billion, matching almost exactly another billion that are badly nourished and underweight.[19]

Westerners, of course, are in the "globeisity" vanguard with America, the United Kingdom, Russia, and Germany all having overweight majorities that seem to be getting heavier by the day, thanks to an energy intake that far exceeds output.[20] Hunter-gatherers expended great amounts of energy in finding their food; farmers did the same in growing theirs. Modern Westerners, by contrast, although metabolically still hunter-gatherers, use little more energy in food acquisition than it takes to push a cart around a supermarket and open their wallets at the checkout counter.

Caloric needs used to be based, in part, on occupation-related energy expenditures, but today's labor-saving machinery has sharply reduced occupational caloric requirements, just as automobiles and elevators have reduced those previously needed for walking and climbing. Television and computers lure us even further into physical inactivity, and the consequences of a growing gap between energy intake and energy output have become terribly evident in the onset of the so-called "chronic" diseases that beset us – coronary artery disease, adult onset diabetes, high blood pressure, and cancer.[21]

The following unsettling numbers lurk behind these modern killers. Between 1988 and 1991, one-third of America's population was overweight; by 1995 estimates indicated that around 55 percent were overweight, and if the young were excluded then 63 percent of men and 55 percent of women over the age of 25 were either overweight or obese.

In 1999, according to an article in *The Journal of the American Medical Association*, 21 percent of male and 27 percent of female Americans were not just overweight but obese, and obesity was killing upwards of 300,000 U.S. citizens annually.[22] In 2001, 65 percent of all Americans were overweight, double the percentage of a few decades earlier, and then in the spring of 2004, *USAToday* told travelers that diet and physical inactivity were doing in 400,000 Americans annually and that obesity was edging out tobacco use as the nation's number one killer. In 2005, the promised revisions to the Food Guide Pyramid corrected its earlier silence on exercise by urging that people exercise between 30 and 90 minutes every day.[23]

Such numbers also lie behind businesses like the weight-loss industry, already doing 5 billion dollars worth of business in 1990. Good for that business, too, was a 1996 Harris Poll report that 74 percent of Americans aged 28 and older perceived themselves to be overweight.[24] If these perceptions seem high, it is a fact that since the 1980s the number of extremely obese Americans has quadrupled despite "low-carb" diets, Slimfast, Richard Simmons, and jazzercise. This has given new meaning to the term "personal expansionism" which has stimulated the clothing industry (in 1985 the most common size for women's sportswear was an 8; in 2003 it was a 14); health-delivery systems (around 250,000 operations to help obese people lose weight are performed annually, and demand for obesity surgeons is skyrocketing); and Medicare, which has tossed its old policy that obesity is not a disease in the wastebasket (thus opening the door to millions of claims for stomach surgery and diet programs). It is also responsible for such novel enterprises as the construction of larger and sturdier couches, chairs, and toilet seats, the manufacture of seat-belt extenders for airlines, extra-wide umbrellas, bathroom scales that can weigh people up to 1,000 pounds, and the production of super-sized caskets with cemeteries offering super-sized plots.

A search for substitute foods and ingredients may have originated for reasons other than weight loss, but it has been spurred on by the current dietary dilemma. Margarine, the first successful substitute food, has been commercially produced in America since 1873 as an inexpensive alternative to butter, although not without bitter opposition from dairy farmers who, at one point, demanded that margarine be dyed purple to discourage its purchase. Unlike butter, margarine lacked vitamins A and D, so that, after the vitamins were discovered, it became obligatory for margarine manufacturers to add these vitamins.[25] By the 1950s, margarine was viewed by the health-conscious not just as a low cost, but also as a low fat alternative to butter. Subsequently, however, doubts emerged about its healthiness.

Margarine is made from those unsaturated vegetable oils praised by nutritionists. The trouble is that in margarine-making the oils are hydrogenated to give them the consistency of butter. It is a process that saturates some of the fat; and worse, it creates trans-fatty acids, shown in the 1990s to raise levels of low-density lipoproteins (the bad cholesterol) and to lower levels of high-density lipoproteins (the good cholesterol). Margarine consumers, therefore, were apparently increasing their risk of a heart attack – substantially so in the estimation of some.[26]

Health considerations also drove the search for a sugar substitute. Saccharin was the first to enter the market at the beginning of the twentieth century. But in 1977, saccharin was shown to be carcinogenic in rats, and the FDA tried to get it banned under the Delaney Clause. Congress, however, enacted a moratorium on the ban (which was renewed several times), and in 1991 the FDA withdrew its ban proposal so that saccharin continues to be used in America as well as in more than ninety other countries.

Aspartame, FDA-approved in 1981 for table use, with only four calories per gram, made possible the wildly successful Diet Coke in 1982 and subsequently became the sweetener of choice for 80 percent of the diet soft drink industry. It is also employed in a range of foods from fruit juices to yogurt products. U.S. aspartame production accounts for about 80 percent of the global market and is added to over 5,000 products in more than 90 countries.[27] These are consumed by most everybody so that a recent campaign of internet terrorism which claimed that aspartame caused multiple sclerosis, Alzheimer's, Parkinson's, and a host of other illnesses scared the daylights out of many. But there was not an ounce of truth in the allegations.

In addition, there are numerous other artificial sweeteners (called low-calorie or non-caloric because the word "artificial" has an ominous ring to it) either on the market, waiting for FDA approval, or still the focus of research. Yet, importantly, low calorie sweeteners have not even shown up as a ripple in the obesity tide because they clearly have not replaced caloric sweeteners. Rather, American sugar consumption has steadily increased despite the use of artificial sweeteners, as has world consumption. In 2004, however, the WHO managed to hammer out an agreement among the world's health ministers that sugar consumption be limited, without the sugar industry destroying it.[28]

Fat substitutes are suspected of precipitating similar unanticipated consequences by increasing the nation's appetite for high-fat foods. These include "carbohydrate" substitutes like Oatrim, protein- based substitutes such as Simplesse, and synthetic fat substitutes, with Olestra a notable example. But in addition to concerns about unintended consequences, there are other unresolved issues of safety and nutrition, notable among them the risk of allergenicity and gastrointestinal distress.[29] Fat substitutes are nothing new, and there are many of them on today's market, but to date, despite considerable publicity, none have proven to be an unqualified success – the bonanza that fake fat manufacturers are shooting for.

Dietary fiber rests on even shakier ground. Although long known as a stimulant for colonic activity, this non-food was pretty well dismissed by medicine as "roughage" until the 1970s. Then suddenly it became a "miracle" preventive of diabetes (by lowering glucose levels), colorectal cancer (by bulking up stools), and heart disease (by reducing cholesterol).[30]

By the 1990s, however, voices questioning the efficacy of fiber were being heard. It was not at all clear that fiber had much, if any, effect on glucose; lots and lots of fiber– (and calorie-) filled foods like cereals and legumes were required to have much of an effect on cholesterol; some fiber-containing cereals like oats were high in calcium (associated with coronary artery disease by a European study group);[31] and no optimal intake of fiber had been determined.[32] Perhaps, if fiber had been taken more seriously as a displacement for fats and other foods by making one feel full, it might have helped slow the obesity epidemic. Yet, fiber by itself contains no nutrients, and heavy fiber intakes deprive the body of nutrient-rich foodstuffs. In the anxiety to shed pounds it was frequently forgotten that the body does have a requirement for dietary fat, in no small part because fatty acids participate in every aspect of cellular life.[33]

Fiber has always had champions, like John Harvey Kellogg, who believed that meat eating was overstimulating and chided "modern people" for the lack of fiber in their diet; and recent writers continue to insist that a lack of dietary fiber is behind various "Western" diseases.[34] Certainly, the nation's 10 million or so vegetarians are convinced that a vegetable diet sustains health and prevents disease, and many believe it is of moral importance as well.[35] The American vegetarian legions, which have increased dramatically since the 1960s, represent the tail end of a long line of vegetarians stretching back to Pythagoras, the Greek natural philosopher who founded a sixth-century BCE religious community based on vegetarianism.[36]

Animal welfare was at the root of early vegetarianism, but medicine also had something to do with its rationale. Some practitioners feared that meat turned putrid after it was consumed (just as it did when not consumed fast enough) which, in turn, brought on ill health, or a nasty disposition, or both. Others felt that undercooked meat could be a curse all by itself. Illustrative was the blood-drenched French Revolution and the tyranny of Napoleon, said in England to be the natural result of a French appetite for rare meat.[37]

Despite the popularity of vegetarianism however, most people, both historically and today, have been underwhelmed by arguments for vegetarianism, in some instances, because of apparently confounding contradictions. For example, despite a heavy meat and fat diet the Eskimos remained remarkably free of the chronic "Western" diseases so long as they continued with their traditional regimen.[38] But when that regimen became "Westernized" – with high doses of saturated fats, sugar, and carbohydrates – Alaskan natives began to develop "Western" afflictions such as obesity, diabetes, hypertension, and heart disease.[39]

Other evidence that meat is far from harmful to human health emerged from a widely-publicized experiment. Two Western volunteers ate a ratio of two pounds of raw, lean meat to one half-pound of raw fat for a year – and nothing else. Both individuals not only survived, but thrived, and one of the two volunteers was judged to be in better health at the end of the experiment than when it began, suggesting, of course, that Western diets may not be all that good for Westerners either.[40] In a similar vein, a study of the Masai of Tanganyika, who consume almost exclusively the meat, blood, and milk of their cattle, turned up no arteriosclerotic disease, purportedly caused by artery-clogging cholesterol.[41]

Pacific Islanders are in a health predicament similar to that of the Eskimos. They, too, have developed extremely high rates of diabetes mellitus II as well as hypertension after the adoption of a "Western" diet.[42] It appears, then, that food globalization can be positively harmful to people – especially those who just yesterday were healthy hunters and gatherers. This, in turn, brings up some questions about what actually constitutes good nutrition, and other questions regarding nutritional adaptation.

The United States government has wrestled with questions about the constituents of good nutrition since 1941, when the Food and Nutrition Board of the U.S. National Research Council established a dietary standard called Recommended Dietary Allowances (RDA). Revised continually, the

RDA is the U.S. nutritional guide, and about forty other countries have also established similar national dietary standards.[43] Then, more recently, in 1992 the USDA established a Food Guide Pyramid to visually depict the amounts of the various foods that make for a balanced diet, the pyramid that was updated in 2005. It puts oils at the top (use sparingly), and bread, pasta, rice, and other cereals at the base (6–11 servings daily).[44] Meat, fish, and poultry, along with dairy products, are right under the oils, but two to three servings from each of the two categories are recommended.[45]

Next came food labeling – this in the wake of a flood of false and misleading health claims about foods, which brought a regulatory crackdown in 1994. Despite howls of financial pain from the food industry, nutrition labeling was made mandatory to let consumers know the macro- and micronutrients contained in the products they buy, and especially the levels of calories, carbohydrates, fats, sodium, and cholesterol.[46] Labeling, however, is tricky because manufacturers can take advantage of the labels to misrepresent their products, so that many assertions remain unblushingly misleading.[47] A good example is "low-fat" or "nonfat" claims for products, which might lead consumers to believe they are slimming. But, as a rule, sugar simply replaces the fat, and the calorie count remains high. Another familiar ploy is ground beef labeled – say – 80 percent lean, which implies that it is low in fat. Yet, what if the label read "20 percent fat" and went on to inform the consumer that a three and a half ounce hamburger patty with 20 percent fat delivers 260 calories, 70 percent of these from fat?[48] Conversely, a lack of labeling can also be dangerous and, until 2006, manufacturers were not required to list the trans fats contained in their products – trans fats or partially dehydrogenated oils that are understood to elevate the risk of heart disease.

The Food Guide Pyramid and labeling requirements clearly represent governmental responses to the nation's obesity epidemic. But from the beginning, the Food Guide Pyramid has been under attack. In part this was because powerful food lobbies such as the National Cattlemen's Association, the National Milk Producers' Federation, and the National Pork Producers Council had a hand in molding it.[49] But it was also the result of carelessness. In the 1992 food pyramid, for example, milk and ice cream were placed in the same category with lentils and bologna; and olive oil and butter with wheat bread and doughnuts.[50] Another problem was the 1992 pyramid did not take into consideration people's age, gender, weight, and exercise patterns, (although this has been corrected to some extent in the 2005 revision).

Then there are deeper objections. Cereal-grains and dairy products have been basic food groups only for the past 500 generations, and some suspect that this has not been enough time for the human body to make all the necessary genetic adjustments to these "new-fangled" foods.[51] Our hunter-gatherer ancestors rarely, if ever, ate from either group, but did take in considerable fats. The Food Guide Pyramid, however, encourages the consumption of much in the way of refined carbohydrates and dairy products and makes all fats, including oils and even fish oils, seem dangerous. But in light of the disastrous nutritional experience of recent hunter-gatherers such as Eskimos, Pacific Islanders, and the Arctic Inuit, who have switched to a "recommended" diet, the question arises of exactly who is supposed to benefit from such nutritional guidance?[52]

The recommendations promote the consumption of a mixed diet of food groups such as cereals, fruits and vegetables, meat and fish, and dairy products, even though the Inuit (and the Eskimos and Pacific Islanders and most people in the world) are lactose intolerant – meaning that they cannot digest many of the recommended dairy products.[53] The traditional Inuit diet consisted almost entirely of caribou, whale, and seal meat, fish, birds, eggs, and meat from other land mammals that could be killed, such as muskoxen (*Ovibos moschatus*). The latter coexisted with mammoths and mastodons, but was hunted so relentlessly by humans for its hides and meat that it was near extinction by the turn of the nineteenth century. Clearly meat was the most important part of the Inuit diet. But the mixed diet tries to steer consumers away from too much meat, lest they develop cardiovascular disease. The Inuit, however, were virtually free of this affliction, along with renal disease, hypertension, and diabetes as are other contemporary foraging peoples.[54]

If the Inuit diet was high in protein and fat, it was extremely low in carbohydrate-containing foods – cereals, fruits, and vegetables – yet the Pyramid recommends that foods high in carbohydrates be consumed in abundance. In short, the Inuit diet is practically a mirror-opposite of the Food Guide Pyramid recommendations. But, like the Eskimos, the Inuit had remarkably good health until they began to eat what the rest of us eat.[55] Nor is this a recent phenomenon. Long ago colonists in New England reported that their Indian neighbors remained healthy so long as they continued to eat those foods they were accustomed to.[56]

This has been labeled the "New World Syndrome" because those who made the rugged journey across the Bering Straits into an icebound New

World would very likely have owed their survival to a thrifty metabolic genotype that they passed along to their descendents. Most likely it can be shown that Pacific Islanders have a similar health dilemma because their ancestors, too, needed such genetic equipment to survive the hardships of long-distance sea voyages.

Polar opposites of the Inuit diet are the cereal-based diets of Southeast Asians and Central and South Americans, which, as we have already seen, can be downright dangerous. As a rule, natives of Asia know how to avoid the deficiencies of thiamine that cause beriberi, just as Native Americans sidestepped niacin deficiency and, consequently, pellagra. But cereal-based diets, low in protein, predispose the young to protein energy malnutrition and can encourage sometimes deadly mineral deficiencies because of the soils the cereals are grown upon.

One example is Keshan disease in the Keshan district of China – with heart enlargement a major symptom – which results from an extremely low concentration of selenium in the region's soil;[57] another example is growth retardation – actually dwarfism – and hypogonadism in the Near and Middle East, which derives from a zinc deficient cereal-based diet containing negligible amounts of animal protein;[58] and, as already noted, goiter stems from iodine-leached soils.[59]

In addition, there are numerous potentially dangerous trace element deficiencies. Many of these trace elements have been known since antiquity, whereas others have only been recently recognized. Nonetheless, they have been deemed essential during the past three or four decades (or are suspected of being essential) because of deficiencies spied in experimental herbivorous animals and in humans receiving prolonged and total parenteral (intravenous) feeding.

In alphabetical order these are: *arsenic,* "the "king of poisons" until the nineteenth century, but now found to be important in animal growth and heart function; *boron,* employed in the past as a food preservative, yet now thought to be important in calcium and protein metabolism as well as brain function; *chromium,* which seems to have a positive effect on glucose and lipid metabolism; *copper,* whose deficiency has been associated with numerous cardiovascular problems; *fluorine,* which protects against abnormal demineralization of calcified tissues; *manganese,* whose deficiency has been linked to osteoporosis and epilepsy; *molybdenum,* needed by nitrogen-fixing organisms and present in animal tissues; *nickel,* which may have something to do with the distribution of calcium, iron, zinc, and other elements in the human body; *selenium*, whose deficiency can produce Keshan disease in humans;[60] *silicon*, essential in bone formation; and *vanadium*, perhaps involved in thyroid metabolism.[61]

Trace element deficiencies are rare for those on meat-based diets because the elements are also essential in the diets of animals used for meat.[62] Meat-based diets are also less toxic than their plant-based counterparts because the bodies of food animals screen the toxins that accompany the plants. Especially in these days of sustainable agriculture and organically grown foods, people have been taught to conceive of food toxins in terms of synthetic herbicides, pesticides, and food additives. But the overwhelming majority of toxins we consume are natural, not synthetic.[63] Plants protect themselves from all sorts of predators – insects, microbes, and animals (including humans) – by synthesizing naturally occurring insecticides and substances toxic for animals, many of which have only been diluted because of selective plant breeding and food processing.[64]

Potatoes, for example, have compounds that can interfere with the autonomic nervous system and nitrates that can form N-nitroso compounds shown to be carcinogenic, not to mention mutagenic, in experimental rodents. The natural pesticides in celery (and the whole parsley plant group) called "psoralins" can precipitate a nasty case of dermatitis, or even serious disease when ingestion is followed by exposure to ultraviolet light; manioc contains cyanide; and peanuts (along with many other plants such as chilli peppers) can be contaminated with aflatoxins that cause liver cancer.[65]

It staggers the imagination to contemplate the wear and tear on our forebears, inflicted by an ongoing trial and error process of determining which foods could be safely eaten, which ones needed special treatment to remove toxins (like manioc), and which ones should be left strictly alone (like deadly nightshade).[66] It puts an added strain on the imagination to comprehend how those same forebears adapted to myriad nutritional environments. But adapt they did – lactose tolerance is a fine example – which brings us back to the question of just who the U.S. dietary guidelines are aimed at.

Like their Arctic counterparts, the Indians of North America also suffer from soaring rates of diabetes (the Pima have the highest in the world), obesity, hypertension, and heart disease – presumably because of a switch to a Western diet. African Americans and Native Hawaiians (who have the worst health profile in the nation) are similarly afflicted.[67] Nor, as already pointed out, are virtually all Native Americans and most Asian and African Americans able to digest milk or utilize many of its products. The point is that U.S. dietary guidelines have not been globalized, but instead are almost exclusively reflective of European food traditions – a point recently made by a congressional Black Caucus. They complained that the fifth edition of *Dietary Guidelines* revealed a "consistent racial bias" by recommending dairy products as a part of a balanced diet when most African Americans over the age of five or so cannot digest the lactose in milk.[68]

The reason they cannot digest milk is genetic, which is probably just the tip of a genetic iceberg. Harkening back to the concept of a "thrifty" gene, it seems apparent that although those of European ancestry have had a centuries-long period of transition from bread and cheese to cheeseburgers, Native Americans, Native Hawaiians, and even African Americans did not have this luxury. The traditional diets of these groups were abruptly "Westernized" leaving them predisposed to the chronic ills of the West. But when there has been a return to the traditional diet as, for example, among some natives in Hawaii, health improvements have been described as miraculous.[69]

Obviously this is not the only bias built in to what is essentially a compromise among the various segments of a food industry determined to sell its products, nutritionists (many of whom are beholden to those segments), and a government sympathetic to the food industry, but one that is also trying to do something about the obesity epidemic. That "something" however, is often clumsily and thoughtlessly done.[70]

Part of the problem is that haranguing the public about matters of food and nutrition has become an occupation and preoccupation for many who can put together a few credentials. Nutritionists, physicians, federal and state officials, food writers, and faddists have all regularly dispensed conflicting, confusing, even misleading nutritional advice and nutritional guidelines, from World War II to the present. Couple this with the scores of magazine and newspaper articles appearing daily on how to eat right, along with competing best sellers laying out dietary regimens, and one might be pardoned for drawing the conclusion that the major accomplishments of such counseling has been to either make eating a nightmare for those paying attention or to bombard generations, past and present, into a weary cynicism that lets them just tune out.[71]

This is doubtless much of the reason why the Food Guide Pyramid seems completely ignored by the millions now rediscovering in *déjà vu* fashion regimens high in protein and low in carbohydrates (they have been around for a century or more), among them the Stillman diet that first appeared in the 1960s, the Atkins diet in use since 1972, and the more recent South Beach and Protein Power diets. High protein–low carbohydrate diets, of course, turn that Pyramid upside down with the counterintuitive notion that calories don't count – that red meats, fats, cheese and other foods high in fat are good foods, but bread, pasta, fruits, and most vegetables are not, even though the world's thinnest peoples eat the most carbohydrates, whereas the heaviest people eat the most protein.

Yet, such diets work, at least in the short run, and are easy enough to stick to so that restaurant menus and supermarkets all tout low-carb foods, and there are over 1,000 such products on their shelves. By contrast, conventional bakers are suffering and restaurants like Panera have developed low-carb bread. Such a faddish backlash against conventional wisdom is also reflected in *The Bad For You Cookbook*, based on the principle that if it can be poached it can be fried; the enthusiasm for high fat and sugared ice cream products like the Haagen-Daz "Mint Chip Dazzler" at an incredible 1,270 calories according to the Center for Science in the Public Interest; and new high in saturated fat, calorie-packed products like Sara Lee's Calzone Creations or Kraft's cheesecake snack bar, denounced by that Center as "food porn."

Yet, such "porn" appeals to women who have a craving for sweets and to men who crave meat for reasons not fully understood, despite some fifty studies during the first half of the 1990s. Some researchers suspect, however, that the differences in gender food cravings boil down to men being ruled by testosterone and women by estrogen.[72] Perhaps related is that metabolism in the brain, especially in those areas associated with addiction, increases significantly at the sight or smell of favorite foods, opening up the possibility that the considerable amount of food stimuli that assaults us daily in the media may have something to do with the obesity epidemic.

THE GLOBALIZATION
OF PLENTY

*The world of food requires unobtrusive erudition. It is well known
that curiosity is the basic thrust toward knowledge, which in turn is
the necessary precondition for pleasure.*

Giovanni Rebora[1]

AS WE JUST SAW, American anguish about weight and well-being has
prompted scientific probes into obscure food-related alleyways. It also
did much to advance food globalization in America. During the 1950s,
Americans with a hankering for the foreign had pizza parlors for eating
out and canned chow mein and chop suey for eating in, but most were still
meat and potatoes people. It was a time when nobody used garlic and only
winos drank wine. But this stolid unimaginative image was chipped away
at beginning with the refined tastes of highly visible Jacqueline Kennedy
and her fondness for French, Italian, and even British foods. Moreover,
Americans took a good look at their waistlines, had their hearts checked,
worried about their fat consumption, and began in earnest to adopt foreign
foods increasingly thought to be healthy.

A stick prodding the public in this direction was the controversial
1977 document entitled *Dietary Goals for the United States*, published
by the Senate Select Committee headed by George McGovern. Its 1978
bombshell edition alleged that the nation was under siege from an epidemic of "killer diseases" – heart disease, stroke, cancer, and diabetes, and
obesity brought on by changes in the American diet during the preceding

half-century. The document called for a more "natural" diet, as well as more nutritional research to counter the epidemic.[2]

The carrot came with an 1980 publication by Ancel Keys and colleagues on the virtues of the Mediterranean diet. These investigators added more than two decades of their own research to earlier explorations of the Mediterranean diet, which, when contrasted with most "Western" diets, revealed a clear relationship between the intake of saturated fats and cholesterol and the incidence of heart disease, diabetes, and certain forms of cancer.[3]

The Mediterranean diet, although based on some consumption of fish, was pretty close to vegetarian – rich in fruits, vegetables, legumes, tomatoes, and grains, with olive oil, a monounsaturated oil, providing most of the fat.[4] It also famously featured alcohol in the form of wine as a regular part of the Mediterranean regimen.[5] It did not take long for scientific research as well as popular writing about the Mediterranean diet to turn into industries, particularly after it became apparent that the diet had a special appeal for those interested in guilt-free alcohol consumption.[6] Indeed, a glass or two (or more) of wine became a dietary imperative for many in the 1990s after the beverage was promoted to the rank of a heart-disease preventive, because some studies showed that it elevates blood levels of high density lipoprotein, the "good" artery cleansing cholesterol.

Appreciation of wine as a miracle worker soared even higher as details of the so-called "French Paradox" began appearing in the media and were featured on the TV series *60 Minutes*. Those details credited red wine drinking among the French with their relatively low rate of heart attacks.[7] Especially impressive was the much lower than expected rate of coronary artery disease among the foie gras–gobbling (but wine drinking) people of Gascony who were also heavy smokers and whose diet incorporated many more cholesterol-laden foods than just goose liver. All of this led to a panel of nutrition authorities from Harvard University and the World Health Organization, which unveiled in 1994 a "Mediterranean Diet Pyramid." This gave olive oil a prominent place, along with cheese, yogurt, and, of course, red wine.[8]

Wine achieving health-food status arrested falling sales of California wines, especially the reds. American tastes had leaned toward white wines as fish and chicken became trendy, but now veered back to red wines while an expanding population of wine drinkers discovered what Californians already knew. California wines had come a long way since the 1960s when

Orson Welles, as a television pitchman for Paul Masson Wines, intoned that "we sell no wine before its time."[9]

The transformation began at the University of California at Davis, where from the 1950s through the 1970s new technologies were applied to turn winemaking and vineyard management into sciences. California wines began to compete favorably with wines the world over and, during the 1990s, the number of wineries in that state jumped from 600 to more than 900.[10] The baby boomers were absolutely charmed by wine and bought plenty of foreign, as well as domestic, offerings. Those of France, Germany, Austria, and Italy began sharing shelf-space with the wines of Spain and Portugal, only to be jostled by New World bottles from Australia, New Zealand, Argentina, and Chile (in 1993, U.S. consumers bought close to two million cases of Chilean wines). Americans began to speak knowledgeably of Viño Cohcha y Toro, a German Kabinett versus a Trockenbeernauslese, and the "Super Tuscans" of Italy, while putting a few bottles of French Bordeaux down in their newly constructed wine cellars.[11] And, in 1999, a new French wine was released, the "Paradoxe Blanc." Named for the "French Paradox," it is a white wine made like a red wine to boost its antioxidant-rich tannins.

But a new appreciation of wine was not limited to the West. In China, a growing health awareness has produced a market for dozens of foreign wines, mostly cheap ones from France, Spain, and nearby Australia. And although the custom of mixing wine with soft drinks like Coca-Cola or Sprite may cause Western connoisseurs to shudder, the Chinese are enjoying the benefits of wine by the pitcher.

Olive oil was also credited with lowering the incidence of heart disease among Mediterranean peoples, and its use in America soared to the point where people became picky wanting more than just "extra-virgin." For many it now had to be "cold-pressed extra virgin," and arguments about the superiority of Greek, or Italian, or Spanish olive oils became as routine as the pesto made from them.[12] Per capita pasta consumption more than doubled between 1968 and 1982, the sale of spaghetti sauces skyrocketed, and America discovered risotto and balsamic vinagar.[13]

The Food Guide Pyramid, which included pasta and rice at its base, pushed up the consumption of both, although Chinese foods were dealt a glancing blow by the 1994 revelation from the Center for Science in the Public Interest that popular Chinese restaurant dishes had high levels of fats, cholesterol, and sodium.[14] The Center also showed that foods served in

Tex-Mex restaurants were ridiculously high in saturated fats.[15] But sushi in Japanese establishments was not and, improbably, after its introduction in the 1960s, Americans gingerly discovered that they could stomach raw fish, and sushi became something of a craze. Food critic Craig Claiborne enthused that sushi was "a great vehicle for maintaining a stable weight and is enormously gratifying to the appetite."[16]

Dim sum – Chinese appetizers – also became popular, as did the French *foie gras*. Yogurt, used in much of the world for ages, remained a novelty in the United States as late as the 1950s. Subsequently, however, it became a U.S. staple, available in myriad flavors and textures from dozens of producers. Annual sales of kosher foods grew from 1.25 million dollars in the 1940s to almost $2 billion by 1993, even though less than a third of the consumers were Jewish.[17] Kosher foods were perceived by the public to be healthier than their non-kosher counterparts. And in 1994, Lean Cuisine varieties of frozen foods that could be microwaved in a few minutes included Cheese Lasagna, Fettucini with Chicken in Alfredo Sauce, Mandarin Chicken, and Teriyaki Stir Fry.[18]

Hawaii may have been the last state to enter the union but it has been first in food globalization. A leading producer of pineapples (an American import), sugar from southeast Asia, and famous for its Kona coffee, which derived from Africa, Hawaii has few food plants of its own. The original Polynesian navigators who apparently arrived from Tahiti were sustained by those they carried with them such as taro, bananas, perhaps sweet potatoes, breadfruit, kava, even coconut palms and, of course, dogs, pigs, and chickens.

The vegetables are called "canoe plants," an acknowledgment of their foreign origin. Had they stuck with this nomenclature such Hawaiian staples as linguiça from Portugal and rice from China would have been called "ship food," and Japanese flavorings like *dashi* and *furikake*, "airplane food." Such migrating ethnic ingredients, which traveled mostly with foreign-born whalers, explorers, and plantation workers from China, Japan, Korea, Portugal and the Philippines, have all been scrambled together to comprise Hawaii's "Pacific Rim" cuisine.

On the mainland, a wholesale acceptance of foreign foods was to some considerable extent also the result of immigration, or perhaps better, the result of a dramatic shift in the origins of immigrants who entered the country during the last half-century and especially after the 1965 Amendments to the Immigration Act.[19] Between 1950 and 1990, the percentage of new arrivals from Europe fell from over 50 to just 15 percent, whereas those from Asia jumped from 6 to 30 percent, and Mexican arrivals more than doubled from 12 to 25 percent.

By the 1990s, the giant food companies had concluded that American tastes had reached a point where "foreign" was perceived as better and they scoured the globe for exotic foods while also giving a foreign cachet to foods produced at home. "Haagen-Dazs," for example, was a name dreamed up to convey the impression that European influences were behind the ice cream's production.[20]

It was in the late 1980s and the decade of the 1990s that so many food globalizing forces coalesced in America that people can now embark on an extensive journey of "culinary tourism" without leaving their hometown.[21] Posters in ethnic restaurants let diners know what is on the menu as matadors face bulls, the Taj Mahal looms, the Tower of Pisa leans, Far Eastern markets beckon, Thai temples glisten, and sleepy European villages lull. In the supermarkets, meat and seafood counters feature ostrich, squid, and escargot, items that few would have dreamed of putting in their mouths in the recent past, along with other foreign delicacies such as Black Forest ham, weisswurst, mortadella, pancheta, and prosciutto. In addition, many of these outlets now have Asian counters featuring sushi, seaweed wraps, wasabi, and soy products.

Produce markets (and farmer's markets) stock cilantro, chayote, jicama, avocados, chilli peppers, tomatillos, and nopales for Mexican dishes; arugula, fennel, fresh basil, radicchio, porcini mushrooms, celery root, and sun-dried tomatoes for Italian meals; leeks, for French and other European dishes; basmati rice, ginko nuts, litchis, shitiake mushrooms, tofu, taro root, and Thai lemon grass for Asian occasions; manioc, papayas, and plantains to be eaten Caribbean (or Brazilian) style. Pomelos, highly valued in Southeast Asia (they are associated with the Chinese New Year), are now readily available in U.S markets.[22]

Fish became globalized so that we regularly eat tilapia – an African fish few Americans ever heard of until a few years ago. Long farmed in Asia and Africa, tilapia is now farmed in the United States and Canada as well as in Central and South America. And Alaska pollock, made into surimi (faux crab, lobster, shrimp, and scallops) has radiated out from Japan to sweep the United States and is poised to engulf the world. Even salt, or rather salts, have gone global so that sea salt in various colors can be obtained from France, South Africa, and Bali, and exotic table salt is also mined in the Himalayas (it is pink), and the mountains of Bolivia.

In 1995, a staff reporter for the *Wall Street Journal* surveying the hinterland from New York reported, "Middle America isn't eating the way it used to."[23] From pot roast, baked potatoes, boiled vegetables, and bread and butter, America's heartland had switched to "chicken burritos, pasta primavera, and grilled salmon" not to mention sautéed shark (in Appleton, Wisconsin), salads constructed with garbanzo and cannellini beans, cilantro, shitiake mushrooms, fresh basil, pinenuts, and the blue cheeses of Denmark, France, Germany, Austria, and Italy.[24]

And Americans learned a whole new vocabulary as they became acquainted with hummus; menudo; bouillabaisse; spaetzle; spaghetti amatriciana, puttanesca, and carbonara; kimchi; sauerbraten; wiener schnitzel; cassoulet; escabeche; tabouleh; tahina; teriyaki; seviche; feijoada; paella, polenta; stroganoff; gazpacho; chicken Kiev, mirepoix, beurre maniè; boquet garni; cotija; and a wide range of South and Southeast Asian curries.

Much of this food education was dispensed in new kinds of upscale "foreign" chain restaurants such as General Mills' Olive Garden – the only national Italian restaurant chain – established in 1982 in a brilliantly successful attempt to piggyback on pizza's thriving prosperity. Here, diners learned about veal marsala and picatta, fettucine alfredo, and cannoli. They also learned more about Mexican cuisine than Taco Bell could teach them in (now floundering) Chi-Chi's, founded (after tacos were well established) in 1976 with its menu vaguely northern Mexico and certainly Tex-Mex. Lessons on Japanese food took place in the Benihana of Tokyo chain with its "teppanyaki" style of cooking – the customers seated around a large grill to watch chefs twirl knives while chopping and slicing vegetables and meats.[25]

While all of this was going on, American foods became further homogenized with "soul" food available in cans. Since the "Jazz Age," New Yorker's had gone uptown to Harlem for grits, greens, ribs, and field peas, and southern black people had their own restaurants for chitterlings, hog jowls, and cornbread. But it took the Civil Rights movement to introduce African American foods to a larger, white audience and longer still (1992) for Glory Foods to begin canning seventeen soul food items such as black-eyed peas, field peas, and collard, mustard and turnip greens. In 1993, Sylvia's, a famous Harlem restaurant since 1962, began expanding into other cities and came out with its own line of soul food products.[26]

Other southern foods such as grits (Bette Midler told a South Carolina audience that grits resembled buttered kitty litter) were elevated to haute status after the election of Jimmy Carter, and recipes for cheese and grits and, especially, shrimp and grits became *de rigueur* in food magazines and cookbooks. Hush puppies crossed the Mason-Dixon line and breakfast menus across the nation offered country ham, grits, and red-eye gravy.

Capitalizing on this growing food savvy of Americans are boutique food enterprises focused on quality that have sprung up in every corner of the country. Their upscale markets, artisan breads, coffee blends, organically grown vegetables, free-range chickens, imported cheeses, even special sugars, salts, peppers, and beers, all present a fascinating counterbalance to fast foods.[27]

At the same time another kind of "fast food" has become a priority of people who cook at home. Instant coffee, minute rice, aerosol cheese, microwaveable oatmeal, macaroni and cheese, and hundreds of frozen meals are all designed for people who want to eat at home in a hurry. "Salads in a bag" often with a package of salad dressing included serve the same purpose, and they obviate the problem of lettuce and other salad materials going bad in the refrigerator. Ditto with bite-sized fresh fruit – melons, grapes, berries, and the like – ready to go in any supermarket.

And, finally, cashing in on the food-related health jitters are companies like Kellogg and Campbell Soups who are marrying pharmaceuticals with food into so-called "nutraceuticals" or "functional" foods. These take low-calorie or "vitamin-fortified" claims to a new high (or low) with promises to lower blood pressure, reduce cholesterol levels, and stimulate immune systems.[28] Just one example: although North American beer makers have shown few qualms in claiming health benefits for their beverages (especially in Canada), they have to be scrambling to match those of a new beer developed in Sweden with the alleged ability to lower blood cholesterol.[29]

FAST FOOD, A HYMN
TO CELLULITE

One taste worldwide.

McDonald's

FAST FOOD MAKES NEWS. In the United States, the Center for Science in the Public Interest periodically exposes the fat and calorie content of fast foods. In 1994 it pointed out, to the consternation of many who thought popcorn was benign, that a large order of this long-time fast food (it became popular during World War II when candy was in short supply), popped movie-style in coconut oil, stuffed its consumer with two days worth of artery-clogging fat – and this before butter was added. With butter, the harmful fat was equal to that packed into nine McDonald's quarter-pounders.[1]

And speaking of McDonald's, a bemused nation recently read that obese adults and youngsters alike were suing the fast food giant for making them fat, and the fast food industry was clamoring for legislation (the so-called "cheeseburger bills") to obviate more obesity suits. But despite considerable anti–fast-food fuming fueled by growing waistlines, fast food establishments were routinely muscling their way into military bases, school cafeterias, university student unions, even into major-league hospitals in a wave of nutritional nihilism that seemed unstoppable.

Abroad, however, where food phobias can take the form of outright terrorism, there were attempts to stop fast food cold. In 1995, Danish anarchists looted, wrecked, and then (adding insult to injury) burned a McDonald's restaurant in Copenhagen – beginning a wave of "McBurnings"

274

and "McBombings" that stretched in Europe from Belgium and England to Greece, France, and Russia, and in South America from Cali to Rio de Janeiro.[2] Why? One of the reasons is that hamburgers have come to symbolize U.S. modernity and efficiency to many of the young, and a global imperialism to others, including their wary elders.

Fortunately, foreign protest is not always violent and, in fact, can be manifested as gentle mockery. Look, for example, at the "Slow Food Movement," an advocacy organization based in Italy that emphasizes local and regional cuisine, rejects food homogeneity, and insists on lengthy cooking times. The movement, which began in 1986 as a protest against the opening of a McDonald's restaurant in Rome, now counts over 65,000 members in close to 50 countries.

The current fast food fuss obscures the reality that such foods are ancient. Fried kibbeh, sausages, olives, nuts, small pizzas, and flat breads have been sold on the streets of Middle Eastern and North African cities for a cycle of centuries; Marco Polo reported barbequed meats, deep-fried delicacies, and even roast lamb for sale in Chinese markets. Specialty shops and stalls featuring noodles, sushi, and tempura were ubiquitous in downtown Edo (now Tokyo) as early as the eighteenth century. In 1762, John Montagu was gambling at London's Beefsteak Club and did not want to waste time sitting down to a meal; so he slapped bread slices around a hunk of meat (fortunately Montagu was the fourth Earl of Sandwich, otherwise we might be calling this fast food a Montagu). A bit later fish and chip shops began opening in London, representing a marriage of still other fast foods – fried fish, which had been sold on London streets since the seventeenth century, and chips or French fries, peddled by pushcart vendors in Paris before the middle of the nineteenth-century.[3]

Needless to say, the fries proved polygamous by marrying other foods, too, in the fast food revolution that radiated out from America in the century just past. Even the name was changed as the French origin was either obscured or ignored. They became known as "American fries" in many countries – an appropriate name given the potato's origin – and briefly "freedom fries" in the United States to express American unhappiness with French objections to "regime change" in Iraq. More American, however, is the potato chip invented, according to one story, in Saratoga Springs around the middle of the nineteenth century by a mischievous chef responding to a customer's complaint that his French fries were too thick.[4]

The hamburger, although slower to catch on, proved the most advantageous marriage for French fries. Its origin is blurred, with some insisting that rounded patties of meat (rissoles) such as the German *Frigadelle* can be traced back to the Tartars who tenderized meats by placing them under their saddles, then ate them raw – the original steak tartare. It was in the seaport of Hamburg, however, that fried *Frigadelle* became popular with sailors during the nineteenth century, hence the name "hamburger" – although in Hamburg it is known as "American steak." The first printed restaurant menu in the United States – that of Delmonico's in 1836 – featured the "hamburger steak" as one of its priciest entrees.[5]

The sandwich part of the hamburger began as a fair food. One claim for its debut is the Outgamie County Fair at Seymour, Wisconsin in 1884, when a concessionaire is said to have made his hamburger steaks portable for wandering fairgoers by stuffing them between two slices of bread. Others claim that the innovation came about in Ohio, at the Akron County Fair in 1892, and, although there are no claims of priority for the St. Louis' 1904 centenary celebration of the Louisiana Purchase, the sandwich, sold by German immigrants, got considerable exposure there.[6]

However, at that same exposition, Pure Food Law advocates and the Fair's Pure Food exhibit were telling the public that much of the nation's meat contained chemical preservatives (among other things). In the following year Upton Sinclair's best-selling book *The Jungle*, exposing meat-packing malpractices, was published and the public, tortured for years by an ongoing debate over the safety of the nation's food supply, now lost its appetite for meat. Meat sales plunged and its sellers were in trouble.

Their counterattack often exhibited moments of sheer brilliance. Nathan Handwerker, for example, (who founded Nathan's Famous Hotdogs in 1916), hired young men in surgeons smocks with stethoscopes dangling from their necks to gather round his cart and eat his sandwiches throughout the day. However, across the nation hot dogs and especially ground beef were regarded as old, tainted, and definitely unsafe to eat. It was this image of ground beef that White Castle undertook to change in the 1920s by creating its own atmosphere of purity and cleanliness.[7]

Founded in 1921 in Wichita, Kansas at the beginning of the Prohibition Era, White Castle restaurants joined other "quick service" establishments like soda fountains, lunch counters (luncheonettes), cafeterias, automats, and diners to provide cheap alternatives to the now vanished saloon "free lunches" – often occupying the same space as these recently defunct establishments.[8] Working men and professionals alike straddled stools for the noon "gobble and git" ceremony.

White Castle elected to concentrate almost exclusively on hamburgers, ostentatiously made with government-inspected beef, and by mid-decade had hit on a white enameled exterior and a white porcelain-enamel interior for their duplicate buildings, which numbered 115 by 1931 – the gleaming buildings pledging cleanliness inside and out. Imitators, such as the White Tower, quickly followed with a castle-like structure – and, like the White Castle outlets, their uniform design doubled as advertising signs.[9]

Still other chains, such as the Toddle House and Little Tavern, joined these early pioneers, and together they elevated the hamburger to respectability in the United States. But because most of these stores were located downtown in the cities, the hamburger did not yet have a mass market, and pork remained the most popular meat in America until after World War II.

The turnaround came in the 1950s with the post-war development of an automobile-centered culture. The interstate highway system began spanning the nation, suburbs spilled over from cities, and trend-setting southern California pioneered in new kinds of fast food restaurants, including drive-ins. The McDonald brothers, who had entered the drive-in business in Pasadena just before World War II, began franchising what had become a self-service restaurant in 1948.

Six years later the now legendary Ray Kroc (then a milk-shake mixer salesman) persuaded the brothers to let him do the franchising, and his first store opened in 1956 – a store utilizing the cleanliness principles of its predecessors. In 1961, he bought out the McDonald brothers and by 1965 had some 700 outlets.[10] But although he learned from the experience of White Castle and its copycats – most importantly by using uniform structures as signs (the golden arches) – he had some ideas of his own. White Castle-type stores were mostly in the inner cities, close to public transportation, with a workingman clientele. Kroc located McDonald's restaurants in the suburbs and along interstate highways – tied to the car and targeting kids – the baby boomers.

An explosive expansion was accomplished by innovative franchising, but with enough attached strings that the parent corporation retained near absolute control. After 1961, franchisees attended the famous "Hamburger University" for degrees in "Hamburgerology," which created a sort of McDonald's corporate culture.[11] By 1990, there were some 8,000

McDonalds eateries (and 30,000 by 2003) whose employees (male only during the early years) were mostly women, teenagers, and immigrants, cheap labor that – although paid minimum wages with few or no benefits and hired and fired as the market dictated – were not likely to organize. Their tasks were routinized by assembly-line procedures – food Fordism – that ensured the same meal at any McDonald's restaurant. Identically-sized hamburgers were shipped frozen to the outlets; French fries were made from Russet Burbank potatoes of uniform size and aged the same length of time to guarantee uniform flavor.[12] This did not, however, completely exclude nods to local tastes and cultures. McLobster sandwiches, for example, are available in Maine, and the mutton Marharaja Mac is served up in India, where a prohibition on beef consumption is widespread.

Kentucky Fried Chicken (founded in 1954) employed similar marketing methods, along with a host of other hamburger hustlers such as Burger King (1954) and latecomer Wendy's (1969). All went after the kids with ruthless marketing techniques that included playgrounds, toys, cartoon character watches, contests, and sweepstakes, even ads placed in the schools and (more recently) on the Internet.

Also competing for the fast food dollar were the ethnic fast food outlets. Beginning in the 1950s, Italian pizza outlets, spearheaded by Pizza Hut, Little Caesar's, and Domino's, radiated across the nation. They utilized the same kinds of marketing and assembly-line techniques as the hamburger chains, as did southern California–born Taco Bell, which blazed a trail in roadside Mexican food. Its tacos, burritos, chalupas, and nachos introduced the nation to the tastes of tortillas, cumin, chilli powder, and pinto beans.

Abroad, American fast food found ready acceptance among the young, even becoming ingrained in youth cultures as exemplified by a group of Japanese Boy Scouts who, when visiting the United States, were relieved to find McDonald's restaurants in Chicago – their anxiety needless since McDonald's stores are everywhere and McDonald's is an Illinois-based corporation.[13] But – the young aside - as already noted, there have been violent objections to American fast foods outside of America triggered by a variety of fears, not the least of which is that globalization in general is rolling over the world like a juggernaut. Fast food is not only the most visible manifestation of economic and cultural globalization, it is synonymous with American cultural imperialism – symbolized by Coca-Cola and by the golden arches of McDonald's that announce over 15,000 restaurants in more than 117 foreign countries.[14]

In underdeveloped countries, American fast food seems a promise of modernization for many; yet others find not so admirable American traits represented in fast food such as assembly-line production, the use of cheap labor juxtaposed with high-tech equipment, and a dedication to efficiency and speed to produce quantity instead of quality.

Other complaints against American fast food are lodged by environmental groups, and these, too, can take the form of anti-Americanism, in no small part because Americans are perceived to be careless, even wasteful of the world's resources, and their government has appeared to be arrogantly opposed to joining any world accord on environmental matters. In fact, the now-famous "McLibel" trial in London put some of the objections to fast food on the front pages of the world press.

In the late 1980s, London Greenpeace (a handful of activists with no connection to Greenpeace International) issued a pamphlet accusing McDonald's of destroying rainforests; producing meat using hormones, pesticides, and antibiotics in cattle feed; dispensing foods often responsible for food poisoning; exploiting workers; aiming its advertising at children; and for good measure – the torture and murder of animals.[15]

The latter, of course, is an animal rights issue, and McDonald's was hardly the only purchaser of ground beef from cattle raised in rainforests. But at two and a half billion pounds annually it is the world's largest beef purchaser and there was no question that the forests of Central America and the Amazon were being turned into cattle pastures mostly because of the fast food industry.[16] Since 1960, over a quarter of the Central American forests have disappeared, along with a number of plant and animal species. It is also true that the methane and nitrous oxide gasses emanating from the world's billion and a half cattle contribute to global warming. And finally, it is true that McDonald's does target children in its advertising – indeed the company got its start with the baby boomers and is now feeding (and feeding on) their grandchildren.

Nonetheless, McDonald's sued London Greenpeace for libel, and in the rigid jurisprudence of Great Britain (which makes those accused of libel prove that they did no such thing), won its case. But because the judge did not find libelous the statements that McDonald's was cruel to animals and exploited children in its advertising, fast food opponents could claim a moral victory.[17]

In the United States similar environmental concerns have surfaced, especially over water pollution from factory farms, and there are plenty of animal rights activists and vegetarians who condemn meat-based diets. Moreover, many are just plain distressed by the development of a fast food culture in the nation. But perhaps the weightiest worries focus on fast food as a major cause of American "overweightness" which brings us back to the obesity epidemic, to fast food, and to the alarm bells proclaiming the United States "the 'fattest' country in the world."[18]

Fast food gets much of the blame. Our somewhat slimmer forebears did not have to contend with super-sized fries, nor with the challenge of all-you-can-eat buffets, "family style" restaurants or too many donuts in the morning, whoppers at noon, and pizzas at night. And the current obesity epidemic, fueled by fat, calories, and sugar – the stuff of fast foods – parallels almost exactly the growth of fast foods. It began in the 1950s with the increasing availability of hamburgers, French fries, pizzas, and fried chicken; by 1975 it was estimated that the average American was consuming three-quarters of a pound of fat and sugar each day;[19] and in 2001, the Centers for Disease Control and Prevention could announce that at least 21 percent of the population, and probably more, was obese and fully *two-thirds* of Americans were overweight. Fast food proliferation had not only kept pace with consumer plumpness but threatened to push up numbers on the bathroom scale even further by dispensing "super-colossal" portions.[20] A swelling fast food industry has also dramatically pushed up the portion of the food dollar that goes toward meals away from home. In 1970 it was 20 cents, but by 1992 this had almost doubled, climbing to 38 cents.

Much of that money buys shortening, cooking oils, and high fat cheeses, along with meat – part of the reason why the Center for Science in the Public Interest found in 1991 that a McDonald's quarter-pounder bristled with 420 calories (even without cheese), 20 grams of fat, and 8 grams of saturated fat, which totaled 40 percent of the recommended daily limit.[21] Add to that a large coke (it is hard to get anything smaller) at 310 calories and Super Size Fries (for just a few pennies more)[22] totaling 540 calories and the reasons behind the obesity epidemic seem less mysterious – particularly because by the early 1990s Americans were consuming an average of two and a half to three hamburgers each week, more than two-thirds of which were bought at fast food restaurants. In fact, on any given day fully one-quarter of the U.S. population eats at least one meal in a fast food restaurant, polishing off the super-sized portions because people will generally eat all of whatever they are given.[23]

That the substantial American weight-gain should correlate well with a doubling of the per capita number of fast food restaurants between 1972 and 1997 seems obvious.[24] Our English cousins have the same sort of problem – and one that shows an even more startling correlation between fast food and weight gain. Between 1984 and 1993, the number of fast food establishments in Great Britain almost doubled and during these same years the adult obesity rate also doubled.[25]

Unfortunately, the nation's young are also fast food feeders, piling on the pounds. Indeed, as Eric Schlosser points out, the eating habits of American kids are viewed by Europeans as a good example of what to avoid with their own children – American kids who get around one-quarter of their vegetable servings in the form of French fries or potato chips.[26]

According to the Third National Health and Nutrition Examination Survey (1988–1991), about 5 million Americans aged 6 to 17 were already "severely overweight" – more than double the rate that prevailed in the 1960s. Fast food is not completely at fault because the young have followed the lead of their parents in becoming inactive. Television and computer games have gotten much of the blame, but children also walk less, bicycle less, and are chauffeured more, or use public transportation to get around.[27] At the same time, physical education has been substantially reduced in the schools – and this at the same schools that at the beginning of the 1990s were serving up lunches with 25 percent more total fat and 50 percent more saturated fat than recommended by the dietary guidelines. The National School Lunch Program, launched in the mid-1940s to make certain that the young got enough nutriments to be well nourished, was now supplying enough of the wrong kind of nutrients to ensure poor nutrition.[28]

Moreover, a growing number of single parents and working women (about 60 percent of all women were in the workforce fulltime by 1999), along with the numerous outside activities of their children, has meant that a dwindling percentage of families eat all that many meals at home.[29] In 1970, youngsters took three meals at home with at least two of these supervised by an adult. Some two decades later many of their offspring were eating some five times a day on a "catch as catch can" basis with no supervision at all. Left on their own, poor food choices are inevitable – especially when so many of these are readily and temptingly available and practically unavoidable in schools that may or may not have hamburger, or Taco Bell, or Pizza Hut franchises in lieu of cafeterias that also sell cheeseburgers, fries, and tater tots. Candy and sugar-laden soft drinks are no further away than a vending machine – the soft drink makers spending big dollars for exclusive "pouring rights" in financially-strapped schools (and universities) whose boards are not bashful about accepting such largess.[30]

The inclusion of the young in the obesity epidemic is a national tragedy and has become a national scandal. French fries are the favorite vegetable of toddlers who, like adults, take in too much fat and sugar, eat too few fruits and vegetables, and receive many more calories than they should. One incredible result is that children are developing the chronic diseases of adults. Among these are "adult onset" type 2 diabetes, high blood pressure, and high blood cholesterol, all of which promise soaring rates of coronary artery disease, stroke, even cancer in the future. In fact, the latest estimates from a diabetes epidemiologist at the CDC are that fully one-third of those born in the year 2003 will develop diabetes – and among black and Hispanic children that percentage will be closer to half.[31] No wonder that there has been recent sentiment for slapping a heavy tax on fast foods – as has been done with cigarettes. It seems only fair to shift some of the tax burden because right now taxpayers are paying more than half of the nation's obesity related medical costs.

The young also suffer psychological consequences of fatness – especially the generation of irrational fears (as opposed to understandably rational fears) of being overweight. Among girls and young women in particular bulimia, binge eating, and purging are responses to these fears. So is anorexia nervosa – a condition of self-starvation inflicted by a distorted body image.[32] The disease seems to have increased in frequency as female film stars and fashion models became impossibly thin and advertising, the media, and fashion – the dominant culture – has projected the notion that thinness connotes success.[33] Unfortunately, the illness is not only difficult to treat but can prove deadly, as Americans learned during the last decades of the twentieth century.[34]

But fast food can be deadly, period, as the 1993 Seattle "Jack in the Box" episode made clear, when hamburgers tainted with *Escherichia coli* bacteria sickened seven hundred individuals (mostly children) in a four state area and killed four of them. Nor, apparently, was this the first such outbreak. Although McDonald's denied it, its restaurants in Michigan and Oregon may have caused the first hamburger-chain epidemic of E. *coli* back in 1982. Since the Jack in the Box outbreak it has been estimated that approximately one-half million individuals (again mostly children) have fallen victim to the disease. Thousands went to the hospital and hundreds have died.[35]

Unhappily, although the disease seems to be on the increase, it cannot be easily eradicated given current livestock feeding practices, which involve the production of cattle feed using ground up dead animals, poultry manure, even cattle manure, and blood. This feeding practice is not dissimilar from that which has been blamed for mad-cow disease (Bovine Spongiiform Encephalopathy) in Great Britain, Canada, and (apparently) in the United States, and it is one that creates ideal conditions for *E. coli* proliferation.[36] So the only real defense is to make certain that beef is cooked to at least 155 degrees in the restaurants. However, at the risk of repetition, this defense is manned by unskilled, underpaid, and generally unmotivated workers.[37]

Yet, cheap labor without benefits and job security is what makes fast food cheap and profits high, with the industry benefiting from the recent phenomenon of a dwindling permanent workforce and a growing reservoir of part-time and temporary workers. Nor is this confined to America. Worker exploitation was another of the accusations leveled at McDonald's in London's McLibel trial. In Canada, Indonesia, and throughout Europe McDonald's has regularly (and fiercely) battled attempts to unionize its employees. Indeed, because McDonald's is known internationally as implacably anti-union, it is somewhat ironic that it spearheaded the advance of American capitalism into Russia, Yugoslavia, and Hungary – all parts of the former Soviet Union that had denounced the company as an "exploiter of child labor."[38]

Recent events, however, have helped to soften McDonald's hard-nosed reputation as the company has fallen on some hard times. At the end of 2002, fast food opponents may have taken some satisfaction in McDonald's announcement that its forty-seven year streak of posting quarterly gains had come to an end. The reasons were several. A two-year price war with Burger King had not produced the hoped-for results. The U.S. fast food market was crowded, and sales abroad had been hurt by concerns over mad-cow disease. A class action consumer lawsuit that blamed McDonalds for the onset of chronic adult diseases in kids had been dismissed, but obesity epidemic worries had not been dismissed by the public and, as a consequence, the company announced that it would be closing under-performing restaurants and pulling out of several countries.

Then, in 2004, its CEO died of a heart attack, and only sixteen days later his replacement underwent surgery for cancer – this just as the McDonalds-bashing documentary *Super Size Me* came out. The "star" of that film, Morgan Spurlock, ate solely at McDonalds three times a day for a month and he supersized portions whenever an employee suggested it. The trio of doctors that accompanied him saw his mental and physical health deteriorate, and his weight increase at an alarming rate. When he began to develop some potentially serious liver and kidney problems, they advised him, unsuccessfully, to quit.

Confronted with this kind of publicity, slumping sales, and the prospect of more obesity suits, not to mention more government regulation, the fast food industry is on the defensive – with part of that defense a posture of corporate responsibility. Kraft foods, for example, sued because of the trans-fat sludge in its Oreo cookies, has now publicly committed to fighting obesity. McDonald's has insisted since 2001 that its beef suppliers abide by FDA feed guidelines, and that the company regularly inspects them to make certain they comply. Burger King and Wendy's have followed suit.

Even before the *Super Size Me* documentary was made public, McDonald's had promised no more super-sized fries and soft drinks and also announced a policy of lowering the trans-fatty acids and saturated fats in its cooking oils. Burger King recently trotted out a BK Veggie Burger, and salads are once more featured at fast food restaurants. For those counting "carbs," burgers can wrapped in lettuce instead of buns. ConAgra and Aramark have developed low fat and low sodium pizzas for the schools, others are sending baked French fries and yogurt drinks to that same market. The McLean burger of a few years ago, which was 91 percent fat free because it incorporated seaweed, was a spectacular failure, but maybe, just maybe, fast food reform will be a silver lining within the black cloud of the obesity epidemic.

PARLOUS PLENTY
INTO THE TWENTY-FIRST
CENTURY

The custom and fashion of today will be the awkwardness and
outrage of tomorrow. So arbitrary are these transient laws.

Alexandre Dumas

LOOKING BACKWARD from this start of a new century (and new millennium for that matter), just a tad more than 600 years have gone by since the Old and New Worlds were united. These are but a small fraction of the ten to twelve thousand years that have elapsed since the beginning of agriculture, but in that short time span the foods of the world have been astonishingly rearranged so that potatoes grow in such diverse climates as those of Siberia and Indonesia, sugar in equally diverse places like Pakistan and Mexico, and pistachios have been transplanted from Iran to California – now the world's second largest producer.

In the Old World, China is now the most important producer of wheat, originally domesticated in the Middle East; China and India dominate the production of rice, which likely began as a Southeast Asian crop; India is the biggest producer of tea, first cultivated in China, and peanuts, first cultivated in South America; tropical Asia produces most of the world's manioc – an American plant that Brazil claims as a native; and China is also the leading producer of white and sweet potatoes, a half-world away from their native Andes. In the New World, Brazil has become the world's most important producer of coffee, originally from Africa, sugar from New Guinea, a big producer of pepper from India's Malabar coast, and the second largest producer of soybeans, which originated in China. North America is a major grower of wheat, the biggest producer of Mesoamerican maize, and leads Brazil in soybean production.

Save for the United States, however, the nations that cultivate the most important of these (now thoroughly shuffled) crops are generally thought of as situated in the developing world. And while residents of the West, and especially the people of the United States, are battling obesity, much of the world lives under the threat of famine – and has for at least the past 6,000 years.[1] China has suffered as many as ninety famines per century over the last 2,000 years, including a recent one between 1958 and 1961; most estimates of the number of dead were at between 14 and 26 million – although some said as many as 40 million. In India at least ninety major famines have occurred over the past 2,500 years. Russia continued to be ravaged by famine – mostly man-made after the Bolshevik Revolution – that claimed millions of lives until the mid-twentieth century; and in Brazil's northeast, climatic and political circumstances have made famine a regular occurrence since these disasters first entered the historical record in 1584.[2] Of course, famines are not just limited to big food producing nations; during the twentieth century they made catastrophic appearances in developing countries in the Horn of Africa, sub-Sahara Africa, and Asia.[3]

The terrible irony is that the ravages of famine are phenomena that globalization – which has precipitated a tremendous expansion of agricultural productivity, a sophisticated system of transport, and globally interlinked markets – could easily prevent.[4] Or it could if the nations of the world would agree that every one of its citizens is entitled to food security as a basic human right.[5] Until that agreement is reached, famines and chronic malnutrition will mar the future as they have the past. And there is something very wrong when some 800 million people in the world are classified as chronically undernourished yet U.S. farmers collect money for not growing food, and northern European farmers produce such an excess of food that the Common Market of the European Union has ordered cutbacks on the production of such items as pork and butter.

Yet, even more devastating than famine-generated hunger is the chronic malnutrition that afflicts some 800 million individuals as we begin the twenty-first century, even though food globalization has helped to narrow the dietary gap between some of the developed and developing countries.[6]

Nonetheless, it seems that the world is losing its war on hunger because the narrowing excludes almost a billion persons for whom even the cost of cooking fuel can be a major expense.[7] In the early 1990s, it was estimated that some 500 million children and adults experienced continuous hunger (and even more were vulnerable to it); that one in three children in the developing world was seriously malnourished; and that over a billion people suffered from nutritional deficiencies. Ironically, these estimates were made at a time when Americans were spending a sum greater than the entire economy of Medieval Europe on their dogs and cats.[8]

In the agrarian societies of developing countries, a sole cereal crop may supply as much as 80 percent of the total caloric intake, and meat is seldom if ever tasted – a situation that has not changed for many over the course of some 10,000 years.[9] Even in Mexico, during a recent recession it was calculated that fully one-half of its estimated 92 million people were getting less than the minimum daily requirement of 1,300 calories.[10]

It is generally acknowledged that adequate infant nutrition is bedrock for the optimal health of a people; yet in under-nourished populations malnutrition begins in the womb. Too often the result is a low birth-weight (LBW) infant, and LBW is the most important determinant of neonatal and infant mortality as well as physical growth until age seven.[11] Although there is a high correlation between maternal weight gain during pregnancy and normal birth weight, many developing country mothers register low, or even negative, weight gains during pregnancy. And together, low maternal weight and LBW continue to be among the leading causes of the world's disease burden.[12]

LBW is not easily corrected after birth, in no small part because of the difficulty of educating developing country mothers who comprise the majority of some 870 million illiterate adults living in those countries.[13] Busy mothers have curtailed breast-feeding since Neolithic women began working in the fields, and substitute infant-feeding methods have left much to be desired ever since. The use of a pap has led straight to protein energy malnutrition, often because the mother's immunological defenses are not transmitted in her milk to the baby. Wet-nursing has proven equally disastrous,[14] and bovine milk is not only hard to digest for human infants but, because iron availability from milk is species-specific, they get less than half the iron from bovine milk than they would from breast milk.[15]

Yet, formula foods – originally developed as low-cost milk substitutes such as INCAPARINA made from corn and cottonseed flour or CSM (corn-soya-milk),[16] also present deadly problems. Practically everybody can recall hearing or reading about multinational corporations aggressively marketing infant formulas to replace mother's milk in Third World nations. Those mothers were deflected from breast-feeding by formulas they could not afford (and thus they over diluted them) and the mother's badly needed antibodies in hostile disease environments did not reach their babies. Perhaps most lethal of all, unhygienic living conditions meant that formulas were prepared with fouled water and there was little understanding of the importance of bottle sterilization. For all of these reasons, countless babies died amid erupting scandal.[17]

Moreover, infancy is just the beginning of the nutritional trials that face Third World youngsters. Those that survive this one and move into childhood, are confronted by another set of hurdles. In many societies men and boys eat first, and females are last in line at the food pot, with female children just ahead of the family dog.[18] Like infants, children are also beset with a high frequency of diarrheal and respiratory diseases that contribute to malnutrition and stem from it because malnutrition lowers resistance to pathogens.[19] It is a synergistic interaction in which each condition worsens the other, and nutritional deficiencies – especially those of protein, vitamin A, and iron – make the child increasingly vulnerable to diseases like measles (a major killer of the Third World young) and nutritional syndromes like PEM.[20]

PEM or protein energy malnutrition consists of a group of nutritional diseases related to an inadequate intake of protein and energy (calories) that chiefly attack infants and young children in poor countries. Its symptomatic poles are *kwashiorkor*, characterized by edema and skin lesions (a rich variety of colloquial names indicates a wide prevalence historically) and *marasmus*, with the victim presenting a "skin and bones" appearance. In the past the swollen bellies of kwashiorkor were sometimes interpreted to signal over-nutrition, but the signs of frank starvation characteristic of marasmus have never fooled anybody.[21]

PEM impairs immunities to infections, produces a fatty and sometimes permanently damaged liver, and, as is the case with severe vitamin deficiencies, has been linked with mental decrement in later life.[22] The illness generally develops when a child is weaned from the protein in mother's milk and placed on a pap. It is prevented by the inclusion of some good quality protein in the weanling's diet. However, this is sometimes not easy to include in places where population growth exceeds food production – making yet another argument for global food entitlements as a part of food globalization.[23]

On a more upbeat note, the globalization of foodstuffs has helped to make enough "extra" protein available to increase the average height for many in the world and to help them start catching up to the stature of our Paleolithic ancestors.[24] This is because of a close association between the average height of a population and its nutritional status, so that height can actually serve as a proxy for protein intake.[25]

Protein intake is also important to the age of menarche. In seventeenth-century Germany, for example, it was noted that peasant girls menstruated later than the daughters of townspeople or the aristocracy.[26] Over the last century there has been a decline in the age of female sexual maturity throughout most of the world[27] although, significantly, the greatest height increases and age of menarche reductions have taken place in the United States and Europe – those regions of the world where improving nutrition and the end of chronic malnutrition have produced declining mortality over the past three centuries or so.[28] But the less affluent countries are now closing the protein intake gap. In the developed world, diets are comprised of ever more sugar, fats, and alcohol, which supply calories yet no protein. By contrast, beans, high in protein, figure heavily in the diets of many in developing countries.[29] It goes without saying, however, that a lowered age of menarche can mean increased fertility, and more mouths to feed makes escape from Third World status just that more difficult.

Moving from food-related health problems in the developing world to others in the developed world, we have already observed that food processing was given a considerable fillip by the onset of industrialization, and it has made incredible progress ever since especially during the last half-century.[30] But government and consumer uneasiness has kept pace with that progress – uneasiness about the use of additives in food processing such as, to single out just one, the venerable preservative nitrate that turns meat red. After all, additives are chemicals, and chemicals can be dangerous. Unquestionably, many of these were in the past, and surely many more will prove to be in the future. So long as there are convenience and processed foods there will be additives. The problem becomes one of when their potential for harm outweighs their usefulness.

Salt is a good example. It is used in near mega-doses by almost all food processors because it makes foods tastier, improves their appearance, increases shelf life, and, not incidentally, adds to profits by adding weight

to products because salt promotes water retention.[31] Because of the intensive use of salt as an additive, however, Americans consume some two teaspoons of the mineral daily even if they do not touch the saltshaker – from which Americans get only about one twentieth of their sodium. But, those two teaspoons are about twice the upper limit of sodium recommended for good health and are pointed to as a major cause of the high blood pressure afflicting some 50 million Americans.

Yet, most Americans find salt tasty, and in the wake of the low sodium craze that peaked in the early 1990s, no longer view it as particularly hazardous, and might even insist that salt as well as other additives are vital to the appearance, texture, flavor, and keeping-quality of foods. Moreover, the use of additives is monitored by governmental authorities and new additives are subjected to rigorous testing, so that the risks they pose may seem acceptable ones.[32]

Regardless of the merits and demerits of food additives, they are unquestionably less dangerous than a number of other constituents of our food supply. Pathogens, for example, ignite food-borne infections, and there are a lot of them about in the form of cestodes, nematodes, trematodes, protozoa, fungi, bacteria, viruses, and at least one prion (the agent that causes bovine spongiform encephalopathy or "mad-cow" disease).[33] In fact, some food- and water-borne infections rank among history's greatest "killer" diseases like cholera, typhoid, and tuberculosis (from infected bovine milk).

Less severe are the diarrheal disorders such as *shigellosis* (bacillary dysentery) and *Escherichia coli* that have rueful, but rollicking monikers like "Montezuma's revenge," "Rangoon runs," "Delhi belly," and "Tokyo trots" – amusing to everyone but the victims of the moment. Other names for these gastro-intestinal ailments like *la tourista*, suggest that they prey mostly on visitors, whereas locals have built immunities to them since early childhood.[34] Yet, North Americans have learned from recent outbreaks of E. *coli* that some strains of the disease are difficult for the body to combat and, therefore, are far from funny.

Other dangers just below the surface of our twenty-first century dietary minefield have to do with food allergies, which children are more likely to suffer from than adults, although they can develop at any age.[35] Among the most common allergy triggers are bovine milk, crustacea (crab, lobster, shrimp), eggs, fish, legumes (especially peanuts and soybeans), shelfish (clams, oysters, scallops), nuts, and wheat.[36] Those who experience allergic reactions to such foods, ranging from the mild (itching and redness) to the severe or even deadly (anaphylactic shock) learn to leave them alone.[37] A problem, however, is that food processors often use terms that conceal rather than reveal the presence of allergenic proteins such as "natural flavorings," which might include soybean or milk proteins. And peanuts, when pressed, deflavored, then reflavored, are sold as other types of nuts, such as almonds. Nonetheless, they retain their allergenic qualities and, therefore, constitute a serious threat to unsuspecting peanut-allergy sufferers.[38]

Careful label reading can help in dodging food allergy hazards (although this is no help when eating out), but globalization has created a situation whereby people may not know they are allergic to a food. So long as familiar foods are eaten, consumers learn what foods should be taboo. But what about the new, unfamiliar foods abruptly made available by globalization? For example, what about the introduction of soybeans to the French diet – soybeans which (despite containing highly touted heart-healthy proteins) now rank third among the most common cause of food allergies in France? Or the kiwi fruit, whose introduction to the United States set off a rash of kiwi fruit allergies?[39] With new and exotic foods increasingly on the market, allergic reaction promises to be an increasing health problem in our new century.

Another unintended consequence of globalization – food intolerances – is already a problem. This can be especially serious when governments act as if they are not a problem as, for example, when a picture of Donna Shalala (then Secretary of Health and Human Services) appeared with a milk mustache in an advertisement for milk in the *New York Times*.[40] Did she even know that millions of Americans are lactose intolerant or realize that her milk mustache was tantamount to a federal endorsement of milk?

Lactose intolerance (as distinct from allergy to milk proteins) has a genetic cause[41] and affects the vast majority of the world's peoples. It has been estimated that although 96 percent of northern Europeans are able to digest milk, some 50 to 75 percent of Africans, Indians, and Eastern Europeans cannot, along with virtually all East Asians and Native Americans.[42] Genetics probably lay at the root of other food intolerances as well, although the line drawn between food intolerances (the result of nonimmunologic mechanisms) and allergies (that stem from immunologic abnormalities) can be fuzzy.

Celiac disease, for example, seems to have familial associations and is thought to be genetic in origin. Those with the condition cannot tolerate a component of gluten, which is a protein present in the grains of the grass family (Gramineae), and especially in wheat.[43] It predominates among people whose ancestry lies in Europe or northern India – both major centers of late wheat cultivation which has suggested a number of things to researchers. Perhaps celiac disease is an artifact of earlier times when the body evolved mechanisms to discourage the consumption of toxic wild grains.[44] Or maybe breeding for better gluten (which forms the tough, elastic framework of wheat breads) in the distant past meant a trait selection that accidentally ordained gluten intolerance for a small minority of wheat bread consumers? Or could it be that the gluten intolerant simply lack a particular enzyme?[45]

Celiac disease patients are advised to seek out "gluten-free" products (not always an easy thing) so as to avoid the diarrhea their affliction produces, which can lead to iron deficiency and a wasting condition, even altered mental capacity.[46] It seems likely that in the past individuals with celiac disease born into societies sustained by wheat would not have lived long enough to reproduce and pass on the disorder, in which case it probably had a significantly greater prevalence in the past than it does today.

There is also a dermatological form of gluten intolerance, but most other food intolerances are provoked by additives such as aspartame, sulfites, tartrazine, (a widely used food dye), and monosodium glutamate (MSG), which first caught public attention in 1968, when the Chinese Restaurant Syndrome (Kwok's disease) was traced to MSG overuse.[47] These are classified as food intolerances because they have not been linked to any immune mechanism and perhaps, like lactose intolerance or celiac disease, were brought to the surface by (in this case a relatively recent) dietary change.

Salt sensitivity, although not classified as a food intolerance, might well be placed under that rubric because past intakes could not have conditioned most humans for the quantities of sodium chloride now consumed daily. Even our ancient ancestors on a fairly salty diet that was 80 percent meat would have taken in less than half – perhaps only a third – of today's average per capita intake in the United States, and to some immeasurable extent such heavy salt consumption bears responsibility for today's mortality generated by kidney disease, stroke, and especially, hypertension (a major cause of heart attacks) in the West, and stomach cancer in developing regions.[48]

Contemporary hunter-gatherer populations consume roughly the same amount of sodium as our foraging forefathers and suffer no hypertension – not even the age-related increase in blood pressure that medicine has resignedly come to call "normal."[49] Part of the reason for the lack of hypertension in hunter-gatherers is that, as a rule, mammals consume more potassium than sodium, and potassium helps the body retain sodium (salt is, after all, crucial to life itself). Contemporary hunter-gatherers take in 10 times more potassium than sodium and, presumably, our hunter-gatherer ancestors did the same.[50]

But beginning around 1,000 years ago, salt became more available and less expensive (despite various taxes on the mineral), and the Europeans doggedly began reversing this ratio. It had been understood for a long time that salt was a preservative (the Egyptians used it to mummify bodies) and now cod, herring, salmon, mackerel, sardines, and eels were all preserved with it. So was Irish beef (Irish corned beef that became a staple of the British navy) along with bacon, ham, cheese, cabbage (sauerkraut), cucumbers, capers, olives, and countless other foods. Much cooking was done in salted water, and salt was again liberally applied at the table.[51] In fact, so much salt was consumed in eighteenth-century England that it has been calculated that the average person was taking in a lethal dose of salt every day.[52] That this did not kill off an entire nation was because of a sodium tolerance that the English (and presumably other northern Europeans) developed. Their bodies adapted by learning to rid themselves of excess salt through urine and perspiration.[53]

By contrast, for other peoples such as sub-Sahara Africans, salt was always a precious commodity. Some, produced locally by evaporating seawater or by exploiting plant resources, could often provide what little salt was used in African cooking. But the salt mined in the desert and carried south in the caravans was the most highly prized – so much so that it was money – a currency – that, in many places, was traded for West African gold and slaves.[54]

As a consequence of this historical experience with salt, people of African origin have bodies that treat the mineral much differently from those of European descent – as something to be conserved and, consequently, they excrete considerably less sodium in urine and perspiration.[55] It is suspected, that this is at least part of the explanation for why African Americans have much higher rates of hypertension and heart disease than European Americans, which, once again, brings up the question of RDAs for whom?[56]

It is difficult to avoid salt in the United States because – as we saw – the food processing industry adds enormous amounts to foods with the result that Americans have turned the 10:1 potassium to sodium ratio consumed by our ancient ancestors upside down. For the first time people are now taking in more sodium than potassium – and at a time when it is beginning to appear that potassium in proper amounts can reduce hypertension.[57]

Iron presents another kind of problem. It is an essential mineral, important for mental development, and a key component of hemoglobin – around 70 percent of the body's iron is in hemoglobin.[58] The rest, which resides in the liver and spleen and especially in bone marrow, is generally on call when needed. Iron balance is crucial. Too much is toxic, too little can precipitate iron deficiency anemia. This – the most common form of anemia – is especially prevalent in developing countries where diets provide little meat (from which iron is efficiently absorbed) but much in the way of vegetable foods (from which iron is poorly absorbed). And some of the vegetable foods contain oxalic or tannic acids that interfere with iron absorption.[59]

Moreover, pathogenic presence has a considerable influence on iron levels. Helminthic parasites, for example (like hookworms that live off of blood), can prosper to the point where they create anemia in the host.[60] Yet, smaller parasites – viruses and bacteria – also need iron to multiply, and these pose a tricky problem. The body tries to deny iron to these parasites by removing it from the blood and putting more of it into storage. The idea is to starve the parasites and forestall their multiplication, which means that iron administration to treat anemia in developing countries may actually work against the patients while benefiting the parasites.

Another kind of problem arises in developed countries. Since most iron is recycled in humans, iron supplementation and food fortification may not be such a good idea after all. In the case of the United States, where the RDA for iron is high and plenty of it is available in foods, iron supplementation has, nonetheless, been carried out on a massive scale since the 1940s. Some feel that it is foolish, even hazardous, to nurture viruses and bacteria in this fashion – pathogens that may lie behind those chronic diseases of ours now on the rise.[61]

PEOPLE AND PLENTY
IN THE TWENTY-FIRST
CENTURY

*There is no more intriguing problem in the history of food than that
of how cultural barriers to the transmission of foods and foodways
have been traversed or broken.*

Felipe Fernández–Armesto[1]

ANOTHER LARGE and daunting twenty-first century problem involves
equal access to food. Today, fertility rates in third-world countries have
decreased sharply even as global per capita calorie consumption has risen,
the twin phenomena casting doubt on predictions of swelling populations
outstripping the globe's food supply.[2] Such predictions were routinely
generated by that alarming increase in the number of people occupying
planet Earth between 1900 and 1990, which was the equal of four times
the sum of all previous increases in the whole of human history.[3] But
although we are now 6 billion, with predictions of an increase to 9 billion
by 2050, it would seem that agricultural advances have probably resolved
concerns about food quantity. There are enough calories for everyone. Yet
fully three-quarters of the world's population derive their calories from
a diet that is low in high-quality protein compared to the other quarter
who consume too much of it in diets that are definitely not tailored for
a small planet. And the problem is, as Tony McMichael points out, that if
food consumption was somehow made equal in terms of quality, the globe

could not currently support our 6 billion; to do so would require two extra planet earths given our current technologies, and to support 10 billion would require four extra earths.[4]

It is both a protein problem and a caloric conundrum. Two extra earths are hard to come by, let alone four. As a rule, per capita food consumption is lowest where population pressure is greatest and the food consumed is of poor quality. But few of us are callous enough to think that it serves the low food consumers right. In the long run, with education and increasing wealth, such populations should shrink, but in the short run, the only way for their food consumption to increase is through the exercise of still more of the new and better technologies that humans have been coming up with since the beginnings of agriculture. One of these is plant breeding – carried out since those beginnings – which today means that we have low carb potatoes, broccolini, and brocoflower; that sunflower yields have been increased by up to 20 percent through utilizing hybrid vigor;[5] and that the soybean, once a subtropical plant, can now be grown in latitudes as far north as 52 degrees, so that U.S. soybean fields begin their march south- ward from Minnesota.[6]

Until now, we have looked at the Neolithic Revolution as if it were something that happened a long time ago. From another angle, however, it is still ongoing – a process of agricultural evolution. It took 10 square kilo- meters to support a single hunter-gatherer. With the advent of traditional farming those 10 square kilometers supported 500 people and as many as 1,000 in fertile river plains. Today's intensive developed-world agriculture can support some 3,000 persons on 10 square kilometers.[7]

The Green Revolution and genetically modified (GM) foods may, there- fore, be regarded as the latest manifestations of an ongoing Neolithic Revo- lution. The Green Revolution, with its roots already growing during World War II, was aimed at increasing the productivity of developing world agri- culture. Not surprisingly, in view of the hemispheric interest of the U.S. government and the Rockefeller Foundation (who might be considered Green Revolution founders), the focus fell first on maize as a revolution- ary crop and Mexico as the place to launch the revolution.[8] By the 1960s, high yielding wheat strains were also under development in Mexico and these, too, subsequently colonized the world.[9] Advances in wheat were paralleled by a Green Revolution in tropical rice, thanks to the efforts of the International Rice Research Institute located in the Philippines, which concentrated on high-yielding semi-dwarf varieties.[10]

Truly sensational yields of rice and wheat and maize followed, but unintended consequences took the edge off the excitement that such yields generated. Technological improvements tend to benefit developed countries most, and the United States managed to double its wheat production in just a quarter of a century.[11] In large part this was because Green Revolution cultivars were heavily dependent on the petrochemical industry for fertilizers, which U.S. farmers could afford even in the face of soaring oil prices in the 1970s. But such prices meant disaster for poor developing world farmers who lost their farms to rich ones.

Another problem – recognized by 1970 – was the displacement and disappearance of a wide variety of cultivars and, consequently, of the genetic variability that had enabled plant breeders to produce those few currently in use. Past corn breeding, for example, now portends potential GM trouble because practically all maize grown commercially comes from a small pool of hybrid seeds whose traits are so unpredictable in the second generation that new seeds must be purchased every year. This is profitable for hybrid seed corn companies, but makes for such genetic uniformity that maize crops are all equally vulnerable to new diseases, pests, and insects and, thus, to widespread crop failure.[12]

Similarly, the new dwarfed and semi-dwarfed wheat and rice plants are also genetically uniform, which means that a growing amount of the world's food supply is at risk from new, or newly mutated, plant pathogens. Nor were the hybrids defending themselves all that well against existing pathogens. More chemicals were brought to bear – especially pesticides whose cost drove still more Third World farmers out of business, and whose effects ignited environmental furor in the developed world.[13]

Finally, perhaps the most discouraging unintended consequence of the Green Revolution was to initiate a tremendous increase in those populations that supposedly were going to be able to feed themselves. Instead, they reproduced to the outer limits of their food supply and, by the 1980s, every country "revolutionized" by the Green Revolution was once again an importer of those staple foods they had expected to be able to export.

Despite this kind of adversity, however, the world's farmers did triple yields between 1965 and the 1990s, and this without yield variability rising significantly. Much of the thanks for this was due the rediscovery of Mendelian Genetics in 1900 that gave rise to food biotechnology a half-century later, which means the use of recombinant deoxyribonucleic acid (rDNA) and cell fusion techniques to introduce new traits into plants, animals,

and microorganisms. Such gene transfers between different species have occurred often enough in nature. But it was only in the aftermath of the mid-century discovery of the roadmap of life (the double helix structure of DNA) by James Watson and Francis Crick that humans have been able to control the process. This has been heralded as the greatest breakthrough in agriculture since its invention – even the beginning of a second Neolithic Revolution – and one that promises even more agricultural transformation and an array of other sparkling possibilities.[14]

As was learned from the Green Revolution, however, its management will require the imposition of some sort of analytic framework – a carefully drawn map if you will.[15] Critics say that this sort of management is impossible but, managed or not, biotechnology is not going to go away. With the prediction of a global population increase from 6 to 9 billion by 2050, technology and science have their work cut out for them, and biotechnology promises a food supply capable of feeding the extra 3 billion of us – even on the poor soils and in the poor climates that characterize many of the developing countries.[16]

GM events have moved at blinding speed since 1994 when the "Flavr Savr" tomato became the first genetically engineered food product approved by the FDA for human consumption in America. Two decades later it was announced that the DNA code of rice had been deciphered, and doubtless the codes of the other major world crops will soon follow, to add still other dimensions to GM foods. At present the United States, Canada, and Argentina account for the bulk of the world's GM food crops (China and South Africa produce GM cotton) and have concentrated on modifying ripening characteristics, and developing resistance to herbicides and insect pests.

The focus was initially confined mostly to soybeans and corn in the United States and canola in Canada but, because of the many uses of these crops as food additives, Americans unwittingly began consuming GM foods almost daily. Fully 80 percent of the nation's soybean crop has been genetically altered with the addition of a gene from a bacterium that makes the plant resistant to a widely-used weed killer, and at least a third of the corn produced has a gene from another bacterium that kills insects. The modification of potatoes and sugar beets has also received much GM attention, and such novelties as melons with edible rinds, fully mature cheeses made barely a week before, and avocadoes with seeds in the skin instead of a pit in the center, are among GM's "near-future" promises.[17]

During much of the 1990s, the controversy that greeted the first GM products on the market seemed to pass right over the heads of Americans, who only took notice of this new development in their food supply when European (and some Asian) governments worried openly about possible health and environmental hazards embedded in GM foods and insisted that they (and products containing GM ingredients) be labeled to give consumers a choice. But because soybeans are employed in over 60 percent of the processed foods Europeans buy from America, this meant that transgenic, herbicide-resistant soybeans from the United States would have to be sorted out from the traditionally grown varieties – a costly procedure. Nonetheless, in the late 1990s the European Union (EU) responded to consumers' fears about the safety of GM foods (85 to 90 percent of Europeans wanted GM foods to be labeled) by enacting a moratorium on their sale.[18]

Such fears of GM foods are as disparate as the groups that voice them. Some object to scientists "playing God." Others worry that consumer ill-health will be the chief harvest of GM foods, and still others are anxious about unintended environmental consequences – GM crops, for example, escaping and crossing with wild relatives to touch off an epidemic of "super weeds."[19] In addition there is the very real possibility that the bugs and weeds GM foods are built to discourage may instead build their own defenses against such efforts. Many, with little confidence in the ethics of GM producers, suspect that the new plants will be outfitted with "terminator" genes to kill them before seed can be collected for planting, thereby chaining developing world farmers to Western agrochemical firms. Still others just don't like big business, or have specific objections to companies like Monsanto with its "seed police" who nose around small towns looking for tips on who might be saving Monsanto seed. Those caught are sued and one poor farmer actually went to prison for the offense.[20]

The food and biotechnology industries denounced the European moratorium as a "knee-jerk" reaction or a "frankenfoods" phobia. Washington (backed by Canada and Australia) claimed that it constituted an illegal trade barrier that would cost U.S. farmers hundreds of millions of dollars annually, and filed a complaint with the World Trade Organization. By the middle of 2003 the smoke was clearing. The European Parliament had passed tough new laws regulating GM foods, to replace the biotech ban – laws that dismayed the U.S. administration. Not only are Europeans getting their labeling, but the regulations state that producers must trace genetically modified organisms at all stages of production. Finally, European growers of GM crops will be regulated so that their fields cannot pollinate other conventional crops.[21]

Knee-jerk or not, the European backlash over the possible health hazards of GM foods augured hard times for the biotechnology industry as the new century got underway. Because of the European moratorium, U.S. farmers already were cutting back on the amount of acreage planted in genetically modified crops when Monsanto became embroiled in a class-action lawsuit filed by soybean growers alleging that this biotech giant had not adequately tested their seed for safety before releasing it. Next, the Kellogg Company made the headlines by shutting down a plant because it could not guarantee that its cereals were free of genetically modified corn. Similarly, Kraft Foods and other manufacturers recalled their tacos made from GM corn, and then the news broke (which the industry denounced as distorted) that pollen from a widely planted genetically tailored strain of corn can kill the larvae of monarch butterflies.

Legitimate demands ensued for more ecological assessments in the regulatory process of agricultural biotechnology, and some Americans (including the Natural Law Party) began demanding labeling laws like those of Europe. For their part, defenders of genetic modification point out that the procedures used are not all that different from those of traditional breeding and insist that the benefits far outweigh the risks,[22] which is about as close as the biotechnology industry has gotten to conceding that there are any risks at all.

But, of course, there are risks; and allergic reaction is a serious one. Illustrative is a new type of soybean that never reached the market because it contained a gene from a Brazil nut, which probably would have done those allergic to tree nuts some real harm.[23] This was a problem caught by testing, but there is a whole generation of new GM foods waiting to be scrutinized by those mindful that the insertion of a single gene can change the constituents of a plant or even alter its entire structure.

On a more positive side, there have been some stunning successes using rDNA techniques. In addition to plants genetically engineered to resist insects, tolerate herbicides, and have a longer shelf life, we now have chymosin, an enzyme used in cheese making. Traditionally extracted from the stomachs of calves and sold in a mixture called rennet, the gene has been transferred to bacteria that can be grown in large quantities – saving much wear and tear on the calves.[24] And on the future front is biotech rice, called "golden rice," because of the hue its beta-carotene content creates – beta-carotene because researchers at a Swiss laboratory spliced three genes into the rice to provide it.

The idea is that "golden rice" could put an end to vitamin A deficiency and consequently to the blindness that many suffer throughout the developing world (including 250,000 children). Obviously, the vitamin-A rich rice could also do much to lower the mortality of underfed and malnourished children.[25] Another kind of biotech rice announced by Cornell University in 2002 was developed by fusing two genes from the E. coli bacterium and placing them in a common rice variety. The new rice is extraordinarily hardy and capable of considerably expanding rice cultivation because it will grow in fields that are much too dry, or too cold, or too salty for ordinary rice.

Earlier, in 1992, American scientists turned out the "hairy potato," whose sticky leaves trap potato pests, and whose gummy sap causes an especially destructive pest to become constipated, swelling its abdomen so that its ovaries are crushed, preventing the growth of future bug generations.[26] A hybrid wheat called "Veery" has been developed that is substantially more hardy and high yielding than other wheat because it contains genetic material from rye, and an "antifreeze" gene is being sought in coldwater fish to help crops like potatoes and strawberries survive unexpected weather changes.

GM rice, maize, millets, soybeans, and manioc that now promise yields some 50 percent higher than unmodified counterparts and are drought, pest, and weed resistant may make unnecessary those extra earths needed to feed developing countries by the middle of the twenty-first century. These will likely be joined in that effort by the so-called bonsai crops – "super dwarfs," such as wheat growing only a few inches tall – that may also benefit everyone environmentally because they will reduce the need for fertilizers, herbicides, and water usage, while at the same time putting less energy into the stems and more into the grain.

Produce consumers will also be pleased with some GM products. In 1996, scientists announced that manipulation of plant genes such as those of tomatoes or lettuce can govern how they develop the hormones that determine a plant's growth rate. Theoretically, the time is near when the rate at which tomatoes ripen can be controlled and the time that lettuce can remain fresh lengthened.[27]

Biotech techniques have also been focused on animals, and that has stirred up even more controversy than GM plants. The jury remains out on cloning, although Monsanto's recent development of recombinant bovine somatotropin (rbST), also known as the Beef Growth Hormone, has done little to ease public suspicion of biotech industry motives. The hormone increases a cow's milk production by 10 to 20 percent, and even though there were concerns that the hormone itself, along with antibiotics in the milk, could be abusive of human health, by 1995 Monsanto claimed to have sold more than 14.5 million doses of rbST to U.S. dairy farmers. Those with concerns are now frustrated because a lack of labeling makes it impossible to know to what extent milk, cheese, yogurt, and ice cream on the market are products of the hormone. Moreover, and more importantly, was such a hormone needed in a nation that was already producing a considerable surplus of milk before it was introduced?[28]

Some chicken design improvements, by contrast, seem more public (and taxpayer) friendly. Americans are eating much more chicken than in the past and are especially partial to the lower-fat white meat, which means breast meat. Poultry breeders have responded by genetically breeding hybrid birds that have larger breasts, are disease resistant, require relatively little feed, and reach five pounds of weight at slaughter in just 35 days.

Scientists are also concentrating on GM functional foods (that deliver health benefits beyond those generally expected of the nutrients) like tomatoes with enhanced levels of cancer-fighters (flavenoids for example), fruits that naturally produce drugs and vaccines, breads that lower cholesterol, and mushroom extracts that boost the immune system.[29] There are other natural foods on the market that some call "functional" foods with no genetic modification like oat fiber, cranberry juice, tomatoes, almonds, soy protein, and olive oil for healthy hearts. Another class of cholesterol-lowering products are butter-like spreads such as Benecol and Pro-Activ that contain plant sterol esters. Then there are "probiotics" that utilize strains of lactic acid bacteria, which seem to produce health benefits when introduced to the microflora of the gut, and a special lactic acid bacteria that can lower blood pressure has just been announced by a Swedish corporation. And finally there are new products like "Reducal" – derived from palm and oat oils – that help in weight management by prolonging the feeling of fullness after eating, along with green and black teas that appear to have myriad health benefits. Such functional foods – some as simple as orange juice fortified with vitamin D – are a wave of the present that promises to achieve tidal proportions in the future.

But functional foods are nothing new. In 1887, Hovis bread was patented in Great Britain. It was and is made with flour containing some five times more of the fatty wheat germ than whole grain bread and was touted as a health food from the outset. Some thirty-five years later vitamin E was discovered, and it turned out that Hovis bread was indeed a health food, loaded with vitamin E. It is now subsumed under the rubric of a nutraceutical.[30]

Among other things, the term "nutraceutical" (coined by the Foundation for Innovation in Medicine around a decade ago) highlights an age-old riddle – to what extent are foods drugs and drugs foods?[31] Honey was a nutriment for the ancient Egyptians but, because of its ability to prevent infection, they also smeared it on wounds; spices made foods taste better in the Middle Ages, but were also employed to aid digestion; and countless foods lining the shelves of nineteenth-century pantries and apothecary shops had histories of medical usage for millennia.[32] Others were created in the nineteenth century. In addition to Hovis bread, there was the "meat extract" of Justus von Liebig and the Graham, Kellogg, and Post contributions like "Graham Crackers," "Grape-Nuts," "Post-Toasties," "Postum," "Corn Flakes," and "All-Bran," which were all marketed as what today we call nutraceuticals.[33]

Citrus fruits have proved themselves against scurvy, and an apple a day probably does pack a wide enough range of nutrients to help keep doctors away, at least most of the time. But perhaps the most venerable of all foods *cum* drugs is garlic, a member of the lily family. Always a seasoning, it has been employed at least since the beginnings of agriculture in amulets to ward off disease. Other uses have been to ease toothache and painful urination, subdue coughs, colds, and hemorrhoids, treat wounds, control epidemics, and, most recently, to reduce plasma concentrations of cholesterol and triglycerides and to inhibit thrombosis. As it turns out, garlic does have antibacterial properties and is about as effective as aspirin as a antithrombotic compound. Moreover, it can help lower levels of low-density lipoproteins while elevating those that are high density. But the catch is that garlic preparations in which garlic's powerful odor is lacking do none of these things. In other words, no way has yet been found to separate the drug from the food in this ancient nutraceutical.[34]

There are also so-called "farmaceuticals" in our twenty-first century world – foods like corn, rice, safflower, barley, even lettuce – that are

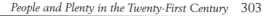

engineered to make biotech drugs. Human antibodies, for example, can be produced with plant proteins that are "biopharmed" (to toss out another new and catchy word). Needless to say, not everyone is enthusiastic about farmaceuticals. A major fear is that crops genetically modified for medicinal purposes could somehow contaminate the food supply, and it is the case that in 2002, stray bits of corn engineered to fabricate a pig vaccine contaminated a Nebraska grain elevator containing soybeans.

Clearly, new GM foods promise combustible issues in the future, but on the future front as well is the expanded production of ancient foods previously garnered mostly from the wild. Sea vegetables in the form of seaweeds are farmed to the tune of more than 4 million tons annually and are put to many uses ranging from making salad dressings and ice cream, to sushi wrappers and nori sheets.

Then there is a slightly different kind of aquaculture that also has a long history, stretching into the distant past, but is very much a part of the present; and, at present, there are some 150 species under domestic culture for human consumption – 90 or so species of fish, 23 species of crustaceans, and 35 species of mollusks.[35] The most important of these are salmon, trout, tilapia, shrimp, oysters, mussels, and eels in the West, carp in much of Asia, and abalone in Japan. In nature, it takes a million fish eggs to beget a single fish. But artificial fertilization is now seeing to it that up to 80 percent of the eggs are fertilized, and aquatic animal cultivation is making, and will continue to make, a significant contribution to the ever-increasing worldwide demand for food, despite problems of elevated pollutants in some farm-raised seafood.[36] Moreover, aquatic farming can lessen pressure on other food resources. Farmed salmon – just one illustration – deliver 15 times more protein per acre than beef cattle.[37]

But, speaking of meat, farming is hardly limited to aquatic animals. Pheasants, squabs, and quail are hatched and raised in captivity So are ostriches, rabbits, bison, deer and elk. And in the plant world, another wild food generated commercially is the mushroom. Mushroom domestication may have begun in China as early as the Han dynasty (206 BCE to 9 AD), but in the West mushrooms were first cultivated in France during the reign of Louis XIV (1643–1715).[38] The original cultivars were the so-called common mushrooms (the *champignon d' Paris*) that were grown in homes and caves very much as they are today.

Common mushroom cultivation reached the United States in 1880, and by 1886 was established in Pennsylvania. In 1925, that state accounted for 85 percent of the nation's supply and still holds onto a 50 percent market share.[39] But there are now many more mushrooms under cultivation, including the wildly popular (and expensive) morel, whose secrets of cultivation have just recently been discovered.[40] Others include the shitake, the oyster mushroom, and the brown-capped common mushroom often called cri-

mini, along with its larger and beefy big brother, the portobello.[41] Shitakes used to be grown only in Japan and criminis only in Italy, but their cultivation is now worldwide and, hopefully, chanterelles, porcinis, and other wild mushrooms will soon follow morels into domestication.

How this wholesale food globalization will play out in the various cuisines of the world remains to be seen because it has sent international cuisines into a dizzying state of flux. The French style has declined in prominence in the face of international competition from Italian and (on the other side of the globe) Japanese cuisines, but fusion cuisines threaten to eclipse them all.[42] Moreover, the food publications that have accompanied growing literacy across the globe, coupled with the Internet, make entire cuisines available to anyone interested, which should ensure a continuation of cuisine changes.[43]

Certainly such developments are threatening to those hoping to preserve old food ways. But, although the history of food and nutrition reflects many millennia of food choices within a process that could almost be viewed along the lines of Darwinian natural selection, there are a couple of constants in that history that may serve to mollify. One is that dietary change has always occurred, and probably always will; the other is that such change has been driven (albeit very slowly at times) by a quest for variety and, again, probably always will.

We have seen a bewildering variety of such changes in the United States, which pioneered in food globalization and now sells cheddar to the English, mozzarella to the French, wines to the Germans, and even Louisiana hot sauce to the Swedes.[44] But the countries of Europe – previously bastions of nationalistic cuisines – are now experiencing the same sorts of changes. These were set in motion by foreign workers and their descendents who responded to post-war labor shortages by migrating to other countries and bringing along their own cuisines. Italian, Turkish, Portuguese, and Greek foods are now widespread and popular throughout Europe, pizza restaurants can be found in even the smallest villages, and, as in the United States, frozen pizzas and other supermarket convenience foods are regularly consumed.

Like the Americans before them, prosperity has made Europeans increasingly reluctant to cook at home. In Germany, traditional restaurants (the Gasthaus in particular) are being supplanted by foreign ones or fast food restaurants because many of the current generation are not interested in the long hours and hard work required to keep them open. The Dutch have moved from potatoes to pasta,[45] and the French have embraced Japanese cuisine as well as that of North Africa.[46] Northern Europeans have become fond of southern European foods and a Chinese food company has moved into Sweden to produce Chinese vegetables.[47] Such revolutionary stirrings are evident even in Moscow, which is dispensing perestroika in all directions. One of its newest wonders is "The Seventh Continent," perhaps the world's largest supermarket, offering a huge selection of foods flown in daily from all corners of the globe. And Moscow's streets bristle with Italian, French, Asian, and Central Asian restaurants.

Clearly, food does not identify and differentiate as it did in the past. Rather, globalization is bulldozing nationalism as well as ethnocentrism. And after 10,000 years of agriculture, for good or for evil, the motor powering the bulldozer is the United States. This is happening at a time when the world's developed countries have gained an unprecedented technological control over their food supply, a control that promises to increase almost daily. The palpable benefits – unprecedented health and longevity – should also increase. The challenge now – and an incredibly complex one – is to pass along this technology and the benefits of what we might call the "Second Neolithic Revolution" to Third World populations on a shrinking planet. It goes without saying that if this is done successfully that revolution, which we could also call a "Post Neolithic Revolution," should signal the beginning of the end of the Third World.

Notes

PREFACE

1. Raymond Grew (ed.), *Food and Global History*, Boulder, CO: Westview Press, 1999, Introduction, 5.
2. William Greider, New York: Simon and Schuster, 1997.
3. F. Fukuyama, New York: Free Press, 1992.
4. Noreena Hertz, London: Heineman, 2001.
5. John Micklethwait and Adrian Wooldridge, New York: Crown Business, 2000.
6. Peter H. Lindert and Jeffrey G. Williamson, "Does Globalization Make the World More Unequal?" *National Bureau of Economic Research, Working Paper 8228*, Cambridge, MA, 2001.
7. Alan M. Taylor, "Globalization, Trade, and Development: Some Lessons from History," *National Bureau of Economic Research, Working Paper 9326*, Cambridge, MA, 2002, 7–8.
8. Brian Murton, "Famine," in Kenneth F. Kiple and Kriemhild C. Ornelas (eds.), *The Cambridge World History of Food*, (hereinafter CWHF), 2 vols., New York and Cambridge: Cambridge University Press, 2000, II: 1421.

INTRODUCTION: FROM FORAGING TO FARMING

1. Harriet Friedmann, "Circles of Growing and Eating: The Political Ecology of Food and Agriculture," in Raymond Grew (ed.), *Food in Global History*, Boulder, CO: Westview Press, 1999, 33.
2. Daniel W. Gade, "Hogs (Pigs)," in Kenneth F. Kiple and Kriemhild C. Ornelas (eds.), *The Cambridge World History in Food* (hereinafter CWHF), 2 vols., New York and Cambridge. Cambridge University Press, 2000, II: 536.
3. Indeed, according to the title of an essay written by Jared Diamond, the invention of agriculture was "The Worst Mistake in the History of the Human Race," *Discover*, 1987, 8(5).

4. See, for example, Tony McMichael, *Human Frontiers, Environments, and Disease: Past Patterns, Uncertain Futures*. Cambridge, UK: Cambridge University Press, 2001.

5. R. E. Hughes, "Vitamin C" and "Scurvy," in CWHF II: 754–62 and 988–1000; See also Kenneth J. Carpenter, *The History of Scurvy and Vitamin C*, Cambridge, UK: Cambridge University Press, 1986, and David I. Harvie, *Limeys*, Cambridge University Press, UK: Sutton Publishing, Phoenix Mills, UK, 2002.

6. Frederick L. Dunn, "Beriberi" in CWHF, I: 915. See also Kenneth J. Carpenter, *Beriberi, White Rice, and Vitamin B*, Berkeley: University of California Press, 2000.

7. Editors, CWHF, I: 10.

8. McMichael, *Human Frontiers*, 30; S. Boyd Eaton, Marjorie Shostak, and Melvin Konner, *The Paleolithic Prescription*, New York: Harper and Row, 1988, 20–1.

9. Clark Spencer Larsen, "Dietary Reconstruction and Nutritional Assessment of Past Peoples," in CWHF, I: 13–33.

10. Donald Ortner and Gretchen Theobald, "Paleopathological Evidence of Malnutrition," in CWHF, I: 34–43; Kristin D. Sobolik, "Dietary Reconstruction as Seen in Coprolities," in CWHF, I: 44–50; Elizabeth S. Wing, "Animals Used for Food in the Past: As seen by Their Remains Excavated from Archaeological Sites," in CWHF, I: 51–7; Ted A. Rathbun, "Chemical Approaches to Dietary Representation," in CWHF, I: 58–62.

11. Mark Nathan Cohen, "History, Diet, and Hunter-Gatherers," in CWHF, I: 63–9.

12. See, for example, Mark N. Cohen and George Armelagos (eds.), *Paleopathology at the Origins of Agriculture*, New York: Academic Press, 1984, and Richard H. Steckel and Jerome C. Rose (eds.), *The Backbone of History: Health and Nutrition in the Western Hemisphere*, Cambridge, UK and New York: Cambridge University Press, 2002.

13. 1950 (orig. 1651), pt. 1, ch. 13.

14. R. Ted Steinbock, "Rickets and Osteomalacia," in Kenneth F. Kiple (ed.), *The Cambridge World History of Human Disease* (hereinafter CWHHD), New York and Cambridge: Cambridge University Press, 1993, 978–80.

15. Susan Kent, "Iron Deficiency and Anemia of Chronic Disease," in CWHF, I: 923.

16. Alfred Jay Bollet and Audrey K. Brown, "Anemia," in CWHHD, 576; Susan Kent, "Iron Deficiency and the Anemia of Chronic Disease," in CWHF, I: 923.

17. Eaton, Shostak, and Konner, *Paleolithic Prescription*, 95–6.

18. Loren Cordain, Janette Brand Miller, and S. Boyd Eaton et al., "Plant-animal Subsistence Ratios and Macronutrient Energy Estimations in Worldwide Hunter-gatherer Diets," *American Journal of Clinical Nutrition*, 2000, 71: 682–92.

19. Stephen Budiansky, *The Covenant of the Wild: Why Animals Chose Domestication*, New York: William Morrow, 1992, 115; Colin Spencer, *The Heretic's Feast*, Hanover, NH and London: University Press of New England, 1995, 23–4, who credits Colin Tudge with the estimate.

20. Eaton, Shostak, and Konner, *Paleolithic Prescription*, 7.

21. Jacqueline L. Dupont, "Essential Fatty Acids," in CWHF, 880; Melissa H. Olken and Joel D. Howell, "Nutrition and Heart-Related Diseases," in CWHF, I:1104.

22. Kenneth F. Kiple, "The Question of Paleolithic Nutrition and Modern Health," in CWHF, II: 1707; R. L. Leibel, M. Rosenbaum, and J. Hirsch, "Changes in Energy Expenditure Resulting from Altered Body Weight," *New England Journal of Medicine*, 1995, 332: 621–8; Leslie Sue Lieberman, "Obesity," in CWHF, I: 1067.

23. Leslie Sue Lieberman, "Diabetes," in CWHHD, 674.

24. Haim Ofek, *Second Nature: Economic Origins of Human Evolution*, Cambridge, UK: Cambridge University Press, 2001: 62–8; Beckerman, "Game" in CWHF, I: 524.

CHAPTER ONE: LAST HUNTERS, FIRST FARMERS

1. H. Leon Abrams, Jr. "Vegetarianism: Another View," in Kenneth F. Kiple and Kriemhild C. Ornelas (eds.), *The Cambridge World History of Food* (hereinafter CWHF), 2 vols., New York and Cambridge, Cambridge University Press, 2000, II: 1571.
2. Stephen Beckerman, "Game," in CWHF, I: 524.
3. Sheldon Aaronson, "Algae," in CWHF, I: 241–4.
4. James L. Parsons, "Sea Turtles and their Eggs," in CWHF, I: 568.
5. Ibid., I: 568, 567.
6. Ibid., I: 569.
7. Naomichi Ishigi, "Japan" in CWHF, II: 1177.
8. Unless otherwise indicated, this discussion of insects is based on Darna L. Dufour and Joy B. Saunder, "Insects" in CWHF, I: 546–53.
9. Brian Murton, "Australia and New Zealand," in CWHF, II: 1342.
10. Sujatha Panikker, "Food-Borne Infection," in CWHF, I: 1031–48.
11. K. T. H. Farrer, "Food Additives," in CWHF, II: 1667. Although, even the healthiness of cooking some foods is now under scrutiny because of their tendency, when cooked at high heat – especially frying, toasting, and roasting – to develop elevated levels of acrylamide, a substance that causes cancer in some experimental animals.
12. Felipe Fernández-Armesto, *Food: A History*, London: Macmillan, 2001, 10; James Trager, *The Food Chronology*, New York: Henry Holt, 1995, 211.
13. Ibid., 9. Reay Tannahill, *Food in History*, New York: Crown Publishers, 1989, 4.
14. Ibid., 12.
15. Naomi F. Miller and Wilma Wetterstrom, "The Beginnings of Agriculture: The Ancient Near East and North Africa," in CWHF, II: 1125–6: Trager, 2, 5.
16. Alfred W. Crosby, *Throwing Fire: Projectile Technology Through History*, New York and Cambridge, UK: Cambridge University Press, 2002, 47.
17. Ibid., 52.
18. Mark Nathan Cohen, "History, Diet and Hunter-Gatherers" in CWHF I: 63–9; Stephen Budiansky, *The Covenant of the Wild: Why Animals Chose Domestication*, New York: William Marrow, 1992, 37, 115.

CHAPTER TWO: BUILDING THE BARNYARD

1. Alan Cromer, *Uncommon Sense: The Heretical Nature of Science*, New York and Oxford: Oxford University Press, 1993, 57.
2. Stephen Budiansky, *The Covenant of the Wild: Why Animals Chose Domestication*, New York: William Morrow, 1992, 33.
3. David R. Yesner, "Caribou and Reindeer," in Kenneth F. Kiple and Kriemhild C. Ornelas (eds.), *The Cambridge World History of Food* (hereinafter CWHF), 2 vols., New York and Cambridge: Cambridge University Press, 2000, I: 481.
4. Budiansky 17.
5. James Trager, *The Food Chronology*, New York: Henry Holt, 1995, 2.
6. Stanley J. Olsen, "Dogs," in CWHF, I: 512–13.
7. Ibid. (p. 15)
8. Trager, 4, 5.
9. Olsen, "Dogs," in CWHF, I: 508.
10. Daniel W. Gade, "Sheep," in CWHF, I578–82 and "Goats," in CWHF, I: 536–41.
11. Gade, "Goats," in CWHF, I: 533.

12. Gade, "Goats," in CWHF, I: 534; "Sheep," in CWHF, I: 577.
13. Gade "Hogs (Pigs)," in CWHF, I: 537.
14. Jack R. Harlan, *Crops and Man*, Madison, WI: Crop Science Society of America, 1975, 41.
15. Gade, "Hogs (Pigs)," in CWHF, I: 539.
16. Ibid., I: 542–5.
17. Ibid., in CWHF, I: 587.
18. Daniel W. Gade, "Cattle," in CWHF, I: 489.
19. Ibid., I: 491.
20. Ibid., I: 489–95.
21. Daniel W. Gade, "Horses," in CWHF, I: 542–5.
22. Stanley J. Olsen, "The Horse in Ancient China and its Cultural Influence in Some Other Areas," *Proceedings of the Academy of Natural Sciences of Philadelphia*, 1988: 140, no. 2, 185.
23. Daniel W. Gade, "Horses," in CWHF, I: 542–3.
24. Elizabeth A. Stephens, "Camels," in CWHF, I: 467–79.
25. Ibid., I: 470–1.
26. Ibid., I: 478.
27. Robert Hoffpauir, "Water Buffalo," in CWHF, I: 583–606.
28. Ibid., I: 585, 588.
29. Ibid., I: 596–8.
30. Ibid., 601.
31. Stanely J. Olsen, "Fossil Ancestry of the Yak, Its Cultural Significance and Domestication in Tibet," *Proceedings of the Academy of Natural Sciences of Philadelphia*, 1990: 142, 73–100.
32. Richard Palmieri, "Yak," in CWHF, I: 607–15.
33. Ibid., 613.
34. Ibid., 608–9; Olsen, "Yak," 90.
35. David R. Yesner, "Caribou and Reindeer," in CWHF, I: 481, 486.
36. Ibid., I: 486.
37. Jean Bottéro, *The Oldest Cuisine in the World: Cooking in Mesopotamia* (tr. Teresa Lavender Fagan), Chicago: University of Chicago Press, 2004, passim.
38. Richard F. Johnston, "Pigeons," in CWHF, I: 561–4.
39. Ibid., I: 563.
40. Harlan, 42–3.
41. William J. Stadelman, "Chicken Eggs," in CWHF, I: 500.
42. Roger Blench and Kevin C. MacDonald, "Chickens," in CWHF, I: 496–8; Stadelman, in CWHF, I: 499–507.
43. Rosemary Luff, "Ducks," in CWHF, I: 517–24.
44. Ibid., 517.
45. Blench and MacDonald, "Goose," in CWHF, I: 529–31.

CHAPTER THREE: PROMISCUOUS PLANTS OF THE NORTHERN FERTILE CRESCENT

1. Naomi E. Miller and Wilma Wetterstrom, "The Beginnings of Agriculture: The Ancient Near East and North Africa, in Kenneth F. Kiple and Kriemhild C. Ornelas

(eds.), *The Cambridge World History of Food* (hereinafter CWHF), 2 vols., New York and Cambridge: Cambridge University Press, 2000, II: 1125.

2. Ibid., II: 1126.
3. Haim Ofek, *Second Nature: Economic Origins of Human Evolution*, Cambridge, UK: Cambridge University Press, 2001, 200.
4. Jared Diamond, "The Worst Mistake in the History of the Human Race," *Discover*, 1987, 185.
5. Joy McCorriston, "Wheat," in CWHF, I: 158, 162–3.
6. Ibid., I: 166–7.
7. Ibid., I: 163–5.
8. Ibid., I: 161.
9. Miller and Wetterstrom, II: 1126.
10. Ibid., 1128.
11. McCorriston, "Wheat," in CWHF, I: 158–74.
12. Joy McCorriston, "Barley," in CWHF, I: 81–9.
13. Phillip A. Cantrell II, "Beer and Ale," in CWHF, I: 619–20.
14. Jack R. Harlan, *Crops and Man*, Madison, WI: Crop Science Society of America, 1975, 187.
15. Editors, "Triticale," in CWHF, II: 1871–2.
16. Hansjörd Küster, "Rye," in CWHF, I: 149–51.
17. John S. Haller, Jr. "Ergotism," in Kenneth F. Kiple (ed.), *The Cambridge World History of Human Disease* (hereinafter CWHHD), New York and Cambridge: Cambridge University Press, 1993, 718–19.
18. Daniel Zohary and Maria Hopf, *Domestication of Plants in the Old World* 2nd ed., Oxford: Clarendon Press, 1994, 77.
19. David M. Petterson and J. Paul Murphy, "Oat," in CWHF, I: 121–31.
20. Lawrence Kaplan, "Beans, Peas, and Lentils," in CWHF, I: 271–80.
21. Zohary and Hopf, 99.
22. Hansjörg Küster, "Northern Europe," in CWHF, II: 1228.
23. Kaplan, CWHF, I: 271–80.
24. Ibid.; Editors, "Chickpea," in CWHF, II: 1752.
25. Zohary and Hopf, 107.
26. Kaplan, CWHF, I: 279–80.
27. Zohary and Hopf, 185.
28. Don Brothwell and Patricia Brothwell, *Food in Antiquity: A Survey of the Diet of Early Peoples*, Baltimore and London: The Johns Hopkins University Press, 1998 ed., 108–9.
29. Ibid.
30. Julia Peterson, "The Allium Species (Onions, Garlic, Leeks, Chives, and Shallots)," in CWHF, I: 249–70; and Brothwell and Brothwell, 108.
31. Delphine Roger, "The Middle East and South Asia," in CWHF, II: 1141, 1145; Miller and Wetterstrom, in CWHF, II: 1128.
32. A. Zaid and P. F. de Wet, "Origin, Geographical Distribution, and Nutritional Values of Date Palm," in Abdelouahhanb Zaid (ed.), *Date Palm Cultivation*, Online, Food and Agricultural Organization of the United Nations, World Wide Web, Rome, 2002.
33. Brothwell and Brothwell, 1: 45–6.
34. Boria Sax, "Apples," in David Schofield Wilson and Angus Kress Gillespie (eds.), *Rooted in America*, Knoxville: The University of Tennessee Press, 1999, 2–3.

35. Editors, "Fig," and "Apple," in CWHF, II, pages 1774 and 1720 respectively.
36. James L. Newman, "Wine," in CWHF, I: 730–7; Miller and Wetterstrom, CWHF, II: 1126.
37. Küster, "Northern Europe," CWHF, II: 1228.
38. Editors, "Flax," in CWHF, II: 1774.
39. Roger, CWHF, II: 1142.
40. Ibid., 1141.
41. Tannahill, 32–3.
42. Charles B. Heiser, *Seed to Civilization: The Story of Food*, 2nd ed., San Francisco: W. H. Freeman, 1981, 12.
43. Colin E. Nash, "Aquatic Animals," in CWHF, I: 456–7.
44. Diamond, 88.

CHAPTER FOUR: PERIPATETIC PLANTS OF EASTERN ASIA

1. Christine Wilson, "Southeast Asia," in Kenneth F. Kiple and Kriemhild C. Ornelas (eds.), *The Cambridge World History of Food* (hereinafter CWHF), 2 vols., New York and Cambridge: Cambridge University Press, 2000, I: 178. CWHF, I: 1151–2; Bruce D. Smith, *The Emergence of Agriculture*, New York: Scientific American Library, 1995, 14.
2. Wilson, "Southeast Asia," in CWHF, I: 1151.
3. Will C. McClatchey, "Bananas and Plantains," in CWHF, I: 178.
4. Don Brothwell and Patricia Brothwell, *Food in Antiquity: A Survey of the Diet of Early Peoples*, Baltimore and London: The Johns Hopkins University Press, 1998 ed., 138.
5. McClatchey, in CWHF, I: 175–80.
6. Brothwell and Brothwell, 139.
7. McClatchey, in CWHF, I: 178.
8. Ibid.
9. Nancy J. Pollock, "Taro," in CWHF, I: 218–30.
10. Wilson, in CWHF, II: 1153.
11. William S. Middleton, "Early Medical Experiences in Hawaii," *Bulletin of the History of Medicine*, XLV: 1971, 446.
12. Pollock, "Taro," in CWHF, I: 224.
13. Patricia J. O'Brien, "Sweet Potatoes and Yams," in CWHF, I: 213.
14. Ibid., I: 207–17.
15. Ibid., 212.
16. H. D. Tindall, *Vegetables in the Tropics*, West Port, CT: Avi Publishing, 1983, 219.
17. Wilson, "Southeast Asia," in CWHF, II: 1152–3.
18. Ibid., II: 1153; Te-Tzu Chang, "Rice," in CWHF, I: 132–48, passim.
19. Editors, "Eggplant," CWHF, II: 1770.
20. Based on Chang, CWHF, I: 132–48, passim.
21. Ibid., I: 138–40.
22. Jeremy Black (ed.), *Atlas of World History*, New York: DK Publishing, 2000, 73; Chang, I: 133–6.
23. Reay Tannahill, *Food in History*, New York: Crown Publishers, 1989, 39.

24. G. Mazza, "Buckwheat," in CWHF, I: 90.
25. Françoise Sabban, "China," in CWHF, II: 1166–7.
26. Ibid., 1166–7.
27. Ibid., 1179.
28. Ibid., 1170.
29. Editors, "Oranges," in CWHF, II: 1826.
30. Editors, "Apricot," in CWHF, II: 1721–2.
31. Editors, "Jujube," in CWHF, II: 1794; Brothwell and Brothwell, 136–8.
32. Sucheta Mazumdar, "The Impact of New World Food Crops on the Diet and Economy of China and India, 1600–1900," in Raymond Grew (ed.), *Food in Global History*. Boulder, CO: Westview Press, 1999, 63.
33. Te-Tzu Chang, "Rice," in CWHF, I: 143.
34. Mazumdar, 62–3.
35. Ibid., 63–4; Mazumdar calls Champa rice "the forerunner of the 'Green Revolution.'" See also Jerry H. Bentley, "Hemispheric Integration, 500–1500 C. E.," *Journal of World History*, 9(2), 1998, 247.
36. Thomas Sorosiak, "Soybean," in CWHF, I: 422–6.
37. Ibid., I: 423.
38. See Chapter 16 in this volume for the history of tea.
39. Sabban, CWHF, II: 1171.
40. Colin E. Nash, "Aquatic Animals," in CWHF, I: 456.
41. Ibid.
42. Colin Spencer, *The Heretic's Feast*, Hanover (NH) and London: University Press of New England, 1995, 70–71; Tannahill, 105–18.
43. Delphine Roger, The Middle East and South Asia in CWHF, II: 1149.
44. J. M. J. De Wet, "Sorghum," CWHF, I: 156.
45. Dorothea Bedigian, "Sesame," in CWHF, I: 413.
46. H. Frederic Janson, *Pomona's Harvest: An Illustrated Chronicle of Antiquarian Fruit Literature*, Portland: Timber Press, 1996, 14.
47. David Maynard and Donald N. Maynard, "Cucumbers, Melons, and Watermelons," in CWHF, I: 305.
48. Ibid.; Maguelonne Toussaint-Samat, *History of Food* (tr. Anthea Bell) Cambridge, MA: Blackwell, 1992, 658.
49. Maynard and Maynard, in CWHF, I: 305.
50. Charles B. Heiser, Jr., *Of Plants and People*, Norman and London: University of Oklahoma Press, 1985, 9.
51. Tannahill, 107.
52. Naomichi Ishige, "Japan," in CWHF, II: 1175.
53. Lois N. Magner, "Korea," in CWHF, II: 1184.
54. Naomichi Ishige, "Sukiyaki – A New Tradition at the Table" in *AJI Communications on Japan's Dietary Culture*, Jan.–Feb. (2): 1980, n.p.
55. Ishige, CWHF, II: 1176–7.
56. Ibid.
57. Magner, CWHF, II: 1188.
58. Ishigi, CWHF, II: 1177.
59. Magner, CWHF, II: 1184–5.

CHAPTER FIVE: FECUND FRINGES OF
THE NORTHERN FERTILE CRESCENT

1. Naomi F. Miller and Wilma Wetterstrom, "The Beginnings of Agriculture," in Kenneth F. Kiple and Kriemhild C. Ornelas (eds.), *The Cambridge World History of Food*, (hereinafter CWHF) 2 vols., New York and Cambridge: Cambridge University Press, 2000, II: 1129.
2. Ibid., II: 1129.
3. Jack R. Harlan, *Crops and Man*, Madison, WI: Crop Science Society of America, 1975, 197.
4. Miller and Wetterstrom, CWHF, II: 1129.
5. Phillip A. Cantrell I, "Beer and Ale," CWHF, I: 620.
6. Borothea Bedigian, "Sesame," in CWHF, I: 415–16.
7. Stephen Budiansky, *The Covenant of the Wild: Why Animals Chose Domestication*, New York: William Morrow, 1997, 23.
8. H. Frederic Janson, *Pomona's Harvest: an Illustrated Chronicle of Antiquarian Fruit Literature*, Portland, Timber Press, 1996, 14. And at some time in the distant past Southeast Asians put monkeys to work harvesting coconuts. Christine S. Wilson, "Southeast Asia," in CWHF, II: 1162.
9. Louis E. Grivetti, "Food Prejudices and Taboos," in CWHF, II: 1497–8.
10. Miller and Wetterstrom, CWHF, II: 1134.
11. Grivetti, CWHF, II: 1498.
12. For a survey of the possible reasons, see Frederick J. Simoons, *Eat Not This Flesh: Food Avoidances from Prehistory to the Present*, 2nd ed., Madison: University of Wisconsin Press, 1994, 98–101.
13. Grivetti, CWHF, II: 1508–9
14. Miller and Wetterstrom, CWHF, II: 1134–5.
15. Michelle Berriedale-Johnson, *The British Museum Cookbook: 4,000 Years of International Cuisine*, New York and London: Abbeville Press, 1992, 36.
16. Miller and Wetterstrom, CWHF, II: 1134.
17. Giovanni Rebora, *Culture of the Fork* (tr. Albert Sonnenfeld), New York: Columbia University Press, 1998, 13–14.
18. James Newman, "Africa South from the Sahara" in CWHF, II: 1330.
19. Ibid., 1332.
20. Jared Diamond, *Guns, Germs and Steel: The Fates of Human Societies*, New York. W.W. Norton, 1997, 389.
21. Ibid.
22. Newman, "Africa South from the Sahara," CWHF, II: 1333.
23. Ibid.
24. National Academy of Sciences, *Lost Crops of Africa: Volume 1, Grains*, Washington D.C.: National Academy Press, 1996, 41.
25. This discussion of sorghum is based on J.M.J. de Wet, "Sorghum," in CWHF, I: 152–8.
26. Ibid., 156.
27. *Lost Crops of Africa*, 215.
28. Ibid., 59.
29. Newman,"Africa South of the Sahara," CWHF, II: 1333.
30. *Lost Crops of Africa*, 80–1.
31. Te-Tzu Chang, "Rice," in CWHF, I: 135.
32. Editors, "Cowpea," in CWHF, II: 1764.

33. K. G. Berger and S. M. Martin, "Palm Oil," in CWHF, I: 397.

34. Ibid., 397, 400.

35. Editors, "Okra," in CWHF, II: 1824.

36. Edmund Abaka, "Kola Nut," in CWHF, I: 681–92.

37. Editors, "Ackee," in CWHF, II: 1713.

38. Editors, "Melegueta Pepper," in CWHF, II: 1812 and Jessica B. Harris, *The African Cookbook*, New York: Simon and Schuster, 1998, 60.

39. David Maynard and Donald N. Maynard, "Cucumbers, Melons, and Watermelons," in CWHF, I: 305–7.

40. Ibid., 306–7.

41. Patricia J. O'Brien, "Sweet Potatoes and Yams," in CWHF, I: 212–14.

42. Diamond, *Guns, Germs, and Steel*, 377, 380–1.

43. James L. Newman, "Africa South from the Sahara," in CWHF, II: 1334–35; MacNeish, 301; Black (ed.), *Atlas*, 73.

44. MacNeish, 220.

45. Hansjörg Küster, "Northern Europe," in CWHF, II: 1228–9.

46. Ibid., 1227.

47. Colin Spencer, "The British Isles," in CWHF, II: 1227.

48. Küster, "Northern Europe," in CWHF, II: 1229.

CHAPTER SIX: CONSEQUENCES OF THE NEOLITHIC

1. Charles B. Heiser, Jr., *Seed to Civilization: The Story of Food*, Cambridge: Harvard University Press, 1990, 2.

2. David Arnold, *Famine: Social Crisis and Historical Change*, Oxford: Basil Blackwell, 1988, passim.

3. Roy Strong, *Feast: A History of Grand Eating*, London: Jonathan Cape, 2002, 8.

4. Stephen Beckerman, "Game," in Kenneth F. Kiple and Kriemhild C. Ornelas (eds.), *The Cambridge World History of Food* (hereinafter CWHF), 2 vols., New York and Cambridge: Cambridge University Press, 2000, I: 524.

5. Reay Tannahill, *Food in History*, New York: Crown Publishers, 1989, 32.

6. Alan Cromer, *Uncommon Sense: The Heretical Nature of Science*, New York and Oxford: Oxford University Press, 1993, 58–9.

7. Harriet Friedman, "Circles of Growing and Eating," in Raymond Grew (ed.), *Food in Global History*, Boulder, CO: Westview Press, 1999, 33–54, passim.

8. Phyllis Pray Bober, *Art, Culture, and Cusine: Ancient and Medieval Gastronomy*, Chicago: University of Chicago Press, 1999, 17. Child limiting was also done by infanticide. See the discussion by Marvin Harris, *Our Kind*, New York: Harper, 1989, 211–14.

9. Sara A. Quandt, "Infant and Child Nutrition," in CWHF, II: 1444.

10. Heiser, *Seed to Civilization: passim*.

11. Susan Scott and Christopher J. Duncan, *Demography and Nutrition: Evidence From Historical and Contemporary Populations*, Malden, MA: Blackwell Science, 2002, 334.

12. Sara Quandt, "Infant and Child Nutrition," in CWHF, II: 1444.

13. The extent of such supplementation is a big, but unanswered question. The ancient Mesopotamians may have suffered from widespread vitamin C deficiency. See Julio César Pangas, "Dental Pathology in Ancient Mesopotamia," *Bulletin of the History of Medicine* 73(2), 1999, 197–207.

14. Clark Spencer Larsen, "Dietary Reconstruction and Nutritional Assessment of Past Peoples: The Bioanthropological Record," in CWHF, I: 15–16.

15. McMichael, 324; J. D. L. Hansen, "Protein-Energy Malnutrition," in CWHF, I: 977–86.

16. Modern day foragers are also relatively free from parasites. See Mark Nathan Cohen, "History, Diet, and Hunter-Gatherers," in CWHF, I: 65–6.

17. William H. McNeill, *Plagues and Peoples*, New York: Anchor Press/Doubleday, 1976, 51.

18. Alfred Jay Bollet and Audrey K. Brown, "Anemia," in Kenneth F. Kiple (ed.), *The Cambridge World History of Human Disease* (hereinafter CWHHD), New York and Cambridge: Cambridge University Press, 1995, 576. These same phenomena occurred in the New World transition to agriculture to be taken up later. See Steckel and Rose (eds.), *The Backbone of History: Health and Nutrition in the Western Hemisphere*; For height, see Cohen, CWHF, I: 68; Robert W. Fogel, "Nutrition and the Decline of Mortality Since 1700," *Working Paper Series of the National Bureau of Economic Research*, Working Paper no. 1807, Cambridge, MA: 1986 and Clark Spencer Larsen, "Biological Changes in Human Populations with Agriculture," *Annual Review of Anthropology* 24, 1995, 185–213. Finally, for stature in Paleolithic times as opposed to that in agricultural times including the present, see S. Boyd Eaton, Marjorie Shostak, and Melvin Konner, *The Paleolithic Prescription*, New York: Harper & Row, 1988, 34, 72, 95.

19. Joseph M. Prince and Richard H. Steckel, "Tallest in the World: Native Americans of the Great Plains in the Nineteenth Century," *National Bureau of Economic Research*, Historical Paper 112, Cambridge MA, 1998.

20. Sheldon Aaronson, "Fungi," in CWHF, I: 315.

21. Jean Bottéro, *The Oldest Cuisine in the World* (tr. Teresa Lavender Fagan), Chicago: University of Chicago Press, 2004, 89–90.

22. Solomon H. Katz and Mary M. Voight, "Bread and Beer: The Early Use of Cereals in the Human Diet," *Expedition*, 28, 1982, 23–34; Reay Tannahill, *Food in History*, New York: Crown Publishers, 1989, 48: Aaronson, "Fungi," in CWHF, I: 314.

23. James L. Newman, "Wine," in CWHF, I: 730–31; Aaronson, "Fungi," in CWHF, I: 315.

24. Newman, "Wine," in CWHF, I: 730–1.

25. Maguelonne Toussaint-Samat, *History of Food* (tr. Anthea Bell), Cambridge, MA: Blackwell, 1992, 34.

26. Tannahill, 29.

27. Toussaint Samat, 26–7.

28. Keith Vernon, "Milk and Dairy Products," in CWHF, I: 693.

29. Ibid., 694.

30. Sean F. O'Keefe, "An Overview of Oils and Fats, with a Special Emphasis on Olive Oil," in CWHF, I: 377.

31. K. T. H. Farrer "Food Additives," CWHF, II: 1668; Bottéro, *Oldest Cuisine* 59–60.

32. Ibid.

33. Mark Kurlansky, *Salt: A World History*, New York: Penguin Books, 2003, 10.

CHAPTER SEVEN: ENTERPRISE AND EMPIRES

1. Edward Gibbon, *Decline and Fall of the Roman Empire*, Ch. 71.

2. Felipe Fernandez-Armesto, *Food: A History*, London: Macmillan, 2001, 156–7.

3. Antonella Spanò Giammellaro, "The Phoencians and the Carthaginians" in Jean-Louis Flandrin and Massimo Montanari (eds.), *Food: A Culinary History*, (ed., English edition, Albert Sonenfeld; tr. Clarissa Botsford et al.), New York: Columbia University Press, 1999, 55–8.

4. Naomi F. Miller and Wilma Wetterstrom, "The Beginnings of Agriculture," in Kenneth F. Kiple and Kriemhild C. Ornelas (eds.), *The Cambridge World History of Food* (hereinafter CWHF), 2 vols., New York and Cambridge: Cambridge University Press, 2000, II: 1134–5.

5. Ibid.

6. Phyllis Pray Bober, *Art, Cuisine, and Culture: Ancient and Medieval Gastronomy*, Chicago: University of Chicago Press, 1999, 90, 92.

7. H. Frederic Janson, *Pomono's Harvest: An Illustrated Chronicle of Antiquarian Fruit Literature*, Portland: Timber Press, 1996, 15.

8. James Trager, *The Food Chronology*, New York: Henry Holt, 1995, 12; Sean Francis O'Keefe, "An Overview of Oils and Fats, With a Special Emphasis on Olive Oil," in CWHF, I: 377.

9. Colin Spencer, *The Heretic's Feast*, Hanover, NH and London: University Press of New England, 1995, 90.

10. Allison Burford Cooper, "Feasting and Fasting in Classical Greece," *Repast*, XX (2): Spring 2004, 1.

11. Maguelonne Toussaint-Samat, *History of Food* (tr. Anthea Bell), Cambridge, MA: Blackwell, 1992, 386.

12. Ken Albala, *Eating Right in the Renaissance*, Berkeley: University of California Press, 2002, 31; Bober, 118.

13. Albala, *Eating Right in the Renaissance*, 19; Michelle Berriedale-Johnson, *British Museum Cookbook*, 21, 23; K. T. H. Farrer, "Food Additives," in CWHF II: 1668.

14. Hansjörg Küster, "Spices and Flavorings," in CWHF, I: 435.

15. Andrew Dalby, *Dangerous Tastes: The Story of Spices*, Berkeley: University of California Press, 2000, 121.

16. Ibid., 120–1.

17. Küster, "Spices and Flavorings," in CWHF, I: 435.

18. O'Keefe, CWHF, I: 378.

19. Brian Murton, "Famine," in CWHF, II: 1412.

20. Reay Tannahill, *Food in History*, New York: Crown Publishers, 1989, 71–2.

21. Toussaint-Samat, 227; Mireille Corbier, "The Broad Bean and the Moray: Social Hierarchies and Food in Rome," in Flandrin and Montanari, 132.

22. Don Brothwell and Patricia Brothwell, *Food in Antiquity: A Survey of the Diet of Early Peoples*, Baltimore and London: The Johns Hopkins University Press, 1998 ed., 147.

23. James L. Newman, "Wine," in CWHF, I: 731.

24. Ray Strong, *Feast: A History of Grand Eating*, London: Jonathan Cape, 2002, 20.

25. Florence Dupont, "The Grammar of Roman Dining," in Flandrin and Montanari, 123–6.

26. Alan Davidson, *The Oxford Companion to Food*, Oxford: Oxford University Press, 1999, 23–4; Bober, 149–50.

27. Ilaria Gozzini Giacosa, *A Taste of Ancient Rome* (tr. Anna Herklotz), Chicago: University of Chicago Press, 1992, 12; Tannahill, 89; Colin E. Nash, "Aquatic Animals," in CWHF, I: 457.

28. Giacosa, 12

29. Ibid., 13; Julia Peterson, "Allium Species," in CWHF, I: 250, 263;". Sheldon Aaronson, "Fungi," in CWHF, I: 316.

30. George W. Hudler, *Magical mushrooms. Mischievous molds*, Princeton: Princeton University Press, 1998, 5.

31. Dorothea Bedigian, "Sesame," in CWHF, I: 413–14.

32. Jansen, 17

33. Dalby, 45; Bruce Karig, "Turkish Yufka and its Offspring," *Repast*, XXI, Winter 2005, 4–5.

34. Stanley J. Olsen, "The Camel in Ancient China and an Osteology of the Camel," *Proceedings of the Academy of Natural Sciences of Philadelphia*, 1988, 140(1): 22–3; Elizabeth A. Stephens, "Camels," in CWHF, I: 478.

35. Delphine Roger, "The Middle East and South Asia," in CWHF, II: 1140.

36. Toussaint-Samat, 492–3.

37. David Maynard and Donald N. Maynard, "Cucumbers, Melons, and Watermelons," in CWHF, I: 305.

38. Kuster, "Spices," CWHF, I: 435.

39. Robert C. Field, "Cruciferous and Green Leafy Vegetables," in CWHF, I: 290–91.

40. Ibid.

41 K. David Patterson, "Russia" in CWHF, II: 1240–1.

42. Editors, "Beet," in CWHF, II: 1730–1.

43. Field, CWHF, I: 293–4.

44. Küster, "Northern Europe," in CWHF, II: 1229.

45. Davidson, 332.

46. Bober, 88–9.

47. Farrer, "Food Additives," in CWHF II: 1669.

48. Arthur C. Aufderheide, "Lead Poisoning," in Kenneth F. Kiple (ed.), *The Cambridge World History of Human Disease*, New York and Cambridge: Cambridge University Press, 1993, 822–3.

49. Peter R. Cheeke, "Rabbits," in CWHF, I: 565–6.

CHAPTER EIGHT: FAITH AND FOODSTUFFS

1. Noel Cohen, *Global History: A Short Overview*, Malden, MA: Blackwell, 2001, 127–9.

2. Daniel J. Boorstin, *The Discoverers*, New York: Vintage Books, 1985, 179–82.

3. Felipe Fernández-Armesto, *Food: A History*, London: McMillan, 2001, 136–7.

4. Delphine Roger, "Southeast Asia," in Kenneth F. Kiple and Kriemhild C. Ornelas (eds.), *The Cambridge World History of Food* (hereinafter CWHF), 2 vols., New York and Cambridge: Cambridge University Press, 2000, II: 1143.

5. Daniel W. Gade, "Goats," in CWHF, I: 533.

6. Roger, CWHF, II:1142.

7. Ibid., 1144–5.

8. Dominique Sourdel, *Islam*, New York: Walker, 1962, 31; Bernard Lewis, *The Arabs in History*, New York: Harper, 1967, 153.

9. Roger, CWHF, II: 1145.

10. Ibid., 1142; Louis E. Grivetti, "Food Prejudices and Taboos," in CWHF, II: 1503.

11. Roger, CWHF, II 1143.

12. Steven C. Topik, "Coffee," in CWHF, I: 642.

13. Kenneth Albala, "Southern Europe," in CWHF, II: 1203–04; Colin Spencer, *The Heretic's Feast*, Hanover, NH and London: University Press of New England, 1995, 118; Grivetti, CWHF, II: 1498–1502.
14. Ibid: 1502–3.
15. Carole M. Counihan, "The Social and Cultural Uses of Food," in CWHF, II: 1515.
16. Spencer, *Heretic's Feast*, 177.
17. Hansjörg Küster, "Northern Europe," in CWHF, II: 1229.
18. K. David Patterson, "Russia," in CWHF, II: 1241.
19. Anneke H. van Otterloo, "The Low Countries," in CWHF, II: 1232.
20. Ibid., 1232; Mark Kurlansky, *Salt: A World History*, New York: Penguin Books, 2003, 110.
21. Küster, "Northern Europe," CWHF, II: 1229.
22. Albala, "Southern Europe," CWHF, II: 1204.
23. Grivetti, "Food Prejudices and Taboos," in CWHF, II: 1503.
24. Mark Kurlansky, *Cod: A Biography of the Fish that Changed the World*, New York: Penguin Books, 1998, 24, and passim.
25. Spencer, *Heretics Feast*, 183: Colin Spencer, "The British Isles," in CWHF, I: 1221.
26. Phillip A. Cantrell II, "Beer and Ale," in CWHF, I: 620; Albala "Southern Europe," CWHF, II: 1205.
27. James L. Newman, "Wine," in CWHF, I: 731–2.
28. Phyllis Pray Bober, *Art, Culture, and Cuisine: Ancient and Medieval Gastronomy*, Chicago: University of Chicago Press, 1999, 207–8.
29. Counihan, CWHF, II: 1519.
30. Colin E. Nash, "Aquatic Animals," in CWHF, I: 458.
31. Van Otterloo, CWHF, II: 1233.
32. Bruno Laurioux, "Medieval Cooking," in Flandrin and Montanari (eds.), 300–01.
33. Fernández-Armesto, 158.
34. James C. Whorton, "Vegetarianism," in CWHF, II: 1553.
35. Paul Rozin, "The Psychology of Food and Food Choices," in CWHF, II: 1478; Grivetti, CWHF, II: 1504–5; Whorton, CWHF, II: 1553.
36. Thomas Sorosiak, "Soybeans," in CWHF, I: 423.

CHAPTER NINE: EMPIRES IN THE RUBBLE OF ROME

1. Jeremy Black (ed.), *Atlas of World History*, New York: DK Press, 2000, 53.
2. William H. McNeill, *A World History*, 2nd ed., New York: Oxford University Press, 1971, 193.
3. Bernard Lewis, *The Muslim Discovery of Europe*, New York: Norton, 1982, 20.
4. Bernard Lewis, *The Arabs in History*, New York: Harper, 1967, 82.
5. McNeill, *World History*, 217, 236.
6. Ibid., 237–8.
7. Reay Tannahill, *Food in History*, New York: Crown Publishers, 1989, 121–2.
8. Black (ed.), *Atlas*, 68–9.
9. Ibid., 68.
10. James Trager, *The Food Chronology*, New York: Henry Holt, 1995, 62.
11. William H. McNeill, *Plagues and Peoples*, New York: Doubleday, 1977, 150.
12. Based on Trager, 62–4.
13. Ibid.

14. McNeill, *World History*, 238–9.
15. Ibid., 237–9.
16. Dominique Sourdel, *Islam*, New York: Walker, 1967, 35.
17. Based on Delphine Roger, "The Middle East and South Asia," in Kenneth F. Kiple and Kriemhild C. Ornelas (eds.), *The Cambridge World History of Food*, 2 vols., New York and Cambridge: Cambridge University Press, 2000, II: 1148.
18. Bruce Kraig, "Turkish Yufka and its Offspring," *Repast*, XXI, Winter 2005, 4.

CHAPTER TEN: MEDIEVAL PROGRESS AND POVERTY

1. Alfred W. Crosby, *Ecological Imperialism: The Biological Expansion of Europe, 900–1900*, New York: Cambridge University Press, 1986, 92.
2. Colin Spencer, "The British Isles," in Kenneth F. Kiple and Kriemhild C. Ornelas (eds.), *The Cambridge World History of Food* (hereinafter CWHF), 2 vols., New York and Cambridge: Cambridge University Press, 2000, II: 1219.
3. Peter R. Cheeke, "Rabbits," in CWHF, I: 565–6.
4. Spencer, "British Isles," in CWHF, II, 1219–21.
5. Massimo Montanari, "Production Structures and Food Systems in the Early Middle Ages," in Jean-Louis Flandrin and Massimo Montarari, (eds.) *Food: A Culinary History from Antiquity to the Present*, New York: Columbia University Press, 1999, 170–2.
6. Ibid., 172–3.
7. Julia Peterson, "Allium Species," in CWHF, I: 263.
8. Spencer, "British Isles," in CWHF, II: 1219–20.
9. Hansjörg Küster, "Northern Europe," in CWHF, II: 1229–30.
10. Alfred W. Crosby, *The Measure of Reality: Quantification and Western Society*, New York and Cambridge: Cambridge University Press, 1997, 52–3.
11. Kenneth Albala, "Southern Europe," in CWHF, II: 1207.
12. Carole M. Counihan, "Social and Cultural Uses of Food," in CWHF, II: 1514.
13. Eva Bartösius, "France," in CWHF, II: 1211; Anneke H. van Otterloo, "The Low Countries," in CWHF, II: 1232.
14. Ibid., II: 1234.
15. Ibid.; K. David Patterson, "Russia," in CWHF, II: 1242.
16. Phyllis Pray Bober, *Art, Culture, and Cuisine: Ancient and Medieval Gastronomy*, Chicago: University of Chicago Press, 1999, 237.
17. Ibid., 248.
18. Stephen Beckerman, "Game," in CWHF, I: 525; Albala, "Southern Europe," CWHF, II: 1207.
19. Antionette Fauve-Chamoux, "Chestnuts," in CWHF, I: 359–63.
20. G. Mazza, "Buckwheat," in CWHF, I: 90.
21. van Otterloo, "Low Countries," CWHF, II: 1233: Küster, "Northern Europe – CWHF, II: 1229; Albala, "Southern Europe," CWHF, II: 1208.
22. Keith Vernon, "Milk and Dairy Products," in CWHF, I: 694.
23. R. E. Hughes, "Scurvy," in CWHF, I: 993.
24. Editors, "Spinach," in CWHF, II: 1856–7.
25. Brian Murton, "Famine," in CWHF, II: 1412; Tannahill, 101.
26. Colin Spencer, *The Heretic's Feast*, Hanover, NH and London: University Press of New England, 1995, 182.

27. Antoni Riera-Melis, "Society, Food, and Feudalism," in Jean-Louis Flandrin and Massimo Montanari (eds.), *Food: A Culinary History From Antiquity to the Present* (tr. Clarissa Botsford et al.), New York: Columbia University Press, 1999, 266.
28. Spencer, "British Isles," CWHF, II: 1221.
29. van Otterloo, CWHF, II: 1233.
30. Ibid.
31. Colin Spencer, *Heretic's Feast*, 183–4.
32. Küster, "Spices and Flavorings," in CWHF, I: 431.
33. Ibid., 436.
34. Thomas G. Benedek, "Food as Aphrodisiacs and Anaphrodisiacs," in CWHF, II: 1525.
35. Hansjörg Küster, "Spices and Flavorings," in CWHF, I: 436.
36. Andrew Dalby, *Dangerous Tastes: The Story of Spices*, Berkeley: University of California Press, 2000, 125.
37. Küster. "Spices and Flavorings," CWHF, I: 435.

CHAPTER ELEVEN: SPAIN'S NEW WORLD, THE NORTHERN HEMISPHERE

1. Juan M. Navia et al., "Nutrient Composition of Cuban Foods II: Foods of Vegetable Origin," *Food Research*, 22: 1956, 131–43. John C. Super and Luis Alberto Vargas, "Mexico and Highland Central America," in Kenneth F. Kiple and Kriemhild C. Ornelas (eds.), *The Cambridge World History of Food* (hereinafter CWHF), 2 vols., New York and Cambridge: Cambridge University Press, 2000, II: 1249. William F. Keegan, "The Caribbean: Early History," in CWHF, II: 1262; Jeffrey M. Pilcher, "The Caribbean from 1492 to the Present," in CWHF, II: 1279.
2. Keegan, in CWHF, II: 1263.
3. Jared Diamond, *Guns, Germs and Steel: the Fates of Human Societies*, New York: W.W. Norton, 1997, 46–7.
4. Stephen Budiansky, *The Convenant of the Wild: Why Animals Chose Domestication*, New York: William Morrow, 1992, 23.
5. David J. Meltzer, "How Columbus Sickened the New World," *The New Scientist*, 136, 1992; Diamond, 46; Hiam Ofek, *Second Nature: Economic Origins of Human Evolution*. Cambridge UK, Cambridge University Press, 2001, 126.
6. Jeremy Black (ed.), *Atlas of World History*, New York: DK Press, 2000, 116.
7. Diamond, *Guns*, 46.
8. Black, *Atlas*, 14
9. Diamond, *Guns*, 47
10. Meltzer, "Columbus," 40–1.
11. Black, *Atlas*, 14.
12. Alfred W. Crosby, *The Columbian Exchange: Biological and Cultural Consequences of 1492*, Westport, CT: Greenwood Press, 1972, 170.
13. Jack R. Harlan, *Crops and Man*, Madison, WI: Crop Science Society of America, 1975, 227.
14. Super and Vargas, CWHF, II: 1248.
15. Ibid., 1249; Gary Irish and Mary Irish, *Agaves, Yuccas, and Related Plants*, Portland: Timber Press, 2000; Editors, "Breadnut," in CWHF, II: 1737.
16. Super and Vargas, CWHF, II: 1249.
17. Joan Peterson, "Maize: Mexico's Gift to the World," *Repast*, XIX (2), 2003, 5.

18. Black (ed.), *Atlas*, 120.
19. Ibid., 171.
20. J. M. J. de Wet, "Millets," in CWHF, I: 113; Ellen Messer, "Maize," in CWHF, I: 100.
21. Sophia D. Coe, *America's First Cuisines*, Austin: University of Texas Press, 1994, 14–15.
22. Sylvanus G. Morley, *The Ancient Maya* (3rd ed., rev. by George W. Brainerd), Stanford: Stanford University Press, 1956, 3.
23. Robert S. Stanley, Thomas Killion, and Mark Lycett, "On the Maya Collapse," *Journal of Anthropological Research*, 42: 1986, 123–50.
24. Morley, passim.
25. Ibid, 7.
26. Susan Kent, "Iron Deficiency Anemia," in CWHF, I: 924–5; Richard Steckel, Paul W. Sciulli, and Jerome C. Rose, "A Health Index from Skeletal Remains," in Richard H. Steckel and Jerome C. Rose (eds.), *The Backbone of History: Health and Nutrition in the Western Hemisphere*, New York and Cambridge: Cambridge University Press, 2002, 67.
27. Rebecca Storey, Lourdes Marquez Morfin, and Vernon Smith, "Social Disruption and the Maya Civilization of Mesoamerica," in Steckel and Rose (eds.), 283–306.
28. Suzanne Austin Alchon, *A Pest In the Land: New World Epidemics in a Global Perspective*, Albuquerque: University of Mexico Press, 2003, 53.
29. Lordes Marquez Morfin, Robert McCaa, Rebecca Storey, and Andres Del Angel, "Health and Nutrition in Pre-Hispanic Mesoamerica," in Steckel and Rose (eds.), 307–38.

CHAPTER TWELVE: NEW WORLD, NEW FOODS

1. For amaranth, see Richard S. MacNeish and M. L. Fowler et al., *Excavation and Reconnaissance, Prehistory of the Tehuacan Valley*, vol. 5., Austin: University of Texas Press, 1975. See also Daniel K. Early, "The Renaissance of Amaranth," in Nelson Foster and Linda S. Cordell (eds.), *Chillies to Chocolate: Food the Americas Gave the World*, Tucson: University of Arizona Press, 1992; and Mary Karasch, "Amaranth" in Kenneth F. Kiple and Kriemhild C. Ornelas (eds.), *The Cambridge World History of Food* (hereinafter CWHF), 2 vols., New York and Cambridge: Cambridge University Press, 2000, I: 75–81.
2. Sophia D. Coe, *America's First Cuisines*, Austin: University of Texas Press, 1994, 90.
3. Ibid., 89–90.
4. Lawrence Kaplan, "Beans, Peas, and Lentils," in CWHF, I: 275.
5. Coe, 31.
6. Kaplan, CWHF, I: 275.
7. Lawrence Kaplan and Lucille N. Kaplan, "Beans of the Americas," in Foster and Cordell (eds.), 62–3.
8. Kaplan, CWHF, I: 274–5.
9. Kaplan and Kaplan, 65.
10. Kaplan, CWHF, I: 275.
11. Coe, 31.
12. Charles B. Heiser, Jr., *Of Plants and People*, Norman and London: University of Oklahoma Press, 1985, 8.
13. Charles B. Heiser, Jr., *The Gourd Book*, Norman and London: University of Oklahoma, Press, 1979, 114–15.

14. Ibid., passim; unless otherwise indicated the following discussion of squash is based on Deena S. Decker-Walters and Terrence W. Walters, "Squash," in CWHF, I: 335–51.
15. Coe, 38.
16. Bruce D. Smith, *The Emergence of Agriculture*, New York: Scientific American Library, 1995, 165.
17. Research by Deena Decker-Walters of the Fairchild Tropical Garden in Florida has established the two independent lineages and domestications of C. *pepo*.
18. Charles B. Heiser, Jr. points out that this earlier arrival in eastern North America may mean that C. *pepo* was domesticated independently north of Mexico. See his *Plants and People*, 16–26.
19. Coe, 39.
20. Ibid., 40.
21. Ibid., 38.
22. Jean Andrews, "Chilli Peppers," in CWHF, I: 283; Janet Long, "Tomatoes," in CWHF, I: 352.
23. Andrews, CWHF, I: 284–5.
24. Jean Andrews, "The Peripatetic Chilli Pepper: Diffusion of the Domesticated Capsicums Since Columbus," in Foster and Cordell (eds.), 83.
25. Andrews, CWHF, I: 281.
26. Long, CWHF, I: 353.
27. Bernal Diaz del Castillo, *Historia verdadera de la conquista de Nueva España*, Mexico, 1980, quoted in Long, CWHF, I: 353.
28. B. de Sahagún, *Florentine Codes, the general history of the things of New Spain*, A. J. O. Anderson and C. Dibble (eds.), Santa Fe, New Mexico, 1951–69, Book 10: 79, quoted by Long, CWHF, I: 353.
29. Long, CWHF, I: 351; Coe, 47.
30. Murdo J. MacLleod, "Cacao" in CWHF, I: 637.
31. John A. West, "A Brief History and Botany of Cacao," in Foster and Cordell (eds.), 105–8.
32. Ibid.; Jonathan D. Sauer, "Changing Perception and Exploitation of New World Plants in Europe, 1492–1800," in Fredi Chiappelli (ed.), *First Images of America: The Impact of the New World on the Old*, 2 vols., Berkeley: University of California Press, 1976, II: 817; Coe, 56.
33. Patricia Rain, "Vanilla: Nectar of the Gods," in Foster and Cordell (eds.), 35–9.
34. Coe, 84–7; John C. Super and Luis Alberto Vargas, "Mexico and Highland Central America" in CWHF, II: 1250.
35. Daniel W. Gade, "South America," in CWHF, II: 1255.
36. Coe, 165.
37. Editors, "Avocado," in CWHF, II: 1774.
38. Sauer, II: 816.
39. Paul W. Sciulli and James Oberly, "Native Americans in Eastern North America: The Southern Great Lakes and Upper Ohio Valley," in Richard H. Steckel and Jerome C. Rose (eds.), *The Backbone of History: Health and Nutrition in the Western Hemisphere*, New York and Cambridge: Cambridge University Press, 2002, 443.
40. Ann W. Stodder, Debra L. Martin, Alan Goodman, and Daniel T. Reff, "Cultural Longevity and Biological Stress in the American Southwest," in Steckel and Rose (eds.), 483–6.
41. Ibid., 492–8.

42. Bruce D. Smith, "Prehistoric Plant Husbandry in Eastern North America," in C. Wesley Cowan and Patty Jo Watson (eds.), *The Origins of Agriculture: An International Perspective*, Washington, DC: Smithsonian Press, 1993, 111.

43. Elizabeth J. Reitz, "Temperate and Arctic North America to 1492," in CWHF, II: 1297.

44. Calvin Martin, "The European Impact on the Culture of a Northeastern Algonquin Tribe: An Ecological Interpretation, in *The William and Mary Quarterly*, XXI: 1974, 3–26; Clark Spencer Larsen et al., "Beyond Demographic Collapse: Biological Adaptation and Change in Native Peoples of La Florida" in David Hurst Thomas (ed.), *Columbian Consequences*, 2 vols., Washington DC: Smithsonian Press, 1990: II: 409–28.

45. C. S. Larsen, A. W. Crosby, and D. L. Hutchinson et al., "A Biohistory of Health and Behavior in the Georgia Bight: The Agricultural Transition and the Impact of European Contact," in Steckel and Rose (eds.), 406–39.

46. Sciulli and Oberly, in Steckel and Rose (eds.), 440–80; Smith, "Eastern North America," 113; Elizabeth J. Reitz, "Temperate and Arctic North America to 1492," in CWHF, II: 1288, 1291–2.

47. Reitz, CWHF, II: 1296.

48. Smith, "Eastern North America," 111.

49. Charles B. Heiser, Jr. "Sunflower," in CWHF, I: 427–30.

50. Because the cucurbit family embraces over 100 genera and upwards of 1,000 species, North America would seem to have been seriously shortchanged. Heiser, *The Gourd Book*, 5; Deena S. Decker-Walters and Terrence Walters, "Squash," in CWHF, I: 345–7.

51. Heiser, *Plants and People*, 163–72.

52. See these entries in François Couplan, *The Encyclopedia of Edible Plants of North America*, New Canaan, CT: Keats Publishing, 1998; See also Reitz, "Temperate and Arctic North America to 1492," for a listing of the foods consumed by Native Americans, CWHF, II: 1289–91.

53. Phillip L. Walker et al., "The Effect of European Contact on the Health of Alto California Indians," in David Hurst Thomas (ed.), *Columbian Consequences*, Washington, DC: Smithsonian Press, 1989, 349–64.

54. J. M. J. de Wet, "Millets," in CWHF I: 113–14.

55. J. Allen Barksdale, "American Bison," in CWHF, I: 450.

56. Richard F. Townsend, *The Aztecs*, London: Thames and Hudson, 1992, 129–30:

57. Coe, 116.

58. For a brief review of how the estimates of Cortés began some of the confusion surrounding the number of Tenochtitlán's inhabitants see Michael E. Smith, "Hernán Cortés on the Size of Aztec Cities: Comment on Dobyns," *Latin American Population History Bulletin*, 25: Spring 1994, 25–7.

59. Sheldon Aaronson, "Fungi," in CWHF, I: 316.

60. Marvin Harris, *Our Kind: Who We Are, Where We Came From, Where We Are Going*, New York: Harper & Row, 1989, 432–6. This contention originated with Michael Harner, "The Ecological Basis for Aztec Sacrifice," *American Ethnologist*, 1979, 4: 117–35. For a brief summary of the debate see Super and Vargas "Mexico and Highland Central America," in CWHF, II: 1249.

61. Harris, *Our Kind*, 432–36; Margaret Visser, *The Rituals of Dinner: The Origins, Evolution, Eccentricities, and Meaning of Table Manners*, New York: Grove Weidenfeld, 1992.

62. This may be an exaggeration. There is considerable debate regarding Pre-Columbian American populations. One student of the decline of Aboriginal populations in Australia has little problem with larger Pre-Columbian American populations that have traditionally been accepted. Wilbur R. Jacobs, "The Tip of an Iceberg: Indian Demography and Some Implications for Revisionism," *William and Mary Quarterly*, 1974, Third Series, XXXI: 123–30. For more on the debate and how rough it has gotten see Henry F. Dobyns, "More Methodological Perspectives on Historical Demography;" Dean R. Snow and Kim M. Lamphear, "More Methodological Perspectives: A Rejoinder to Dobyns;" and David Henige, "On the Current Devaluation of the Notion of Evidence," all in *Ethnohistory*, 1989, 36(3): 285–98, 299–303, and 304–07, respectively.

CHAPTER THIRTEEN: NEW FOODS IN THE SOUTHERN NEW WORLD

1. Sophia D. Coe, *America's First Cuisines*, Austin: University of Texas Press, 1994, 182.
2. Daniel W. Gade, "Llamas and Alpacas," in Kenneth F. Kiple and Kriemhild C. Ornelas (eds.), *The Cambridge World History of Food* (hereinafter CWHF), 2 vols., New York and Cambridge: Cambridge University Press, 2000, I: 555–9.
3. Daniel W. Gade, "Muscovy Ducks," in CWHF, I: 559.
4. Ibid., I: 560.
5. Daniel W. Gade, "South America," in CWHF, II: 1254–5.
6. Ibid.; Ellen Messer, "Potatoes (White)," in CWHF, I: 188–9. For the classic study of *The History and Social Influence of the Potato*, see this work by Redcliffe Salaman, and edited by J. G. Hawkes, Cambridge, UK: Cambridge University Press, 1985 (first published in 1949).
7. Ellen Messer, Barbara Haber, Joyce Toomre, and Barbara Wheaton, "Culinary History," in CWHF, II: 1372.
8. Patricia J. O'Brien, "Sweet Potatoes and Yams," in CWHF, I: 208.
9. Ibid., 210–12.
10. Noel Vietmeyer, "Forgotten Roots of the Incas," in Nelson Foster and Linda S. Cordell (eds.), *Chilies to Chocolate*, Tuscon: University of Arizona Press, 1992, 98; A. D. Livingston and Helen Livingston, *Edible Plants and Animals: Unusual Foods from Aardvark to Zamia*, New York: Facts on File, 1993, 229; Alan Davidson, *The Oxford Companion to Food*, Oxford: Oxford University Press, 1999, 547.
11. Vietmeyer, 98–9; Davidson, 35; Editors, "Arracacha," in CWHF, II: 1723.
12. Douglas H. Ubelaker and Linda A. Newson, "Patterns of Health in Prehistoric and Historic Ecuador," in Richard H. Steckel and Jerome C. Rose (eds.), *The Backbone of History: Health and Nutrition in the Western Hemisphere*, New York and Cambridge: Cambridge University Press, 2002, 347.
13. Phillip A. Cantrell II, "Beer and Ale" CWHF, I: 623.
14. Gade, "South America," CWHF, II: 1255.
15. Ibid.; Editors, "Cañihua," in CWHF, II: 1743–4.
16. Johanna T. Dwyer and Ritu Sandhu, "Peanuts," in CWHF, I: 364–5; Editors, "Peanut," in CWHF, II: 1830–31.
17. Mary Karasch, "Manioc," in CWHF, 1: 181–6.
18. Maguelonne Toussaint-Samat, *History of Food* (tr. Anthea Bell), Cambridge, MA: Blackwell, 1992, 67.

19. Quoted in Raymond Sokolov, *Why We Eat What We Eat*, New York: Summit Books, 1991, 21–2.

20. Alfred W. Crosby, *The Columbian Exchange: Biological and Cultural Consequences of 1492*, Westport, CT: Greenwood Pub. Co., 1972, 77; William F. Keegan, "Caribbean: Early History," in CWHF, II: 1272.

21. Coe, 18.

22. Karash, CWHF, I: 183.

23. Gade, "South America," CWHF, II: 1255; Editors, "Achira," in CWHF, II: 1713.

24. Editors, "Malanga," in CWHF, II: 1807; Nancy J. Pollock, "Taro," in CWHF, I: 221; Tindall, *Vegetables in the Tropics*, 59–62.

25. Gade, "South America," CWHF, II: 1255.

26. Steckel and Rose (eds.), passim.

27. Jeremy Black (ed.), *Atlas of World History*, New York: DK Press, 2000, 144–5.

28. Ibid.

29. Ibid., 146–7.

30. John V. Murra, "Rite and Crop in the Inca State," in Daniel R. Gross (ed.), *Peoples and Cultures of Native South America*, New York: Doubleday, 1973, 377–87.

31. Ubelaker and Newsome, in Steckel and Rose (eds.), 369.

32. Walter Alves Neves and Veronica Weslowski, "Economy, Nutrition, and Disease in Prehistoric Coastal Brazil: A Case Study from the State of Santa Catarina," in Steckel and Rose (eds.), 376–400.

CHAPTER FOURTEEN: THE COLUMBIAN EXCHANGE AND THE OLD WORLDS

1. *The Diariy of Christopher Columbus's First Voyage to America, 1492–1493*. Abstracted by Fray Bartolomé de las Casas. Transcribed and Translated into English with Notes and a Concordance of the Spanish, by Oliver Dunn and James E. Kelley, Jr., Norman, OK: University of Oklahoma Press, 1989, 93.

2. Tony McMichael, *Human Frontiers, Environments, and Disease: Past Patterns, Uncertain Futures*, Cambridge, UK: Cambridge University Press, 2001, 128–30.

3. Brian Murton, "Famine," in Kenneth F. Kiple and Kriemhild C. Ornelas (eds.), *The Cambridge World History of Food* (hereinafter CWHF), 2 vols., New York and Cambridge: Cambridge University Press, 2000, II: 1412.

4. William H. McNeill, "American Food Crops in the Old World," in Herman J. Viola and Carolyn Margolis (eds.), *Seeds of Change*, Washington and London: Smithsonian Institution Press, 1991, 43–59.

5. Alfred W. Crosby, *The Columbian Exchange: Biological and Cultural Consequences of 1492*, Westport, CT: Greenwood Press, 1972, 171.

6. Ken Albala, *Eating Right in the Renaissance*, Berkeley: University of California Press, 2002, 236–7.

7. Jonathan D. Sauer, "Changing Perceptions and Exploitation of New World Plants in Europe, 1492–1800," in Fredi Chiappelli (ed.), *First Images of America: The Impact of the New World on the Old*, 2 vols., Berkeley: University of California Press, 1976, II: 824.

8. Jean Andrews, "Diffusion of Mesoamerican Food Complex to Southeastern Europe," *Geographic Review*, 1993, 83(2): 194–204.

9. Theresa Mélendez, "Corn," in David Schofield Wilson and Angus Kress Gillespie (eds.), *Rooted in America*, Knoxville, University of Tennesse Press, 1999, 42.

10. Sauer, II: 824.
11. Mélendez, "Corn," 45–8.
12. Crosby, *Columbian Exchange*, 180; K. David Patterson, "Russia," in CWHF, II: 1242.
13. Colin Spencer, *The Heretic's Feast*, Hanover, NH and London: University Press of New England, 1995, 178.
14. Vladimir G. Simkhovitch, "Hay and History," *Political Science Quarterly*, September 1913, XXVIII, no. 3: 394–95.
15. Thomas G. Benedek, "Aphrodisiacs and Anaphrodisiacs," in CWHF, II: 1527.
16. Sauer, II: 825.
17. Redcliffe Salaman, *The History and Social Influence of the Potato*, New York: Cambridge University Press, 1987, 142.
18. Messer, "Potatoes (White)," in CWHF, I: 191.
19. Ibid.
20. Ibid., I:193; Editors, "White Potato," in CWHF, II: 1879–80.
21. Ibid., 1879.
22. Stewart Lee Allen, *In the Devil's Garden*, New York: Ballentine Books, 2002, 137.
23. Hansjörg Küster, "Northern Europe," in CWHF, II: 1230; Patterson, "Russia," CWHF, II: 1242.
24. Ibid. II: 1243.
25. Janet Long, "Tomatoes," in CWHF, I: 354–8.
26. Paul Rozin, "The Psychology of Food and Food Choice," in CWHF, II: 1482.
27. Jean Andrews, "The Peripatetic Chilli Pepper: Diffusion of the Domesticated Capsicums since Columbus" in Nelson Foster and Linda S. Cordell (eds.), *From Chillies to Chocolates*, Tuscon: University of Arizona Press, 1992, 81–93; Jean Andrews, "Chilli Peppers," in CWHF, I: 281–4.
28. Stanley J. Olsen, "Turkeys," in CWHF, I: 579–80.
29. Ibid., I: 578–9, 581.
30. Sophia D. Coe, *America's First Cuisines*, Austin: University of Texas Press, 1994, 124.
31. Jean Anthelme Brillat-Savarin, *The Physiology of Taste or, Meditations of Transcendental Gastronomy* (tr. M. F. K. Fisher), New York: Harcourt Brace, Jovanovich, 1978, 80.
32. Reay Tannahill, *Food in History*, New York: Crown Publishers, 1989, 211.
33. Ibid., 210–11
34. Thomas McKeown, *The Modern Rise of Population*, New York: Academic Press, 1976; John M. Kim, "Nutrition and the Decline of Mortality," in CWHF, II: 1383; Although most concede that nutrition was a factor in the mortality decline, many insist other factors were equally or even more important. For a summary see William Muraskin, "Nutrition and Mortality Decline: Another View," in CWHF, II: 1389–96. For the importance of the fall in total infant mortality in England's population boom after 1750, see Susan Scott and Christopher J. Duncan, *Demography and Nutrition: Evidence From Historical and Contemporary Populations*, Malden, MA: Blackwell Science, 2002, 235.
35. Roger Scofield, "The Impact of Scarcity and Plenty on Population Change in England, 1541–1871," *Journal of Interdisciplinary History*, 1983, XIV(2): 270; Olwen Hufton, "Social Conflict and Grain Supply in Eighteenth-Century France," *Journal of Interdisciplinary History*, 1983, XIV(2): 303.
36. Robert W. Fogel, "Nutrition and the Decline of Mortality since 1700," *Working Paper Series of the National Bureau of Economic Research*, Working Paper no. 1802, Cambridge, MA: 1986, 572.
37. Hufton, 305.

38. Simkhovitch, 400.
39. William L. Langer, "Europe's Initial Population Explosion," in Kenneth F. Kiple and Stephen V. Beck (eds.), *Biological Consequences of the European Expansion, 1450–1800*, Aldershot, Hampshire Great Britain: Ashgate, 1997, 344.
40. Giovanni Rebora, *Culture of the Fork* (tr. Albert Sonnenfeld), New York: Columbia University Press, 1991, 118.
41. Andrews "Chilli Peppers," CWHF, I: 282.
42. James L. Newman, "Africa South from the Sahara," in CWHF, II: 1335.
43. Ibid.
44. John A. West, "A Brief History and Botany of Cacao," in Foster and Cordell (eds.), 109.
45. Sucheta Mazumdar, "The Impact of New World Food Crops on the Diet and Economy of China and India, 1600–1900," in Raymond Grew (ed.), *Food in Global History*, Boulder, CO: Westview Press, 59.
46. Christine S. Wilson, "Southeast Asia," in CWHF, II: 1154.
47. Ibid., 68–9; Françoise Sabban, "China," in CWHF, II: 1170; Ping-Ti Ho, "The Introduction of American Food Plants into China, *American Anthropologist*, 1955, 57(2): 191–201.
48. Mazumdar, in Grew (ed.), 66–8.
49. Crosby, *Columbian Exchange*, 196–7.
50. Naomichi Ishige, "Japan," in CWHF, II: 1181.
51. Lois N. Magncr, "Korea," in CWHF, II: 1185.
52. Leonard Blussé, "An Insane Administration and an Unsanitary Town: The Dutch East India Company and Batavia (1619–1799)" in Robert J. Ross and Gerard J. Telkamp (eds.), *Colonial Cities*, Dordreck: Martinus Nijhoff, 1985, 70.
53. Wilson, "Southeast Asia," CWHF, II: 1159–60.
54. Küster "Spices and Flavorings," CWHF, I: 436.
55. Andrew Dalby, *Dangerous Tastes: The Story of Spices*, Berkeley: University of California Press, 2000, 62–3.
56. Johanna T. Dwyer and Ritu Sandhu, "Peanuts," in CWHF, I: 366, 364.
57. Mary Karasch, "Amaranth," in CWHF, I: 78.
58. Delphine Roger, "The Middle East and South Asia," in CWHF, II: 1150.
59. Karasch, "Amaranth," in CWHF, I: 72–3.
60. Felipe Fernández-Armesto, *Food: A History*, London: McMillan, 2001, 163.

CHAPTER FIFTEEN: THE COLUMBIAN EXCHANGE AND THE NEW WORLDS

1. William Shakespeare, Merry Wives of Windsor, Act II, Sc. 2.
2. Nancy Davis Lewis, "The Pacific Islands," in Kenneth F. Kiple and Kriemhild C. Ornelas (eds.), *The Cambridge World History of Food* (hereinafter CWHF), 2 vols., New York and Cambridge: Cambridge University Press, 2000, II: 1353.
3. Ibid. II: 1353–4.
4. H. Michael Tarver and Allan W. Austin, "Sago," in CWHF, I: 201–6.
5. Hugh C. Harries, "Coconut," in CWHF, I: 388–95.
6. Will C. McClatchy, "Bananas and Plantains," in CWHF, I: 175–81.
7. Lewis, "Pacific Islands," in CWHF, II: 1353–6.
8. Ibid., II: 1352; Brian Murton, "Australia and New Zealand," in CWHF II: 1339.
9. Ibid. II: 1340.
10. Murton, "Australia and New Zealand," in CWHF, II: 1342.
11. Ibid., 1339–40.

12. Ibid., 1340.
13. Jane Clarke, "Super Drug: Honey's healing powers help take the sting out of conventional treatments," *The Observer Magazine*, 2 July, 2000, 43.
14. Murton, "Australia and New Zealand," in CWHF, II: 1344–5.
15. Lewis, "Pacific Islands," in CWHF, II: 1354.
16. Patricia J. O'Brien, "Sweet Potatoes and Yams," in CWHF I: 211. Douglas E. Yen explores this question in a chapter on "Construction of the Hypothesis for Distribution of the Sweet Potato" in Carroll L. Riley et al. (eds.), *Man Across the Sea: Problems of Pre-Columbian Contacts*, Austin: University of Texas Press, 1971, 328–42.
17. O'Brien, "Sweet Potatoes and Yams," in CWHF, I: 211–12.
18. Alfred W. Crosby, *Ecological Imperialism: The Biological Expansion of Europe, 900–1900*, New York: Cambridge University Press, 1986, 230.
19. Ibid., 180–1.
20. Peter R. Cheeke, "Rabbits," in CWHF, I: 566.
21. Ibid.
22. Unless otherwise indicated, the following is based on Murton, "Australia and New Zealand," in CWHF, II: 1346–50.
23. Felipe Fernández-Armesto, *Food: A History*, London: McMillan, 2001, 211.
24. Frederick W. Clements, *A History of Human Nutrition in Australia*, Melbourne: Longman House, 1986, 34.
25. Alan Davidson, *The Oxford Companion to Food*, Oxford: Oxford University Press, 1999, 41.
26. Alfred W. Crosby, "Metamorphosis of the Americas," in Herman J. Viola and Carolyn Margolis (eds.), *Seeds of Change*, Washington and London: Smithsonian Institution Press, 1991, 70–89 and passim.
27. Daniel W. Gade, "Hogs (Pigs)," in CWHF, I: 538.
28. Alfred W. Crosby, *The Columbian Exchange: Biological and Cultural Consequences of 1492*, Westport, CT: Greenwood Publishing, 1972, 76; Jeffrey M. Pilcher, "The Caribbean from 1492 to the Present," in CWHF, II: 1279.
29. Ibid.
30. Daniel W. Gade, "Cattle," in CWHF, I: 493; William F. Kegan, "The Caribbean: Early History," in CWHF, II: 1272.
31. J. H. Parry, *The Spanish Seaborne Empire*, New York: Alfred A. Knopf, 1966, 97–8.
32. Gade, "Cattle," CWHF, I: 493–4.
33. Daniel W. Gade, "Sheep," in CWHF, I: 578.
34. Daniel W. Gade, "Goats," in CWHF, I: 533.
35. Stanley J. Olsen, "The Horse in Ancient China and its Cultural Influence in Some Other Areas," *Proceedings of the Academy of Natural Sciences of Philadelphia*, 1988, 140, no. 2, 165.
36. Ibid., 164.
37. Crosby, *Ecological Imperialism*, 183.
38. George F. Carter, "Pre-Columbian Chickens in America," in Carroll L. Riley et al. (eds.), *Man Across the Sea*, 178–218; Page Smith and Charles Daniel, *The Chicken Book*, San Francisco: North Point Press, 1982; Blench and MacDonald, "Chickens," in CWHF, I: 498.
39. William J. Stadelman, "Chicken Eggs," in CWHF, I: 506; Smith and Daniel, 31.
40. Crosby, *Ecological Imperialism*, 188–90.
41. Joy McCoriston, "Wheat," in CWHF, I: 170; John C. Super and Luis Alberto Vargas, "Mexico and Highland Central America," in CWHF, II: 1250.

42. Crosby, *Columbian Exchange*, 67–8, 98.
43. Pilcher, "The Caribbean CWHF, II: 1288.
44. Hansjörg Küster, "Rye," in CWHF, I: 151.
45. H. Frederic Janson, *Pomona's Harvest: An Illustrated Chronicle of Antiquarian Fruit Literature*, Portland: Timber Press, 1996, 98.
46. Pilcher, "The Caribbean," CWHF, II; McClatchey, "Bananas and Plantains," CWHF, I: 178; Super and Vargas, CWHF, II: 1251.
47. Julia Peterson, "Allium Species," in CWHF, I: 252.
48. Ibid., 251, 257.
49. Thomas G. Benedek, "Aphrodisiacs and Anaphrodisiacs," in CWHF, I: 1525.
50. H. C. Harries, "The Evolution, Dissemination and Classification of Cocos Nucifera L." in *The Botanical Review*, 1978, 44: 280.
51. Ibid.
52. Pilcher, "The Carribbean," in CWHF, II: 1279.
53. Robert C. Field, "Cruciferous and Green Leafy Vegetables," in CWHF, I: 288–98.
54. See the Chapter on "Weeds" in Crosby's *Ecological Imperialism*, 145–70.
55. Ibid., 191–2.
56. William M. Denevan (ed.), *The Native Population of the Americas in 1492*, Madison: University of Wisconsin Press, 1976; See Suzanne Austin Alchon, *A Pest in the Land: New World Epidemics in a Global Perspective*, Albuquerque: University of New Mexico Press, 2003, for a recent effort to balance the ravages of disease with other reasons for Native American population decline; Marshall T. Newman, "Aboriginal New World Epidemiology and Medical Care and the Impact of New World Disease Imports," *American Journal of Physical Anthropology*, 1976, 45: 667–72.
57. The final paragraphs in this chapter are based on my own notes of The History of the Carribbean but can be found in summarized form in J. H. Parry and Philip Sherlock. A Short Histroy of the West Indies 3rd ed., London: Macmillan, 1971.

CHAPTER SIXTEEN: SUGAR AND NEW BEVERAGES

1. J. H. Galloway, "Sugar," in Kenneth F. Kiple and Kriemhild C. Ornelas (eds.), *The Cambridge World History of Food* (hereinafter CWHF), 2 vols., New York and Cambridge: Cambridge University Press, 2000, I: 437.
2. Ibid., I: 442.
3. Ibid., I: 443.
4. Sidney W. Mintz, *Sweetness and Power: The Place of Sugar in Modern History*, New York: Viking, 1985, 32.
5. Galloway, "Sugar," CWHF, I: 443.
6. J. H. Parry and Philip Sherlock, *A Short History of the West Indies* 3rd ed., London: Macmillan, 1971, 63–80.
7. For a survey of sugar and slavery, see Philip D. Curtin, *The Rise and Fall of the Plantation Complex*, New York: Cambridge University Press, 1990.
8. K. David Patterson, "Russia," in CWHF, II: 1242; Galloway, "Sugar," CWHF, I: 445.
9. Ibid., I: 445–6; Maguelonne Toussaint-Samat, *History of Food* (tr. Anthea Bell), Cambridge, MA: Blackwell, 1997, 560–1.
10. Murdo J. MacLeod, "Cacao," in CWHF, I: 636.
11. Sophia D. Coe, *America's First Cuisines*, Austin: University of Texas Press, 1994, 53.
12. MacLeod "Cacao," CWHF, I: 636–7.
13. Ibid., I: 637.

14. Ibid., I: 638.
15. Thomas G. Benedek, "Aphrodisiacs and Anaphrodisiacs," in CWHF, II: 1529.
16. Steven C. Topik, "Coffee," in CWHF, I: 641.
17. Toussaint-Samat, 581.
18. Topik, "Coffee," CWHF, I: 641; James Trager, *The Food Chronology*, New York: Henry Holt, 1995, 77.
19. Toussaint-Samat, 586.
20. Topik, "Coffe," CWHF, I: 643; Tannahill, 275.
21. Topik, "Coffee," CWHF, I: 648–9.
22. Ibid., I: 648.
23. Alan Davidson, *The Oxford Companion to Food*, Oxford: Oxford University Press, 1993, 202.
24. Topik, "Coffee," CWHF, I: 650.
25. Ibid.; Toussaint-Samat, 587.
26. Kevin Knox and Julie Sheldon Huffake, *Coffee Basics*, New York: John Wiley and Sons, 1996.
27. John H. Weisberger and James Comer, "Tea," in CWHF, I: 713.
28. Ibid.
29. Reay Tannahill, *Food in History*, New York: Crown Publishers, 1989, 127.
30. Ibid., 714.
31. Trager, 59.
32. Weisburger and Comer, CWHF, I: 713–14.
33. William H. Ukers, *The Romance of Tea*, New York: Knopf, 1936, 20–5.
34. Giles Brochard, "Time for Tea," in *The Book of Tea* (ed.) Ghistlaine Bavoiledt, Italy: Flammarion, 1992, 130, 132.
35. Newman, "Wine," in CWHF, I: 732.
36. Bailey W. Diffie and George D. Winius, *Foundations of the Portuguese Empire*, Minneapolis: University of Minnesota Press, 1977, 381.
37. Ibid., 714.
38. Ibid, 430; C. R. Boxer, *The Dutch Seaborne Empire: 1600–1800*, New York: Alfred A. Knopf, 1965, passim.
39. Tannahill, 267; Elisabeth Lambert Ortiz, *The Encyclopedia of Herbs, Spices, and Flavorings*, New York: Dorling Kindersley, 1992, 268.
40. Boxer, 277.
41. Trager, 129.
42. Ibid., 140, 147.
43. Henry Hobhouse, *Seeds of Change*, New York: Harper and Row, 1985, 108–12.
44. Trager, 246.
45. Mintz, 138; Trager, 177.
46. Brochard, 160.
47. Trager, 146; Toussaint–Samat, 597.
48. Mintz, 135–6; Nadine Beauthéae, "Tea Barons" in *The Book of Tea*, 61; Trager, 179.
49. Trager, 126; Brochard, 174.
50. Tannahill, 254–6; Pauline Maier, "Crisis of Empire: British" in Jacob Ernest Cook (ed.), *The Encyclopedia of the North American Colonies*, 3 vols., New York: 1993, III: 712–19.
51. Hobhouse, 114–15; Brochard, 174; Maier, 712–19.
52. Howard Chapelle, *The History of American Sailing Ships*, New York: Bonanza Books, 1935, 283–7; Trager, 242, 244.

53. Hobhouse, 116–18.
54. Ibid.; Beauthéac, 65.
55. Hobhouse, 123–4.
56. Trager, 383.
57. Artemas Ward, *The Grocer's Encyclopedia*, New York: Union Square, 1911.
58. Ibid., 395; Harold McGee, *On Food and Cooking*, New York: McMillan, 1984, 216.
59. Robert Kroes and J. H. Wineburger, "Nutrition and Cancer," in CWHF, I: 1095.
60. Toussaint-Samat, 598.
61. Anthony Burgess, "Preface" to *The Book of Tea*, 16; Rudyard Kipling, *Under the Deodars (Collected Works of Rudyard Kipling)*, New York: Classic Books, 2000; Diary of John Adams, 3 vols., Cambridge, MA: Harvard University Press, 1961–1964, December 17, 1773.
62. Alain Stella, "Tea Gardens," in *The Book of Tea*, 44.
63. Catherine Donzel, "The Taste of Tea," in *The Book of Tea*, 212; Ortiz, 269.
64. Ward, 100.
65. Unless otherwise indicated this section is based on Christopher Hamlin, "Water," in CWHF, I: 720–9.
66. Unless otherwise indicated this section is based on Colin Emmins, "Soft Drinks," in CWHF, I: 703–12.
67. Trager, 337.
68. Ibid., 323–4.
69. Trager, 323, 336, 342, 349, 359, 360.
70. Ibid., 324, 335, 453.
71. Jeffrey M. Pilcher, "Food Fads," in CWHF, II: 1488.
72. Emmins, CWHF, I: 703.
73. Newman, "Wine," CWHF, II: 733.
74. Ibid., I: 733–4.
75. Stewart Lee Allen, *In the Devil's Garden*, New York: Ballentine Books, 2002, 141.
76. James Comer, "Distilled Beverages," in CWHF, I: 656–9.
77. Patterson, "Russia," in CWHF, II: 1243–4; Colin Spencer, "British Isles," in CWHF, II: 1223.
78. Comer, "Distilled Beverages," in CWHF, I: 658–9.
79. Ibid., I: 659–61.

CHAPTER SEVENTEEN: KITCHEN HISPANIZATION

1. Hernando Cortés, *Five Letters of Cortés to the Emperor 1519–1526* (tr. J. Bayard Morris), New York: Norton, 1991, 271–2.
2. Woodrow Borah and Sherburne F. Cook, "Conquest and Population: A Demographic Approach to Mexican History," *Proceedings of the American Philosophical Society*, 1969, 113(2): 182.
3. Luis Bértola and Jeffrey G. Williamson, "Globalization in Latin America Before 1940," *National Bureau of Economic Research, Working Paper 9687*, Cambridge, MA, 2003.
4. Rachel Laudan, "Where Do Mexican Culinary Traditions Come From? Or 'We Never Ate Mexican Food'" *Repast*, 2003, XI, (2): 2.
5. Ibid., 1.
6. Daniel W. Gade, "South America," in Kenneth F. Kiple and Kriemhild C. Ornelas (eds.), *The Cambridge World History of Food* (hereinafter CWHF), 2 vols., New York and Cambridge: Cambridge University Press, 2000, II: 1257.

7. Ibid.
8. Ibid., II: 1259.
9. Ibid., II: 1256–7.
10. Ibid., II: 1256.
11. Ibid., II: 1257.
12. Alan Davidson, *The Oxford Companion to Food*, Oxford: Oxfort University Press, 1994, 34.
13. Gade, "South America," CWHF, II: 1257.
14. James L. Newman, "Wine," in CWHF, I: 734.
15. Stuart Walton, *The World Encyclopedia of Wine*, New York: Smithmark Publishers, 1996, 216–17.
16. Margarette De Andrade, *Brazilian Cookery*, Rio de Janeiro: A Casa do Livro Eldorado, n.d., passim.
17. Gade, "South America," CWHF, II: 1257.
18. Ibid.
19. Davidson, *Companion to Food*, 597.
20. Gade, "Cattle," in CWHF, I: 493.
21. John C. Super and Luis Alberto Vargas, "Mexico and Highland Central America," in CWHF, II: 1253.
22. Ibid., II: 1251–3.
23. William F. Keegan, "The Caribbean: Early History" in CWHF, II: 1262–8.
24. Jeffrey M. Pilcher, "The Caribbean from 1492 to the Present," in CWHF, II: 1278–9.
25. Elisabeth Lambert Ortiz, *The Complete Book of Caribbean Cooking*, Edison, NJ: Castle Books, 1995, 33, 291–2, 280.
26. Kenneth F. Kiple, *The Caribbean Slave: A Biological History*, New York and Cambridge: Cambridge University Press, 1984, passim.
27. Robert Dirks, *The Black Saturnalia: Conflict and its Ritual Expression on British West Indian Slave Plantations*, Gainesville: University of Florida Press, 1987, passim.
28. Jerome S. Handler, Arthur C. Aufderheide, and Robert Corruccini, "Lead Contact and Poisoning in Barbados Slaves: Historical, Chemical, and Biological Evidence," in Kenneth F. Kiple (ed.), *The African Exchange: Toward a Biological History of Black People*, Durham, NC: Duke University Press, 1987, 140–66.
29. Kiple, *Caribbean Slave*, 46.
30. Jeffrey M. Pilcher, "The Caribbean From 1492 to the Present," in CWHF, II: 1283.
31. Ibid., II: 1284.
32. Ibid.
33. Ibid., II: 1286.

CHAPTER EIGHTEEN: PRODUCING PLENTY IN PARADISE

1. Elizabeth J. Reitz, "Temperate and Arctic North America to 1492," in Kenneth F. Kiple and Kriemhild C. Ornelas (eds.), *The Cambridge World History of Food* (hereinafter CWHF), 2 vols., New York and Cambridge: Cambridge University Press, 2000, II: 1288.
2. Alfred W. Crosby, *Ecological Imperialism: The Biological Expansion of Europe, 900–1900*, New York and Cambridge: Cambridge University Press, 1986, passim.
3. Alfred Crosby coined the term, which he used as a title for his *Ecological Imperialism*.
4. James Comer, "North America from 1492 to the Present," in CWHF, II: 1305.

5. Jay Mechling, "Oranges," in David Schofield Wilson and Angus Kress Gillespie (eds.), *Rooted in America*, Knoxville: University of Tennessee Press, 1999, 124.

6. Editors, "Peach," in CWHF, II: 1830.

7. David Maynard and Donald N. Maynard, "Cucumbers, Melons, and Watermelons," in CWHF, I: 306.

8. Trager, 123. Waverley Root and Richard de Rochemont, *Eating in America: A History*, New York: William Morrow and Company, 1976, 46–7, 65–7.

9. Reitz, "Temperate and Arctic North America," CWHF, II: 1298–9.

10. Linda J. Reed, "The Arctic and Subarctic Regions," in CWHF, II: 1325.

11. Dean R. Snow and Kim M. Lanphear, "European Contact and Indian Depopulation in the Northeast: The Timing of the First Epidemics," *Ethnohistory*, 1988, 35: 15–33.

12. Alfred W. Crosby, *Germs, Seeds, & Animals: Studies in Ecological History*, Armonk, New York: M. E. Sharpe, 1994, 109.

13. Quoted in Crosby, *Ecological Imperialism*, 208.

14. Jonathan D. Sauer, "Changing Perception and Exploitation of New World Plants in Europe, 1492–1800," in Fredi Chiappelli (ed.), *First Images of America: The Impact of the New World on the Old*, 2 vols., Berkeley: University of California Press, 1976, II: 814.

15. James W. Baker, "Plymouth Succotash and Forefather's Day," *Mayflower Quarterly*, December 2000, 340; Reitz, "Temperate and Arctic North America," CWHF, II: 1288.

16. G. Mazza, "Buckwheat," in CWHF, I: 90.

17. Evan Jones, *American Food: The Gastronomic Story*, New York: E. P. Dutton, 1975, 3, 5.

18. Ibid., 15.

19. Comer, "North America," CWHF, II: 1306–7.

20. Robert F. Huber, "There were no Tea Parties for the Pilgrims in Plymouth," *Mayflower Quarterly*, 2000, 66: 250.

21. Editors, "Apples," in CWHF, II:1720; Boria Sax, "Apples," in Wilson and Gillespie (eds.), 5.

22. Alan Davidson, *The Oxford Companion to Food*, Oxford: Oxford University Press, 1999, 76.

23. H. Frederic Janson, *Pomona's Harvest: An Illustrated Chronicle of Antiquarian Fruit Literature*, Portland: Timber Press, 1996, 98; Sax, "Apples," Wilson and Gillespie (eds.), 5.

24. Ibid., 6–8.

25. Janson, 183.

26. J. M. J. De Wet, "Sorghum," in CWHF, I: 156; Jahanna T. Dwyer and Rita Sandhu, "Peanuts," in CWHF, I: 365.

27. Stanley J. Olsen, "Turkeys," in CWHF, I: 581.

28. Crosby, *Ecological Imperialism*, 187–90; Reitz, "Temperate and Artic North America," CWHF, II: 1296.

29. Daphne L. Derven, "Wholesome, Toothsome, amd Diverse: Eighteenth-Century Foodways in Deerfield Massachusetts," and Michael D. Coe and Sophia D. Coe, "Mid-Eighteenth Century Food and Drink on the Massachusetts Frontier," both in *Foodways in the Northeast: Annual Proceedings of the Dublin Seminar for New England Folklife*, Boston: Boston University, 1984, 47–65 and 39–46, respectively.

30. James Trager, *The Food Chronology*, New York: Henry Holt, 1995, 146.

31. Maguelonne Toussaint-Samat, *History of Food* (tr. Anthea Bell), Cambridge, MA: Blackwell, 1992, 701, 706.

32. *The Williamsburg Art of Cookery or Accomplish'd Gentlewoman's Companion*, (facsimile of the 1742 edition), Williamsburg, VA: Colonial Williamsburg, 1966, 105–5: *The First American Cookbook*: A facsimile of "American Cookery," by Amelia Simmons, New York: Oxford University Press, 1958, 13.

33. Ibid., passim.

34. Thomas Sorosiak, "Soybean," in CWHF, I: 423.

35. Harvey Levenstein, "The Perils of Abundance: Food, Health, and Morality in American History," in Jean-Louis Flandrin and Massimo Montanari (eds.), *Food: A Culinary History From Antiquity to the Present* (tr. Clarissa Botsford et al.), New York: Columbia University Press, 1999, 517.

36. James Comer, "Distilled Beverages," CWHF, I: 661.

37. Ibid.

38. Ibid.

39. Stefan Gabányi, *Whisk(e)y*, New York: Abbeville Press, 1997, 54; Root and de Rochemont, 380.

40. Keith Vernon, "Milk and Dairy Products," in CWHF, I: 696.

41. Timothy J. Hatton and Jeffery G. Williamson, "What Fundamentals Drive World Migration?" *National Bureau of Economic Research, Working Paper 9159*, 2001, 9.

42. Elaine N. McIntosh, *American Food Habits in Historical Perspective*, Westport, CT: Prager, 1995, 89; Trager, 313.

43. Richard Osborn Cummings, *The American and His Food*, Chicago: University of Chicago Press, 1940, 53–74 and passim; Root and de Rochemont, 146–60 and passim; Mechling, "Oranges" and Virginia S. Jenkins, "Bananas," both in Wilson and Gillespie (eds.), 124 and 24, respectively.

44. Trager, 383.

45. Robert L. Morris, "Feeding the Hungry: High Technology or a Corporal Work of Mercy?" in Marianne Postiglione and Robert Brungs (eds.), *The Science and Politics of Food*, St. Louis: Itest Press, 1995, 103; McIntosh, *American Food Habits*, 97–8.

46. Reay Tonnahill, *Food in History*, New York: Crown Publishers, 1989, 328; Trager, 300–1.

47. The story of the late nineteenth-century *Crusaders for Fitness: The History of American Health Reformers* (Princeton, NJ: Princeton University Press, 1982) has been skillfully told by James C. Whorton. See also Ronald Numbers for his study of the *Prophetess of Health: A Study of Ellen G. White*, New York: Harper and Row, 1976.

48. Tannahill, 329–31; Trager, 285–8 and passim; Joseph Hotchkiss, "Development of Trends in Food Science" in Jennie Brogdon and Wallace C. Olsen (eds.), *The Contempory and Historical Literature of Food Science and Human Nutrition*, Ithaca and London: Cornell University Press, 1995, 7.

CHAPTER NINETEEN: U.S. FRONTIERS OF FOREIGN FOODS

1. Leslie Brenner, *American Appetite: The Coming of Age of a Cuisine*, New York: Avon Books, 1999, 15–16.

2. James Comer, "North America from 1492 to the Present," in Kenneth F. Kiple and Kriemhild C. Ornelas (eds.), *The Cambridge World History of Food* (hereinafter CWHF), 2 vols., New York and Cambridge: Cambridge University Press, 2000, II: 1313–14.

3. James Trager, *The Food Chronology*, New York: Henry Holt, 1995, 284.
4. Evan Jones, *American Food: The Gastronomic Story*, New York: E. P. Dutton, 1975, 50–1.
5. Trager, 284.
6. David W. Gade, "Cattle," in CWHF, I: 494.
7. Trager, 127, 161, 213, 281.
8. Jones, *American Food*, 58–9.
9. Piero Camporesi, *Exotic Brew: The Art of Living in the Age of Enlightenment* (tr. Christopher Woodall), Cambridge, MA: Polity Press, 1994, 33.
10. Terry Thompson, *Creole-Cajun Cooking*, Tucson: H. P. Books, 1986, 6–7.
11. Sybil Kein, "Louisiana Creole Food Culture: Afro-Caribbean Links" in Sybil Kein (ed.), *Creole: The History and Legacy of Louisiana's Free People of Color*, Baton Rouge: Louisiana State University Press, 2000, 244–51.
12. Paul F. Lachance, "The Foreign French" in Arnold R. Hirsch and Joseph Logston (eds.), *Creole New Orleans: Race and Americanization*, Baton Rouge: Louisiana State University Press, 1992, 101–30.
13. Clement Eaton, *A History of the Old South*, 3rd ed., New York: Macmillan, 1975; Jones, *American Food*, 43.
14. Ibid., 67–70.
15. Daniel W. Gade, "Hogs (Pigs)," in CWHF, I: 538: Trager, 207.
16. Phillip A. Cantrell II, "Beer and Ale," in CWHF, I: 623.
17. Although hard cider is now making a comeback in New England, on one side of the North American continent, and Oregon and California on the other side.
18. Cantrell, "Beer and Ale," in CWHF, I: 624.
19. Editors, "Cranberry," in CWHF, II: 1764; Root and de Rochemont, 418–19.
20. Robert J. Goode, Jr., "Pilgrim and Early New England Recipes," *Mayflower Quarterly*, March 2000 40, 43.
21. Mark Kurlansky, *Cod: A Biography of the Fish that Changed the World*, New York: Penguin Books, 1998, 78.
22. Ibid., 79–81.
23. Tad Tuleja, "Pumpkins," in David Scofield Wilson and Angus Kress Gillespie (eds.), *Rooted in America: Folklore of Popular Fruits and Vegetables*, Knoxville: University of Tennessee Press, 1999, 145.

CHAPTER TWENTY: CAPITALISM, COLONIALISM, AND CUISINE

1. Jared Diamond, *Guns, Germs, and Steel: The Fates of Human Societies*, New York: Norton, 1999, 400–01.
2. Ellen Messer, Barbara Haber, Joyce Toomre, and Barbara Wheaton, "Culinary History," in Kenneth F. Kiple and Kriemhild C. Ornelas (eds.), *The Cambridge World History of Food* (hereinafter CWHF), 2 vols., New York and Cambridge: Cambridge University Press, 2000, II: 1368.
3. Felipe Fernández-Armesto, *Food: A History*, London: McMillan, 2001, 216–17.
4. Sandra Sherman, "Alimentary Nationalism in England," *Repast*, Summer 2004, XX (3): 4.
5. Ibid., 5.
6. Eva Barlösius, "France," in CWHF, II: 1210, 1212–13.
7. Jeffrey M. Pilcher, "Food Fads," in CWHF, II: 1486–7.

8. Colin Spencer, "British Isles," in CWHF, II: 1222.
9. Ibid., II: 1223; Robert W. Fogel, "Changes in the Disparities in Chronic Disease during the Course of the Twentieth Century," *National Bureau of Economic Research, Working Paper 10311*, Cambridge, MA: Feb. 2004, 13.
10. Spencer, "British Isles," in CWHF, II: 1224.
11. Carol F. Helstosky, "The State, Health, and Nutrition," in CWHF, II: 1579.
12. Ellen Messer, "Potatoes (White)," in CWHF, I: 193.
13. George W. Hudler, *Magical Mushrooms, Mischievous Molds*, Princeton, NJ: Princeton University Press, 1998, 36.
14. Messer, "Potatoes (White)," CWHF, I: 193.
15. James Trager, *The Food Chronology*, New York: Henry Holt, 1995, 205, 207, 210.
16. Messer, "Potatoes (White)," CWHF, I: 193.
17. Trager, 237; Hudler, 39.
18. Messer "Potatoes (White)," CWHF, I: 193; Hudler, 39–40.
19. Keith Vernon, "Milk and Dairy Products," in CWHF, I: 696.
20. Kevin H. O'Rourke and Jeffrey G. Williamson, "When Did Globalization Begin?" *National Bureau of Economic Research, Working Paper 7632*, Cambridge, MA, 2000.
21. John Burnett, *Plenty and Want*, London: Thomas Nelson, 1966, cited by Sidney W. Mintz, *Sweetness and Power: The Place of Sugar in Modern History*, New York: Viking, 1985, 129.
22. Mintz, 130.
23. Spencer, "British Isles," CWHF, II: 1224; Brian Murton, "Australia and New Zealand," in CWHF, II: 1346.
24. Fernández-Armesto, 157.
25. Laura Tabili, "Imperialism and Domestic Society" in Peter N. Sterns (ed.), *Encyclopedia of European Social History*, 5 vols, New York: Charles Scribner's Sons, 2001, I: 509.
26. Annekke H. van Otterloo, "The Low Countries," in CWHF, II: 1232, 1238.
27. Hansjörg Küster, "Northern Europe," in CWHF, II: 1231.
28. Based on Murdo J. MacLeod, "Cacao," in CWHF, I: 639–40.
29. Steven C. Topik, "Coffee," in CWHF, I: 651–2.
30. John H. Weisburger and James Comer, "Tea," in CWHF, I: 717.
31. Nancy J. Pollock, "Kava," in CWHF, I: 664–70.
32. Based on Clarke Brooke, "Khat," in CWHF, I: 671–83.
33. Based on Edmund Abaka, "Kola Nut," in CWHF, I: 684–91.
34. S. Jenkins, "Bananas," in David Schofield Wilson and Angus Kress Gillespie (eds.), *Rooted in America: Folklore of Popular Fruits and Vegetables*, Knoxville: University of Tennessee Press, 1999, 24–5; McClatchey, "Bananas and Plantains," CWHF, I: 179.
35. Kolleen M. Guy, "Food and Diet," in Sterns (ed.), V: 502.
36. Yves Péhaut, "The Invasion of Foreign Foods," in Jean-Louis Flandrin and Massimo Montanari (eds.), *Food: A Culinary History From Antiquity to the Present* (tr. Clarissa Botsford et al.), New York: Columbia University Press, 1999, 457–70.
37. Ibid., 458–9.
38. Hugh C. Harris, "Coconut," in CWHF, I: 394.
39. K. G. Berger and S. M. Martin, "Palm Oil," in CWHF, I: 399, 400.
40. Ibid., I: 405.
41. Péhaut, 458–9.
42. Ibid., 459: Johanna T. Dwyer and Ritu Sandhu, "Peanuts," in CWHF, I: 365.
43. Ibid., I: 365, 367.

44. Dorothea Bedigian, "Sesame," in CWHF, I: 418.

45. Péhaut, 457, 461.

46. Ibid., 462.

47. Sean Francis O'Keefe, "An Overview of Oils and Fats, with a special emphasis on Olive Oil," in CWHF, I: 384.

48. Thomas Sorosiak, "Soybean," in CWHF, I: 424–5.

49. Maquelonne Toussaint-Samat, *History of Food* (tr. Anthea Bell), Cambridge, MA: Blackwell, 1992, 51.

50. Colin E. Nash, "Aquatic Animals," in CWHF, I: 459–62.

51. Heather Munroe Prescott, "Adolescent Nutrition and Fertility," in CWHF, II: 1454–5.

52. Ibid., II: 1455; Robert Hudson, "Chlorosis," in CWHD, I: 638–41.

CHAPTER TWENTY-ONE: HOMEMADE FOOD HOMOGENEITY

1. Ellen Messer, Barbara Haber, Joyce Toomre, and Barbara Wheaton, "Culinary History," in Kenneth F. Kiple and Kriemhild C. Ornelas (eds.), *The Cambridge World History of Food* (hereinafter CWHF), 2 vols., New York and Cambridge: Cambridge University Press, 2000, II: 1368.

2. Alan L. Olmstead and Paul W. Rhode, "The Red Queen and the Hard Reds: Productivity Growth in American Wheat, 1800–1940," *National Bureau of Economic Research, Working Paper 8863*, Cambridge, MA: 2002, 5.

3. Robert L. Morris, "Feeding the Hungry: High Technology or a Corporal Work of Mercy?" in S. Marianne Postiglioni and Robert Brungs (eds.), *The Science and Politics of Food*, St. Louis: Itest Press, 1995, 103; Agricultural expansion received much government support in the form of a second Morrill Act passed in 1890, which provided for the establishment of experiment stations, extension services, and agricultural research stations. See James Trager, *The Food Chronology*, New York: Henry Holt, 1995, 242, 266, 334.

4. Harvey A. Levenstein, *Revolution at the Table: The Transformation of the American Diet*, New York: Oxford University Press, 1988, 3.

5. Jame C. Whorton, "Vegetarianism," in CWHF, II: 1561.

6. Burton Kline, "American Cusine," *American Mercury*, January, 1925, 4: 69–70.

7. Whorton, "Vegetarianism," in CWHF, II: 1561.

8. Waverley Root and Richard de Rochemont, *Eating in America: A History*, New York: William Morrow & Company, 1976, 276.

9. Richard J. Hooker, *Food and Drink in America: A History*, Indianapolis and New York: Bobbs-Merrill, 1981, 317–19.

10. Messer, Haber, Toomre, and Wheaton, "Culinary History," CWHF, II: 1368; Hooker, 321–2; Trager, 352.

11. Hooker, 336–40.

12. John L. Hess and Karen Hess, *The Tastes of America*, New York: Grossman Publishers, 1977, 2, 224.

13. James Beard, *James Beard's American Cookery*, New York: Little Brown, and Company, 1972, 5–6.

14. James Comer, "North America from 1492 to the Present" in CWHF, II: 1324.

15 Trager, 328, 386, 386.

16. Ibid., 419.

17. Stewart Lee Allen, *In the Devil's Garden*, New York: Ballentine Books, 2002, 139.

18. Trager, 272, 284.
19. Ibid., 333.
20. Ibid., 453.
21. Ibid., 410.
22. Ibid., 543.
23. Ibid., 640.
24. Trager, 649.
25. Levenstein, "The Perils of Abundance" in Jean-Louis Flandrin and Massimo Montanari (eds.), *Food: A Culinary History From Antiquity to the Present* (tr. Clarissa Botsford et al.), New York: Columbia University Press, 1999, 528.
26. Leslie Brenner, *American Appetite: The Coming of Age of a Cuisine*, New York: Avon Books, 1999, 99–100.
27. Trager, 596, 603.

CHAPTER TWENTY-TWO: NOTIONS OF NUTRIENTS AND NUTRIMENTS

1. Kenneth J. Carpenter, *Protein and Energy: A Study of Changing Ideas in Nutrition*, New York and Cambridge: Cambridge University Press, 1994, 219.
2. Kenneth Albala, "Southern Europe," in Kenneth F. Kiple and Kriemhild L. Ornelas (eds.), *The Cambridge World History of Food* (hereinafter CWHF), 2 vols., New York and Cambridge: Cambridge University Press, 2000, II: 1207.
3. Jeffrey M. Pilcher, "Food Fads," in CWHF, II: 1489.
4. Harvey A. Levenstein, *Paradox of Plenty: A Social History of Eating in Modern America*, Berkeley: University of California Press, 2003, 184.
5. Louis E. Grivetti, "Food Predjuices and Taboos," in CWHF, II: 1503.
6. Harvey A. Levenstein, *Revolution of the Table: The Transformation of the American Diet*, New York: Oxford University Press, 1988, 30–43, 152–60.
7. Vivek Bammi, "Nutrition, the Historian, and Public Policy: A Case Study of U.S. Nutrition Policy in the 20th Century," *Journal of Social History*, 1981, 14: 629–30.
8. Keir Waddington, "Unfit for Human Consumption: Tuberculosis and the Problem of Infected Meat in Late Victorian Britain," *Bulletin of the History of Medicine*, 2003, 77: 636–7.
9. Upton Sinclair, *The Jungle*, New York: New American Library of World Literature, 1905, 1906. Sinclair was a young radical novelist who hoped to expose the horrible conditions under which packing house employees worked, to show corruption in Chicago politics and to advance the cause of socialism. But it was his depiction of the unsanitary conditions under which meats were processed that aroused a middle-class readership. Sinclair is reputed to have said of that readership, "I aimed for their hearts and hit their stomachs." George Donaldson Moss, *America in the Twentieth Century*, 3rd ed., Upper Saddle River, New Jersey: Prentice Hall, 1997, 53.
10. Waverley Root and Richard de Rochemont, *Eating in America*, New York: William Morrow & Company, 1976, 40–1.
11. K. T. H. Farrer, "Food Additives," in CWHF, II: 1670.
12. Clayton A. Choppin and Jack High, "Umpires at Bat: Setting Food Standards by Government Regulation," *Business and Economic History*, Second Series, 1992, 21: 109–18.

13. Moss, 53; Laura Shapiro, *Perfection Salad: Women and Cooking at the Turn of the Century*, New York: Farrar, Straus, and Giroux, 1986, 196; Laura S. Sims, *The Politics of Fat: Food and Nutrition Policy in America*, New York: Armonk, 1998, 49; Eliza Mojduszka, "Food Labeling," in CWHF, II: 1622.

14. Levenstein, *Revolution*, 40–1.

15. C. F. Langworthy, "Food and Diet in the United States," *Yearbook of the United States Department of Agriculture, 1907*, Washington D.C.: Government Printing Office, 1908, 361–78.

16. James Trager, *The Food Chronology*, New York: Henry Holt, 1995, 391.

17. Stewart Lee Allen, *In the Devil's Garden*, New York: Ballentine Books, 2002, 104.

18. Levenstein, *Revolution*, 178–9; Richard Osborn Cummings, *The American and His Food*, Chicago: The University of Chicago Press, 1940, 174. For the early twentieth-century crisis of health experienced by two groups of southerners see Edward H. Beardsley, *A History of Neglect: Health Care for Blacks and Mill-Workers in the Twentieth-Century South*, Knoxville: University of Tennessee Press, 1987.

19. Leon A. Congden, *Fight for Food*. Philadelphia: J. B. Lippincott, 1916.

20. See, for example, P. J. Atkins, "White Poison? The Social Consequences of Milk Consumption, 1850–1930," *Social History of Medicine* 1992, 5: 207–27.

21. Ibid.

22. Peter R. Shergold, *Working-Class Life: The "American Standard" in Comparative Perspective, 1899–1913*, Pittsburgh: University of Pittsburgh Press, 1982, 191.

23. E. C. Shroeder, "Some Facts about Tuberculous Cattle," *Yearbook of the U.S. Department of Agriculture, 1908*, Washington D.C.: Government Printing Office, 1909, 223.

24. Werner Troesken, "Lead Water Pipes and Infant Mortality in Turn-of-the-Century Massachusetts," *National Bureau of Economic Research, Working Paper 9549*, Cambridge, MA: 2003.

25. Congden, 192–206.

26. Peter J. Pellet, "Energy and Protein Metabolism," in CWHF, I: 906.

27. George Wolf, "Vitamin A," in CWHF, I: 741–50.

28. For the story of protein, see Kenneth J. Carpenter, *Protein and Energy: A Study of Changing Ideas in Nutrition*, Cambridge and New York: Cambridge University Press, 1994, and his essay on "Proteins" in CWHF, I: 882–8.

29. Editors, "The Nutrients-Deficiencies, Surfeits, and Food-Related Disorders," in CWHF, I: 739.

30. Daphne A. Roe, "Vitamin B Complex, *Thiamine, Riboflavin, Niacin, Panothenic Acid, Pyridoxine, Colbalamin, Folic Acid*," in CWHF, I: 751.

31. Frederick L. Dunn, "Beriberi," in CWHF, I: 918. See also Kenneth J. Carpenter, *Beriberi, White Rice, and Vitamin B: A Disease, A Cause, And A Cure*, Berkeley: University of California Press, 2000.

32. Dunn, "Beriberi," in CWHF, I: 918–19.

33. Roe, "Vitamin B Complex: CWHF, 1: 751. The last "e" was dropped when it was discovered that not all vitamins contained nitrogen; Nevin S. Scrimshaw, "Infection and Nutrition: Synergistic Interactions," in CWHF, II: 1398.

34. Kenneth J. Carpenter, *The History of Scurvy and Vitamin C*, Cambridge, UK: Cambridge University Press, 1986, vii.

35. R. E. Hughes, "Scurvy," in CWHF, I: 988–99.

36. Wolf, "Vitamin A," CWHF I: 743.

37. Stephen V. Beck, "Scurvy: Citrus and Sailors" in Kenneth F. Kiple (ed.), *Plague, Pox, and Pestilence*, London: Weidenfeld and Nicolson, 1997, 68.

38. Adolphus Windeler, *The California Gold Rush Diary of a German Sailor* (W. Turrentine Jones, ed.), Berkeley: Howell-North, 1969, 31; Alfred E. Harper, "Recommended Dietary Allowances and Dietary Guidance," in CWHF, II: 1607.

39. H. H. Draper, "Human Nutritional Adaptation," in CWHF, II: 1468.

40. Sir James Watt, "Medical Aspects and Consequences of Cook's Voyages," in Robin Fisher and Hugh Johnston (eds.), *Captain James Cook and His Times*, Seattle: University of Washington Press, 1979, 129–58; David I. Harvie, *Limeys*, Phoenix Mill, UK: Sutton Publishing, 2002.

41. Carpenter, *History of Scurvy*, 145.

42. Beck, "Scurvy: Citrus and Sailors," in Kiple (ed.), 73; R. E. Hughes, "Vitamin C," in CWHF, I: 756; Harper, "Recommended Dietary Allowances," CWHF, II: 1607.

43. Daphne A. Roe and Steven B. Beck, "Pellagra," in CWHF, I: 960–61; Elizabeth W. Etheridge, "Pellagra," in Kenneth F. Kiple (ed.), *The Cambridge World History of Human Disease* (hereinafter CWHHD), New York and Cambridge: Cambridge University Press, 1993, 918–23.

44. The discovery was made by E. Kodichek, "Nicotinic Acid and the Pellagra Problem," *Bibliotheca "Nutritio et Dieta,"* 1962, 4: 109–27.

45. Roe and Beck, "Pellagra," in CWHF, I: 961.

46. Ibid., I: 962.

47. Sophia D. Coe, *America's First Cuisines*, Austin: University of Texas Press, 1994, 14. Draper, "Nutritional Adaptation," in CWHF, II: 1473.

48. Etheridge, "Pellagra," in CWHHD, 920–1.

49. Kenneth F. Kiple and Virginia H. Kiple, "Black Tongue and Black Men: Pellagra in the Antebellum South," *Journal of Southern History*, 1977, 43:3, 411–28.

50. Betty Fussell, *The Story of Corn*, New York: North Point Press, 1992, 203.

51. Ibid.

52. Etheridge, "Pellagra," in CWHHD, 922–3.

53. T. Ted Steinbock, "Rickets and Osteomalacia," in CWHHD, 978.

54. Herta Spencer, "Calcium," in CWHF, I: 785.

55. Glenville Jones, "Vitamin D," in CWHF, I: 763.

56. Steinbock, "Ricketts and Osteomalacia," in CWHHD, 978–9.

57. Marvin Harris, *Our Kind: Who We Are, Where We Came From, Where We Are Going*, New York: Harper & Row, 1989, 113–14.

58. K. David Patterson, "Lactose Intolerance," in CWHF, I: 1057–62.

59. Kenneth F. Kiple and Virginia H. King, *Another Dimension to the Black Diaspora: Diet, Disease, and Racism*, New York: Cambridge University Press, 1981, 84.

60. Jones, "Vitamin D," in CWHF, I: 765.

61. Stephen V. Beck, "Rickets: Where the Sun Doesn't Shine," in Kiple (ed.), *Plague, Pox, and Pestilence*, 133; Jones, "Vitamin D," CWHF, I: 764.

62. Kiple and King, 106; Vera Phillips and Laura Howell, "Racial and Other Differences in Dietary Customs," *The Journal of Home Economics*, 1920: 410–11.

63. Jones, "Vitamin D," in CWHF, I: 763; Steinbock, "Rickets and Osteomalacia," in CWHHD, 978.

64. Spencer, "Calcium," CWHF, I: 785.

65. Steinbock, "Rickets and Osteomalacia," CWHHD, 980.

66. Jones, "Vitamin D," in CWHF, I: 766.

67. Ibid., I: 766–8.
68. Robert P. Heaney, "Osteoporosis," in CWHF, I: 951.
69. Ibid., I: 951–3.
70. Spencer, "Calcium," in CWHF, I: 785–93; Carpenter, "Proteins," in CWHF, I: 888.
71. John J. B. Anderson, "Phosphorous," CWHF, I: 835–6.
72. Heaney, "Osteoporosis," in CWHF, I: 959.
73. Basil S. Hetzel, "Iodine and Iodine-Deficiency Disorders," in CWHF, I: 797; Sheldon Aaronson, "Algae," in CWHF, I: 231.
74. Ibid., I:797–8.
75. Susan Scott and Christoher J. Duncan, *Demography and Nutrition: Evidence From Historical and Contemporary Populations*, Malden, MA: Blackwell Science, 2002, 242; Kenneth F. Kiple, "Scrofula" in Kiple (ed.) *Plague, Pox, Pestilence*, 44–9.
76. Hetzel, "Iodine and Iodine Deficiency Diseases," in CWHF, I: 799–800.
77. Clark T. Sawin, "Goiter," in CWHHD, 750–4; Hetzel, "Iodine and Iodine-Deficiency Diseases," in CWHF, I: 800.
78. Renate Lellep Fernandez, *A Simple Matter of Salt: An Ethnography of Nutritional Deficiency in Spain*, Berkeley: University of California Press, 1991.
79. James L. Newman, "Africa South from the Sahara," in CWHF, II: 1337.
80. Hetzel, "Iodine and Iodine Deficiency Disorders," in CWHF, I: 809; Donald T. Simeon and Sally M. Grantham-McGregor, "Nutrition and Mental Development," in CWHF, II: 1458.
81. Based on Margaret J. Weinberger, "Pica," in CWHF, I: 967–75.
82. Glenville Jones, "Vitamin E," in CWHF, I: 769–73.
83. Myrtle Thierry-Palmer, "Vitamin K and Vitamin K-Dependent Proteins," in CWHF, I: 774–82.
84. Theodore D. Mountokalakis, "Magnesium," in CWHF, I: 825–6.
85. Ibid., I: 830–1.
86. Ibid., I: 832.

CHAPTER TWENTY-THREE: THE PERILS OF PLENTY

1. Harvey Levenstein, *Paradox of Plenty: A Social History of Eating in Modern America*, New York: Oxford University Press, 1993, 27.
2. Richard J. Hooker, *Food and Drink in America: A History*, Indianapolis and New York: Bobbs-Merrill, 1981, 307–9; Janet Poppedieck, *Breadlines Knee-Deep in Wheat: Food Assistance in the Great Depression*, New Brunswick, NJ: Rutgers University Press, 1986, 83.
3. Levenstein, *Paradox of Plenty*, 67; James Trager, *The Food Chronology*, New York: Henry Holt, 1995, 546.
4. Ibid., 714.
5. Daniel W. Gade, "Cattle," in Kenneth F. Kiple and Kriemhild C. Ornelas (eds.), *The Cambridge World History of Food* (hereinafter CWHF), 2 vols., New York and Cambridge: Cambridge University Press, 2000, II: 1196–7.
6. Trager, 543: Marion Nestle, "The Mediterranean," in CWHF, II: 1196–7.
7. Joel Howell, "Concepts of Heart-Related Diseases," in Kenneth F. Kiple (ed.), *The Cambridge World History of Human Disease* (hereinafter CWHHD), New York and Cambridge: Cambridge University Press, 1993, 97–8.
8. K. T. H. Farrer, "Food Additives," in CWHF, II: 1675–6.

9. Trager, 592–3, 597.
10. Marion Nestle and Sally Guttmacher, "Hunger in the United States," *Nutrition Reviews*, 1992, 50: no. 8, 242–3.
11. Ibid., 244.
12. H. H. Draper, "Human Nutritional Adaptation: Biological and Cultural Aspects," in CWHF, II: 1475.
13. Leslie Sue Lieberman, "Obesity," in CWHF, 1069–70; Marion Nestle, *Food Politics, How the Food Industry Influences Nutrition and Health*, Berkeley: University of California Press, 2002, 13.
14. Trager, 390; Beverly Bundy, *The Century in Food*, Portland, OR: Collectors Press, 2002, 8.
15. Lieberman, "Obesity," CWHF, I: 1069; Marion Nestle, "Food Biotechnology," in CWHF II: 1645.
16. Leslie Sue Lieberman, "Diabetes," in CWHHD, 672–4; S. Boyd Eaton, Marjorie Shostac, and Melvin Konner, *The Paleolithic Prescription: A Program of Diet and Exercise and a Design for Living*, New York: Harper and Row, 1988, 88.
17. Nestle, "The Mediterranean," CWHF, II: 1195. The author warns that these data are for rough comparisons only because such surveys are not truly comparable.
18. Trager, 579.
19. Gary Gardner and Brian Halwell, "Underfed and Overfed: The Global Epidemic of Malnutrition," *Worldwatch Paper 150*, Worldwatch Institute, 2000.
20. Lester R. Brown, "Worldwide: Obesity is a Threat to World Health," *American Fitness*, May 2001, 1–2.
21. Peter L. Pellett, "Energy and Protein Metabolism," in CWHF, I: 896.
22. Lieberman, "Obesity," CWHF, I: 1064; Ali H. Mokdad, Mary K. Serdula, and William H. Dietz, et al., "The Spread of the Obesity Epidemic in the United States, 1991–98," and David B. Allison, Kevin R. Fontaine, and JoAnn E. Manson, et al., "Annual Deaths Attributal to Obesity in the United States," both in *The Journal of the American Medical Association*, 1999: October 27, 1519 and 1530–8, respectively.
23. Pellet, "Energy and Protein Metabolism," CWHF, I: 897; *USA Today*, March 10, 2004, 1A.
24. Trager, 693; Lieberman, "Obesity," CWHF, I: 1074.
25. Farrer, "Food Additives," CWHF, II: 1672.
26. Beatrice Trum Hunter, "Substitute Foods and Ingredients," in CWHF, II: 1677–8; Jean Anderson and Barbara Deskins, *The Nutrition Bible*, New York: William Morrow and Company, 1995, 244.
27. Hunter, "Substitute Foods and Ingredients," CWHF, II: 1678–9.
28. Ibid., 1681.
29. Ibid., 1681–3.
30. Lieberman, "Diabetes," CWHF, I: 1084; Robert Kroes and J. H. Weisburger, "Nutrition and Cancer," in CWHF, I: 1090–1; Melissa H. Olken and Joel D. Howell, "Nutrition and Heart-Related Disorders," in CWHF, I: 1105.
31. Stephen Seely, "The Cardiovascular System, Coronary Artery Disease, and Calcium: A Hypothesis," in CWHF, I: 1119.
32. R. E. Hughes, "Nonfoods as Dietary Supplements," in CWHF, II: 1688–9.
33. Jacqueline L. Dupont, "Essential Fatty Acids," in CWHF, I: 876, 881.
34. Kenneth J. Carpenter, "Proteins," in CWHF, I: 884.
35. James C. Whorton, "Vegetarianism," in CWHF, II: 1559–62; Paul Rozin, "The Psychology of Food and Food Choice," in CWHF II: 1482.

36. Whorton, "Vegetarianism," CWHF, II: 1554.

37. Ibid., II: 1556.

38. H. Leon Abrams, Jr., "Vegetarianism: Another View," in CWHF, II: 1568–69. This is not to say that like other Native Americans the Eskimos were not ravaged by the contagious diseases that arrived with the Europeans. Robert Fortune, "The Health of the Eskimos, as Portrayed by the Earliest Written Accounts," *Bulletin of the History of Medicine*, XLV: 1971, 97–114.

39. Linda J. Reed, "The Arctic and Subarctic Regions," in CWHF, II: 1327–8.

40. Abrams Jr., "Vegetarianism: Another View," CWHF, II: 1568.

41. Ibid., II: 1569.

42. Nancy Davis Lewis, "The Pacific Islands," in CWHF, II: 1363–4.

43. Alfred E. Harper, "Recommended Dietary Allowances and Dietary Guidance," in CWHF, II: 1606–7.

44. Marion Nestle, "Food Lobbies and U.S. Dietary Guidance Policy," in CWHF, II: 1628.

45. Ibid., II: 1628–41 and passim. (See also her *Food Politics: How the Food Industry Influences Nutrition and Health*, Berkeley: University of California Press, 2002.).

46. Eliza Mojduszka, "Food Labeling," in CWHF, II: 1621–8.

47. Ibid., 1628.

48. *University of California, Berkeley Wellness Letter*, May 2000, 16(8): 3–5.

49. Nestle, "Food Lobbies," CWHF, II: 1628–41.

50. Center for Science and the Public Interest, "CSPI's Healthy Eating Pyramid," *Nutrition Action Health Letter 19*, December 1992, no. 10, 8–9.

51. Loren Cordain, "Cereal-Grains: Humanity's Double-Edged Sword," *World Review of Nutrition and Dietetics*, 1999, 84: 19–73; Seely, "The Cardiovascular System," CWHF, I: 1119.

52. Marilynn Larkin, "Little Agreement About How to Slim Down the *USA*," *The Lancet*, November 2, 2002, 360: 1400.

53. Draper, "Human Nutritional Adaptation: CWHF, II: 1471–2.

54. Mark Nathan Cohen, "History, Diet, and Hunter-Gatherers," in CWHF, I: 69.

55. Draper, "Human Nutritional Adaptation," CWHF, II: 1466–75; Reed. "Arctic and Subarctic Regions," CWHF, II: 1325–7.

56. J. Worth Estes, "Food as Medicine," in CWHF, II: 1546.

57. Yiming Xia, "Keshan Disease," CWHF, I: 939–46; Forrest H. Nielsen, "Other Trace Elements," in CWHF, I: 862–3.

58. Ananda S. Prasad, "Zinc," in CWHF, I: 868–72.

59. Basil S. Hetzel, "Iodine and Iodine Deficiency Disorders," in CWHF, I: 797–810.

60. Xia, "Keshan Disease," CWHF, I: 939–46.

61. Forrest H. Nielson, "Other Trace Elements," in CWHF, I: 856–65.

62. Draper, "Nutritional Adaptation," CWHF, II: 1473.

63. Gordon L. Klein and Wayne R. Snodgrass, "Food Toxins and Poisons from Micro-organisms," in CWHF, II: 1696.

64. Michael W. Pariza, "Food Safety and Biotechnology," in CWHF, II: 1664; Draper, "Human Nutritional Adaptation," CWHF, II: 1473–4.

65. Klein and Snodgrass, "Food Toxins," CWHF, II: 1697–8; Michael W. Pariza, "Food Safety," in CWHF, II: 1666.

66. Harper, "Recommended Dietary Allowances," CWHF, II: 1607.

67. Lieberman, "Diabetes," CWHHD, 669, and "Obesity," CWHD, 1063. See also Stephen J. Kunitz, *Disease and Social Diversity: The European, Impact on the Health of Non-Europeans*, New York: Oxford University Press, 1994, passim.

68. Draper, "Human Nutritional Adaptation," CWHF, II: 1475; Nestle, *Food Politics*, 73.

69. Laura Shapiro, "Do Our Genes Determine Which Food We Should Eat?" *Newsweek*, August 9, 1993, 64.

70. Nestle, *Food Politics*, passim.

71. Rozin, "Psychology of Food," CWHF, II: 1484.

72. Suzanne Hamlin, "Researchers Find Cravings Hard to Resist," *New York Times*, Feb. 22, 1995, B1.

CHAPTER TWENTY-FOUR: THE GLOBALIZATION OF PLENTY

1. Giovanni Rebors, *Culture of the Fork*, New York: Columbia University Press, 2001, 167.

2. William J. Broad, "Nutrition's Battle of the Potomac," *Nutrition Today*, 1979, 14 (4): 7.

3. A. Keys, F. Fidanza, and H. Blackburn et al., *Seven Countries: A Multivariate Analysis of Death and Coronary Artery Disease*, Cambridge, MA: Harvard University Press, 1980; Melissa H. Olkin and Joel D. Howell, "Nutrition and Heart-Related Diseases," in Kenneth F. Kiple and Kriemhild C. Ornelas (eds.), *The Cambridge World History of Food* (hereinafter CWHF), 2 vols., New York and Cambridge: Cambridge University Press, 2000, I: 1097–1109.

4. Aldo Mariani-Costantini and Giancarlo Libabue, "Did Columbus Also Open the Exploration of the Modern Diet?" *Nutrition Reviews*, 1992, 50(11): 313–19.

5. Marion Nestle, "The Mediterranean (Diets and Disease Prevention)," in CWHF, II: 1193–1203.

6. Such scientific research has gone beyond the Mediterranean. See, for example, Ram B. Singe, Gal Dubnov, and Mohammad A. Niaz, et al., "Effect of an Indo-Mediterranean Diet on the Progression of Coronary Artery Disease in High Risk Patients (Indo-Mediterranean Diet Heart Study): A Randomized Single-blind Trial," *The Lancet*, 2002, 360: 1455–61.

7. See, for example, S. Renaud and R. Gueguen, "The French Paradox and Wine Drinking," in *Novartis Foundation Symposium*, 1998, 216: 208–17; A. L. Klatsky, "Alcohol and Cardiovascular Diseases: A Historical Overview," in *Novartis Foundation Symposium*, 1998, 216: 2–12; and M. H. Criqui, "Do Known Cardiovascular Risks Mediate the Effect of Alcohol on Cardiovascular Disease?" in *Novartis Foundation Symposium*, 1998, 216: 159–67.

8. Michael W. Miller, "Call for a Dose of Wine Ferments Critics," *The Wall Street Journal*, June 17, 1994, B1.

9. Dennis Overstreet, *Overstreet's New Wine Guide*, New York: Clarkson/Potter Publishers, 1999, 24.

10. Stuart Walton, *The World Encyclopedia of Wine*, New York: Smithmark, 1996, 205. The beginning of the twenty first century, however, is seeing something of a wine glut, with part of the problem that the children of the baby boomers are not so enthusiastic about wine as their parents.

11. James Trager, *The Food Chronology*, New York: Crown Publishers, 1989, 703.
12. Leslie Brenner, *American Appetite: The Coming of Age of a Cuisine*, New York: Avon Books, 1999, 180–1.
13. Trager, 655.
14. Ibid., 702, 708.
15. Ibid., 715.
16. Craig Claiborne, *Craig Claiborne's The New York Times Food Encyclopedia*, New York: Random House, 1985, 436.
17. Trager, 704–5.
18. Ibid., 704–5, 711.
19. Ximena Clark, Timothy J. Hatton, and Jeffrey G. Williamson, "Where Do U.S. Immigrants Come From, and Why?" *National Bureau of Economic Research, Working Paper 8998*, Cambridge, MA, 2002, 1.
20. Michael J. McCarthy, "Food Companies Hunt for 'Next Big Thing' But Few Can Find One," *The Wall Street Journal*, May 6, 1997, A1.
21. Lucy Long, "Culinary Tourism: A Folkloristic Perspective on Eating and Otherness," *Southern Folklore*, 1998, 55 (3): 181–204.
22. Christine Wilson, "Southeast Asia," in CWHF, II: 1160.
23. Kathleen Deveny, "America's Heartland Acquires Global Tastes," *The Wall Street Journal*, Oct. 11, 1995, B1.
24. Ibid.
25. John A. Jackle and Keith A. Sculle, *Fast Food: Roadside Restaurants in the Automobile Age*, Baltimore: The Johns Hopkins University Press, 1999, 253, 261–2, 285.
26. Trager, 702, 709; Brenner 89, 207.
27. John C. Super, "Food and History," *Journal of Social History*, Fall, 2002, 170.
28. McCarthy, "Food Companies Hunt," *Wall Street Journal*, May 6, 1997, A1.
29. *Oresund Food Excellence Newsletter*, November, 2004, 1.

CHAPTER TWENTY-FIVE: FAST FOOD, A HYMN TO CELLULITE

1. Center for Science in the Public Interest, "Popcorn: Oil in a Day's Work," *Nutrition Action Health Letter*, May, 1994, 21(4): 9.
2. Eric Schlosser, *Fast Food Nation: The Dark Side of the All-American Meal*, Boston and New York: Houghton Mifflin, 2001, 244–5.
3. Delphine Roger, "Middle East and South Asia," in Kenneth F. Kiple and Kriemhild C. Ornelas (eds.), *The Cambridge World History of Food* (hereinafter CWHF), 2 vols., New York and Cambridge: Cambridge University Press, 2000, II: 1147; Naomichi Ishige, "Japan," in CWHF, II: 1181, and Colin Spencer, "British Isles," in CWHF, II: 1223.
4. Editors, "White Potato," in CWHF, II: 1880.
5. Alan Davidson, *The Oxford Companion to Food*, Oxford: Oxford University Press, 1999, 369; Waverley Root and Richard de Rochemont, *Eating in America: A History*, New York: William Morrow and Company, 1976, 308; John F. Mariani, *The Dictionary of American Food and Drink*, New Haven and New York: Ticknor and Fields, 1983, 187–8; James Trager, *The Food Chronology*, New York: Henry Holt, 1995, 224.
6. Ibid., 320, 339, 380.
7. Ibid., 380, 381, 385; Schlosser, 197–8.

8. Levenstein, *Paradox of Plenty*, 187–93; Dorothy Sue Cobble, *Dishing It Out: Waitresses and the Unions in the Twentieth Century*. Urbana and Chicago: University of Illinois Press, 1991, 22–3.

9. Trager, 445; John A. Jackle and Keith A. Sculle, *Fast Food: Roadside Restaurants in the Automobile Age*, Baltimore: The Johns Hopkins University Press, 1999, 38–9.

10. Trager, 503, 531, 550, 568.

11. Jackle and Sculle, 70–1, 151.

12. Levenstein, *Paradox of Plenty*, 229; James Comer, "North America from 1492 to the Present," in CWHF, I: 1319.

13. Emiko Ohnuki-Tierney, "We Eat Each Other's Food to Nourish Our Body: The Global and the Local as Mutually Constituent Forces," in Raymond Grew (ed.), *Food in Global History*, Boulder, CO: Westview Press, 1999, 259.

14. Alan M. Taylor, "Globalization, Trade, and Development: Some Lessons from History," *National Bureau of Economic Research, Working Paper 9326*, Cambridge, MA, 2002, passim; Schlosser, 229.

15. Marion Nestle, *Food Politics: How the Food Industry Influences Nutrition and Health*, Berkeley: University of California Press, 2002, 160.

16. It should be noted that, unlike Burger King, McDonald's denies importing cheap beef from Central and South America and has threatened to sue anyone who states or infers that it does. But, in truth, the USDA beef labeling system makes it impossible to ascertain the origin of beef.

17. Nestle, *Food Politics*, 161.

18. C. Wayne Callaway, "U.S. Leads Global Obesity Epidemic," in *Global Health and Environment Monitor*, 1989, 6: 4–5; Marilynn Larkin, "Little Agreement About How to Slim Down the USA," *The Lancet*, November 2, 2002, 360: 1400.

19. Sidney W. Mintz, *Sweetness and Power: The Place of Sugar in Modern History*, New York: Viking, 1985, 199.

20. Samara Joy Nielsen and Barry M. Popkin, "Patterns and Trends in Food Portion Sizes, 1977–1998," *Journal of the American Medical Association*, 2003, 289: 450–3.

21. Trager, 697.

22. Until recently, fast food establishments preferred to compete with serving sizes rather than price for obvious reasons. See Leslie Sue Lieberman, "Obesity," in CWHF, I: 1066. See also Jackle and Sculle, *Fast Food*, passim, and page 326 for a "Stuff Yourself" billboard advertising the Maverick Family Steak House with its food bars in Springfield, Illinois. See also Schlosser, 3, and finally see Larkin, 1400.

23. Schlosser, 241, 198; Trager, 707.

24. Matt Nesvisky, "An Economic Analysis of Adult Obesity," *The* NBER *Digest*, February, 2003, 1.

25. Schlosser, 242.

26. Ibid., 243.

27. Thomas N. Robinson, "Reducing Children's Television Viewing to Prevent Obesity," *The Journal of the American Medical Association*, 1999, 282 (16): 1561–7.

28. Trager, 508.

29. "Research Summaries: Gender-Related Shifts in the Distribution of Wages" in *Family Economics and Nutrition Review*, 1995, 8(2): 34–5.

30. Ibid.; Richard J. Hooker, *Food and Drink in America: A History*, Indianapolis and New York: Bobbs-Merrill, 1981, 351–2; "For the assertion that even in the

middle 1980s some 75 percent of American families ate breakfast and dinners together on the average of only three times a week or less, see Mintz, *Sweetness and Power*, 205.

31. Nestle, *Food Politics*, 7–8.
32. Heather Munro Prescott, "Anorexia Nervosa," in CWHF, I: 1001.
33. Carol M. Counihan, "The Social and Cultural Uses of Food," in CWHF, II: 1514.
34. Although thought to be rare until fairly recently, anorexia nervosa rates have skyrocketed in the United States since the 1960s and may strike as many as 1 in 250 females aged 12–16 years. See Heather Munroe Prescott, "Anorexia Nervosa," in Kenneth F. Kiple (ed.), *The Cambridge World History of Human Disease*, New York and Cambridge: Cambridge University Press, 1993, 577–81.
35. Trager, 708; Schlosser, 198–9.
36. Claude Fischler, "The 'Mad Cow' Crisis: A Global Perspective," in Grew (ed.), 208.
37. Schlosser, 202–3.
38. Laza Featherstone, "The Burger International Revisited," *Left Business Observer*, August 1999, 91.

CHAPTER TWENTY-SIX: PARLOUS PLENTY
INTO THE TWENTY-FIRST CENTURY

1. Brian Murton, "Famine," in Kenneth F. Kiple and Kriemhild C. Ornelas (eds.), *The Cambridge World History of Food* (hereinafter CWHF), 2 vols., New York and Cambridge: Cambridge University Press, 2000, II: 1412.
2. Ibid., 1412–13; K. David Patterson, "Russia," in CWHF, II: 1246–7; Francisco Viacava , Célia Maria Poppe de Figueiredo, and Walmir Andrade Oliveira, *A Desnutrição no Brasil*, Petrópolis: Editora Vozes, 1983; Fernando Homen de Melo, *O Problema Alimentar no Brasil*, Petrópolis, Rio de Janeiro: Paz e Terra, 1983: Roger Cunniff, "Drought Region (Brazil)" in Barbara A. Tenenbaum (ed.), *Encyclopedia of Latin American History and Culture*, 2 vols., II: 406.
3. Susan Scott and Christopher J. Duncan, *Demography and Nutrition: Evidence From Historical and Contemporary Populations*, Malden, MA: Blackwell Science, 2002, 75.
4. Ibid., 1411.
5. Carole M. Counihan, "Social and Cultural Uses of Food," in CWHF, II: 1514; William H. Whitaker, "Food Entitlements," in CWHF, II: 1585–93.
6. Adam Drewnowski, "Fat and Sugar in the Global Diet: Dietary Diversity in the Nutrition Transition," in Raymond Grew (ed.), *Food in Global History*, Boulder, CO: Westview Press, 1999, 194–205.
7. Ellen Messer, Barbara Haber, Joyce Toomre, and Barbara Wheaton, "Culinary History," in CWHF II: 1371.
8. Murton, "Famine," CWHF,II: 1411; Penelope Nestel, "Food Subsidies and Interventions for Infant and Child Nutrition," in CWHF, II: 1593: Stephen Budiansky, *The Convenant of the Wild: Why Animals Chose Domestication*, New York: William Morrow, 1992, 3.
9. Loren Cordain, "Cereal Grains: Humanity's Double-Edged Sword," *World Review of Nutrition and Diet*, 1999, 84: 23.
10. "Mexico: Restless Poor are Hungry," *Latinamerica Press*, Sept. 19, 1996, 1.
11. Eileen Kennedy and Lawrence Haddad, "The Nutrition of Women in Developing Countries," in CWHF, II: 1439.

12. Ibid.; Nestel, "Food Subsidies and Interventions," CWHF, II: 1593, Majid Ezzati, et al., "Selected Major Risk Factors and Global and Regional Burden of Disease," *The Lancet*, November 2, 2002, 360: 1347.
13. Nestel, "Food Subsidies," CWHF, II: 1604.
14. Antoinette Fauve-Chamoux, "Breast Milk and Artificial Infant Feeding," in CWHF, I: 626–34.
15. Susan Kent and Patricia Stuart-Macadam, "Iron," in CWHF, I: 813.
16. Nestel, "Food Subsidies," in CWHF, II: 1600.
17. Sara A. Quandt, "Infant and Child Nutrition," in CWHF, II: 1450–1.
18. William H. Whitaker, "Food Entitlements," in CWHF, II: 1587.
19. Kennedy and Haddad, "Nutrition of Women," CWHF, II: 1441.
20. Nevin S. Scrimshaw, "Infection and Nutrition: Synergistic Interactions," in CWHF, II: 1397–1406; George Wolf, "Vitamin A," in CWHF, I: 749.
21. J. D. L. Hansen, "Protein Energy Malnutrition," in CWHF, I: 978–9.
22. Donald T. Simeon and Sally M. Grantham-McGregor, "Nutrition and Mental Development," in CWHF, II: 1461, 1457.
23. Hansen, "Protein-Energy Malnutrition," CWHF, I: 977–86.
24. Bernard Harris, "Height and Nutrition," in CWHF, II: 1427–35.
25. Ibid., 1434.
26. Heather Munro Prescott, "Adolescent Nutrition and Fertility," in CWHF, II: 1454.
27. Ibid., II: 1453–4.
28. R. Floud, "Anthropometric Measures of Undernutrition" and Robert W. Fogel, "Second Thoughts on the European Escape From Hunger: Famines, Chronic Malnutrition, and Mortality Rates" both in S. R. Osmani (ed.), *Nutrition and Poverty*, Oxford: Clarendon Press, 1992, 231 and 280, respectively. See also the discussions by John M. Kim, "Nutrition and the Decline of Mortality" and William Muraskin, "Nutrition and Mortality Decline: Another View," in CWHF, II: 1381–8, and 1389–97, respectively.
29. Kenneth J. Carpenter, "Proteins," in CWHF, I: 887.
30. Tannahill, passim; Jeffrey M. Pilcher, "Food Fads," in CWHF, I: 1487.
31. Thomas W. Wilson and Clarence Grim, "Sodium and Hypertension," in CWHF, I: 853.
32. K. T. H. Farrer, "Food Additives," in CWHF, 1667–76; Robert Kroes and J. H. Weisburger, "Nutrition and Cancer," in CWHF, I: 1093.
33. Sujatha Panikker, "Food-Borne Infection," in CWHF, I: 1032.
34. Ibid., 1031–48.
35. Judy Perkin, "Food Sensitivities: Allergies and Intolerances," in CWHF, I: 1049.
36. Susan L. Hefle, "Food Allergies," in CWHF, I: 1024.
37. Perkin, "Food Sensitivities," CWHF, I: 1050.
38. Hefle, "Food Allergies," CWHF, I: 1027–8.
39. Ibid., I: 1025.
40. Marion Nestle, *Food Politics: How the Food Industry Influences Nutrition and Health*, Berkeley: University of California Press, 2002, 81–2.
41. K. David Patterson, "Lactose Intolerance," in CWHF, I: 1058.
42. Keith Vernon, "Milk and Dairy Products," in CWHF, I: 693–4; Linda J. Reed, "The Arctic," in CWHF, II: 1328.
43. Donald D. Kasarda, "Celiac Disease," in CWHF, I: 1008–17.
44. Kenneth F. Kiple, "The Question of Paleolithic Nutrition and Modern Health," in CWHF, II: 1706.

45. Ibid. The absence of celiac disease in northern China, however, still needs explaining. Kasarda, "Celiac Disease," in CWHF, I: 1010.
46. Perkin, "Food Sensitivities," CWHF, I: 1052.
47. James Trager, *The Food Chronology*, New York: Henry Holt, 1995, 594.
48. Kiple, "Paleolithic Nutrition," CWHF, II: 1706; Wilson and Grim, "Sodium and Hypertension," CWHF, I: 852–3.
49. Mark Nathan Cohen "History, Diet, and Hunter-Gatherers," in CWHF, I: 69.
50. S. Boyd Eaton, Marjorie Shostak, and Melvin Konner, *The Paleolithic Prescription*, New York: Harper and Row, 1988, 81, 86.
51. Mark Kurlansky, *Salt: A World History*, New York: Penguin Books, 2002, 144–61.
52. Kiple, "Paleolithic Nutrition," CWHF, II: 1706.
53. Ibid.
54. Ibid., I: 1707. Wilson and Grim, "Sodium and Hypertension," 848; Kurlansky, *Salt*, 50–1, 89, 205, who points out that salt was also used as money in areas as diverse as the China of Marco Polo and Native Americans of the Yucatan. R. J. Harrison Church, *West Africa*, London: Longman's Green and Company, 1957, 141.
55. Kenneth F. Kiple, *The Caribbean Slave: A Biological History*, New York and Cambridge: Cambridge University Press, 1984, 46–7.
56. David S. Newman, "Potassium," in CWHF, I: 847; Kiple, "Paleolithic Nutrition," CWHF, II: 1707; Wilson and Grim, "Sodium and Hypertension," CWHF, I: 851.
57. Eaton, Shostak, and Konner, *Paleolithic Prescription*, 116–17; Wilson and Grim, "Sodium and Hypertension," CWHF, I: 853; Newman, "Potassium," CWHF, I: 847.
58. Kent and Stuart-Macadam, "Iron," CWHF, I: 811; Simeon and Grantham-McGregor, "Nutrition and Mental Development," CWHF, II: 1458.
59. Eaton, Shostak, and Konner, *Paleolithic Prescription*, 119–21; Alfred Jay Bollet and Audrey K. Brown, "Anemia," in Kenneth F. Kiple (ed.), *The Cambridge World History of Human Disease*, New York and Cambridge: Cambridge University Press, 1993, 571–6; Kent and Stuart-Macadam, "Iron," CWHF, I: 811–12.
60. Nevin S. Scrimshaw, "Infection and Nutrition: Synergistic Interactions," in CWHF, II: 1403.
61. Kent and Stuart-Macadan, "Iron," CWHF, I: 812–13: Kent, "Iron Deficiency and Anemia of Chronic Disease," CWHF, I: 933–4.

CHAPTER TWENTY-SEVEN: PEOPLE AND PLENTY
IN THE TWENTY-FIRST CENTURY

1. Felipe Fernández-Armesto, *Food: A History*, London: McMillan, 2001, 156.
2. Robert W. Fogel, "Reconsidering Expectations of Economic Growth after World War II from the Perspective of 2004," *Working Paper Series of the National Bureau of Economic Research, Working Paper 11125*, Cambridge, MA, 2005.
3. Robert W. Fogel, "Changes in the Disparities in Chronic Disease during the Course of the Twentieth Century," *National Bureau of Economic Research, Working Paper 10311*, Cambridge, MA, 2004, 11–12.
4. Tony McMichael, *Human Frontiers, Environments and Disease: Past Patterns, Uncertain Futures*, Cambridge, UK: Cambridge University Press, 2001, 357.
5. Charles B. Heiser Jr., "Sunflower," in Kenneth F. Kiple and Kriemhild C. Ornelas (eds.), *The Cambridge World History of Food* (hereinafter CWHF), 2 vols., New York and Cambridge: Cambridge University Press, 2000, I: 429–30.

6. Thomas Sorosiak, "Soybean," in CWHF, I: 425.
7. McMichael, 142–3.
8. Jack Ralph Kloppenburg, Jr., *First the Seed: The Political Economy of Plant Biotechnology, 1492–2000*, New York and Cambridge: Cambridge University Press, 1988, 157–61.
9. Fernández-Armesto, 233.
10. Te-Tzu Chang, "Rice," in CWHF, I: 145.
11. Fernandez-Armesto, 233.
12. Joan Peterson, "Maize: Mexico's Gift to the World," *Repast*, XIX, (2), 2003, 6.
13. Christine S. Wilson, "Southeast Asia," in CWHF, II: 1153–4.
14. Michael W. Pariza, "Food Safety," in CWHF, II: 1666.
15. Marion Nestle, "Food Biotechnology: Politics and Policy Implications" in CWHF, II: 1643; Lawrence Busch et al., *Plants, Power, and Profits: Social, Economic, and Ethical Consequences of the New Biotechnology*, Cambridge, MA: Blackwell, 1991; Rosamond Taylor, Walther Falcon, and Eirka Zavaleta, "Variability and Growth in Grain Yields, 1950–94: Does the Record Point to Greater Instability?" *Population and Development Review*, 1997, 21(1): 41–58.
16. Nestle, "Food Biotechnology," CWHF, II: 1644.
17. Irena Chalmers, *The Great Food Almanac*, San Francisco: Collins Publishers, 1992, 59.
18. Nestle, "Food Biotechnology," CWHF, II: 1651.
19. Ibid., 1650.
20. Nick Nuttal, "Fruit with a Twist," *The MM Times: The World at the Millenium*, Week 6, Food, 30.
21. Xavier Bosch, "Europe Moves to Loosen Restrictions on GM Foods" *The Lancet*, December 14, 2002, 360: 1945.
22. Nestle, "Food Biotechnology," CWHF, II: 1645–6.
23. Ibid., 1646.
24. Ibid., 1654.
25. *Science Magazine*, January 21, 2000; Nevin S. Scrimshaw, "Infection and Nutrition," in CWHF, II: 1397–8, 1404: William H. Whitaker, "Food Entitlements," in CWHF, II: 1585.
26. Ken Ringle, "Stalking the Wild Potato," *The Washington Post*, Tuesday, December 1, 1992, C1.
27. Pariza, "Food Safety and Biotechnology," CWHF, II: 1664.
28. Nestle, "Food Biotechnology," CWHF, II: 1655–9.
29. Nuttall, "Fruit with a Twist," *The MM Times: The World at the Millenium*, Week 6, Food, 30.
30. Glenville Jones, "Vitamin E," in CWHF, I: 771.
31. J. Worth Estes, "Food as Medicine," in CWHF, II: 1534.
32. Ibid., II: 1534, 1537, 1539.
33. Ibid., II: 1542, 1544–5.
34. Ibid., II: 1549–51.
35. Colin E. Nash, "Aquatic Animals," in CWHF, I: 466.
36. Ibid., I: 466–7.
37. Fernández-Armesto, 85.
38. Sheldon Aaronson, "Fungi," in CWHF, I: 315–16.
39. George W. Hudler, *Magical Mushrooms, Mischievous Molds*, Princeton: Princeton University Press, 1998, 167.
40. Ibid., 150.

41. Editors, "Mushrooms," in CWHF, II: 1818–19.
42. Eva Barlösius, "France," in CWHF, II: 1216; Anneke H. van Otterloo, "Low Countries," in CWHF, II: 1239.
43. Ellen Messer, Barbara Haber, Joyce Toomre, and Barbara Wheaton, "Culinary History," in CWHF, II: 1373.
44. Helene Cooper and Scott Kilman, "Trade Wars Aside, U.S. and Europe Buy More of Each Other's Foods," *The Wall Street Journal*, Tuesday, November 4, 1997, A1.
45. Hansjörg Küster, "Northern Europe," in CWHF, II: 1230–1; van Otterloo, "Low Countries," CWHF, II: 1239.
46. Barlösius, "France," CWHF, II: 1216.
47. Küster, "Northern Europe," CWHF, II: 1231; *Orsund Food Excellence Newsletter*, November 2004, 1.

Index

Dave Chasen's restaurant, 233
Davis, Adel, 253
Delaney Clause, 254, 258
Delaney, James J., 254
delicatessens, 231
Delmonico, Lorenzo, 231
Delmonico's restaurant, 229, 231, 232
Derby, Elias Hackett, 176
diabetes mellitus II, 5, 256, 259–260, 264,
          268, 282
Diat, Louis, 232
Diaz, Bernal, 118–119, 159
Dickens, Charles, 248
Dietary Goals for the United States, 267
*Directions for Impregnating Water
          With Fixed Air*, 179
Dirks, Robert, 190
The *Divine Husbandman*, 45
The *Divine Ploughman*, 45
dog domestication, 15, 16
   in the Americas, 15
   in the British Isles, 15
   in the Pacific, 15
   in the Swiss Lake region, 15
Dole, James D., 234
Don the Beachcomber restaurant, 232, 233
Don Quixote, 142
Doomsday Book, 99
Dorés restaurant, 231
Drake, Francis, 139, 161
duck, 24, 60
   domestication, 24
   eggs, 24
Dutch in the Caribbean, 161
   and Dutch West India Co., 162
   and salt, 161
   and sugar revolution, 162

eddoes, 39
Edict of Purity (Bavaria), 182
Egypt (ancient), 51–54
   animal domestication failures, 53
   barley, 51, 54
   barnyard animals, 53
   beer, 52, 54
   bread, 54
   cattle, 53
   chicken, 53
   diet, 47–48
      elite, 71
      peasant, 71
   expanding Sahara Desert, 51, 70, 71
   food prohibitions, 53
   ful medames, 52
   goat, 53

melokhia leaves, 52
melon, 52
Middle East plant complex, 51
Nile fish, 51, 53
Nile River, 51
Osiris worship, 53
pig, 53
pork avoidance, 53
sheep, 53
watermelon, 52
wheat, 51
wine, 52
Eijkman, Christiian, 242
einkorn (wild), 13
elephant, 48
emmer (wild), 13
empanadas, 188
Erie Canal, 199
ergotism, 193
   and Salem "witches", 193
Escoffier, Auguste, 232
Europe to the Renaissance
   hunter-gatherer horticulture, 59–60
      foxtail millet, 60
      lentils, 60
      peas, 60
   under the Romans
      bread-making, 80
      cruciferous vegetables, 79–80
      fruit, 79, 80
      grapes, 60
      oats, 60, 80
      rye, 60, 80
      viticulture, 76
   Middle Ages (*see also* Monasteries below)
      aquatic animals, 89, 97
      barnyard animals, 98
      buckwheat, 100
      chestnut, 100
      cider, 98
      collective farms, 98
      cooking styles
         north, 89, 102
         south, 89, 102
      crops, easiest to grow, 98
      diets
         commoners, 99–101
         elite, 99–101
      Dutch, 99
         butter, 99
         cheese, 99
         horticulture, 99
      English
         fall of Rome, 81, 97
         gin and taxes, 174